The Living I Ching

元 亨 利 貞

THE LIVING
I CHING

Using Ancient Chinese Wisdom to Shape Your Life

DENG MING-DAO

HarperSanFrancisco
A Division of HarperCollinsPublishers

Note on the frontispiece: The four words shown are *yuan heng li zhen,* the central phrase in the *I Ching.* The phrase can be translated in different ways. Please see appendix 2 for a more complete discussion.

The title page motif is *Zhouyi,* the title of the *I Ching* prior to the Han Dynasty.

Design, layout, and all illustrations by Deng Ming-Dao

Chinese text typeset by ASCO Typesetters, Ltd., Hong Kong

HarperCollins books may be purchased for educational, business, or sales promotional use. For information please write: Special Markets Department, HarperCollins Publishers, 10 East 53rd Street, New York, NY 10022.

HarperCollins Web site: http://www.harpercollins.com

HarperCollins®, ⛰ ®, and HarperSanFrancisco™ are trademarks of HarperCollins Publishers.

FIRST EDITION

Library of Congress Cataloging-in-Publication Data is available.
ISBN-13: 978–0–06–085002–9
ISBN-10: 0–06–085002–7

06 07 08 09 10 RRD(H) 10 9 8 7 6 5 4 3 2 1

FOR MORTON MARCUS

poet, teacher, friend

Contents

Acknowledgments

One of the recurring phrases in the *Changes* is "beneficial to see the great person." In my case, Morton Marcus was the great person who provided encouragement, guidance, and tutoring. He is a loyal and compassionate man, a devoted husband and father, and a man who has earned his views through hard experience as a poet, Air Force veteran, college professor, union leader, film critic, radio host, and promoter of the arts. He has made a serious study of poetry from around the world, with particular emphasis on classical Chinese poetry. As a college student, he told Professor Yi-Pao Mei that he wanted to study the Chinese poets. The professor began the traditional way, by having him copy poems repeatedly—stroke by stroke with brush and ink.

I met Mort just as I was looking for the courage to write this book. I had been a guest speaker in a college class on Chinese history and poetry that he was coteaching. He gave me a several books of his poetry, and I recognized one of them, *The Santa Cruz Mountain Poems,* which I had read in a library more than a quarter-century before. As we talked informally, I told him about my planned book, saying off-handedly that I might write it once I had retired. I thought I was being modest with such a grandiose idea. After all, Confucius supposedly did not consider himself mature enough to study the *Changes* until he was past fifty.

"You cannot wait. Not if you're a creative person," he told me. "Being a father is fine. Being a businessman is fine. But if you are a writer, you write because you must. You write because it keeps you sane. Waiting to retire before you write this book is too—Confucian."

It was a remark as abrupt as that of any Chinese teacher, but it also signaled support. Mort read many drafts as the book took form. I could not have continued without his tutelage and, in many cases, his hand pulling me back from precipices as I groped for the right approach. Sometimes he would telephone me and say, "Stop writing like this!" or "I hate those rhymes!" Unlike the traditional Chinese teacher, though, he was also encouraging, and he could demonstrate what he was suggesting by improvising lines.

Our friendship is about the magic of poetry, and how poems can live in a person for years after just a few readings. We have pulled our families into our friendship, and together we have indulged our love of food. It is therefore with the greatest respect and affection that I dedicate this book to Mort.

This book also benefited from discussions with Mark Salzwedel, who was my editor for a number of previous books. Before there was even a manuscript, we discussed my ideas, and he instantly understood what I was attempting. I am fortunate that he lent his critiques to this project.

I must also extend my appreciation to Pearl Weng Liang Huang, who helped me translate several passages (especially the lengthy extracts in the appendixes) and who discussed words and phrases particularly difficult to understand. Our discussions affirmed how challenging translation is, and how important it is to look beyond meanings to understanding.

My thanks also go to Eric Brandt, my editor, who took a great deal of time with the work and who helped to shape the book with great sensitivity.

Other readers to whom I am most grateful are Moss Roberts, Betty Gee, Alison Jade Ong, Robert Dato, and Ralph Kilmann. I thank them all for their comments and suggestions.

Calling this book an act of madness, folly, and vanity would be to elevate it too much. Calling it stupid would be too thin a description. This is not a scholarly book; I am not qualified. Neither is it the work of a master; I have no lofty authority. Since the *Changes'* model virtue is humility, let me simply acknowledge this: What I search for is the concern of neither the scholar nor the master. It is a personal search for direct communion with the *Changes* itself. If the trail leads others to that voice, this folly will have been worthwhile.

Preface

The search for wisdom to shape our lives often takes us through the world's great books: the Bible, the Quran, the Talmud, the Buddhist and Hindu scriptures, and many others. We can also delve into Greek, Roman, Norse, Mesopotamian, Native American, and Asian myths, explore philosophers from every culture, and look deeply into literature. Sooner or later, our search will lead to China. There we have such important books as the *Daodejing*, the *Zhuangzi*, and the *Analects of Confucius*.

The wisdom of China flows in three main streams: Buddhism, Confucianism, and Taoism. Usually, these schools hold themselves distinct, but there is one remarkable book that predates them all, has been accepted by them all, and yet stands apart from them in its own right. That book is the *I Ching*.*

I, pronounced "yi," means "change." *Ching*, pronounced "jing," means "canon." For simplicity and clarity, we will refer to the *I Ching* simply as the *Changes*. The *Changes* is a compilation of texts and commentaries from as early as the 12th century B.C.E. It has been used as a source of wisdom and as a book of divination. It is mainly built around sixty-four hexagrams (groups of six lines). Each hexagram has a Statement, attributed to the Zhou dynasty founder King Wen; comments about each of the six lines, attributed to the Duke of Zhou (son of King Wen); and an Image, attributed to Confucius. Later editions carry commentaries by other scholars.

How did this book exist with the three great streams of Chinese thought? The Buddhist version of the *Changes* was clearly meant to graft Buddhism to the indigenous Chinese wisdom of the *Changes*. (Buddhism originated in India). Confucianism placed the *Changes* in a central position for all imperial governments from the Han dynasty (established 206 B.C.E.) to the Qing dynasty (ended 1911 C.E.) by making it one of the Five Classics (or Canons)

---

* The title *I Ching* is spelled in an older form of transliteration. *Yijing* is the title transliterated under the pinyin system. Established by the People's Republic of China in the mid–twentieth century, pinyin has become the predominant form of romanization used around the world. However, we have retained the older spellings in the title as well as for the word *Tao* because those versions are more familiar to Western readers.

Prior to the Han dynasty, the *I Ching* was known as the *Zhouyi*. The name means "The Changes of the Zhou dynasty," because the book was one of the primary forms of divination and because it came to be the repository of two of the Zhou dynasty's early leaders—King Wen and his fourth son, the Duke of Zhou.

of Confucianism. These books formed the basis of orthodox Chinese thought for over two thousand years. Finally, since the *Changes'* central tenet is that all circumstances result from the interaction of nature's impersonal forces rather than divine intervention, Taoism found an ancient tradition that blended seamlessly with its own. In turn, various editors added Taoist influences back into the *Changes.* This strong link between Taoism and the *Changes* is so important that anyone who wants to understand Tao must also study the *Changes.*

Most people who have heard of the *Changes* think of it as a book of divination. They are intrigued that a book can be consulted by thinking of a question and then either tossing three coins or counting out yarrow stalks. In that process, one draws a "hexagram," or a stack of six lines. Depending on the kind of lines one draws, one then looks up one or more entries in the *Changes* that address one's question. (See pages xix and 86–89 for more information.) The advice we receive is hardly the normal kind of language we might expect from "fortune telling." The *Changes* never gives "yes" or "no" answers, but instead reveals a picture of the situation, often through poetic images, and then provides guiding philosophy, reassurance—and sometimes pithy reminders of what we should do.

If one uses the book over a long period of time, one may well find that it shapes one's life. But that is not enough. There is a consistent and profound philosophy hidden in the book. In fact, great thinkers throughout Chinese history have insisted that the value of the *Changes'* wisdom is far greater than its role as oracle.

In order to discover this deeper wisdom, *The Living I Ching* takes readers through the sometimes abstruse classic in a gradual and progressive way. The goal is to absorb the knowledge directly, even to the point of eschewing the divinatory aspects. Readers can then indeed use the *Changes* to directly shape their own lives.

If you would rather plunge right in, the Brief Overview that follows will give you a quick orientation. You can try divining right away by following the instructions on page xix. If you would like to go slowly and first learn more about the background of the *Changes* and the goals of this book, you are invited to begin your exploration at the introduction on page xxvi. No matter which choice you make, the *Changes* will clearly reward a lifetime of study.

Brief Overview

When the sun rises, the moon sets.
When the moon sets, the sun rises.

These lines describe life as cyclical movement, and represent one of the fundamental assertions of the *Changes*.

This brief orientation introduces the minimum number of concepts for a basic understanding of the *Changes'* underpinnings. More detailed background information and further explanations can be found in the appendixes beginning on page 357.

The philosophical basis of the *Changes* begins with the limitlessness that is our origin.

The first movement out of limitlessness is into yin and yang, the world of opposites: light and dark, male and female, hot and cold, hard and soft, and so on. They are symbolized as a straight line, yang ▬▬ ; and a split line, yin ▬ ▬ . These opposites are not static; their balance is in constant flux.

The four possible pairings (2^2) of these lines represent the initial interaction of yin and yang.

| Old | Young | Young | Old |
| Yang | Yin | Yang | Yin |

If we recombine the four pairs of lines with the primary yin and yang lines, we can express a further level of complexity (2^3). This set is called the Eight Trigrams. A trigram is a formation of three lines called a *gua*.

| Heaven | Lake | Fire | Thunder | Wind | Water | Mountain | Earth |

Each of the trigrams' names symbolizes more than its literal meaning. This is clear because the trigram names are esoteric rather than ordinary words. For example, the heaven trigram is named *qian* instead of the more ordinary *tian* (sky). In the same way, the water trigram doesn't use the common word for water, *shui,* but uses *kan,* a word that means a pit in the earth.

The Eight Trigrams are organized into an octagonal pattern called the *bagua* (*ba* means eight, *gua* means trigram). There are two versions. The first is called the Early Heaven sequence and is sometimes named after Fu Xi, the man credited with its creation.

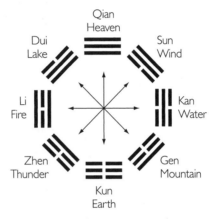

The trigrams are arranged in polar opposites: heaven-earth, water-fire, wind-thunder, lake-mountain. Each pair's relationship stands for fundamental principles:

heaven-earth: creation, nature, the cosmos

water-fire: forms of energy

wind-thunder: movement, development

lake-mountain: consolidation, social interaction.

The Eight Trigrams squared (8^2) generate the Sixty-Four Hexagrams shown below. A hexagram is a formation of six lines. The Early Heaven hexagram arrangement follows a binary number sequence.

The top three lines of each row repeat the trigram order shown on page xiii: Heaven, Lake, Fire, Thunder, Wind, Water, Mountain, and Earth. The upper trigrams of each row are identical. If one reads down the lower trigrams in the first column, the same order is repeated.

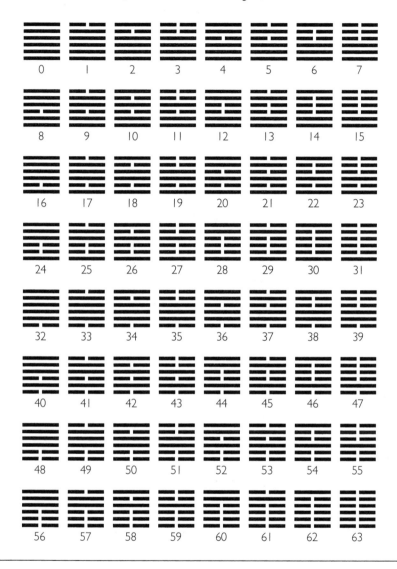

Fu Xi's sequence of hexagrams was revised by a feudal prince posthumously known as King Wen. In his formation, shown on the following page, the trigrams are arranged in a cyclical progression, read clockwise from the top. The trigrams were also assigned compass directions and seasonal associations:

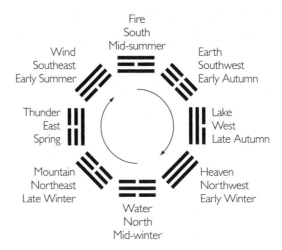

King Wen arranged his hexagrams in pairs. He changed each odd-numbered hexagram into its opposite to generate the subsequent even-numbered one. Most are an overturning of the six lines. For example Hexagram 11 shows the Earth trigram above the Heaven trigram. Hexagram 12 inverts the lines:

Those few hexagrams which would be the same when turned upside down are reversed line for line (substituting a yin line for a yang line, and vice versa). Hexagrams 61 and 62 are an example.

Fu Xi's Eight Trigrams are arranged as *opposites,* but his hexagrams are arranged in *numerical* order. King Wen's Eight Trigrams are arranged *cyclically,* but his sequence of hexagrams is arranged as *pairs of opposites.* Overall, King Wen's order, shown on the following page, begins with all yang (Hexagram 1) and yin (Hexagram 2) lines, and ends with perfect alternation of yin and yang lines (Hexagrams 63 and 64).

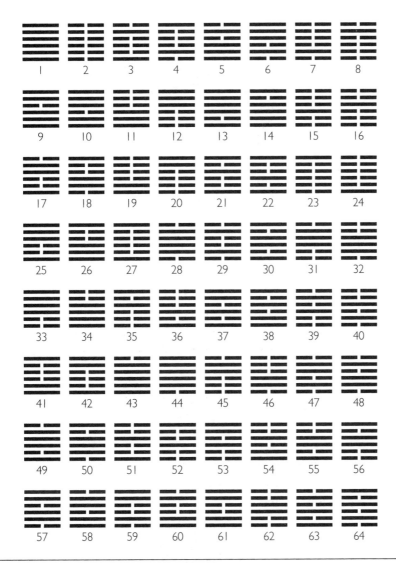

The sixty-four hexagrams have titles. We do not whether King Wen named them, or whether he was using preexisting names.

Each hexagram in the *Changes* has three core texts; additional commentaries vary according to different editions. The three core texts shown in Circle Seven of this book are:

The Statement: A short text attributed to King Wen, with such repeated phrases as "good fortune," "no error," or "misfortune," combined with poetic images.

The Lines: A poetic comment on each line of each hexagram by King Wen's fourth son, the Duke of Zhou.

The Image: Advice to a "noble one," which could mean a ruler or a wise individual. This text is attributed to Confucius.

Most editions of the *Changes* also include a group of appendixes called the *Ten Wings,* written by Confucius or later scholars.

While a complete view of the *Changes* requires years of study, the following eight points summarize the philosophy of the *Changes.*

1. Nature, society, and individuals all act through cyclical change.
2. Cycles of change are driven by polar opposites named yin and yang.
3. A cycle reaching its zenith descends toward its nadir. Likewise, the only path from nadir is ascent.
4. A cultivated person and an enlightened society act in accord with these cyclical movements, remaining aware of the numerous cycles they instigate each day. Ethical acts reinforce community and maintain beneficial cycles. Selfish acts increase isolation and generate destructive cycles.
5. A wise person engages in constant self-cultivation to become more sensitive to change.
6. Cultivated persons are not sad when misfortune occurs. They use the occasion to seek errors within themselves. By cultivating humility, they fend off further misfortune. They are modest and careful in times of great fortune. They are grateful and reverent. They will also consolidate their gains, search for nascent seeds of misfortune, and prepare for the future.
7. A person who can discern the cycles of life can learn to utilize them for his or her own ends. The *Changes* advocate spirituality, humility, reverence, and service to others as the highest standards.
8. All endings are only transitions.

Simple Divining Ritual

The simplest method of divination for the *Changes* uses three coins:

Compose yourself in a quiet and clean room. Let no one disturb you.

Place the *Changes* and three like coins before you. These coins can be either antique or modern but should be reserved only for divination.

Consider the question you have, meditate on it, and write it down on a clean piece of paper or in a notebook. Here are some examples of how to phrase the inquiry: "Will this course of action bring success?" or "How can I—?" or "What will happen if—?" Avoid asking either-or questions. The more specific your question, the more specific the answer will be. Concentrate on your question, and concentrate on addressing that question directly to the *Changes*.

Pick up the three coins, shake them in your hands, and then cast them onto a table. One of four combinations will result:

Head + Head + Head	Old Yang Line	—O—
Head + Head + Tail	Young Yin Line	▬ ▬
Tail + Tail + Head	Young Yang Line	▬▬▬
Tail + Tail + Tail	Old Yin Line	▬X▬

Write this first line down. Take up the coins again, and repeat the ritual to draw each of the next five lines from the bottom up. When you have a hexagram of six lines, you have completed the ritual. In order to find your hexagram, refer to the table on the inside back cover.

If all the lines are either Young Yin or Young Yang lines (meaning they don't change), just read the hexagram that they form. If there are Old Yang or Old Yin lines (meaning that they will change), you must derive a second hexagram by substituting the opposite line for each of these "old" lines.

Read the material related to the first hexagram, including the comments about each changing line that you drew.

Then derive a new hexagram by substituting the old lines for their opposites. Read this new hexagram's text (but none of its line commentaries).

The first hexagram is your situation at the moment. The lines modify that hexagram's content. The second hexagram is the situation as it might someday become. (See page 89 for more information.)

Book Format

The Eight Circles of Change

Aside from divination, it's important to understand the principles of the *Changes*. *The Living I Ching* is designed to be read sequentially to allow just such an exploration of the *Changes'* underlying meanings.

This sequence consists of eight circles, mapped to the mandala on the opposite page. The diagram is read from the inside outward.

1. *Wuji:* The open circle at the center has no divisions. It represents the great limitlessness that is our origin.
2. *Yin and Yang:* The solid line represents yang, and the broken line represents yin. Yin and yang are the first separation after limitlessness.
3. *The Four Images:* Yin and yang take on their first pairings with one another, forming four combinations.
4. *The Early Heaven Eight Trigrams:* This is Fu Xi's arrangement of the Eight Trigrams. The arrangement is read counter clockwise. Opposite trigrams are arranged across from one another.
5. *The Early Heaven Sixty-Four Hexagrams:* This arrangement is read from the top and center outward on either side. One begins from heaven (at the "top" of the circle) and meets the other side at the "bottom" on earth. One can begin from heaven, only to find all lines reversing themselves after passing the point marked by earth.

   A blank band between the fifth and sixth circle marks King Wen's revolutionary rearrangement of the Eight Trigrams and the Sixty-Four Hexagrams.
6. *The Later Heaven Eight Trigrams:* King Wen's Eight Trigrams pattern, expressing the cyclical, seasonal, and directional nature of change. This pattern unites the Five Phases (see appendix 7, page 388) and the Eight Trigrams. It is read clockwise.
7. *The Later Heaven Sixty-Four Hexagrams:* The sequence is read clockwise. Odd-numbered hexagrams generate the following even-numbered hexagram by reversing their lines in a yin-yang exchange. Thus, every other hexagram is the inverse of the preceding one. In turn, even-numbered hexagrams are linked to subsequent hexagrams. Each hexagram is built from six lines, and these lines symbolize time and

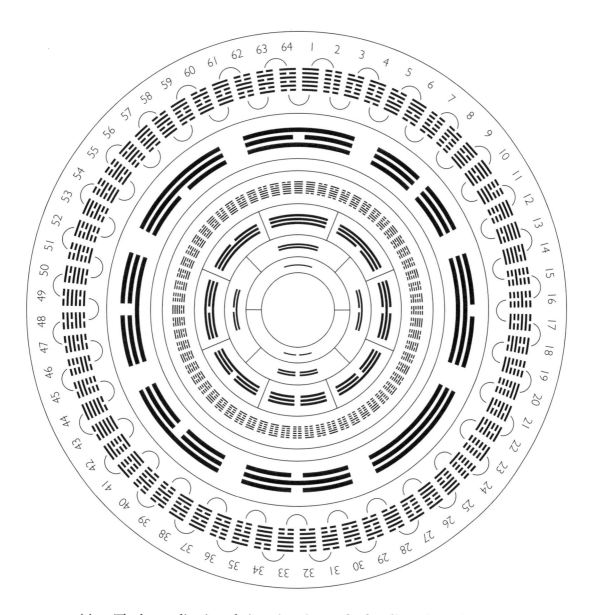

position. The lowest line is early in a situation and subordinate in position. The highest line is late in a situation and retiring in position. By the logic of the *Changes*, that which is late in a cycle changes to its opposite, and generates a new cycle. Thus, each hexagram represents a cycle.

8. *Voice of the Oracle:* A consideration of how we can hear the voice of the *Changes* directly.

The presentation of two of the circles is more complicated than the others. Circle Four introduces the Eight Trigrams and attaches both introductions and commentaries to each one.

Circle Seven is even more complicated because of all the commentaries and associations that have been attached to the hexagrams. Details on reading Circles Four and Seven follow on the next pages.

Reading Circle Four

The core pages of Circle Four focus on the Eight Trigrams. Each trigram is treated with one set of facing pages. The left page has two columns. The

Trigram   Ideogram   Title and poem

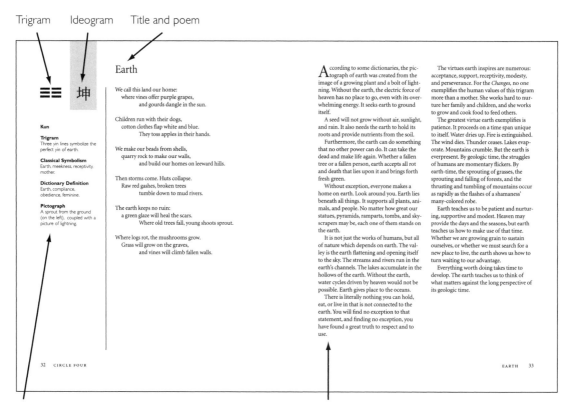

Earth

We call this land our home:
    where vines offer purple grapes,
        and gourds dangle in the sun.

Children run with their dogs,
    cotton clothes flap white and blue.
        They toss apples in their hands.

We make our beads from shells,
    quarry rock to make our walls,
        and build our homes on leeward hills.

Then storms come. Huts collapse.
    Raw red gashes, broken trees
        tumble down to mud rivers.

The earth keeps no ruin:
    a green glaze will heal the scars.
        Where old trees fall, young shoots sprout.

Where logs rot, the mushrooms grow.
    Grass will grow on the graves,
        and vines will climb fallen walls.

Kun

Trigram
Three yin lines symbolize the perfect yin of earth.

Classical Symbolism
Earth, meekness, receptivity, mother.

Dictionary Definition
Earth, compliance, obedience, feminine.

Pictograph
A sprout from the ground (on the left), coupled with a picture of lightning.

According to some dictionaries, the pictograph of earth was created from the image of a growing plant and a bolt of lightning. Without the earth, the electric force of heaven has no place to go, even with its overwhelming energy. It seeks earth to ground itself.

A seed will not grow without air, sunlight, and rain. It also needs the earth to hold its roots and provide nutrients from the soil.

Furthermore, the earth can do something that no other power can do. It can take the dead and make life again. Whether a fallen tree or a fallen person, earth accepts all rot and death that lies upon it and brings forth fresh green.

Without exception, everyone makes a home on earth. Look around you. Earth lies beneath all things. It supports all plants, animals, and people. No matter how great our statues, pyramids, ramparts, tombs, and skyscrapers may be, each one of them stands on the earth.

It is not just the works of humans, but all of nature which depends on earth. The valley is the earth flattening and opening itself to the sky. The streams and rivers run in the earth's channels. The lakes accumulate in the hollows of the earth. Without the earth, water cycles driven by heaven would not be possible. Earth gives place to the oceans.

There is literally nothing you can hold, eat, or live in that is not connected to the earth. You will find no exception to that statement, and finding no exception, you have found a great truth to respect and to use.

The virtues earth inspires are numerous: acceptance, support, receptivity, modesty, and perseverance. For the *Changes*, no one exemplifies the human values of this trigram more than a mother. She works hard to nurture her family and children, and she works to grow and cook food to feed others.

The greatest virtue earth exemplifies is patience. It proceeds on a time span unique to itself. Water dries up. Fire is extinguished. The wind dies. Thunder ceases. Lakes evaporate. Mountains crumble. But the earth is everpresent. By geologic time, the struggles of humans are momentary flickers. By earth-time, the sprouting of grasses, the sprouting and falling of forests, and the thrusting and tumbling of mountains occur as rapidly as the flashes of a shamaness' many-colored robe.

Earth teaches us to be patient and nurturing, supportive and modest. Heaven may provide the days and the seasons, but earth teaches us how to make use of that time. Whether we are growing grain to sustain ourselves, or whether we must search for a new place to live, the earth shows us how to turn waiting to our advantage.

Everything worth doing takes time to develop. The earth teaches us to think of what matters against the long perspective of its geologic time.

Basic background information for this trigram: transliteration of Chinese name, description of trigram, classical symbolism, contemporary dictionary definition of the word, and what the pictograph depicts

Commentary on the trigram

left-hand column shows the trigram, the ideogram, and basic background information about the trigram.

This background information consists of the transliterated form of the title, an explanation about the basic interpretation of the graphic form of the trigram, and the classical symbolism explaining the usual associations with the trigram. It also includes a definition that shows what contemporary dictionaries list as the meanings of the trigram names. The last section shows the pictograph interpretation. Many Chinese words are pictures, and understanding the symbolism of each name can lead to deeper insights.

The right-hand page contains commentary on the trigram. The main purpose of this commentary is to understand the trigram's meaning and role in the Eight Trigrams. Traditional associations are taken into account but are balanced against the role the trigram plays in the set of Eight Trigrams as a whole.

Reading Circle Seven

The core pages of Circle Seven focus on the Sixty-Four Hexagrams. Each hexagram is treated with two consecutive sets (spreads) of facing pages.

The left page of the first spread has two columns. The left-hand column shows the hexagram, the ideogram, and basic background information about the trigram.

This background information consists of:

1. the number of the hexagram in the assigned sequence of sixty-four;
2. the two constituent trigrams;
3. the traditional interpretations of how the two trigrams interpret basic associations;
4. the transliterated form of the title, and dictionary definitions;
5. the sequence and the link, which gives an interpretation of how the hexagram fits into the traditional sequence of the hexagrams.

An introductory poem follows to complete the first page of the spread.

Once the basic information has been given, together with the poem to sketch out possible ways in which the hexagram symbols can be illustrated, the right-hand page gives the full core texts of the *Changes*. These three traditional texts are:

Introductory Material to the Hexagram

Hexagram   Ideogram   Title and poem

The Traditional Core Texts of the *Changes*

The Statement, attributed to King Wen

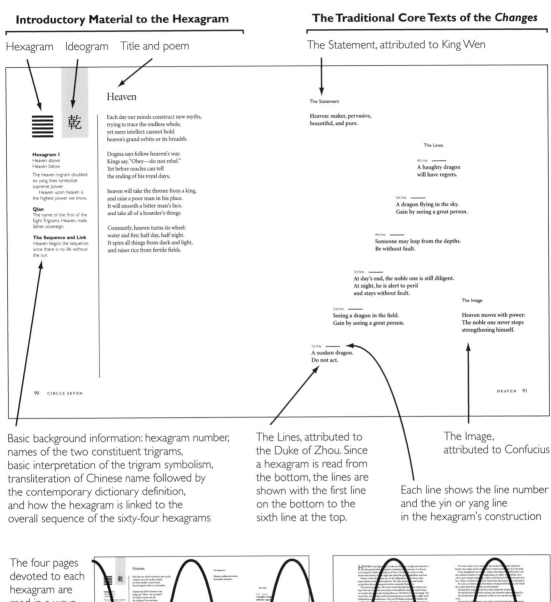

Heaven

Each day our minds construct new myths,
trying to trace the endless whole,
yet mere intellect cannot hold
heaven's grand orbits or its breadth.

Dogma says follow heaven's way.
Kings say, "Obey—do not rebel."
Yet before oracles can tell
the ending of his royal days,

heaven will take the throne from a king,
and raise a poor man in his place.
It will smooth a bitter man's face,
and take all of a hoarder's things.

Constantly, heaven turns its wheel:
water and fire; half day, half night.
It spins all things from dark and light,
and raises rice from fertile fields.

Hexagram 1
Heaven above
Heaven below

The heaven trigram doubled:
six yang lines symbolize
supreme power.
    Heaven upon heaven is
the highest power we know.

Qian
The name of the first of the
Eight Trigrams. Heaven, male,
father, sovereign.

The Sequence and Link
Heaven begins the sequence,
since there is no life without
the sun.

The Statement

Heaven: maker, pervasive,
bountiful, and pure.

The Lines

6th line
A haughty dragon
will have regrets.

5th line
A dragon flying in the sky.
Gain by seeing a great person.

4th line
Someone may leap from the depths.
Be without fault.

3rd line
At day's end, the noble one is still diligent.
At night, he is alert to peril
and stays without fault.

2nd line
Seeing a dragon in the field.
Gain by seeing a great person.

1st line
A sunken dragon.
Do not act.

The Image

Heaven moves with power:
The noble one never stops
strengthening himself.

90   CIRCLE SEVEN

HEAVEN   91

Basic background information: hexagram number,
names of the two constituent trigrams,
basic interpretation of the trigram symbolism,
transliteration of Chinese name followed by
the contemporary dictionary definition,
and how the hexagram is linked to the
overall sequence of the sixty-four hexagrams

The Lines, attributed to
the Duke of Zhou. Since
a hexagram is read from
the bottom, the lines are
shown with the first line
on the bottom to the
sixth line at the top.

Each line shows the line number
and the yin or yang line
in the hexagram's construction

The Image,
attributed to Confucius

The four pages
devoted to each
hexagram are
read in a wave-
pattern like
the yin-yang
cycles of the
Changes.

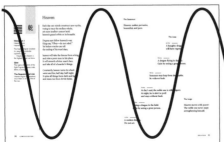
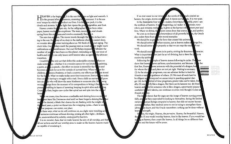

1. the Statement, attributed to King Wen;
2. the Lines, attributed to the Duke of Zhou;
3. the Image, attributed to Confucius.

The reading of the right-hand page is of particular importance. Since the traditional way to read a hexagram is from the bottom up, the lines are arranged from bottom to top. The sections are arranged on a slant to reinforce this order. Each one of the lines is numbered and shows whether it is a yin or a yang line.

The first spread is followed by a second one that contains two pages of commentary on the hexagram. In this commentary, there is a general essay, together with specific sections regarding the *Statement,* the *Lines,* and the *Image.* These passages are signaled by mentioning the name of that core text of the *Changes* in **semibold italic.**

On the right side of the second spread are two hexagrams with ghosted lines. This is a graphic representation of the "ideal" line positions believed by many commentators to be an essential key to understanding the nature of the hexagram lines.

The commentators posited that there was an ideal arrangement of lines. This arrangement is a perfect alternation of yin and yang lines, beginning with a yang line at the bottom and ending in a yin line at the top. Any hexagram is then compared to this ideal line arrangement, and lines that coincide with that arrangement are deemed to be in their "proper place." The graphic shows which lines are in their right places by showing them completely black. All other lines are ghosted in gray. The example here shows that in Hexagram 32, only lines 3 and 6 are in their proper places.

Reading the two spreads together leads the eye through a subtle sine wave, reinforcing the yin-yang nature of the *Changes.* By reading Circle Seven in groups of four pages to each hexagram, a reader can consider all that can be interpreted from that hexagram, and then go on to contemplate how each one is linked with the next. In total, then, every part of the commentary, the text, and the graphics links all the hexagrams into the hidden message of the *Changes:* all change is one circle.

Introduction

Prologue

Many years ago, when I was both younger and more daring, I joined others in buying a piece of country land. The agent told us that the most important factor in buying undeveloped acreage was the water supply. This land had a good well—one so plentiful that a thirty-foot geyser had erupted when the well was first dug. The land had trees, meadows, a good garden for growing food, even a huge outcropping of stone that seemed perfect for building walls and paths.

Before we finalized the purchase, I did something I had not done for many years. I consulted the *I Ching*.

I should explain why it had been such a long time since I had used this book, even though I valued it so highly. I first stumbled upon the *I Ching* when I was a teenager. The book was tucked on a shelf in the basement of a neighborhood bookstore. It meant something to me that I found it within walking distance of my home, because I didn't think one should have to look "outside of one's own yard" to find needed wisdom. Later, I bought my first set of yarrow stalks (used in the divining process) at a nearby shop.

I wore out the book consulting it over the two problems that most plagued me then—what to do about a career and what to do about love relationships. After about five years, however, I realized that I had become completely dependent on the *I Ching*. Instead of making decisions as they became necessary, I had to rush home to divine. This was clearly a disadvantage. I even felt it was a weakness.

One day, I took the book down from its high storage place (the *I Ching* is supposed to be stored above shoulder level), unwrapped the book from its silk sheathing, and put it on a shelf with other books. I can remember feeling strongly that it would be better to absorb the wisdom of the *I Ching* and make right actions instead of being crippled by dependency on an oracle.

Although I put the book away, I never stopped applying its principles to my life. This led to both mistakes and doubts. Still, I tried all the principles in real life and in many different contexts.

So, decades after putting the book away, I took it out again and consulted it about the purchase of the land. I received a single hexagram—the Well— with no changing lines:

Well. A city may change,
but the well does not.
It does not lose, it does not gain.
In spite of all who come and go from a well,
it remains a well.
But if the rope cannot reach,
or if the well's vase is upended:
misfortune.

Although I was used to the *I Ching,* I was still startled. The hexagram seemed eerily appropriate. I did note the warning, "But if the rope cannot reach, or if the well's vase is upended: misfortune." In other words, if I could not get to the water or if I spilled the water, it would be bad.

Then everything was going to be fine, I concluded. What could go wrong? The well was strong and certified by a consultant, and the pipes were good. The water was surely reachable. It was not until several years had passed that the statement took on a different meaning.

The property was over a three-hour drive away, and I went there with less frequency. The well was still good—"In spite of all who come and go from a well, it remains a well"—but we simply couldn't get to the land often enough to maintain it or enjoy it. Then I saw a different meaning in the warning "... if the rope cannot reach..." Eventually, we sold the land without having used it or enjoyed it much.

This experience taught me that the readings of the *Changes* may take years to manifest themselves. That in turn gave further weight to what the ancients maintained: that it takes many years to understand the *Changes.* Moreover, it reaffirmed my earlier feelings that it was essential to learn the wisdom of the *Changes* rather than simply relying upon a book.

Decades have passed since those early experiences with the *Changes,* and I have studied with many teachers. I have especially concentrated on Taoism. Being interested in the *Changes* as I am, it would seem natural for me to study the book with every teacher possible. However, I have found difficulties with the established approaches to the *Changes.*

There are two kinds of teachers of the *Changes:* the masters and the scholars. Ultimately, I found that neither could reveal all the substance of this great tradition. Let me explain, for I mean no disrespect to either side.

Chinese masters accept the *Changes* at face value. They accept all aspects of the *Changes* as fact. When these masters are asked to explain why the *Changes* exists as it does, they answer that the sages created it—so no more questions should be asked. For anyone trained in Chinese cultural norms, this is familiar. For anyone who thinks critically, such an assertion is unsatisfactory. Meanwhile, the masters maintain that if we only spend some thirty to fifty years reverently and unquestioningly approaching the *Changes,* we will come to the right understanding on our own. But will we?

By contrast, scholars scrutinize every aspect of the book. They search for truth by deconstructing the text as much as possible. They compare different editions, they debate the origins of the book's imagery, and they combine their efforts with archaeology and even astronomy. (Current research shows that constellations might have inspired some of the images in the *Changes.*) What they most pointedly do not do is teach people how to *use* the *Changes* to shape their lives, nor do they teach its philosophy for practical applications. In fact, many university professors begin their classes by pointedly warning students that they are not there to answer a student's religious or spiritual questions.

Moreover, it is easy for both traditional masters and scholars to establish an exclusionary air about the *Changes.* This may be unintentional, but they effectively discourage any innocent exploration of this great classic. The masters exclude people who don't know the Chinese language, aren't faithful enough, or have not spent enough time contemplating the esoteric qualities of the *Changes.* The scholars exclude anyone who cannot take the time to follow the research, who won't delve into the debates over the *Changes*—or who insists that he or she would like to make practical use of the book.

There has to be a different approach to the *Changes.* There must be a step-by-step way of absorbing the *Changes* directly. There must be a way to explore the *Changes* beyond both traditional interpretations and scholarly inquiries. In short, there must be a way to answer these three questions:

What does the *Changes* mean?
How can it be used?
How can we hear it directly?

Answering these questions is the goal of *The Living I Ching.* Follow this book through the eight circles (see page xx). You will discover the wisdom of the *Changes* that neither masters nor scholars have yet shown us.

Why Eight Circles?

The eight circles form a pilgrimage. There is a reason why this metaphor of a spiritual journey has been used. All pilgrimages have two common features: a *circle* (one travels with the intention of returning to normal life) and *change* (one returns with insight and spiritual strength). The *Living I Ching* is a virtual pilgrimage. We will make a circle and return with insight into what drives all movement in our world.

The idea of a circular journey was inspired by the original title of the *Changes—Zhouyi*. Aside from its meaning as the name of the Zhou dynasty, *zhou* means "circumference," "circle," "complete," "everywhere," and "provide." These definitions provide remarkable inspirations for our search. Circumference—to encompass an understanding of all change. Circle—all change occurs in cycles; fortune and misfortune follow one another unendingly. Complete—we must gain a thorough understanding. Everywhere—the process of change is pervasive. Provide—all answers and support will come to us if we act according to the *Changes*.

The word *yi* also has multiple meanings. It means "change." It also means "exchange" and "easy." "Exchange" reminds us that yin and yang drive all change. "Easy" promises that someone who masters the *Changes* will find the way eased. The word *yi* itself is a pictograph of a lizard. A quick lizard and a chameleon changing color both resonate with the idea of change.

Thus, if we contemplate all the meanings of the word *zhouyi*, we can imagine a lizard running in a circle, its body undulating. For all these reasons, the journey through the *Changes* has been arranged in circular form.

The aim of walking these eight circles is to find the voice of the *Changes* itself. The clues that such a voice exists lie in the passages where the *Changes* speaks in the first person. (See appendix 10 for a complete listing.) There is a voice in the *Changes,* one that is reverent and strict, holy and yet familiar with sorrow, determined and yet also knowing regret. The *Changes* is not a supernatural oracle. It is a human one.

This, then, is the reason why the book is conceived as a pilgrimage: we go to hear the *Changes* speak to us. We go beyond the exclusionary airs of the master and scholars: no one can deny that a person has gone on a pilgrimage. A pilgrimage puts the possibility of spiritual success under our own control. It is a self-propelled journey. No god does it for us. No one can substitute for us. Privilege is no aid; poverty is no disadvantage. We must travel in person. We need no other qualifications, sponsorships, or status. Everyone can benefit by completing their circles. When we return, having heard the voice of the *Changes,* that will be supreme success.

周
易

Zhou
yi

About the *Changes*

Why is the *Changes* important? If we are looking for wisdom upon which to base our lives, it makes sense not to rely on temporary or untested knowledge. The problems of our existence are perennial. They are problems that every generation has faced, and it's important to find a body of knowledge that transcends the limitations of our times. Besides, we don't want to revisit or experiment with some of the dreadful disasters of human history—slavery, war, genocide, and natural calamity—but we do want to learn from these past events. Thus, in searching for wisdom, we must search for the deepest traditions.

The great age of the *Changes* and the fact that it has had many revisions and additions throughout the centuries make it ideal for such a search. Following the *Changes* back through its texts will lead us to the very roots of human consciousness. The recent history of the *Changes* in the West is just the surface of this book's vast history. Two thousand years ago, before our Web sites and offset lithography books, there were older books printed with wooden type on paper. About fifteen hundred years before that, we find books of handwritten bamboo strips tied together with leather thongs. Even earlier still, in the Bronze Age, we find passages scratched onto ox scapulae and turtle shells. By following the *Changes* back to neolithic times, we can gain access to some of the earliest and deepest levels of human experience. The book's survival over thirty centuries attests to the power of its words and the necessity of its message. Its images and wisdom are archetypal and tested by generations of people. As a result, the *Changes* offers a near-universal philosophy.

As a book of divination, the *Changes* has no obvious mechanism for making its pronouncements. No one claims that there is a god speaking through the book. No one claims that there is anything supernatural about it. The *Changes* speaks of impersonal forces and utilizes the most impersonal of these forces to activate its own oracular function: chance. When one wants to use the *Changes,* one uses randomly cast yarrow stalks, coins, or even a computer randomizer to build a series of six lines called a hexagram. One uses this hexagram to find the corresponding passages in the book. The method of arriving at the hexagram may be one of pure chance, and yet a completely individual and personal reading emerges. That puzzle of how the book "knows" makes it all the more intriguing.

It is significant that the *Changes* is an oracle that needs no intermediary. Other divination methods require an interpreter—meaning that there will be a separation between the inquirer and the source. There are obvious issues of privacy, fallibility, access, and even affordability in all traditions that require an intermediary. The *Changes* requires none of these prerequisites.

What it does require is that a person be sincere and attuned to the question. A period of meditation prior to asking the question is an integral part of the process. The more one is centered on the question, the more apt the answer is likely to be. In other words, one should be so absorbed during the building of the hexagram that the passages from the *Changes* will seem like swift enlightenment. It should be as if someone said some words to us as we were struggling with a problem, triggering a sudden perception: "Of course!" we blurt out, and our problem suddenly becomes clear.

The *Changes* makes no promises. Instead, it exposes the principles behind our inquiry, and it gives advice based on farsighted wisdom, unshakable ethics, and harmony with nature. The *Changes* has absorbed the experiences of rising and falling kingdoms, of great heroes and scheming villains, of humble sages and demonic demagogues. To the extent that any individual's life travels—from the heights of exalted heaven to the depths of lonely dilemmas—the *Changes* will have a wider, deeper, and more lengthy record.

Thus, the book aims to open a reader's mind to the full nature of change instead of just giving an "answer." The *Changes* emphasizes an individual's mental abilities and moral character as the greatest factors for shaping the future. Most radically—for a book of divination—the *Changes* asserts that the future is *not preordained* but is in constant flux and can therefore be influenced by the actions of an enlightened person.

The *Changes* places such an enlightened person into an overall cosmic order. The forces that affect us—and which we can affect in turn if we are cultivated enough—are shown to us dispassionately. Heaven, earth, water, fire, wind, thunder, mountain, lake—nature is integral to the *Changes'* philosophy. The book itself models what it would have us all do: align ourselves with nature and act in harmony with nature.

Modern living, as refined as it is, does not supply all the answers we need. Even if we follow the most recent trends, read the latest research, and buy new products, we are still unable to find all the guidance we want. When we open the newspaper each day, we are confronted with more disasters. What troubles us most are the questions that have mystified every generation: self-knowledge, the meaning of life, family relationships, marriage, and children, work—followed by the even larger problems of migration, war, famine, torture, and genocide. These issues confront each of us with harsh riddles.

The only reason to use the *Changes* is that it works. It is alive and it is useful. Its imagery is primal, profound, and based on nature. Its language goes to the root of all things. If we want access to wisdom that goes beyond our own limited experiences, if we want wisdom that guides us into the future, the *Changes* is the book not only to study, but also to absorb and internalize so that we too can act as the *Changes* would have us do.

The Difficulties of Translation

There can be no perfect translation of the *Changes*. As soon as one settles on a translation for one context, it is wrong when seen from another setting. It's impossible to encompass all the implications of ancient Chinese in another language. The goal of this book is thus more modest—to find at least one intelligible translation given that it is impossible to provide all the shadings of the original language. We will briefly examine some of the problems of translation here. (For a deeper discussion, see appendix 2.)

The language of the *Changes* is ancient. Even today's literate Chinese cannot read it well. Although most words in the *Changes* are still used today, many definitions have been altered over the last three millennia. Words in their present-day meanings make no sense when read in the *Changes*. What's more, some words have so fallen out of use that they now exist nowhere but in the *Changes*.

From early on, the *Changes* required masters who specialized in its old language. The written versions were regarded as mere prompts to oral traditions transmitted through competing schools. There were differences of opinion, misunderstandings, and—because Chinese scholarship placed a premium on memorization—mistakes. Even in Confucius's time (551–479 B.C.E.), the language of the *Changes* had become obscure. In fact, it was Confucius's ability to interpret the old texts that made him so valuable a scholar.

Since the Chinese language sprang from many dialects among groups isolated by rivers and mountains, early definitions and word usage was imprecise. Standardization by imperial decree began only in the third century B.C.E., when Qin Shihuang united several separate states to make what became the nation of China. However, the *Changes* had already been in use—with nonstandardized language—for some eight hundred to fifteen hundred years.

There have been several points in history where the *Changes,* as well as other ancient books, was endangered. By the end of the Qin dynasty (206 B.C.E) for example, many books and libraries were destroyed by years of war. Decades later, some books were found again (in one case, a cache was discovered inside a wall where a scholar had hidden them) or reconstructed.

Furthermore, there were certainly accidental changes in the texts. First, the books were reproduced by manual transcription until the use of movable type after 1045 C.E. Such a process was vulnerable to scribal error. Second, scribes frequently used homonyms—because of genuine ambiguity, as a shortcut, or because the word might have carried the correct meaning before the standardization of the language. (For more discussion, see appendix 4.)

Adding to this uncertainty are the number of editions we have from different points in history, ranging from the Zhou dynasty (12th–3rd centuries B.C.E.) to as late as the Qing dynasty (15th–20th centuries C.E.). Translators have brought out English versions of each of the surviving editions. These versions differ, sometimes dramatically, and it is difficult to name any single edition as being definitive. So as we undertake the translation of the *Changes,* we have to ask ourselves, "Which version?"

One answer might be "Use the earliest version," on the assumption that it is the most "authentic" and "pure." But does that make all the other commentary of later generations wrong? True, other people added to the *Changes,* but they did so in clearly separate passages. We have to assume that scholars over the past two thousand years have had a closer vantage point to the meanings of the *Changes* than we have now, and we should not automatically discount what they have written.

Should we therefore use the latest editions (already several hundred years old)? Those versions are burdened with didactic Confucian language that doesn't carry as much meaning for us today. At least for the purposes of this book, then, I've used the latest versions, but have tried to edit out the feudal concepts that either are irrelevant or seem negative to us. For example, the word *fu* can mean either "confidence" or "captured war slaves." I've chosen to translate the word as "confidence." Likewise, Hexagram 54 shows the feudal practice of marrying two sisters to a great chief. I've tried instead to frame this in terms of a person forced into an unfortunate and subordinate relationship. (For more discussion, see appendix 1.)

A final complication for translation is the extremely compressed language of the *Changes.* There are usually no articles, pronouns, conjugations, or indication of past, present, or future tenses to help us determine the context of a given passage. In addition, ancient Chinese used no punctuation, and a passage's meaning can differ significantly depending on how it is punctuated. We cannot translate the texts strictly. We have to interpret them in a more open way.

Take Hexagram 9, *Xiao Chu,* for example. How should we translate the word *chu?* In one translation (Wilhelm/Baynes), *chu* is translated as "taming power," while in another (Richard John Lynn) it is rendered as "domestication." If we research the word, it means a dumb creature, an animal, livestock. It is also a verb, meaning to raise livestock. The Oracle's advice may not necessarily be to raise livestock, but to tame ourselves and our situation. We clearly do not have a word in English with all the equivalent meanings.

However, there may be other ways to access the meaning. It can be helpful if we relax. If we dream, and let the words and images connect, the hexagram can become more meaningful:

> *Chu.* A domesticated animal. *Xiao,* meaning little or slight. Not that the animal is small, but that the degree of domestication is superficial. The animal is wild. Our situation is wild, just coming under control. The animal is still straining at the rope, rubbing against the fence. Then the rain is also being held back, just as the animal is barely restrained. The clouds strain against what's holding them, just as the animal threatens to break loose or rebel against the labor demanded of it.

Now, in the dream of this hexagram comes comprehension. Any question we put to the *Changes* can go into the swirl of images and give us insight. Somehow, we need to connect with the dream level, where all concepts are carried not in words like *domestication, prevalence,* and *furthering,* but in images of vivid color.

It can even be said that the Confucian scholars have drained the *Changes* of its drama. They insist on interpreting concrete imagery as being allusions to abstract principles. For example, in the case of Hexagram 54, which we mentioned before, they will define the "marrying sister" as the emperor's minister and shape the wisdom of the *Changes* into narrow advice for a bureaucrat. What if we instead accept the raw power of the *Changes'* language? Consider some of these images from the *Changes:*

> Waiting in a bloody cave.
> Get out!
> (Hexagram 5, Line 4)

The well is dredged, but no one drinks.
My heart is anguished. Water
could be drawn. If the king understood,
we would instantly receive happiness.
(Hexagram 48, Line 3)

Wild swans gradually reach the shore.
A man journeys but does not return. A wife,
pregnant; does not give birth. Misfortune.
Gain by guarding against raiders.
(Hexagram 53, Line 3)

Early in this project, it became clear that merely translating the *Changes* would not uncover all that needed to be found. It was then that poetry suggested itself. The poems in this book allow exploration of the *Changes'* themes without restriction to the strict interpretation of translation.

Grasping the Whole Through Metaphor

The use of poetry to probe the *Changes* is appropriate because it is similar to how the *Changes* conveys its meaning. It is said that each line of the sixty-four hexagrams addresses all possible human situations. That yields only 384 possibilities, and there are surely more situations than that. However, if we look at the fact that any inquiry might yield a pair of hexagrams, and that all readings of the *Changes* are meant to interact with the questioner, the potential of greater complexity becomes apparent. More important, the *Changes* is built on a complex system of symbols and metaphors so that each hexagram and each word can suggest a multiplicity of meanings.

Like a human body, where atoms form molecules, which in turn form cells, then form living tissue that obeys the commands of the brain, the smallest parts of the *Changes* are built on words that are whole metaphors in themselves. These parts are joined with others to form larger metaphors—all while embodying living observations of the world. Those words are further bound into names, trigrams, and hexagrams to form the whole of the *Changes.*

This is a complicated idea, so some explanation may be in order. As examples, let's examine the line patterns of the hexagrams themselves, the trigram system, and finally, a hexagram.

Let's look at the lines first. As has been detailed in the Brief Overview (see page xiii), the most basic graphic expression of the Changes is the solid line, meaning yang ▬▬▬ ; and the split line ▬▬ ▬▬ , meaning yin.

When we see the eight trigrams, we see the various ways in which these lines are combined, and yet we still need to keep the yin and yang elements in mind. When we see the eight possible trigrams, we can see the presence of yin and yang. Interestingly enough, it is the single *unlike* line that determines the yin or yang character of the trigram.

Heaven   Lake   Fire   Thunder   Wind   Water   Mountain   Earth

The yang (meaning, light, heat, and male) hexagrams are heaven, thunder, water, and mountain. The yin (meaning dark, cold, and female) hexagrams are earth, wind, fire, and lake. This in turn leads to family associations— heaven is father, thunder is the eldest son, water is the second son, and mountain is the youngest son. Earth is mother, wind is the eldest daughter, fire is the second daughter, and lake is the youngest daughter. (See page 70 for further discussion.) There are many extensions to these metaphors, but for now, it's enough to suggest how the basic elements of yin or yang extend throughout the book.

For a second approach to tracing the path of metaphors in the *Changes*, let's look at the trigrams themselves. We've already seen how their yin or yang characteristics have made them metaphors for family relationships. In addition, the trigrams have been made into metaphors for natural phenomena as shown earlier and as discussed on pages 30–45. The trigram of three solid lines, for example, is seen as triple yang. What could be more supremely yang than heaven? Accordingly, the three solid lines are indeed the symbol of heaven, and then other meanings are assigned to it as well— creative force, masculine energy, imperial power, and even fatherhood. These additions expand on the metaphor of heaven. Note that being all yang is not necessarily a good thing. The Heaven hexagram's sixth line warns against haughtiness.

When the eight trigrams are combined into the two trigram combinations, the overall formation of trigrams forms more layers of metaphor. The Early Heaven formation (see page 23) teaches us of opposites. The Later Heaven formation (see page 53) teaches us of seasons, family relationships, and the cyclical nature of change. We will go into this in greater detail in the book, but for now, it's enough to show how the basic metaphors of the *Changes* are combined to yield greater meanings.

As a final example, let's look at the language itself. Each word in the *Changes* has a multiplicity of meanings, and the *Changes* uses the words in all their variations. Thus, one needs to understand the meanings of the words that are being used, and then one needs to see how those meanings are consciously combined and contrasted with one another. We've already seen a little of that with our examination of the word *chu* on page xxxiv. Let's look at one other word, *guo.*

There are two hexagrams that have this word in their titles. Each of them occupies a strategic location in the sequence of hexagrams—exactly two hexagrams away from the end of the upper and lower sections of the sixty-four hexagrams (the upper section ends at Hexagram 30). Hexagram 28 is *Da* (big) *Guo.* Hexagram 62 is *Xiao* (little) *Guo.*

The strange thing is that *guo* means both "to exceed," and "to cross," and *guo* is used in both senses in the hexagrams. The Statement of Hexagram 28 speaks of a sagging ridgepole, so this is *da guo* in the sense of "big excess." However, in the sixth line of that hexagram, the *Changes* speaks of fording a river. Surely this is a conscious play on the idea of *guo* as "crossing." When the line reads: "Fording, wading, head submerged. Misfortune, but without fault," it is combining both crossing and excessiveness into a warning.

When we come to Hexagram 62, *Xiao Guo,* we find the Statement: "Small matters can be done, but not large matters." *Guo* in the sense of crossing works better here—we can make small attempts (like crossings), but we cannot make grand ones. What's more, the second, fourth, and sixth lines use the word *guo* both in the sense of crossing (or meeting) and as a warning to guard against excess.

The fact that words are used in more than one meaning—actually almost opposite meanings—is the case with every hexagram. If you'll recall that the basis of the book is yin and yang, we could even say that the theme of each hexagram has its yin and yang aspects as well. For example, Hexagram 18, Poison, seems to refer to the decay of our ventures, the decline of our fathers' and mothers' affairs (and perhaps our fathers and mothers themselves). At the same time, there is also a strong implication that some "poison" is beneficial—as in the case of fermentation. Without fermentation, we would not have wine, some teas, and other foods. Hexagram 27, as another example, refers to nourishing in its title, and so it is clearly concerned with feeding. But then it goes on to examine how the motivations of others are revealed by the movements of their jaws and by what they seek to "fill their mouths." Even Hexagram 4, Youth, which is the *Changes'* direct, first-person rebuke to a foolish youth, still admits that this is a gainful omen and it refers to the joys of a family in Line 3. Again, the metaphors of yin and yang intersect with the language metaphors to create a complex and highly sophisticated web of meanings.

The overall point is simply to demonstrate that the metaphors of the *Changes* are consciously manipulated as the basis of its philosophy. Invocation of the *Changes* is said to activate the hexagrams. The hexagrams establish the basis for the commentaries. When the reader is conscious of the layers of metaphor, the intuitive associations that will give insight into the problem at hand become possible. Metaphor becomes the basis for spirituality.

The best metaphors establish their meanings faster than rational thought. That is why metaphor's cousin, the joke, can fly under our inhibitions and make us laugh before we catch ourselves. Metaphors force us to link disparate images and recognize larger meanings.

Metaphor thus takes advantage of our deep tendencies to make connections. From birth, we are trying to connect events to find meaning in them. If we can accept that, the divinatory aspects of the *Changes* can be understood. We are all parts of a greater whole, and every event reflects that whole. The *Changes* reflects the pace of those events just as the pulse reflects the health of a person. The changes of life are self-propelled by the dynamic shifting of yin and yang without the agency of any god or personage to manipulate or control them. The words and images of the *Changes* are made to reflect the greater whole of the cosmos.

The Shape of Change

The shape of change is a circle. This means that all events in the world move in cycles. The original usage of the *Changes* as a means of divination reflects a desire to know the future. But trying to know the future through any form of divination is too slow, too artificial, too primitive. There is another way to know the future, and that is to understand the inevitable trajectories of our daily events. Then, we can surely know the future simply by observing the present.

We already do this every day. Here are some obvious examples: If we miss our train, we're going to miss our appointments. If we go out into a blizzard, we have a greater risk of accident than on a spring day. But what happens when we have to make plans for a career, or decide whom we will marry, or try to set forth a plan to raise our children? What happens if we're a leader and we have to make decisions for our organization or set forth plans for thousands of followers? In those cases, we have to go from merely seeing how a set of circumstances will affect us to looking at how *we* can affect circumstances. In other words, it's not enough to just know how change works on us. We also need to know how we can influence change for the better.

This, then, is what the *Changes* finally means: it means absorbing the principles of change so that we can not only sense them intuitively, but also make intelligent decisions for the future to yield positive benefits. This is also the best way to understand the *Changes'* moral structure. The *Changes* constantly emphasizes humility, upright character, kindness, and service to others as its core values. After all, manipulating the future is open to the character of the people doing it. Disaster as well as benefit exists in the future. A madman can launch a hundred wars, or a kind person can lift the lives of the wretched. Which future will we have? It won't come by itself. A good future will come only if it is husbanded by the enlightened.

That is why the *Changes* constantly addresses itself to a "noble one." Originally, these words meant a prince or a gentleman, because the *Changes* were originally used by royalty and the elite, not the general population. But our society doesn't exist that way anymore. Each of us has to make decisions of enormous weight each day. Now, each of us needs the wisdom of the *Changes*. We are the noble ones whom the *Changes* addresses. We are the noble ones who are responsible for the future.

Use the *Changes* as a tool of divination. Use the *Changes* to strengthen your moral and ethical conviction, and that will be even better. Use the *Changes* to understand the basis of all events. Use the *Changes* to see that the wisdom to shape the future has been tested for thousands of years. Above all, though, use the *Changes* and your life will be immeasurably improved.

Join us in this journey through the *Changes*. Follow the circles and return changed. You can read this book in sequential order. You can read it by skipping around in it. You can read it simply by using the coin or yarrow-stalk method of divination. You could even read it backward, from the last circle to the first.

After all, a circle has no front or back. It has no beginning and it has no end. What is most important is that you enter the circle. Once you do that, and once you open yourself, the journey will begin. The *Changes* will speak to you. When you hear that voice of the *Changes* directly, you will know that the wisdom of change can shape your life. You need only hear that voice, and afterward you will have no doubts about it. Then, confidence in the future will be yours.

Invocation

Like exiled immortals, we have a memory of a previous paradise, even as we confront the daily frustration of being human. It is as if we are doomed to wander the earth for offending heaven. Perhaps we wrote a couplet that did not please, or perhaps we overindulged in kitchen pleasures.

Being flung back to earth is worse than death: At least death would mean reincarnation and the wonder of new life. No, the opposite of immortality is the pain and turmoil of constant change—of sweating and groaning and squinting in darkness, bereft of divine sight.

In that darkness, the *Changes* whispers to us with the voice of one who has seen both the sorrows of being human and the joy of heavenly palaces. It is the voice of one who has trudged the mountainsides and flowed into the sunset clouds. The *Changes* is a spirit reborn in more people each generation, until it is a consciousness rooted in millions of souls. It is a spirit that learns and grows with each act of divination, a spirit who chooses to live neither in heaven nor on earth but who dwells in the human heart. It is from that seat that the *Changes* speaks from both earthly pain and heavenly clarity.

Talk to us now, voice in the darkness.

More than twenty-five centuries ago, most people heard you. Our ancestors made their own art, poetry, music, and dance, even as they led the country, studied numbers, followed the stars, reared children, farmed, picked medicinal herbs, and acted as their own diviners. It was natural that they communed directly with the spirits. Thousands of years later, you are still here in millions of us, but many ignore you. There are not enough of us to listen for you.

That deafness is our loss, for you are well worth hearing. You are the voice of wisdom and the emotion of memory. You obey your own rules, which are the rules of nature, far beyond the concepts that people have invented. You are blood and semen and milk and sweat as well as sparks shooting from the human spirit.

Your voice sounds through thousands of years, travels thousands of miles, emerges from the pages of your book. Your voice is the collective made into one. Your voice is the sound of a flute played by a solitary wanderer perched on the edge of a cliff with only the ice-colored moon above. Your voice is that sobbing music, made by inhalations that make ribs ache and by exhalations that take faith to let all air out.

You are like water. None of us can live far from some stream. We must drink water to nourish our thoughts, our blood, our flesh. By body alchemy, we change water into the juices we need. When water takes our waste, it also takes traces of us with it, and every drop returns to the great stream.

As water nourishes all beings, you animate our voices. As water leaves each being to return to the great stream, our voices return to you.

You are not a god separate from us. You are not a distant personage to be supplicated. When we approach you, we are not at the mercy of whims and capriciousness. You have the honesty of one whose hands have broken rocks, dug in the soil, and planted trees.

You have wandered, you have run, you have stumbled, you have fallen. Lost, you clawed through the brush. Proud, you plunged ahead only to confront mountains upon mountains. Careless, you eventually walked back to your village, only to find that too much time passed. You understood how important it was to return. Return to your own Tao, you said. How can that be wrong?

You have cried. You have fled from marauding horsemen. You have trekked to wilderness meadows and cleared them for houses. You have made sacrifices to heaven and earth, knelt down before the fire and pulled ox bones from the ash to squint at the cracks for signs. You have bowed to friends who joined you. You have stood with them to till the fields, to lift sticks against bandits, to scythe wheat, rice, and millet. You have gathered silkworms into baskets, and cast bronze vessels to share the bounty of your labor.

You are sharing still, sharing your wisdom, sharing of the millions of souls who have strengthened you. Sharing to help us face our troubles and celebrate our joys.

When people first hear the rumors about your existence, they rush to you. They are moved, sometimes terrified, at your knowing words. Then they may continue to invoke you without ever going deeper into the darkness where you dwell, or they put you aside, unwilling to live with your wisdom.

Still, there are some who want to know you better. There are those who want to enter into the same mysteries you know so well. They study you. They look into your words. Yet your words can too often be as mystifying as the truths they represent. After much effort, we realize that we will not find you by merely translating the old words of those who first recorded your utterances. No translation can accurately convey what you said then. The problem of looking for you in the written word occurred even before the Zhou dynasty was over, when the original language of the *Changes* became arcane. Even in the time of Confucius, only a handful of people understood your words. Within a few dynasties, merely reading your book became hopeless. Interpreters sprang up, and for thousands of years most people knew you only through someone else's words. That is why today we must instead find a way to hear you ourselves.

Let us hear the words that bring sighs of release. When you cry out, sob, shout, or laugh, let us feel that inside ourselves. When you flash lightning and dry oceans by your sun, let us behold it. When you tell stories of armies battling for walled cities, kings moving whole countries, farmers harvesting, let us be there too. When you reveal the omens—wild swans flying across the water, rising floods, dragons in the field, a poisoned well, a mare roaming among burial mounds—let the people shudder. We will feel you as surely as we feel our own hearts beat.

We will make our pilgrimage to you. When pilgrims visit a holy place, each pilgrim's experience is his or hers forever. We journey to experience the *Changes* as a pilgrim travels to Tai Shan or Mecca, Borobudur or Jerusalem, Ujiyamada or Varanasi. Let us walk your circles of change, absorbing your power and your voice, and let us return, transformed, and fortified to face the change that marks our daily lives.

Talk to us now, voice in the darkness. Show us the way.

The Origin

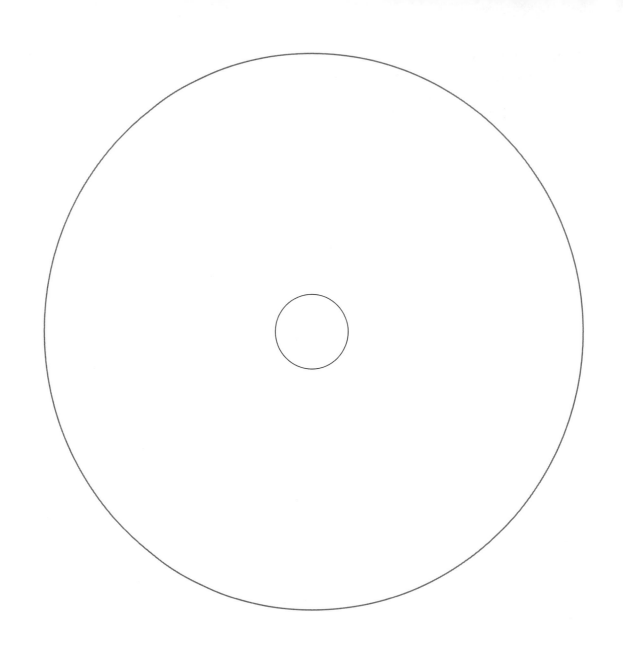

The dawn when someone first mapped the changes was so early that we can no longer distinguish legend from fact. Like someone squinting at a desert horizon, shapes flicker and fade, and we fear we are seeing our own wishes more than the robes of a far-off person.

When one figure is pointed out as a king named Fu Xi, we strain to see him. He remains ever-distant. If each year between him and us were a yard, he would stand more than forty-eight hundred yards away.

Some have colored his outline with their own stories. In the most flamboyant folk legend, Fu Xi is the brother of Nu Wa, the woman who created people from river mud. Those early humans lived simply, hunting deer and gathering berries. One day, all was almost destroyed when the gods of fire and water battled for control of the earth. Fire set all the forests ablaze. When the gods' blows broke a hole in the northwest quadrant of heaven, the heavenly river gushed out, brimming valleys and flooding mountains. Nearly all the early people died. Struggling to save them, Nu Wa repaired heaven by melting stones of five different colors, plugging the hole with glistening jewels.

This woman who birthed our ancestors, who nursed and taught them and who made heaven whole again, was half-woman and half-snake. The legends say Fu Xi was such a being too—a man with a serpent's body instead of legs. He had a man's intelligence and skills—in some ancient murals, he's shown with a try square—yet the serpent's body points to a more primitive and limbic body. He has eyes to see the stars, hands to measure his world, but a body fully in touch with the earth.

Scholars scoff that Fu Xi is a mirage. They say he seems large because he merely represents a group of people who established early civilization on the banks of the Yellow River. They question whether a single "primitive" person could be the father of advanced wisdom. Yet during that time, cultures already existed in other parts of the world. Cities stood along the Nile River. Cuneiform writing recorded transactions in the land between the Tigris and Euphrates Rivers. Cities in the Indus River valley were rich with copper and bronze vessels.

Perhaps it is possible, then, to give some credence to what the traditionalists believe: Fu Xi was a ruler. He observed the moving stars and changing moon above. He observed the patterns of the earth below, learning the habits of birds and animals, and turning the soil with his hands. He helped create written language, and he knew tallying and calculation. Most important, Fu Xi began the long effort to understand change.

So let us agree that Fu Xi is too far away for us to see him clearly. Let us agree that we are looking through layers of myth, legend, historical fact, and philosophical ideas. If each year was represented by a yard, some forty-eight hundred yards would separate us from him. At that distance it would be hard to distinguish one layer of air from another. Even if we could walk toward Fu Xi, those layers would be disturbed by our very presence.

Nevertheless, we can learn from the stories of Fu Xi—even the tale that he was half-snake. A snake's sleeping coils have tremendous potential. They might be nest, spring, or strangulating muscle. The snake's coils are a circle enclosing an empty center. In the same way, the moment before all movement is empty—pure future waiting to explode.

That is how we understand our origin today: an emptiness with a past so unknowable that we cannot name it, a power so great that the future springs from it. We call this *wuji*—a void with neither light nor shadow.

Wuji means "no limits." Think of the highest beam in your house—the high point of every rooftop, the limit of every building. If we can imagine that which needs no ridgepole, that which no roof could contain, that which has no inside and no outside, we can begin to grasp what no limits means.

Wuji is at the center and the beginning of our pilgrimage. As we make our pilgrimage, we are reproducing the entire evolution of this world. It began from nothing, as we begin from nothing—as each of us begins our mornings from nothing. Whenever we create—and that might be something as simple as deciding what to do next or as involved as composing music—we begin from nothing.

Thus, saying that *wuji* is at the center of all things is not some impenetrable philosophy. It is a state we are all familiar with each day.

This truth is valid on any scale. The origin of the universe must also be nothing. If we wish for an irreducible source for our world, then only nothingness can be that source. Every other assertion—whether we credit a god or any other intervening force—leaves open the question of further investigation. If this world was made by gods, then who made the gods? Only nothingness can satisfy the question of origin. Being came from nonbeing. Nothing but nothingness can answer the question.

Some people believe that as long as we can split distinctions into the smallest parts, we will find the origin of the world. This reductive process will never be satisfying. Just as we cannot parse the distance to Fu Xi, we cannot find the ultimate origin of our world in the pieces of the world. If we try to split things into tinier particles, we will find smaller parts to separate in turn.

Taking the world down to its finest subatomic level does not necessarily tell us about the way things work. We can suggest how all the pieces of the world fit together, from the simplest atom to the most complicated social structures, but we also need to know how those pieces *function* as a whole. We cannot understand a dance of molecules by lab tests. Grasping the whole of our existence requires a leap of intuition, a flash of insight. It means seeing all that we know around us at the same time that we see our history, back to the beginning of nothingness. The origin lies not in sharper distinctions but in a moment before distinctions existed.

Mathematics was limited until the discovery of zero. The study of change was not fully successful until we could conceive of emptiness as source. Although this philosophical discovery happened about a thousand years after Fu Xi, we can best understand the system he began by considering emptiness.

Emptiness is silence. It is not the stillness of the grave. It is midnight silence, when the wind rests, birds sleep, and the sun is hours from rising. It is the quiet that falls with snow, when the fields of labor are covered in white and trees have withdrawn into patience. That quietness is not the cessation of shouts, pounding feet, and pumping arms, but their origin. It is the source of day and the origin of spring. Silence is not the end. It is the beginning.

Wuji is essential stillness, the packed potential before the beginning. It is the beginning of the beginning. Only after silence breaks into sound does emptiness become all things.

Yin and Yang

In the source, in *wuji,* all is nothingness. There can be no movement, no consciousness. All is whole. When all is whole, there are no events until there is separation. Only with that division is there the beginning of all we know. Beyond that, the divisions continue: ours is a world of myriad distinctions.

If we sit on one side of a river valley we can watch the hills across from us lit by sunlight. The summer grass is golden, and the contours are defined by shadows. We can watch those shadows travel across the hills as the day lengthens, until the gold turns to cinnabar in the sunset and the shadows stretch to touch the looming night.

This image of the sunlit side and the shadow side of a hill is the image of yin and yang. We cannot see one without the other. Take away the light, and you have no end to shadow. Take away the shadow and you cannot see the edges of light.

The same is true of our feelings. What would sadness be if it was unrelieved by happiness? What would joy be without conflict? Indeed, every conflict lays bare the workings of yin and yang.

We encountered *wuji* in our previous circle. In this circle, we come to *taiji.* *Tai* means "great," and is written by adding one more dot to the word for "large." Great is bigger than what is largest. *Ji* is the same word as in *wuji* and means "limit." *Wuji* is to be without limits and thus to be without distinctions. As soon as there are distinctions, *wuji* ends and *taiji* begins. *Taiji* brings us into the world of dualities named yin and yang.

Yin is dark, female, cold, lower, under, yielding, soft.

Yang is light, male, heat, higher, above, firm, and hard.

Neither is better than the other. Neither can be cut from the other.

Something yin in one sense can be yang in another. For example, the top of a hill might be considered yang when compared to a valley, but if it is compared to a mountain, it would be yin. A woman would normally be considered yin, and yet if she commanded an army, she would be considered yang.

Yin and yang are not discrete forces but ways to conceive of a universal principle. We cannot find an entity, substance, or energy with those names, as we might detect magnetism or gravity. We cannot find why shadows move across the hills by digging and sifting the soil. We cannot do double-blind studies, because yin and yang change as each moment passes. Yin and yang are not things and they are not forces. Yin and yang are the names for pure interaction.

If there is a preponderance of yin, there will still be some yang. Eventually the balance will shift, because nothing is fixed. No matter how rapid that shifting might be, there can never be a gap between yin and yang. The balance is dynamic, and both create one another.

The balance of yin and yang can be subtle. One grain of rice tips the scales; one dot turns the large into *tai*. One shadow colors the sunlit wall. If you can look at an entire riparian forest moving with the wind, tracking each shadow of every sunlit leaf along with every rippling reflection in the water below, and still notice the hopping of water-striders below the flight of honeybees, you have an idea of what it takes to detect the balance of yin and yang.

Inhalation and exhalation are yin and yang. Reading is yin and yang. Each time your eye stops, you perceive. That moment is yang. As the eye moves again—albeit in a fraction of a second—and there is no thought, that moment is yin.

Our daily lives are divided into periods of sleep and activity. Our relationships are a balance between male and female. Our work lives are periods of effort and rest. Yin and yang account for every experience.

This understanding of yin and yang can be viewed from a pragmatic angle by considering the unique martial art Taijiquan. A Taiji fighter establishes a yin-yang tie by constantly touching the opponent during the match. Whenever the opponent moves, the Taiji fighter will counter with an opposite movement. That is instantaneous because it is not the fighter responding to the movement but rather the yin side responding to the yang of the opponent. If the Taiji fighter is an expert, he is like a shadow to whatever his opponent does. The opponent, in effect, is fighting himself.

We can follow the example of a Taiji fighter and strive for that same sensitivity in our daily lives as well. Whatever we face, we can be highly successful if we simply bring yin and yang into balance. We need not passively accept the panorama of circumstances that come our way. That would be like the Taiji fighter passively watching whatever happened, thinking, then trying to formulate a response. Not only is that too slow, but it completely misses the idea of completing a yin-yang pairing. On the other hand, if we understand yin and yang, we step into the flux of movement, acting on a reflexive level to bring balance into our lives.

Yin and yang represent polarity. There is tension between positive and negative. These opposites create movement in dynamic balance. The relentless process of dark pushing into light and light pushing into dark, of hard mixing with soft, of thrusting and receiving, of fire and water, of male and female is all there is to this world. Accepting that takes strength. A true acceptance of yin and yang destroys fate, gods, and luck. There is no predestination. There is no script. There is no god pulling strings. There is only the alternation of yin and yang, the polarity that describes every experience and everything we know.

Fu Xi sensed all this and wanted to understand this balance. In his time, people used tally marks to count. They knotted ropes to record transactions. They cut notches in sticks to count their sheep. So it must have been natural for him to notate yin and yang with lines. According to what we believe, he made two lines. A solid line ▬▬▬ meant all that we understand as yang. A line with a split ▬ ▬ meant all that we understand as yin. We can imagine him sitting on the sand and picking up a twig to scratch those two kinds of lines. It is from these two simple notations that Fu Xi began to tabulate his understanding.

The Four Images

Fu Xi must have asked himself how to show yin and yang's interaction. Just as tally marks are combined to show larger sums, it was logical for him to have made combinations of the two lines. There are four possible pairs:

Old Yang   Young Yin   Young Yang   Old Yin

This set was eventually named the Four Images, and each pair received a further name. The double yin line was called Old Yin, and the double yang line was called Old Yang. The pair with the yang line above was called Young Yang, and the pair with the yin line above was called Young Yin. These names introduce time into our understanding of yin and yang.

The Four Images symbolize change over time: extremes become their opposites. The Four Images show this clearly. Yang or yin doubled—their greatest extreme—are labeled old. They are on the wane. Young yin or young yang is actually more balanced. The two polarities are joined; their internal tension animates them and generates energy. Momentum is great; decline is distant.

When a situation reaches its extreme, symbolized by a double yang or a double yin, there must be a change. A limit has been reached and the pendulum must swing the other way, moving through combinations of yin and yang in varying proportions until the opposite extreme is reached.

We can visualize this by imagining a scoop on a waterwheel as it rotates out of the water and begins its ascent. When it reaches the top, water flows into a trough and the emptied scoop begins its descent. The scoop was rising—we can call that yang—until it reached the top of the curve. Immediately after passing that point it turned downward, entering the yin part of the cycle. At the bottom, underwater, it is in extreme yin. It must rotate upward again.

It the same way in nature. A full moon begins to wane. When the night is darkest, dawn approaches. Once the winter solstice passes, spring is on its way. Once the summer solstice passes, autumn is inevitable.

Social history demonstrates these same ideas. An empire at the peak of its glory succumbs to decadence, decay, and eventual destruction. Rome, Byzantium, Babylon, and the great Zhou empire all declined after their peaks. In modern times we have elections and democracy as a means of incorporating change into our political process. Rather than allowing the sporadic, violent, and ultimately negative process of dynastic succession, revolt, or invasion, we have a process to regularly change our governments.

Individual life spans have the same rhythms. There are seasons in one's life, from the spring of youth to the winter of old age. Within that overall scheme, there are smaller periods when we find ourselves at the height of a particular set of powers. In one's teen years and twenties, for example, one's physical prowess is generally at its greatest. In the middle years, one has matured enough to work hard and lay the foundations for future years. Many of us begin families. Later years ideally involve less physical labor, teaching the young, and contemplating the meaning of one's life. Yin and yang is inherent in our very process of aging.

The Four Images hold the basic idea of a cycle. If we know that cycles change from one extreme to another, we can search for the moment when that transition will occur.

No circumstances in life change from yin to yang and back again in simple and regular alternation. That would require a closed system. More commonly, another influence will enter this perfect system from the outside. The concept of the Four Images is balanced, symmetrical, and therefore static. But life is most emphatically not static. It is asymmetrical and complex. The Four Images cannot address all the complexities of change by themselves. Fu Xi needed to express more.

We might have some idea of why this was necessary if we consider that change usually comes out of anomaly. Our lives are perfect, and then we fall in love, and our lover disturbs us and excites us, causing us to act in ways we would never act otherwise. Into perfect summer, rain falls, wind comes up unexpectedly, and thunder surprises everyone. Just as a great city builds its highest walls and gilds its rooftops, marauders storm the gates. In every way, change happens when something touches the spinning top, or the carriage suddenly goes downhill, or some strange thought shimmers up from our subconscious and we set off in a direction that none of our calculations can justify. Change comes from asymmetry.

In the legends, Fu Xi sits on a riverbank in meditation. Just as he opens his eyes, a "dragon-horse" appears. Fu Xi was inspired by the patterns on the horse's back and made an enormous leap of thinking into finding a new graphic representation.

Two squared is four. Two cubed is eight. A set of eight combinations of yin and yang lines is the heart of Fu Xi's accomplishment, for with these eight lines he summed up the interactions of yin and yang. He then took those sets of three lines, called trigrams, and set them in an octagonal pattern inspired by the markings on the horse's back.

We know that diagram today as Fu Xi's Eight Trigrams. It is also called the Primal Arrangement, or the Early Heaven Eight Trigrams.

The Early Heaven Eight Trigrams

Fu Xi's Eight Words

In sorrow, we kneel to heaven
and offer rice and pears to earth.
We fast, then bathe in calm water,
scent our robes in sandalwood fire,
and whisper prayers into the wind.
But we cower before thunder
and weep for those who left our lake
to drink cold dew on the mountain.

Should you also climb that mountain
as your stepping-stone to heaven?
Should you pool your blood like a lake,
run like a mare over the earth,
and chant the sutras like thunder?
If you returned, skins of water
would still dribble dry in the wind
and bodies would be laid in fire.

Each day, raiders hack with swords, fire
bombards farms beneath the mountain,
and mad tyrants poison the wind.
Fields crack. Locusts drop from heaven.
Temblors knock brick walls to the earth,
corn withers. When rain falls, the lake
brims, and pines topple in water.
Hard to see that the same thunder

that uproots trees is the thunder
that brings spring to refill the lake.
Left and right must be one, as earth
bears ice waiting for sun. Mountain
is high and valley low, heaven
sets night to follow day. Wind is
both breath and storm. We cook with fire,
and we douse that fire with water.

So we search for those like water,
who stand while men flee from thunder,
who watch stars blaze into dawn fire,
and gaze as geese circle the lake;
who see snow engulf the mountain,
who track both deer roaming the earth
and planets turning through heaven:
they know when to sail with the wind.

Yet they build walls to block the wind,
and dig trenches for snow water.
They dance to the drums of heaven,
pluck herbs to heal body thunder,
and gather swords to melt in fire.
They would never move a mountain:
they stay low to serve all on earth
as hollow is bed for the lake.

Let us follow them to that lake:
where wolf and deer both drink; where fire
will kindle our hearts; where thunder
strikes gongs and blows songs on the wind.
Let us be like plunging water
and accept the will of heaven
with the wide stance of a mountain
and the summer richness of earth.

Our souls dwell nowhere else but earth,
the voice we want is on the wind.
There is a spring on the mountain—
our source. We crawled from that water.
Drink it into your belly's lake,
let kindness rise from your heart's fire,
let your movements be like thunder:
be both child and lord of heaven.

The Early Heaven Eight Trigrams of Fu Xi, also called the *bagua,* set forth eight fundamental principles to describe change. These eight are heaven and earth, water and fire, thunder and wind, mountain and lake. In their graphic arrangement, the pairs of trigrams are set as opposites.

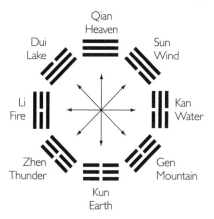

We can easily see heaven and earth as opposites. Water and fire are equally clear. However, thunder and wind, along with mountain and lake, may be less apparent pairings and are worth further exploration.

Heaven and earth establish our basic place in the cosmos. Heaven is above, the source of weather, the seasons, light, and warmth—as well as the sun, moon, and stars by which we measure time. Earth provides us with a place to live, food to eat, all the riches of precious minerals, oil, salt, clay—and thousands of other benefits.

We live between heaven and earth, and all our needs are fulfilled by them. There is nothing we could manufacture for ourselves without first being gifted by heaven or earth. The air we breathe, the sun that warms us, the wells that quench our thirst, the land that supports us, the food we eat, timber and stone for shelter—everything we need is given to us. We, in our naked softness, can do nothing without heaven and earth.

Water and fire benefit us in ways just as fundamental. We need both drink and warmth to survive. Without water, we could not live. Without fire to warm us, to use for cooking, and to use for forging our tools, we could die in the wilderness. We make water and fire our metaphors for the way energy works—the chilling and the downward-flowing is water. The blazing and the upward-shooting is fire.

In the *Changes,* additional meanings were attached to the symbols of the water and fire trigrams. Water was given a name that referred to a pit (water is in sunken places) and was classified as the symbol for danger. Fire was made the symbol for illumination, brightness, and enlightenment.

If thunder and wind, the next two trigram pairs, seem more associated with each other than opposites, we need to look more closely at their metaphorical content. Aside from its literal meaning, thunder also represents the arousing force of growth. A seed that sprouts, for example, is compared to thunder. Thunder is sometimes then expanded to symbolize an entire forest. A leader calling people to action is compared to thunder. Thunder also means the force of sound itself.

Just as thunder represents the sudden overcoming of inertia, wind also represents movement, but in a far different mode. Where thunder is arousing and forceful, wind represents the gentle and steady. Where thunder explodes with great impact, wind symbolizes thorough permeation. Where thunder expands rapidly, wind spreads, seeps, interweaves, and penetrates. The symbol of wind is also associated with wood; the steadily growing tree with its slowly spreading roots carries the idea of the gentleness of wind. Thunder and wind therefore represent the two extremes of growth.

The last two trigram pairs are mountain and lake. In addition to their natural meanings, they bring the social world into the eight trigrams. Mountain represents stillness, and can be associated either with a serene meditator or with a person standing in anger. Mountain therefore represents stoppage, consolidation, and the solitary.

Lake is set in contrast to mountain. It is level and liquid. Where the mountain is a consolidation of rock, the lake pools. The gathered water becomes clear as its impurities settle to the lake bed.

Like mountain, lake is used to symbolize an aspect of human interaction. Where mountain represents the solitary, lake represents gathering. Where the mountain is the meditator or the person isolated in stubbornness, lake is the marketplace and festival ground. It is the delight of friendship.

The eight trigrams combine to depict our environment, model how energy moves, conceptualize the kinds of growth, and address the extremes of social interaction. The octagonal pattern itself graphically capsulizes one of the basic assumptions of change: that change arises from the tension between polar opposites. Thus, the early positing of yin and yang as the two forces that make all movement in our world is carried through to a more sophisticated form. By assigning one of three places in a trigram to either a yin or a yang line, the binary begins to take on a greater range.

Each trigram is still yin or yang. The yin trigrams consist of earth, with three split lines plus trigrams with only one yin line (wind, fire, lake), while the yang trigrams are heaven, with three solid lines plus the trigrams with only one yang line (thunder, water, mountain). With a little experimentation, we can take any one pair and consider their opposing natures. If we see where they are antagonistic and where they are complimentary, if we realize that all pairs are in constant tension and yet at the same time make each other possible, we will already have gained much insight into the philosophy of change.

These eight fundamental images make the expansion to even more complex and far-reaching ideas possible. It is critical to absorb the whole of what each trigram can teach us if we are to go further in the discovery of change. Let us consider each of the eight trigrams.

Qian

Trigram
Three yang lines, symbolizing
the perfect yang of heaven.

Classical Symbolism
Heaven, strength, creativity,
father.

Dictionary Definition
Heaven, male, father,
sovereign.

Pictograph
The sun seen through the
trees, combined with the
sign for rising vapor.

Heaven

Windows still dark, we leave our beds
to kneel to the gold-dusted dawn.

Oriole song shakes azaleas,
dew steams through the green-bud branches.

Underneath the sun-furrowed sky,
we plow the earth and sow our seeds.

We may scratch tallies of the days
in our calendars and almanacs,

but our empire of stone and bronze
is just a blossom on the breeze.

Far better to bow to heaven
as it unfolds our days and years,

the heaven we breathe in and out,
that mingles others' breaths with ours.

From the earliest times, we have looked to heaven as the origin of all things outside ourselves. We regard it as the source of mysteries, and see the home of gods in its unlimited vastness. It has always been this way, and it will always be so.

Every generation before us has measured time by heaven. Though measurements were less exact thousands of years ago, and though we have better methods of accuracy today, our clocks, maps, calendars, nautical navigation, meteorology, and astronomical calculations still depend on heaven.

Few of us can manage without a clock, weather reports, and a calendar. These things alone remind us that heaven provides the context for our lives.

Nothing we have accomplished in our civilization alters the seasons. Nothing changes the solstices and equinoxes. Nothing we have made can eliminate the need to conform to day and night, or the need to make plans with the weather and time of year in mind.

We forget how supreme weather is, sometimes allowing people to perish in flood, hurricane, or snow because of our folly. We forget how necessary farming is to us. Without the heaven of rain cycles, and snow, and the sunshine that makes plants and oceans vital, we would quickly die.

Imagine yourself in a maze, with so many openings surrounding you that it would take too long to count them. The openings change. Some close seamlessly as new ones appear. Some give the illusion of being portals, when they are really solid. If you go through an opening, you find yourself in another chamber like the one you were in, a chamber the size of a stadium—with more doors around the perimeter. It would take too much time to try every opening, even if they were not shifting kaleidoscopically.

This is like the human condition heaven gives us. Heaven is time and the conditions that affect us. Some people superstitiously refer to that as "heaven's will" or "fate." Instead of believing in strange forces, devils, or gods, we should understand heaven as simple context. When faced with the panoply of change heaven provides us, we act according to those circumstances, but our actions must come from our hearts. No intellectual system alone can guide us.

In that sense, we must become the heaven that sets situations in motion. We can go through gates instead of standing paralyzed. We can become heaven—the heaven like a father who acts, who fights when necessary, who leads, who works. We must act, and benefit all that we touch as surely as the sky sends sun and rain.

Heaven creates time and circumstances. We must accept that. At the same time, we must find heaven in ourselves. We create with what heaven gives us, and in so doing, we become heaven itself.

Kun

Trigram
Three yin lines, symbolizing the perfect yin of earth.

Classical Symbolism
Earth, meekness, receptivity, mother.

Dictionary Definition
Earth, compliance, obedience, feminine.

Pictograph
A sprout from the ground (on the left), coupled with a picture of lightning.

Earth

We call this land our home:
   where vines offer purple grapes,
      and gourds dangle in the sun.

Children run with their dogs,
   cotton clothes flap white and blue.
      They toss apples in their hands.

We make our beads from shells,
   quarry rock to make our walls,
      build our homes on leeward hills.

Then storms come. Huts collapse.
   Raw red gashes, broken trees
      tumble down to mud rivers.

The earth keeps no ruin:
   a green glaze will heal the scars.
      Where old trees fall, young shoots sprout.

Where logs rot, mushrooms grow.
   Grass turns to sod on new graves,
      and vines creep up fallen walls.

According to some dictionaries, the pictograph of earth was created from the image of a growing plant and a bolt of lightning. Without the earth, the electric force of heaven has no place to go, even with its overwhelming energy. It seeks earth to ground itself.

A seed will not grow without air, sunlight, and rain. It also needs the earth to hold its roots and provide nutrients from the soil.

Furthermore, the earth can do something that no other power can do. It can take the dead and make life again. Whether a fallen tree or a fallen person, earth accepts all rot and death that lies upon it and brings forth fresh green.

Without exception, everyone makes a home on earth. Look around you. Earth lies beneath all things. It supports all plants, animals, and people. No matter how great our statues, pyramids, ramparts, tombs, and skyscrapers may be, each one of them stands on the earth.

It is not just the works of humans but all of nature that depends on earth. The valley is the earth flattening and opening itself to the sky. The streams and rivers run in the earth's channels. The lakes accumulate in the hollows of the earth. Without the earth, water cycles driven by heaven would not be possible. Earth gives place to the oceans.

There is literally nothing you can hold, eat, or live in that is not connected to the earth. You will find no exception to that statement, and, finding no exception, you have found a great truth to respect and to use.

The virtues earth inspires are numerous: acceptance, support, receptivity, modesty, and perseverance. For the *Changes,* no one exemplifies the human values of this trigram more than a mother. She works hard to nurture her family and children, and she works to grow and cook food to feed others.

The greatest virtue earth exemplifies is patience. It proceeds on a time span unique to itself. Water dries up. Fire is extinguished. The wind dies. Thunder ceases. Lakes evaporate. Mountains crumble. But the earth is ever present. By geologic time, the struggles of humans are momentary flickers. By earth time, the sprouting of grasses, the sprouting and falling of forests, and the thrusting and tumbling of mountains occur as rapidly as the flashes of a shamaness's many-colored robe.

Earth teaches us to be patient and nurturing, supportive and modest. Heaven may provide the days and the seasons, but earth teaches us how to make use of that time. Whether we are growing grain to sustain ourselves, or whether we must search for a new place to live, the earth shows us how to turn waiting to our advantage.

Everything worth doing takes time to develop. The earth teaches us to think of what matters against the long perspective of its geologic time.

Kan

Trigram
Two yin lines, one above and one below a yang line. Water is soft on the outside but strong inside. The trigram can also be seen as a picture of a chasm seen from above.

Classical Symbolism
Water, danger, difficulty, second son.

Dictionary Definitions
Pit, hole, depression. The sound of percussion. A snare, crisis.

Pictograph
The earth coupled with a picture of a yawning man; by extension, a huge pit in the earth.

Water

Cutting
    fissures cold and black,
water seeps with silent force.
It will flow through any crack,
penetrating mountain blocks
    until it spurts
    from the rock.

We stand
    at the chasm's edge,
toes on overhanging walls.
Water drips in unplumbed depths:
no one ever ventures down
    where the bottom
    is unknown.

Drowning
    is a sailor's fear,
sinking is a boatman's curse.
Still we set sail on the waves,
braving storms to keep our course:
    to heal our wounds
    and find our source.

Like all the trigrams, water has a series of meanings, and the combination of those meanings gives it profundity. Water's meanings are like a pentatonic chord; the totality of the chord's scale is its significance.

At its root, the name of this trigram means a pit in the earth. While there is a word for water, the written character for *kan* uses the earth radical instead. That indicates that we must not limit ourselves to thinking of water solely in its liquid state. *Kan* is water splashing over rocks in a ravine; to drink, we must climb down into a dark and slippery pit. That is why *kan* means both water and danger.

The next note in our chord of understanding focuses on how water remains uncompromised by danger. Water streams in chasms that frighten us, and yet it emerges unscathed. Water falls from black clouds, from high cliffs, or through ravines. It can squeeze through miles of aquifers and emerge intact. Accordingly, we have made it the symbol of remaining true to oneself. Water may represent flowing downward, coldness, darkness, and liquidity—but it also shows eternal integrity. Whether a single drop or a vast ocean, whether ice or steam, water will always re-form itself into its purest state.

For the third note, we must recall that all life evolved from water. Many creatures still live in water. All creatures drink water. Our bodies are predominantly water; the layers that make us human are thin. We may need the air of heaven, the nourishment of the earth, but we also need the quenching power of water.

We all have to drink water, and this leads to the fourth note. Not only is water an essential part of maintaining our health, but it can help us heal. It flushes toxins from our system. It provides an essential part of new cells. All over the world, people soak in hot springs, bathe in sacred pools, or drink the waters of remote artesian wells in their efforts to renew themselves.

For the highest note, we examine the virtues of water worth emulating. Noble persons seek to be as "fearless" as water. They "spread" their personalities: instead of holding rigidly to one doctrine, they give equal emphasis to all parts of their personalities. They change as quickly as water. They adapt to circumstance as water fills any void—and yet they maintain their integrity.

Pure water is clear, and this is the ideal of an evolved personality. By facing change with the clarity of water, we act without prejudice and preconceived ideas. Like water flowing into a cavern pool, we enter a situation and fill it completely. Like water that always finds its level, we maintain equilibrium. Like water that always flow downward, we never shirk any task that will serve others.

Turbulent waters obscure streambeds; still waters let us see clearly. A good mind is clear enough that it perceives, fluid enough that it does not fear danger. The trigram water represents both life and danger. The wise person accepts that the two are one, and calmly follows any situation.

Li

Trigram
Two yang lines, one above and one below a yin line. Fire is yang (hot) on the outside but yin (insubstantial) on the inside.

Classical Symbolism
Fire, light, elegance, intelligence, second daughter.

Dictionary Definitions
Brilliance. To leave, depart, separate. To defy, to go against. Distant from, apart from. To run into, to meet. To act in tandem.

Pictograph
A hand reaching for a bird caught in a net.

Fire

As a hand grabs for a snared bird,
so we snatch at the winging fire.
　We cage it in our forge and kiln.
　We use it in our hearth and stove.
　　We may trap it,
　　but we never tame it.

For all its strength it cannot stand.
It perches like a shaking bird—
　just as thinking cannot be freed
　from what we hear and what we see,
　　what we know comes
　　from eyes, nose, ears, mouth, touch.

Heaven's river cannot be spanned
by any measure we devise.
　Our only way is with the light
　of what ignites within our minds—
　　like a lantern
　　floating on a night sea.

As water is the beginning of life, fire is the beginning of civilization. The emperor before Fu Xi was named Suiren—Fire Maker—indicating the importance of fire as the beginning of advanced culture. Pottery, smelting, casting, forging, welding, glassmaking, chemistry—none of these would be possible without fire. Heating of homes, cooking, and lantern light—we need fire for them all.

Every time we use a force of nature, we must be careful that it does not destroy us. Water can drown us and flood our fields. Fire can burn us, blast our homes, and incinerate entire forests. A spark to flammable fumes, a break in a natural-gas line, a log fallen from a fireplace, a match carelessly thrown into dry grass—all show us the slim margin between using fire properly and letting it explode unchecked. We must be watchful. Fire can be channeled. It cannot be tamed.

The sun and stars are orbs of fire. We use the fire of light to measure light-years in space. We need light to work. We eat grain and vegetables that grow only because they gained energy by converting sunlight. We need light to read, to find our way at night, to signal to others, to make our computer screens readable.

We need warmth to counter the winter. We revel in the warmth of our own bodies too—the embrace of our loved ones, the rush of energy we feel as athletes. True to fire's dual meaning, though, fire can signal destruction: the heat of a serious fever, the rising rage when we have lost our temper.

Spiritually, fire represents brilliance, insight, and intelligence. It also symbolizes the heart, and the creative and intuitive powers that emanate from it.

Light can scatter. It can be fractured into different colors. Our concentration can flicker in the same way. But consider what happens when light is concentrated through a lens. It can make ordinary sunlight burn. It can cut like a laser. Concentrated light is a powerful force. Imagine if we could take the fire of our own intelligence and focus it through a lens. Imagine if the fire of our insight was not scattered to die in ashen heaps but ignited other minds.

Our heart is our hearth. It is the center of our being. Warmth, vitality, and the light for perceiving all emanate from it. We must constantly stoke those inner fires to work, to heal, and to burn away impurities. Whenever we discover errors in our character, we should smelt them and make ourselves better. In the same way, when we have been hurt by others, we can also burn away the injustices thrown at us. Fire is our center of vitality, as the sun is the center of the solar system, as the hearth is the center of a home. Act from that warmth and all will be well.

If we are to realize our own brilliance, we must constantly tend our fire. So we must purify ourselves, view the world by strong light, and focus ourselves. Our brilliance can light the world.

Zhen

Trigram
A single yang line appears suddenly to two yin lines.

Classical Symbolism
Thunder, motion, agitation, eldest son.

Dictionary Definitions
To shake, to tremble. To excite, to shock. Scared, terrified. Thunder, thunderclap.

Pictograph
The rain, with a word pronounced *chen,* indicating the sound of thunder. Among other meanings, the word *chen* means "time" and "heavenly bodies."

Thunder

It is cloud clamor—
skittering tongues rending
the vaults of starless space.

It is bombardment—
splitting hearts, blasting minds,
quaking heaven and earth.

It is ground shudder—
the robin's winging way
trembling a waiting leaf.

It is rain splatter—
on green shoots unfurling
while we are curled in sleep.

Every song starts with a beat. Whether it is soft or dramatically martial, the first note is a rousing from silence. The trigram thunder reminds us that change begins from sudden initiative. It takes great force to break inertia. The drumbeat signals the army. The announcement gathers a group. The song excites the lover. The chant of holy people calls us to worship.

Understanding what thunder symbolizes can be hampered by how overwhelming it is. Yes, thunder is loud, and when it comes, we look up and fall quiet as we wait for the next crescendo. When thunder explodes directly overhead, followed by a downpour of rain like a thousand sticks on cymbals, we become children, overwhelmed by the force of nature. One of the traditional ideas of thunder is that it awes us and calls us to reverence. All of that is true, yet we must look deeper, for thunder is also a metaphor for further subtle ideas.

Thunder indicates the beginning of all change. Change is cyclical, but cycles must have beginnings. Rolling waves had their origins far in the oceans, and yet something had to start their movement. Thunder comes each year, and each storm is familiar because we have experienced storms before. Their trembling registers as muscle memory in our very limbs. At the same time, each storm is different, and the havoc it may cause as well as the reactions it stirs will vary. Each season occurs in perfect order, yet each season is new in itself. All events are therefore both cyclical repetition and unique occurrence. Thunder teaches us to search for new beginnings within myriad cycles.

Thunder challenges us to adjust our view so that even the slightest movements can be noticed with the same attention that a storm demands. As an amplifier makes the seemingly inaudible detectable, we must adjust our sensitivity toward the small. There is no other way to know how change begins.

Traditionally, thunder is also compared to a forest. That may be a starling association. A forest grows by yang force through the open ground of the yin earth. Roots look like lightning forking the night-dark soil. A tree's seed is a sudden and shocking growth, breaking its husk and splitting the dirt.

Thunder is our first grunt as we put our shoulder to the wheel. It is the instant we lift our hand to a task. It is the first pen stroke on a blank piece of paper. It is the moment when a seedpod splits. It is the joining of oxygen and hydrogen to make water. It is the energy released when atoms cleave.

We should not be surprised when confronted with a looming situation. Instead, we should ask, "How did this enormous event happen?" Then we must look for the answer. An enormous event—something with the magnitude of a thunderstorm—had a tiny beginning. The thunder trigram is a single yang line hidden beneath two yin lines. Seeking to learn that hidden impetus gives us the mental force of thunder.

巽

Sun

Trigram
Two yang lines above a yin line. Wind seems soft, but can accomplish yang effects.

Classical Symbolism
Wind, wood, penetration, pliancy, eldest daughter.

Dictionary Definitions
Subservient, submissive, mild, bland.

Pictograph
Four hands on a loom.

Wind

Warp pulled
to weft,
wrapping the planet, knotting peaks,
    threading through caves,
            netting
forests, tangling ravines.

    Crane bones
    hollow
as if to let whistling through.
    Tree branches forked,
            giving
way to the shuttle's tug.

    Weaving
    itself,
unraveling itself each night,
    the wind ties us,
            like beads,
on endless threads of breath.

Think of a loom with four hands, the four hands implying a weaver working twice as fast. The fingers touch every part of the fabric, pulling it into a magnificent design.

That is the idea of wind. It can be as soft as cloth, weaving in and out of spaces. It penetrates, as threads penetrate a body of fabric. Where thunder is sudden, shocking, and arousing, wind is gentle influence. It transforms from an ongoing and interweaving pattern.

While a weaver is working, few can discern the final design of her work. She, however, imagines it clearly. She may have even woven the pattern before. She keeps her plan well in mind; the pattern grows from the very first knot tied. Similarly, once set in motion, the blowing of the wind cannot be stopped. It began long before, tied meticulously with many different strands. We cannot change the wind; we can only engage it.

At best, we might seek shelter from a storm. We might put up a barrier. Or we might work with the wind, hoisting sails on boats, or pumping water with windmills, or simply flying a kite. The wind makes its grand design, and we work either to shield ourselves from it or to make use of its energy.

When the weaver's design is finally seen, admirers gasp in wonderment and awe over the skill it took to make the cloth. They will praise the weaver, who both foresaw the pattern and was able to create it thread by thread, knot by knot, color by color.

No one thread makes the entire design, just as no one breeze makes a storm. But when the winds are combined, as in a tornado or hurricane, the sum is formidable. Wind, concentrated and amplified, can erode cliffs and uproot trees.

The trigram wind also stands for wood. That may be a curious association, a forcing of two metaphors together. We may even balk at having to hold both images at once. Nevertheless, the association makes sense if we look more deeply.

The roots of wood weave into the earth. The growing tree does not burst into existence but grows gradually—as anyone who has planted trees or has counted the tight growth rings of a stump knows. Branches interweave with one another, and spread in the sky, "rooting" themselves in the light, air, rain—and wind—of heaven as much as the tree spreads through the earth below. Forests, with their millions of trunks, form a pattern woven into this world. Wind can be seen as the warp, the trees as the weft.

Since thunder is seen as representing forests, so wind and thunder represent two kinds of growth—wind, the gentle and permeating; thunder, the explosive and sudden.

Wind. It weaves the atmosphere around our planet into a design of oxygen for our breathing, scatters pollen and seeds for new growth, lofts migrating birds thousands of miles so that new generations can be born. Wind: on its gentle and penetrating currents, a thousand forms of life find movement in the grandest of tapestries.

Gen

Trigram
One yang line above two yin lines. A mountain pushing upward to its pinnacle.

Classical Symbolism
Mountain, obstruction, stoppage, stillness, youngest son.

Dictionary Definitions
Tough, leathery food. Straightforward, outspoken. Simple clothing. Honest and upright personality.

Pictograph
A man stopping in mid-stride, turning to glare angrily.

Mountain

The prince rides to the highest peak,
dismounting at the great divide.
One side of the valley is his,
but nomad tents dot the far side.
He tells his men to plant their flag,
orders masons to unpack their tools.
Every nation needs good borders;
a strong defense will be his way to rule.

Descending the mountain toward home,
he encounters a sitting sage.
His beard is white, his clothes are patched.
He raises clasped hands in the shade.
The prince remains in his saddle,
the sage puts his head to the ground.
"I know why you come," the sage says.
"Among rulers you strive to be the first."

As his horse snorts and snorts again,
the prince glares and yanks on the reins.
"There," says the sage, "is your answer.
As you drive flags to stake your claim,
and patrol your borders to rule,
so must your anger be curtailed."
The prince dismounts, falls to his knees,
and touches his head to the dusty trail.

A mountain is unmoving. A mountain is a lofty upthrusting of rock. A mountain separates one plain from another. Its base is wide, sometimes occupying hundreds of square miles, its peak so high that trees die from the altitude and can grow no higher, leaving only snow and ice at the crown.

The mountain as supreme barrier symbolizes limits. A mountain can block the wind and rain. It can mark a border, defining a nation's territory and protecting it from invaders as no brick ramparts could ever do.

The mountain symbolizes stillness. For all of our consideration of the momentum of ongoing transformation, the mountain represents cessation. Sometimes that might mean a walling off of movement. Sometimes that might mean a culmination or solidification of movement. Like a volcano rising from the folding of the earth's crust, the mountain is a petrification of force.

Heaven and earth move, yet we see only solid things. We must understand that all molecules and atoms are bound together temporarily. Even though some bonds may outlast a human life span, they will eventually break. Thus, we can speak of constant flux and still include solidity in our contemplation of change. We need to give solidity a time frame, for what appears solid is moving so slowly that it only gives the illusion of being fixed. We must be prescient enough to know that there is no true permanence.

The mountain represents two types of behavior: meditation and anger. If that seems surprising, consider that both have to do with being solitary. One is solitude for a spiritual purpose; the other is solitude that degenerates into alienation. Both have to do with stoppage.

Spiritual persons withdraw for meditation. They practice being motionless, like a mountain. They may live a hermit's life on a mountain. On the other hand, those who stop to confront others by glaring in anger also isolate themselves. When the warrior takes a stance to issue a challenge, he stands alone against his opponent.

We need to apply the lesson of the mountain to the phenomenon of the mountain itself. In other words, we must limit even limits. Endless spiritual pursuit is not encouraged when there is so much more both to spiritual practice and to helping the needy in this world. Anger and the way of the warrior may have its place, but we must be mindful of what that place is. We must put limits on our rage. Every mountain has its summit. We must identify the peak of each limit we establish or meet.

Ultimately, the stillness of the mountain represents the culmination of what we do: it means placing limits on limits. The proper understanding of how to move and stop, how to be flowing and then firm, is the peak of moving and stilling at the right times.

Lake

Dui

Trigram
A yin line on top of two yang lines. A lake appears insubstantial on the surface, but has depth and power below.

Classical Symbolism
Marsh, lake, pleasure, joy, eloquence, youngest daughter.

Dictionary Definitions
To exchange, to barter.

Pictograph
A person throwing arms up in joy, mouth open in a shout.

She is the youngest of six,
trotting and laughing behind
her three older brothers
            and
   her two sisters.

At the outdoor market
they lay out the wild herbs
each has gathered by hand.
          "Come!"
  The crowd gathers.

"Must I really stay here?
Look! Acrobats and sweets!"
The eldest two pause, turn,
         smile
  and let her go.

Soy milk. Candy and pears.
Live turtles. Geese and ducks
and a boy's somersault
        all
  are her delight.

When dusk comes, off they trek,
past the lotus wetlands
where returning cranes are calling
         mates
  in the night marsh.

Mother and father wait
beside the hearth, smiling.
Eight at the table, they
        share
  their salted rice.

In contrast to the mountain as concentration culminating in solidity, the lake is concentration through pooling. Where the mountain is proud upthrusting, with the danger of excessive isolation, the lake is gathering through lowness: it is where waters run together.

Wherever waters form a lake, life springs from it. Fish swim in the currents, plants grow on the shores, and animals come to the banks to drink. When a man and woman give pleasure to one another, there is also pooling, and new life can result.

Gathering together in friendship, coupling together in love, even the uniting of body fluids in lovemaking are like the lake, and so this trigram is the sign for pleasure.

When essences are pooled together, there are chemical reactions leading to new emergence. Exchange has occurred. This exchange can also mean purification. Muddy streams flow into the lake, but when the silt settles out, the water is clear again.

The trigram also alludes to a marsh, bog, or wetland. Here is where the image of exchange expands. Think of a wetland and how much it is a place of exchange. Thousands of birds stop at a wetland during their migrations. They eat the insects and plants that grow there. In turn, their trampling and their droppings contribute to the fertility of the wetland, making wetlands perfect locations for growing rice.

A salt marsh is another example. In a salt marsh, water flows into the sloughs, and over distance and time, blue water gradually becomes heaps of pure crystallized salt. In the process, birds, fish, shrimp, insects, and bacteria live in the various pools of salinity, feeding off each other. An endless number of exchanges happen in a salt marsh.

On a social level, the lake as symbol of exchange reminds us of the pleasures of festivals and marketplaces. The market is where so much of our social intercourse takes place. There is barter. There is trade. There is selling and buying. In rural areas, where people live far apart, they will gather together—as at a lakeshore—for commerce and celebration. This coming together for exchange fits the metaphor of the lake and wetlands.

Finally, although the study of change is serious business, this trigram reminds us that there is a legitimate place for joy. Just as the trigrams are meant to represent the entirety of all change, they must also represent the entirety of our revolving emotions as well. We are social beings. We love exchange.

We study change so that our exchanges with others will be joyful.

The Early Heaven Hexagrams

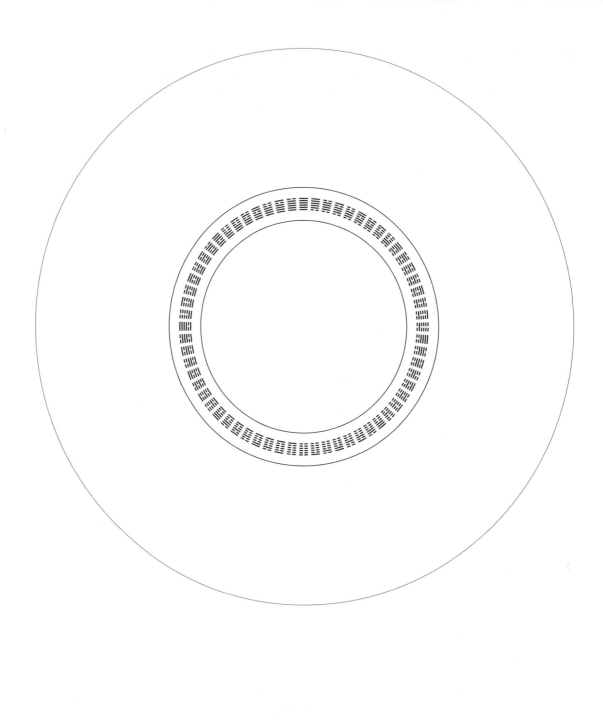

What follows from the Early Heaven Eight Trigrams is an arrangement of sixty-four hexagrams in a perfectly logical order. Whether due to a some undocumented loss in history, or whether subsequent revisions rendered those commentaries obsolete, we do not have any written wisdom on this arrangement—only the graphic forms. Nevertheless, we need to understand them in order to comprehend what comes later.

The Early Heaven Hexagrams are perfectly derived from yang and yin. The illustration below, based on a drawing by Shao Yung (1011–1077 C.E.), a philosopher of the Song dynasty, shows this scheme. *Wuji* is at the base of the drawing. Then it splits into yang and yin, and then into finer distinctions. There are six layers. Each layer will either be black (yin) or white (yang). In this way, all sixty-four hexagrams are generated.

The lower drawing makes this explicit. All yang boxes, which generate Heaven, or Hexagram 1, are on the left. A stack of six yin boxes, which generate Earth, or Hexagram 2, is on the opposite side.

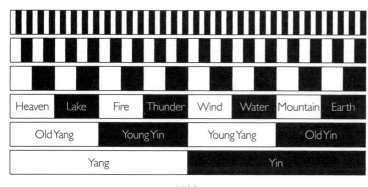

Wuji

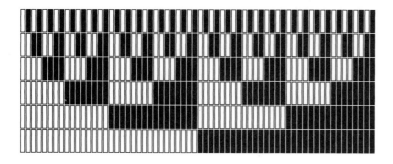

The generation of the Early Heaven Hexagrams from *wuji*. *Wuji,* at the base of the upper diagram, splits into yang and yin, which in turn split into the Four Images. Next come the Eight Trigrams. Note that their names indicate the top line of that trigram, and not necessarily whether a trigram is considered yin or yang.

The lower drawing clearly shows how each stack of six boxes duplicates the yin and yang pattern in the full set of hexagrams.

There are two arrangements of the Early Heaven Hexagrams that have come to us today. One is a square arrangement:

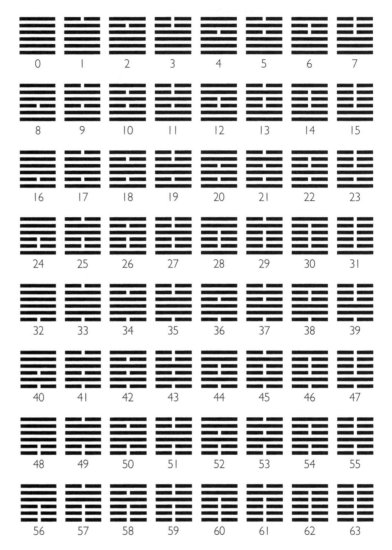

The other is the circular arrangement that is the map of this circle. This arrangement corresponds perfectly with the Early Heaven Eight Trigrams. If we start at the center, we begin from *wuji.* Then we come to the first yang line. The next circle has the two Old Yang lines. Adding the primal yang with the two Old Yang gives us the three yang lines of the Heaven trigram at the top of the circle. Each of the trigrams can be generated by the same method.

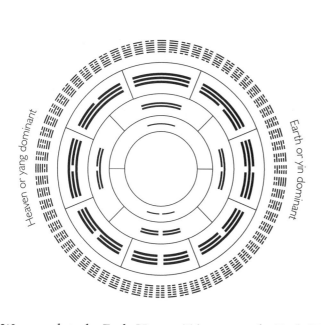

Heaven or yang dominant

Earth or yin dominant

The Early Heaven Hexagrams are derived from all the circles within it. The lower trigram of each hexagram is aligned with its position on the next inner circle. For example, fire is the lower trigram of the hexagrams adjacent to fire in the eight trigrams. On the left side, heaven is on top of each cardinal hexagram, on the right, earth is on top. Looking counter-clockwise, there is a progression from heaven at the top to earth at the bottom, and then a progression back to heaven on the right side.

We can relate the Early Heaven Trigrams to the Early Heaven Hexagrams in the same way. The heaven hexagram, a doubling of the heaven trigram, is at the top. Each of the eight trigrams occupies the lower position of the hexagram centered and adjacent to it, combined with heaven (on the left side) or earth (on the right side) as the upper trigrams. Therefore, the left side of the circle is dominated by heaven, or yang, and the right side is dominated by earth, or yin.

For example, when we read in a straight line from the inside out, we can see the fire trigram take the lower position of the hexagram next to it in the outermost ring shown above. Heaven takes the upper position. All the fire hexagrams (as defined by the lower trigram) are grouped together next to the fire trigram.

What this means is that our understanding of cycles is now made even more sophisticated. Our basic analogy of a waterwheel still stands. But we can now see that the stages of turning can go through tremendous variation. If we say that extreme yang becomes extreme yin, we can now see that there may be many phases to that transformation. Whichever direction you travel, and from whichever point you begin, the extremes vary, mix together, coalesce momentarily into their pure states, and then begin a new cycle again.

Then, in the eleventh century B.C.E., a prince named Ji Chang, later known as King Wen, would take both the eight trigrams and the sixty-four hexagrams and drastically rearrange them.

The Later Heaven Eight Trigrams

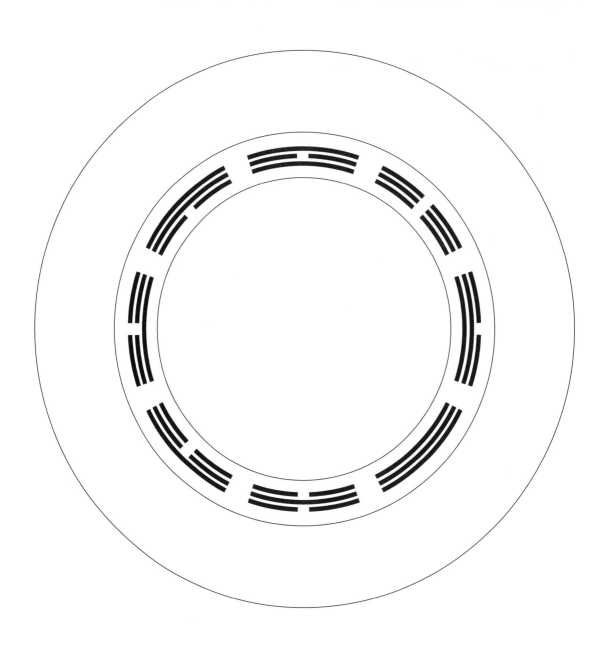

King Wen: Hidden Lines

I

Strong and just was King Wen.
He knew the will of heaven.
Though he wept tears of blood,
He never lost his clear vision.

O Ji Chang! Where are you? We are here, thousands of years and thousands
of miles from you, far from the mountains and streams you loved, far
from the valley where your grandfather and his loyal people made exo-
dus from tribes who demanded their land.

How your country has changed! How your people have changed! Perhaps
you foresaw that, and yet, as in so many things, you are silent. You knew
how to keep a secret in your heart, as a nightingale in a palace courtyard
is unheard by wild birds.

We find no more pieces of shell, bone, or bronze with your name, and people
argue over how tall you were or what sounds flew from your throat.

Those who paw words on rotting silk, who dig like ghouls for your bones, can
never know how cherished you are. People have kept you alive in the
blood of their hearts, on their lips as they kiss their children good night,
in the memories they summon like talismans when demons wail on
foggy nights.

You were the leader of Zhou, vassal state to the great Shang kingdom. You
taught your people to till the fields, to marry and have children, to care
for the elderly, to study the words of the ancients, to train themselves
through archery, and to celebrate their harvests.

You lived in forests no ax had touched, with clear streams and good soil,
where dreams drifted on dawn mists, and starlight streaked the night
like blessings from a thousand gods. It was a land where it was easy to
know the spirit of each rock, each piece of moss, each flower, and each
tree.

You were grateful, and you made reverence, you, a prince, who would be
named King Wen, who clasped heaven and earth together, who called
people to temples because a life without gratitude was a life of grunting
and rolling with pigs.

When the sun and the moon tugged the myriad things together, when waters
    burst from clouds and springs, when devils and sprites battled gods and
    ancestors with explosions and black smoke, you held your clean palms
    to the sky.
And yet, one man hated you, his tongue stiff in his hunger to crush you.

II

Strong and just was King Wen.
He knelt in the tyrant's den.
He was seized for a sigh,
and locked in a dark prison.

O Ji Chang! If, like you, we had been summoned to the palace and we had
    walked into the court of Di Xin, king of Shang, and smelled how he cut
    open pregnant women and once hacked the heart from a sage who
    criticized him, could we have been so calm?
Did you pause when Minister Feizhong rubbed his palms on his robes?
Did you know that Prince Hu whispered to Di Xin that the population in
    your land was growing, that your armies were strong, and that your cof-
    fers were full?
Could you foresee that Di Xin, though clutching his concubine Daji, was
    drinking himself flaccid?
Did you know of the forest with lakes of wine—venison and hams hung
    from branches, girls and boys prancing nude—where he and Daji
    sported on couches laid with leopard and tiger skins? How they ate
    camel, rhinoceros, and ginseng roots dug from nameless patches where
    men had died cursing and raging?
Did you know the spectacle that made Daji and him laugh and touch? Where
    a condemned man was chained to a bronze pillar rubbed with oil, a
    bonfire lit at his feet to force him to shimmy up, palms singeing, loins
    grilling, only to have him fall back repeatedly until king and concubine
    could savor the charred flesh?
How you must have known all this, and still you went when Di Xin
    demanded your appearance, because your sense of duty was firm, you
    knew that your country was not yet stronger than Shang, and you kept
    yourself as a man of honor.

How you must have mastered yourself, to glance at his red leer and bristling
    beard as he sat his bloat in layers of stiff green, black, and purple silk,
    regarding you as a wolf eyes a crippled doe.
How you must have searched for some omen when Di Xin appointed you
    and two other princes—Prince Jiu and Prince E—as his high counse-
    lors, but never sought a word of advice.
How you must have wanted your battle armor when he jailed you three
    princes behind lacquer doors.
How you must have counseled restraint when, months later, Prince Jiu sent a
    virgin as bribe for his freedom.
How you must have wanted to call your generals when the maiden gasped
    and turned her head as Di Xin disrobed, and he struck her down, and
    ordered Prince Jiu minced alive for the kitchens.
How you must have wanted to grab Prince E before he shouted.
How you must have wanted to close your eyes when, before the echoes were
    still, a dagger pierced his flesh.
Hemmed in by soldiers, surrounded by glaring princes, the blood of two
    friends smeared on the palace stones, you sighed.
Prince Hu heard that and said that proved your treason.
Afraid of your brothers, afraid of your sons, but feeling powerful in the fury
    spurting in his blood, Di Xin ground his molars together, a beast about
    to spit black gore, a scoundrel scheming tricks and traps, and he
    ordered you thrown into Deer Terrace at Youli:
where the rain dripped off the eaves and mists flew through the barred win-
    dows like ghosts of those dismembered;
where chiseled walls trickled dampness, glistening like coagulating blood;
where you had one wooden table, one candle;
where you turned to the hexagrams, which your jailers could not understand,
    and you sat, facing north, counting the lines.

III

Strong and just was King Wen.
He could read the portents.
Yet he still sacrificed
to keep the Way of reverence.

O Ji Chang! Who among us could survive seven years without pounding at
the door, tearing out our hair, ripping at our cheeks, weeping tears into
dust until our eyes were like two marbles rolled to the corners of our
heads?

Your jailers bowed, addressed you as prince, but once they closed the door,
they snickered and joked, and ticked off on thick fingers the hundreds
of tortures and maimings they loved.

Did your ribs heave as you stifled your cries for explanation from your ancestors? For you were taught that your ancestors, Houji first among them,
were more precious than all the jewels, and that they protected and
blessed your every step.

How it must have maddened you that you could not kneel at their altar as the
moon rose.

You were not a man to shriek blame: you searched for the mistake in yourself.

So you completely reshaped divination and reordered wisdom.

You began your rebellion against Shang by altering the very cosmology by
which every person thought and acted.

You rearranged the trigrams even as longing rocked in you like a bucking
stallion.

You clutched for sanity by building a paradise in your mind.

You imagined yourself at home in your valley, the sky and mountain behind
you, rivers flowing eastward.

You longed to see the eastern dawn, the westerly sunset, hear the thunder,
and feel the desert wind coursing from the west.

You missed the warm breeze from the southwest.

You wanted to throw your arms open to the summer skies and the goodness
of the earth as you remembered the smiling citizens who brought
you baskets of millet, wheat, soybeans, sorghum, corn, apples, pears,
peaches, and melons.

You would not give Di Xin hints of your churning. You would not compose
elegies, sing dirges, or paint pastorals. Instead, you remade the trigrams
and the hexagrams.

You let Di Xin hiss when the guards reported how you had scrambled the
oracular orthodoxy.

You stayed silent. Turning those lines must have secretly showed you a way
out of misery, as they arranged and rearranged themselves, linking and
unlinking, until they made a ladder that you climbed into heaven.

IV

Strong and just was King Wen.
He found a brilliant man
who fished with a straight hook,
while he laid his battle plans.

O Ji Chang! Among all whom you missed, among your brothers and ten
    sons, including crown prince Ji Fa and your genius fourth son, Ji Dan,
    among their mother, Taisi, among your concubines and advisers,
    among the people in the fields, you missed one man above all others.
His name was Taigong.
You remembered when you once were about to go hunting and the diviners
    set to work, drilling holes in turtle shells and ox scapulae, firing them
    until they cracked, finally pronouncing something startling:
"Neither a dragon nor a serpent, neither a tiger nor a bear, but something far
    more useful to a prince."
Wondering, wandering, tracking, you and your hunting party arrived on the
    northern shore of the Wei River, and there, beside Sandy Rock Creek, a
    seventy-two-year-old man sat with a fishing pole.
He pulled the line from the waters. There was no bait, and the hook had been
    straightened.
You saw his eyes and his straight back, and you wanted to know the straight-
    ness of his mind. Impressed within a few questions, you called him
    Teacher Uncle, and took him home in your own chariot. All others
    would call him Taigong, the Great Man.
You thought no less of him when he told you he had been dismissed from Di
    Xin's service, how his businesses as a butcher and then as a rice dealer
    were both unsuccessful.
You listened when he told you how his wife divorced him as a failure and
    hired men to chase him from their home. You nodded when he said he
    came to Zhou, waiting months for a chance to meet you.
Friendship—unlike the love found in harems, or the selfless love for the peo-
    ple, or the dutiful love for ancestors—flashed and instantly bound the
    two of you together.
It was the love of two halves for their whole.
From that day on, you conferred with Teacher Uncle over every matter.

Taigong drew troops directly from the fields, as subterranean water flows from the earth. It was an army to fight, but also to do public works, to chase robbers and raiders, to guard taxes and levies, and to hunt.

Taigong's army was the first to use chariots in formation, mowing down foot soldiers, rolling wheel to wheel against the enemy, hacking limbs with halberds, scraping the inside of skulls with spears, the blood on the battlefield rising in a flood that filled threshing pits until the pestles floated.

This old warrior was never defeated in battle, yet he never attacked while you were held hostage.

How you appreciated that.

How he tried through every other form of diplomacy and bribery to free you.

Across rivers and battlefields, the comrade with whom you had fought shoulder to shoulder, whom you loved as both teacher and uncle, the one who was closer to you than any kin—this man searched for the lever that would pry you from Di Xin.

V

Strong and just was King Wen.
He gave fertile fields to tend.
Mulberry around homes
fed silkworms and screened the wind.

In your dreams, you saw two travelers, and you puzzled over why they were on the road heading west.

You saw them, walking sticks in hand, dressed in cotton tunics and conical hats of woven bamboo. There was white in their beards, and lines around their eyes from squinting against the sun.

You saw them trudge to the border of Zhou, and stop at the checkpoint. They were surprised that there was neither toll nor tax.

They watched guards let farmers pass without stealing from the carts.

They strode down the road as the sun settled orange, and they whispered your name, nodding.

In your dreams, you remembered the time you ordered a pond dug. The diggers found a skeleton, and the officer in charge reported it to you.

"Bury the dead properly," you commanded.

"But no one is responsible for him," said the officer.

"He who claims the world is responsible for every person in it. He who claims a princedom is responsible for every person in it. Am I not responsible for this dead man?"

The bones were collected and reburied with clothing, coffin, and full rites.

In your dreams, you saw old men in courtyards, hair white and wispy, bones wrapped awkwardly in padded clothes, who sat all day with no wives and no children to call their names.

You saw women whose faces froze when their husbands died, graven wrinkles forming the ideograms for wind-pierces-the-chambers-of-the-heart— words no one wanted to mouth, ever.

You saw those who stood by trees, teeth grinding, hair falling out in clumps, feet skewed, as they gnawed on their wrists.

You saw babies abandoned by the roadsides, pale as ice and too afraid to cry, and frowning orphans clutching any nearby adult.

You asked all these people to walk ahead of you.

You ordered the laws carved into wood and bamboo tablets so that all could see them and no official could bully on their own whims.

You built schools for children so they could read those laws and read the great books.

You completed an academy for commoner and noble alike, surrounded by a moat to bring the clear sound of water to young minds.

You welcomed any qualified person to become an officer of your court and paid pensions to their wives and children.

You gave each family a home, and around each one you ordered mulberry trees planted to cut the wind and to feed silkworms so the old would be cushioned in silk.

You gave each family five brood hens and five brood sows, so that everyone would have eggs and meat.

You divided the fields into squares, each square subdivided into nine smaller squares, one to each man so that he could feed a family of eight from his one hundred *mu*.

In your dreams, you saw two shadows at your border.

You would never know them; only sense the presence of Boyi and Shuqi, two sons of the Prince of Guzhu from the northwestern steppes.

When their father died, they went to Shang, but detested the rule of Di Xin.

Hearing how you cared for the old and the poor, they walked to Zhou, and settled secretly in your land.

VI

Strong and just was King Wen.
His men said, take revenge!
But he held each one back,
looking for signs from heaven.

O Ji Chang! While you paced in Youli, trying to measure the future, Di Xin
tottered over wine jars, and sank his head in Daji's breasts.
His ministers whispered hoarsely through the screens: The princes are rest-
less! Return to your throne!
Di Xin responded by inviting hundreds of princes to a grand hunt.
Dressed in gold and crimson, his bow and arrows ready, he led hundreds of
horsemen. But his eyes rolled. His face reddened as he gripped the reins.
He wobbled in the saddle. He saw the unspeaking princes around him,
and his lips twisted.
When he returned to the capital, a foot soldier dashed in, panting: the Yufang
tribes had revolted!
Di Xin summoned armies to crush them.
Many princes sent men, but they also submitted a petition: if Ji Chang's
imprisonment continued, they would come to the capital to share the
same incarceration.
Di Xin's hands closed on the arms of his throne like a tiger who misses its
prey and seizes a root.
Just then, dispatched by Taigong, San Yisheng arrived with gifts to be presented through Minister Feizhong.
Green bile leaching his tongue, Di Xin received the envoy. Saliva on his teeth
glinted as he gaped at the zebras, white foxes, and giant tortoises crowd-
ing into his court.
"Your prince is loyal to send such exotic gifts! Any one of them is worth his
release, and yet you give me so many!"
He sat back, his eyes two slits.
You were brought to him, and as you knelt, Di Xin presented you with bows,
arrows, axes, halberds, and appointed you his Field Marshal of the West,
with the authority to wage war in his name against the rebellious tribes.
For seven years, you had cultivated yourself. For seven years, you had remade
the hexagrams so that they spoke more clearly. Calculating quickly, you

ceded ten thousand square *li* of your territory between Shang and Zhou
to Di Xin. His chest relaxed.
You thanked him. You assured him your allegiance was unshakable.
He nodded, then added: "How tragic that Prince Hu framed you."
You returned to Zhou, where your sons and Taigong welcomed you with
celebration but cried for you to punish both Prince Hu and Di Xin.
You said you were a righteous prince loyal to his king.

VII

Strong and just was King Wen.
Strangers came, he welcomed them.
They saw peace in his land
and found towns of eager friends.

O Ji Chang! You rode your chariot through grain high as a man's ear. Farmers
on far slopes stooped in a row, mowing the furrows, sickles in hand.
You stopped beneath a tree. Its spirit felt young and wild.
In Di Xin's country, spouse and children were punished with the criminal.
Your courts tried only the accused.
In Shang, a peasant was a peasant for life, yellow as the dirt. A warrior was a
warrior until the end, brittle as his armor. A prince held his land for life,
rooted as a tree. Di Xin would rule as an eternal god with bronze fists
who snorted fire.
You gave land freely to any young family who moved to Zhou.
One day, the Prince of Rui and the Prince of Yu both claimed a stretch of land
between them. Battle flags had been unfurled, but they had agreed to let
a third man judge.
They could have gone to Shang, but Feizhong grasped for gold and Di Xin
grabbed for wine.
The two princes came to Zhou. Citizens yielded the road with courteous
words. Farmers halted work until they passed. In the villages, they saw
men and women walk in separate but orderly groups. No one with
white hair carried heavy loads.
They stopped at a government office. One officer was urging his superiors to
give his promotion to another man.
The two princes looked at each other, then down at their feet.

They came to you, Ji Chang, and you saw their pasts in their eyes: arrow
    against spear, horse against man, battle-ax against flesh, flag against
    drumbeat.
You ordered a bronze cauldron of fresh food to be put between them, and six
    men lifted it into place.
In sharp relief around its girth were the faces of ancestors and ancient words
    of peace. The words were writings with curves languid as an elephant's
    trunk, corners as precise as constellations.
All the assembled drank wine from three-legged bronze cups, and the atten-
    dants ladled steaming food from the cauldron and the two princes ate.
The Prince of Rui and the Prince of Yu put their states under your protection.
Then they sent messengers. In response, forty states, including Ruan and
    Gong, made alliances with you.
In the years that followed, your armories smoked day and night. The clang-
    ing of hammer and tong was a song of armored men and bloody eyes,
    whirling swords and war cries.
You inspected your troops, and Taigong glanced at you, yet your lips did not
    move.
When you moved your troops, it was to defend Zhou against attack from the
    Kunyi tribes to the west.
When you moved your troops, it was against the Prince of Mi, ally of Prince
    Hu, who had invaded Ruan and Gong.
When you moved your troops, it was to turn the armies of the Prince of Li,
    on the borders of Shang.
You could have turned your reins toward Prince Hu, and your men would
    have gladly followed.
You could have sent spies and scouts into Shang, and your men would have
    gladly followed.
Taigong glanced at you, but you turned toward home, and he had to ground
    the lightning of his eyes in the earth of Zhou.
Through the trees, you saw women bent over vats of boiling water, reeling
    silk. Fingers unaware of the steam and bubbling water, they picked up
    the white cocoons and drew the silk out in gossamer filaments. One jerk
    would snap the thread.
You spoke to your son Ji Dan about your seven years. He understood, and
    wrote poetry to the lines of each hexagram.
You remarked to Taigong that more than two-thirds of the princes surround-
    ing Shang had put themselves under your protection.

Neither your sons nor your Teacher Uncle saw the threads you pulled with
steady hands.

VIII

Strong and just was King Wen.
Though he died before Shang's end,
his flame still lights our nights,
guides the way beyond our ken.

O Ji Chang! For six years after your release from prison, conscripts labored to
pile stones and build the walls of Prince Hu's city of Chong higher and
thicker. For six years, he rallied other princes against you, and gathered
armies to destroy you.

Finally, the *Changes* spoke to you. Taigong prepared the scaling ladders and
the assault towers.

Outside Chong, you told your troops: "Do not kill civilians. Do not raze
homes. Do not bury wells. Do not chop trees. Do not steal livestock."

You laid siege to Chong in the valley of Wei. For three months, your ladders
and assault towers toppled. Then, as you neared one hundred days of
war, Chong fell.

You took Prince Hu's head in exchange for seven years.

You pulverized his city walls, just as you crushed the alliances against you.

And still Boyi and Shuqi stayed in Zhou, for they knew your war was according to heaven's omens.

You liked the valley plateau of Wei so much that you built a new city to the
east of it and named it Feng. Mountains to the north, west, and south
formed walls larger than Prince Hu could ever have built, and the Yellow River flowed through the east.

From that platform, all the plains of Shang were lower.

Ji Chang, master of the hexagrams, noble shaman who mouthed the oracle
lines: Taigong outlived you. Your sons Ji Fa and Ji Dan outlived you. You
were a pious man, who steadily sacrificed to your ancestors.

Ji Chang, founder of Feng, city of fire and thunder named Abundance: you
became an ancestor.

Ji Chang: We can only guess what you saw beyond the white hair hanging
over your face.

Ji Chang: Even after your death, your silk threads pulled taut.

Ji Chang: Di Xin, slumped drunkenly on his throne, woke and slurred, "What day is it? What hour is it?" The courtiers could not hear the timekeeper's chime, but they could hear the whetstones in the kitchens, and they soothed, "We do not know."

Ji Chang: Di Xin sent a messenger to the Grand Tutor, a man so learned he could have used the bronze pillar as a sundial. "No one knows the day or hour in all the palace save me. Doom!"

Ji Chang: The tutor said, "Tell his majesty that I do not know." Plucking one string of his lute, he undid his hair and went to live among the slaves.

Ji Chang: Did you foresee that crown prince Ji Fa would conquer Shang, slay Daji, and put Di Xin's head on a pike?

Ji Chang: Boyi and Shuqi smelled the smoke of burning cities. They heard the cries of women and children. They felt the trembling of trapped warriors. They tasted blood in the food of Zhou. They saw all your silken patience rent by ax strokes.

Ji Chang: Boyi and Shuqi said, "Had the Prince of Zhou lived, the Shang would have voluntarily opened their gates to him. Instead, his son charges with the hooves of a horse and the claws of a tiger. Woe!"

Ji Chang: Your food had been nectar in their mouths. Now it tasted of putrid blood. They climbed up Shouyang Mountain, preferring to eat wild grass.

Ji Chang: Boyi and Shuqi starved themselves to death, even as your son Ji Fa was crowned with the name War—King Wu.

Ji Chang: Your son declared the beginning of the Zhou dynasty and gave you the posthumous name Culture—King Wen.

Ji Chang: Could you have foreseen that three thousand years later, your adversaries and your sons, your cities and your bamboo chronicles would be dimly known, but that you would still shine?

Ji Chang: Your light of peace, your light of wisdom, your light of virtue still blaze from an unseen source.

Ji Chang: In confusion we have sought wisdom, but today, we know how: the broken lines of your light show us the way.

W hen we first encounter King Wen's Later Heaven Trigrams, we face a mystery. Where Fu Xi's Early Heaven Trigrams were simple pairs of opposites, the Later Heaven Trigrams seem to lack such order. Initially, we see Fire across from Water, and what we have learned of yin and yang seems assured. But we may well ask why Heaven and Earth are moved to seemingly secondary positions. If we would learn from King Wen, we must study what he left us so that we may follow him.

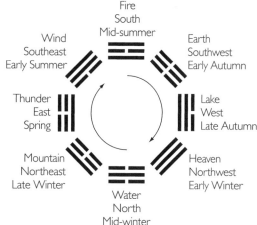

Let us start with the basics of what the tradition gives us. The Later Heaven Trigrams have been interpreted with these features:

Seasonal associations

Directional associations

Family relationships

Concordance with the Five Phases

We do not know if King Wen intended all these concordances, although we can pinpoint no other person as the arranger of the Later Heaven Eight Trigrams. Nevertheless, these associations have existed for thousands of years. Regardless of who formulated them, the Later Heaven Eight Trigrams are held to be a cosmological representation as functional as a mathematical formula. They are a calculator for change.

Seasonal Associations

The Later Heaven Trigrams were given seasonal associations that eventually encompassed other ideas of time, including the solstices, equinoxes, and hours of the day. Since the arrangement is circular, we could begin at any trigram, but for simplicity's sake, we will begin with water at the bottom of the octagon and read clockwise:

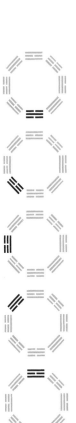

Water—cold, downward-flowing, and dangerous—begins midwinter. If we remember that water is a chasm in the earth and therefore even lower than the ground we stand on, we can see why it is the darkest and lowest of the hexagrams.

Mountain—consolidation, stopping, stillness—is late winter, snow-covered mountains, ice, frozen lakes and streams, and the dormant trees.

Thunder—growth, shocking, energy, growing plants—is spring, a time of thunderstorms, thawing, new growth, and movement everywhere from the melting snows to the sprouting branches.

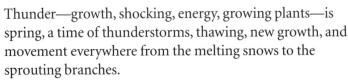

Wind—gentle influence, pervasive movement, and growing trees—follows. Warm breezes signal the fullness of spring. Pollen, bees, insects are borne on the wind. Trees are in full leaf.

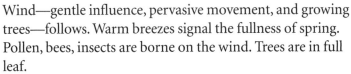

Fire—brilliance, light, heat, glory—is the height of summer.

Earth—fecund—represents early autumn, when harvest is near and the bounty of the earth seems almost unlimited.

Lake—gathering—alludes to harvest gatherings, and also to the consummation of all the processes that have come before, as the stream flows into the lake, as mud settles into wetlands, repository for layers of life from bacteria to birds.

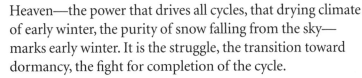

Heaven—the power that drives all cycles, that drying climate of early winter, the purity of snow falling from the sky—marks early winter. It is the struggle, the transition toward dormancy, the fight for completion of the cycle.

Then comes the continuation of the cycle with water again.

This cycle has turned since before there were humans to observe it, and this cycle will continue for every generation. It is the constancy of change.

Directional Associations

It is easy to see the compasslike divisions of the *bagua*. The Later Heaven Trigrams place the south at the top of the circle, and if we look at each of the cardinal points, we can find both geographical and meteorological meanings.

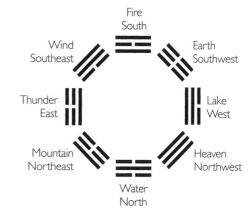

These associations originated in northern China. There is a vivid picture here of that Middle Kingdom. But we should not take the influence of the countryside literally. We should take these directions metaphorically, extrapolate, and derive meaning for wherever we are in the world.

Water is north, toward the cold.

Fire is south, toward the sun.

Thunder is east, where the sun rises.

Lake is west, where the sun sets.

In looking at the directions between the cardinal points, we can still find a perfect correspondence:

Heaven is in the northwest. In northern China, the early winter winds blow from the north and northwest, precisely during the season assigned to heaven in the Later Heaven Trigrams. If we remember that Heaven means the drying power of the sun, and we look at the climate in China, we can see that it is most dry (least rainfall) in that direction. In addition, all gods and the emperors have traditionally sat with their back to the north as they faced south.

Mountain is in the northeast. There are mountains to the north and northeast of central China. The mountain ranges in modern Shaanxi may be the literal model for this *bagua*. Due to two influences—the cold north wind, and numerous invasions from the north—the Chinese have always valued mountains on their northern border. The mountain as symbol of stopping and barrier thus fits perfectly. The metaphor was extended still further by the building of the Great Wall.

Wind is in the southeast. As spring moves into early summer, the north and northwest winds shift to the south and southeast. Thus, the trigram wind is in this direction, and again corresponds with the season as well.

Earth is in the southwest. From central China, that would indicate parts of the Yellow River and Yangzi River valleys and beyond. Crops in this direction have been barley, millet, corn, and rice.

Altogether, the Later Heaven Trigrams correspond to geographical features in China. We should understand this as the inspiration for and the reasoning of the assignment and not restrict ourselves to thinking solely in terms of China. At all times, the Later Heaven Trigrams should be seen in relationship to where we are.

Family Relationships

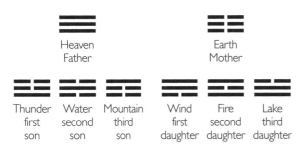

The trigrams are also believed to have a family relationship. Heaven is father, Earth is mother. Thunder is the eldest son, Wind is the eldest daughter. Water is the middle son, Fire is the middle daughter. Mountain is the youngest son, Lake is the youngest daughter.

There are two ways of looking at this idealized relationship. At first glance, we can regard these relationships as being a simple mnemonic device. The relationships indicate the position of the lines within each trigram. Heaven is all yang ☰, earth is all yin ☷. If we remember that the trigram lines are always counted from the bottom up, like the floors of a building, the position of the one *unlike* line defines the family position.

For example, the single yang line in Thunder's first position ☳ means the first and eldest son. The single yin line in Wind's first position ☴ means the first and eldest daughter. The single yang line in Water's second position ☵ means the second son. The single yin line in Fire's second position ☲ means the second daughter. The single yang line in Mountain's third position ☶ means the third and youngest son. The single yin line in Lake's third position ☱ means the third and youngest daughter. Thus, all the trigrams can be easily remembered by referring to family relationships.

If we extend the metaphor, we can arrive at a further understanding of the Later Heaven Trigrams with a comforting picture of the ideal family.

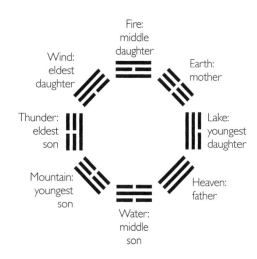

Father and mother, on the right side of the arrangement and keeping their youngest daughter between them, send their eldest two children out as the vanguard of the next generation. Thunder is the eldest son, as spring is the first movement of the new year, the east is the rising sun of a new day. The eldest daughter is beside him, the herald of summer, the direction of morning, the maker of new growth. The eldest two siblings, being the most mature, are farthest from mother and father.

Father keeps the middle son beside him for further instruction, as mother keeps the middle daughter beside herself. Both of these siblings have considerable responsibility, however, for they must carry on what the two oldest children have initiated: Fire, the glory of summer, furthers what her sister began, as Water furthers what Heaven began.

Father and mother keep their youngest daughter between them. The youngest son is protected by his two brothers. It is up to the youngest two siblings to bring all things to completion, and this fits with their attributes of consolidation. The youngest two receive all that their parents and older siblings have created, and they bring climax to all efforts. Mountain, the youngest son, represents culmination, whether the stopping of a venture or a lifting to the highest spiritual peak. Lake, the youngest daughter, represents the final receiving of all the riches, the importance of exchange, and the joy of celebration.

The family relationships of the Later Heaven Trigrams are as familiar and fundamental as the natural images of the Early Heaven Trigrams. They are another way of reassuring us of the rightness of these trigrams. They take the natural, seasonal, and directional aspects of the *bagua* and project them directly onto the most fundamental of human relationships. In this way, the Later Heaven Trigrams bring all of the cosmos directly into our homes, and show us an ideal way to structure our families.

When we look beyond the names of the trigrams to the phenomena that the names indicate, we see an endless movement from one trigram to another. Their movement is a direct indication of the movement of life.

This sense of circulation is crucial to the Later Heaven Trigrams. We are not meant to pick one station and stay there. We are meant to shift constantly from one trigram to another. This change is quick and constant. We change, as all circumstances are ever changing. Thus, the most important thing we can do is act with that change.

The Later Heaven Trigrams make the process of change immediate, personal, and everyday. Change becomes something that happens in us, and through us. It is intimately connected to us. In fact, to borrow the imagery of Wind, it is like the threads of wind that weave through every opening. Whether through molecular openings or wrapping the entire planet, it weaves all things together. If we accept this hidden message of the Later Heaven Trigrams, we will no longer regard change as something that happens *to* us. Instead, it is a process that happens *with* us.

From there, it is only a short leap of logic to see that since we are as much a part of change as anything else, and since we have consciousness, we can influence the process of change. There are two ways this can happen.

First, since we are connected to all other parts of this existence, what we do, say, think, and feel will have an influence on the enormous web. Second, we have control over our own thoughts, emotions, and decisions, and we can change within ourselves to accommodate whatever is going on outside. In every case, we are part of change, not passive and helpless objects upon which change acts.

The Imagination of King Wen

In contrasting the Early Heaven Trigrams with the Later Heaven Trigrams, it should be clear that there is a radical difference between the two. The restructuring of the first set to the second was such a leap of imagination, such an expansion of possibilities, that it truly emphasizes the brilliance of King Wen (reigned 1171–1122 B.C.E.).

Many of China's historical figures became mythologized, but this has never happened with King Wen. Immediately following his death, he was held up as a paragon of enlightened rule, and Confucius counted King Wen as a paragon of the sage-king, but no one tried to explain his intelligence with claims of divinity.

Nevertheless, many masters have invested King Wen's innovations as dogma. So great is their awe that they have made him a rigid example for themselves and their disciples. By doing this, they go against King Wen's example. King Wen did not bind himself by rigidity or fanatical classicism. His was not the insight of the orthodox master, but the vision of a shaman-prince.

If King Wen had been orthodox in his thinking, he might well have died in Di Xin's prison. He survived, not by thinking along common lines—Prince Jiu is the obvious example of this—but by completely changing his approach. This may well be King Wen's greatest example of change: when faced with the overwhelming nature of change itself—with his nation, his family, his freedom, and his life in dire jeopardy—he changed himself and the entire basis of his thinking.

It is said that the word for change shows a lizard, and we all know how quick a lizard is. King Wen changed as quickly as a lizard. The word *yi* means not only "change" but "easy." We can see that King Wen changed easily, and created a system that may seem complicated but is easy to follow—and improvise upon—once it is learned.

This, then, is the final hidden message of King Wen: do not cling to orthodoxy, but change as quickly as change itself.

The Later Heaven
Sixty-Four Hexagrams

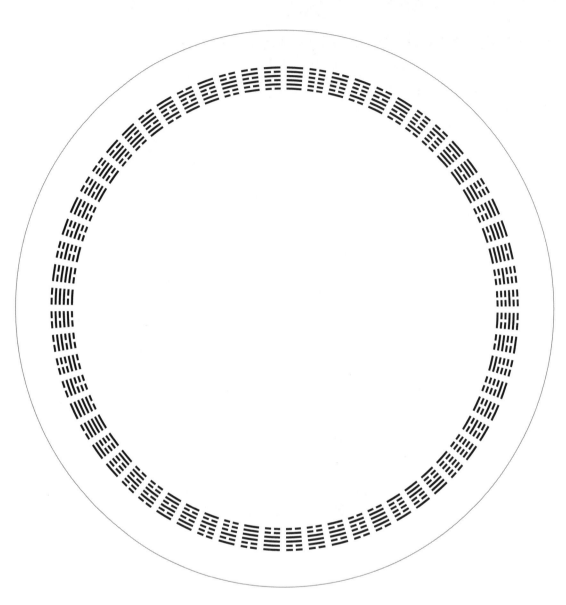

King Wen and the Sixty-Four Hexagrams

We believe that there were at least two sequences of hexagrams after Fu Xi. One was called *Lianshanyi—Changes of Linked Mountains*. The other was named *Guicanyi—The Changes That Return and Store*. Both arrangements and their commentaries have been lost. All that we know is that King Wen turned away from these sequences and created his own, adding a statement to each hexagram.

With his subtle mind, King Wen took the idea of polar opposites and reprised them in his sequence. He viewed each hexagram as a pair of trigrams. Every hexagram has one of the following pairs of trigrams: yang-yang, yin-yang, yang-yin, or yin-yin. The Sixty-Four Hexagrams extend the yin-yang formation of the Four Images onto the trigram level and use that extension to generate the Sixty-Four Hexagrams.

After pairing the trigrams, he then went on to pair the hexagrams: each even-numbered hexagram is either the inverse (turning over) or reverse (reversing yin for yang lines and vice versa) of the preceding odd-numbered hexagram. This embodied the idea that any occurrence that has reached its zenith changes into its opposite. Fu Xi paired the trigrams as opposites; King Wen paired hexagrams as opposites.

The overall sequence of these hexagram pairs is punctuated by the eight hexagrams composed of doubled trigrams. The hexagram sequence opens with Heaven and Earth, and closes its first section near the middle with Water and Fire. In the second section, Thunder and Mountain, Wind and Lake occupy places close to the end of the section. The final two hexagrams are the only two where the yin and yang lines fall in perfect alternation. So the sequence opens with the complete yang of heaven and the complete yin of earth and ends with the perfect mixing of yin and yang lines.

The position of each line within its hexagram is also considered meaningful: the first and lowest line is early and peripheral to a situation, the fifth line is generally the climax of a situation, and the sixth and highest line is late and outside the situation. Thinkers after King Wen posited an ideal alternation of yin and yang lines. Many of the interpretations of a given line come from its position in the overall hexagram and its relationship to this ideal sequence.

King Wen advanced the study of change with yin-yang precision, and he added his own intuitive perception. His work was carried farther by the work of his fourth son, known as the Duke of Zhou.

The Duke of Zhou

King Wen's fourth son was Ji Dan, the Duke of Zhou. As a statesman and warrior, a poet and scientist, a musician and builder of cities, he brilliantly composed a statement for each line of the hexagrams for a total of 384 lines.

> *The Duke wrote in the Lines:*
> A dragon flying in the sky.
> Gain by seeing a great person.

Except on one occasion, the Duke never spoke of himself. That one exception was when King Wu—his older brother and successor to King Wen—was ill. The Duke went to the temple and offered himself in sacrifice, saying to the gods: "I beseech the Lord Above to let me, Ji Dan, be the king's substitute. I was lovingly obedient to my father. I possess many talents that fit me to serve the spirits. Your Principal Descendant does not have as many talents as I have for serving the spirits. He received the Mandate of Heaven, and established your descendants in this lower world. Do not let the Mandate of Heaven fall to the ground. May you, our former emperors, hold it and secure it forever."

> *The Duke wrote in the Lines:*
> Unexpected illness.
> Recovery from sickness brings joy.

He rejoiced when the king recovered, and he sealed the divination in a bronze coffer and forbade the diviners to ever speak of it.

> *The Duke wrote in the Lines:*
> Return to your own Way.
> How can this be bad?

He once said to his son, the Marquis of Lu, that on any day of his life he wished he could find "ten men to have as teachers, thirty to have as friends, one hundred to talk with at leisure, and one thousand helpers who could help me and to whom I would always listen."

The Duke wrote in the Lines:
    Beholding my life:
    advance or retreat?

He said, "When I wash my hair, I often have to hold it up three times; when I dine, I stop frequently: I am always fearful that I will have missed meeting good men." He dispatched princes to report on the conditions of the common people. He wanted to know if they were suffering from cold or hunger, if the laws were just, and if all had work. People still say today, "The Duke of Zhou let his meals be interrupted, and won the hearts of the whole world."

The Duke wrote in the Lines:
    Through delight, the great attains.
    Do not doubt it! Friends gather
    like hair in a clasp.

We believe that he composed or edited forty-five of the poems in the *Odes.* His words are preserved in all of the Five Classics—*Odes, Documents, Rites, Spring and Autumn Annals,* and the *Changes.*

The Duke wrote in the Lines:
    Surviving on old favors: a perilous sign.
    In the end: fortune.
    One may undertake royal service,
    but without personal success.

When the Zhou dynasty was established, he composed the music called *Great Triumph,* and he also composed *Three Elephants* and *Following in the Footsteps of the Ancestors.*

The Duke wrote in the Lines:
    Someone increases by ten groups of turtles no one
    can defy. Everlasting firmness
    and fortune. The king makes offerings to god.
    Fortune.

King Wu died only six years after establishing the Zhou dynasty. His son, then only thirteen years old, became King Cheng. The young king appointed the Duke as his prime minister, but within a few months, he made him regent.

The Duke wrote in the Lines:
　　Hide your talents, but stay steadfast
　　if you would be of royal service.

Their older brother, Prince Guan, and two other brothers refused to attend King Wu's burial as outright defiance of the young king's rule. The Duke stationed himself in the eastern part of the empire between them and the capital.

The Duke wrote in the Lines:
　　Armed and lying in ambush,
　　under the thicket. Looming above
　　is their high mound.
　　For three years, there is no rising.

For three years, the Duke was away from the court as he strained to prevent war. The young king listened to rumors in court, and he began to doubt his uncle. That autumn, thunder and lightning destroyed the crops. Frightened, the king went to the temple to divine. He found the bronze coffer, ordered it opened, and discovered how the Duke had offered himself as a human sacrifice. "The divination is unnecessary," wept the sixteen-year-old king. "The duke has toiled so hard, but I, being small, was ignorant of it. Now heaven sends down its terrors to light the virtue of the Duke of Zhou. I must go welcome him back in person."

The Duke wrote in the Lines:
　　Distressed by vines and creepers.
　　With anxious speech and acts, one repents. Repent and go forward to
　　fortune.

The Duke went back to the capital and joined his nephew.

The Duke wrote in the Lines:
　　Returning alone
　　in the middle of the road.

Almost immediately, rebellion began. The three princes and the last heir of the Shang dynasty joined together to make war against their own family and country. The Duke did not want to fight; for him, civil war was family war.

The Duke wrote in the Lines:
    No increase when someone attacks.
    Setting the heart without constancy:
    misfortune.

King Cheng declared war and commanded the Duke to lead the army.

The Duke wrote in the Lines:
    The king's servant hindered—
    though he did not personally cause it.

The last heir of Shang was slain. Prince Guan, the treacherous older brother, hanged himself. The other two princes were captured.

The Duke wrote in the Lines:
    The king goes to battle.
    Admirably, he humbles the chieftains
    and captures vile rebels. No fault.

The Duke of Zhou was a warrior. He led Zhou armies when the Shang dynasty was overthrown. He led expeditions against invading barbarians. He fought against his own brothers and the resurgent Shang.

The Duke wrote in the Lines:
    Pure fortune. Regrets vanish. Terrifyingly
    attack the Gui Fang. In three years,
    there will be rewards in a great country.
    Pure fortune. No regrets.

The Duke was also a mathematician, and his dialogues with Shao Gao are recorded in *Zhou Bi Suan Jing,* the Zhou dynasty book of numbers, and his mathematical concerns joined with his concerns about astronomy and the calendar.

The Duke wrote in the Lines:
    Plentiful screens.
    Seeing the northern stars at noon.
    Meeting one's great lord. Fortune.

In the *Odes* he wrote of the tall millet, and the joys of harvest. He felt the seasons, and understood how important it was to plant during the day even as he studied those stars at night.

The Duke wrote in the Lines:
    A calling crane in the shade:
    its young are at peace.
    I have a good wine goblet.
    I will share its excellence with you.

He was as much a scientist in his time as anyone else. When a diplomatic delegation from what is now Vietnam journeyed to the Zhou capital, they despaired over finding their way home. The Duke gave them chariots equipped with the earliest known compasses—with needles that always pointed south.

The Duke wrote in the Lines:
    Pure fortune. Regrets vanish.
    The hedge breaks: entanglement is gone.
    Strong as a great car's axle blocks.

The Duke of Zhou had the insight to write poetry to each line of the *Changes*. He talked with his father about the imprisonment at Youli and his insights into the *Changes*. With his knowledge of poetry, music, mathematics, astronomy, earth science, agriculture, governance, and military science, the Duke of Zhou was the perfect person to expand the *Changes*.

The Duke wrote in the Lines:
    Nothing but gain:
    Modest and humble.

Confucius

The noble work of King Wen and the Duke of Zhou established a powerful oracle for their dynasty. Yet the empire began to wane in less than a millennium. The oracle might have perished too, except for the work of one man and those who followed him. That man was Confucius (Kong Fuzi).

Without him, the oracle was too hard to understand, the visions of King Wen and the Duke of Zhou too hard to grasp, and the records of the diviners' utterances too difficult. No one would have even known what the texts meant had it not been for the efforts of Confucius to explain and preserve the *Changes.*

Confucius was born in the state of Lu in 551 B.C.E. He grew to over six feet in height. As a young man, he worked in the granaries of the Qi clan and was made their minister of works.

The annals do not record why, but Confucius was dismissed from the Qi clan and he traveled from the state of Lu. This brought him no comfort. He was driven out of Sung and Wei, and encountered trouble in Chen and Cai, before returning to Lu.

There, Confucius found new employment with the Duke of Lu. Eventually, the duke gave him a carriage, horses, and a page boy, and sent him to Zhou to study the rites. It was there that Confucius met Laozi.

"I have heard that the rich and great offer farewell gifts of money, while the good offer advice," said Laozi as Confucius was departing after his time with him. "I am neither great nor good, but, unworthy as I am, I have been called good. Let me offer you a few words of advice: A shrewd observer who criticizes others risks his own life. A learned man who exposes the faults of others endangers himself. Neither a filial son nor a loyal subject should push himself forward."

Laozi stood for the natural, the mystical, the nonconforming individual who should "return to the source," and be as an "uncarved block of wood." Yet he was expert enough in the rites that Confucius went to study with him. Confucius was no less expert a scholar, no less mysterious a sage. A disciple once said: "We can hear the master's views concerning culture, but he does not tell us anything about nature and fate." That may be, and yet he revered the *Changes,* a book that shows us nature and fate.

Confucius returned to Lu from Zhou and gathered disciples. Sima Qian says of him, "In his teaching, Confucius emphasized four things: culture, conduct, loyalty, and honesty. He avoided four things: hasty conclusions, arbitrary views, obstinacy, and egotism. He advocated caution during sacrifice, war, and sickness. He rarely spoke of profit, fate, or goodness. He preferred earnest pupils: if he gave one corner of a square and the pupil could not infer the other three corners, he would not repeat himself."

He had three thousand pupils. Seventy-two of them would become famous as his primary disciples. Only they mastered the Six Arts he advocated: rites, music, archery, charioteering, writing, and mathematics. He based his writings on the ancient classics. He gathered the records into the *Documents,* arranging them chronologically from the time of Yao and Shun, and he edited the *Rites.* He then went on to compile the *Odes,* and among them were songs of praise for both King Wen and the Duke of Zhou.

He loved the *Changes.* Sima Qian reports that he never grew tired of examining the hexagrams, and he read all the commentaries of his day. He studied the book so much that the leather thongs binding the wooden tablets wore out three times. "Give me a few more years," he said, "and I shall become quite proficient!"

One of his followers once sighed, "The more I look up, the higher his teaching is above me. The deeper I probe, the harder it becomes. One moment I think I have it, but the next, it eludes me again. How skillfully and systematically the master leads us on! He has broadened me with culture, and restrained me with the rites. Even if I wanted to, I could not stop."

Confucius traveled from one lord to the next, in an attempt to bring order to a land where the countries were constantly at war, but his efforts at diplomacy and government were unpopular with the warlords and princes of his time.

Once, Confucius had an audience with Duke Qing. The duke questioned him about government, and Confucius replied, "Let the prince be a prince, the minister a minister, the father a father, and the son a son." The duke was ready to award Confucius a fief for this answer, but his adviser called Confucius an arrogant and self-willed windbag—a leader of scholars who would bankrupt themselves for a scrumptious funeral, and whose prescriptions for appearance, dress, and behavior would take more than a lifetime to learn. So the duke dismissed Confucius.

The highest office Confucius attained was as prime minister to Duke Ding. Within three months, vendors of pork and lamb controlled their prices, men and women walked on different sides of the road, no one took anything that did not belong to them, and travelers were safe and welcome. This frightened the state of Qi. They sent eighty of the most beautiful dancing girls with sixty pairs of dappled horses to Duke Ding. When the ruler accepted them, to the neglect of state affairs and attendance to the rites, Confucius resigned and left the country.

When he was living in Cai, the state of Chu wanted him to join them, and he would have gone, except that Cai feared any state led by Confucius. They sent assassins to kill him and his followers on the road. The battle lasted for days as his disciples fought back. They ran out of food and water. Fortunately, the King of Chu sent troops. Otherwise, Confucius might have died there.

The King of Chu wanted to give land to Confucius. The king's advisers said that Confucius would surely make any amount of land into a great nation that would someday destroy Chu. The king did nothing, and died that autumn. That was Confucius's last chance at having a position of power.

He once described himself as a man "who never wearies of studying the truth, never tires of teaching others, who in his eagerness forgets his hunger and in his joy forgets his bitter lot, and who does not worry that old age is creeping on him."

King Wen strained against Di Xin, and suffered imprisonment and death before his country could be established. The Duke of Zhou fought to give the Zhou the Mandate of Heaven, and struggled to maintain a young country so that his nephew could rule a stabilized land. Confucius admired the golden era of the early Zhou and wanted to return to that time. All three men aimed for perfection. Perfection eluded all three. Still, they have influenced generations and countries far beyond their own, and their striving assured us of the oracle we have today.

The Divining Ritual

Through the wisdom of Fu Xi, King Wen, the Duke of Zhou, and Confucius, the *Changes* became an extraordinary book, unique not simply because it was composed of words but because those words could be accessed through a divining ritual.

One point is undeniable: there is no answer until one divines. Whether you would ask the oracle to speak to you, or whether you would seek the wisdom of thousands of years, you must first approach and inquire in order to receive.

It is our initiative, not the happenstance gift or the intervention of others, that gives us the most reliable way of being. For everything we want to do—plant a crop, build a house, travel abroad, know the future—we must begin.

All spiritual matters require us to take the first steps. Then there will be a response. The spiritual never pursues us first. The spiritual is there only when we initiate the encounter. That is why every religion has ritual. It is through the reading, the bodily participation, the worship in consecrated places that we realize the spiritual.

The Yarrow Stalk Oracle

The *Changes* is approached by a divining ritual. The simplest ritual is one using three coins (see page xix). The more elaborate one uses yarrow stalks. Due to its more lengthy process, it offers more opportunity to consider one's question, and the process of counting the sticks can become reassuring in itself. Here is how the ritual is done:

Divining the First Line, Part One

Compose yourself in a quiet and clean room. Let no one disturb you.

Place the *Changes* and fifty yarrow stalks before you on a table.

Consider the question you have, meditate on it, and write it down on a clean piece of paper or in a book of your own. The question should be phrased as an inquiry about your situation, like "Will this course of action bring success?" or "How can I—?" or "What will happen if—?" Avoid asking an either-or question. The more specific your question, the more specific the answer will be. Concentrate on your question, and concentrate on addressing that question directly to the *Changes*.

Take up the fifty yarrow stalks. Pull one stalk from the bunch and put it aside. It will not be used again for the remainder of this ritual.

Divide the remaining forty-nine stalks randomly into two heaps.

Take one stalk from the right-hand heap and place it above the *Changes*.

Hold the left-hand heap with your left hand. Using your right hand, subtract groups of four stalks from this bunch until four or fewer stalks are remaining. Add this number to the single stalk from the right-hand heap.

Hold the right-hand heap in your left hand. Using your right hand, subtract groups of four stalks from this bunch until four or fewer stalks are remaining. Add this number to the single stalk from the right-hand heap and the four or fewer stalks from the left-hand heap. There should be a total of either five or nine stalks.

Gather the previously discarded stalks from both the left and right sides into one group. Then divide them at random into two bunches.

Divining the First Line, Part Two

As before, take one stalk from the right-hand heap and place it above the *Changes*.

As before, hold the left-hand heap with your left hand. Using your right hand, subtract groups of four stalks from this bunch until four or fewer stalks are remaining. Add this number to the single stalk from the right-hand heap.

As before, pick up the right-hand heap in your left hand. Using your right hand, subtract groups of four stalks from this bunch until four or fewer stalks are remaining. Add this number to the single stalk from the right-hand heap, the four or fewer stalks from the left-hand heap, and the stalks from the first counting. There should be a total of either nine, thirteen, or seventeen stalks.

Gather the previously discarded stalks from both the left and right sides into one group. Then divide them at random into two bunches.

Divining the First Line, Part Three

As before, take one stalk from the right-hand heap and place it above the *Changes*.

As before, hold the left-hand heap with your left hand. Using your right hand, subtract groups of four stalks from this bunch until four or fewer stalks are remaining. Add this number to the single stalk from the right-hand heap.

As before, hold the right-hand heap in your left hand. Using your right hand, subtract groups of four stalks from this bunch until four or fewer stalks are remaining. Add this number to the single stalk from the right-hand heap, the four or fewer stalks from the left-hand heap, and the stalks from the first and second counting. There should be a total of either thirteen, seventeen, twenty-one, or twenty-five stalks.

Gather the previously discarded stalks from both the left and right sides into one group. You should have either thirty-six, thirty-two, twenty-eight, or twenty-four stalks in your hand. If you do not have one of these numbers, there has been an error, and you must begin the process again.

Divining the First Line, Conclusion

Divide the total number of stalks in your hand by the number four. There are four possible quotients: nine, eight, seven, or six.

These are their meanings:

Nine is an Old Yang Line   ━O━
Eight is a Young Yin Line   ━ ━
Seven is a Young Yang Line   ━━━
Six is an Old Yin Line   ━X━

Write this first line down on your page. This concludes the divining of the first line. You must now repeat the entire procedure in order to determine each of the five subsequent lines.

When you have a hexagram of six lines, you have completed the ritual. In order to identify your hexagram, refer to the table on the inside back cover.

What the Lines Mean

If the line is a Young Yin or Young Yang line, it does not change. An Old Yang or Old Yin line is a *changing* line and becomes its opposite. A hexagram with all young lines is static, and only that hexagram statement applies to you.

If there are any old lines in your hexagram, you must draw a second hexagram beside your first one. Beginning from the bottom, copy the lines of the first hexagram. Whenever you arrive at an Old Yang line, draw a Young Yin line in its place in your second hexagram. Whenever you arrive at an Old Yin line, draw a Young Yang line in its place in your second hexagram. Consult the hexagram statement of the first hexagram, read the line statements only for any changing lines, and then read the second hexagram. Usually, the first hexagram describes your current situation, the line commentaries describe subtleties of or exceptions to the situation, and the second hexagram is a discussion of what your situation could become.

Sample hexagram
as first cast. Lines 2
and 5 are changing lines.
The other lines do
not change.

Find the hexagram
in the table by
looking at the bottom
trigram, Mountain
and the top trigram,
Lake. This is Hexagram 31.
Read the commentary
for the hexagram
and for Lines 2 and 5.

When Lines 2 and 5
change to their
opposites, a new
hexagram is formed.
Find the hexagram in
the table by looking
at the bottom trigram,
Wind, and the top trigram,
Thunder. Read the
hexagram commentary.

In the example above, the divining ritual has formed a hexagram with an Old Yin line in the second place, and an Old Yang line in the fifth place. The first hexagram that is formed is Hexagram 31. It can be found at the intersection of the lower trigram, Mountain, and the upper trigram, Lake, in the table. The second hexagram formed is Hexagram 32. It is found at the lower trigram, Wind, and the upper trigram, Thunder. In this example, one would read the commentaries of Hexagram 31, its lines 2 and 5 (and no others), and then the hexagram commentary of Hexagram 32 without reading any of its line commentaries.

Heaven

乾

Hexagram 1
Heaven above
Heaven below

The Heaven trigram
doubled: six yang lines
symbolize supreme power.
　Heaven upon heaven is
the highest power we know.

Qian
The name of the first of the
Eight Trigrams. Heaven, male,
father, sovereign.

The Sequence and Link
Heaven begins the sequence,
since there is no life without
the sun.

Each day our minds construct new myths,
trying to trace the endless whole,
yet mere intellect cannot hold
heaven's grand orbits or its breadth.

Dogma says follow heaven's way.
Kings say, "Obey—do not rebel."
Yet before oracles foretell
the ending of his royal days,

heaven will take the throne from a king,
and raise a poor man in his place.
It will smooth a bitter man's face,
and take away a hoarder's things.

Constantly, heaven turns its wheel:
water and fire; half day, half night.
It spins all things from dark and light,
and raises rice from muddy fields.

The Statement

**Heaven: maker, pervasive,
bountiful, and pure.**

The Lines

6th line ———

**A haughty dragon
will have regrets.**

5th line ———

**A dragon flying in the sky.
Gain by seeing a great person.**

4th line ———

**Someone may leap from the depths.
Be without fault.**

3rd line ———

**At day's end, the noble one is still diligent.
At night, he is alert to peril
and stays without fault.**

The Image

2nd line ———

**Seeing a dragon in the field.
Gain by seeing a great person.**

**Heaven moves with power:
the noble one never stops
strengthening himself.**

1st line ———

**A sunken dragon.
Do not act.**

HEAVEN is the beginning. It is the sun that gives us light and warmth. It is the ground after a rainstorm, steaming in the summer. It is the seasons' tempo by which we conduct our lives. It is the snow pack; it is the clouds and streams. It is the light that ripens the grain, vegetables, and fruit.

Heaven creates from open sky. As the calligrapher begins from white paper, heaven works from emptiness. The stars, moon, sun, and clouds spring from this emptiness and revolve constantly through it.

The sun rises and sets. The moon travels through the night, its face turning to the sun. Many of us, deep in the darkness when we cannot sleep, wonder about the stars turning above us. We think of our own aging. The clock ticks. Our holidays mark the passing years as much as they might mark celebrations or remembrances. Our own birthdays impassively tabulate the number of years we have been on this planet, reminding us that our store of health and vitality can only lessen until heaven takes us again in the ultimate transition.

Creativity is the only act that defies this undeniable constant. When we make something—whether it is a wooden spoon for our kitchen, a painting, a poem, a song, a speech—the effort we invest is stored for the future and becomes a vehicle that lets us live outside of normal time. When we care for children, organize a business, or lead a country, our efforts are likewise stored for the future. What we make today saves time tomorrow. Every tool we make frees us from having to struggle with a task. Every child we nurture will grow into an adult who will show the same kindness to someone else. Every song we sing springs from the moment of its composition to bring itself fresh into the present, doubling its layers of meaning, keeping its spirit alive and dancing. Creativity, then, begins new cycles that spiral out and spin into the coils of heaven.

When we create, time becomes a malleable and shining force we can fold layer upon layer like Damascus steel until we have forged a shining blade that cannot be denied, a blade that cleaves the air, flashing with the weight of a thousand years, a point we thrust into the wrapping cycles—there to establish our purpose, our center, our place.

In these ways, what we do will continue on, as a light wave traveling across the universe continues without slowing, joining all other light—brilliant, free, unencumbered by solidity, unstopped by barriers.

It is no wonder, then, that we make heaven the aim of all worship, and that all our actions and all our worship aim to make us like heaven: heaven made us capable of emulating it.

If we ever waver in our reverence, the words of the Oracle remind us: heaven, the origin, moves unimpeded. It ripens our harvests. It is ever pure.

In the *Statement,* four words—*maker, pervasive, bountiful, pure*—are the symbols of heaven. It is our beginning, our *maker.* It is *pervasive,* and remains everlasting. It gives us the harvest with a power *pure* and firm. When we divine, the answer comes from that source, clear, and perfect.

Yet even as we learn of the benevolence of all-powerful heaven, the Oracle also makes these four qualities moral examples:

We should be as great as the force that created this universe.

We should strive for profuse success, just as heaven makes all things live.

We should strive to act properly so that we can reap the results of our work.

We should emulate heaven in its purity, striving for firmness of character. What is important is not just the act of divining, but to have the purity to receive the spiritual.

Following the example of heaven means following its cycles. The *Lines* show that heaven knows earliness, synchronization, and lateness. (**1**) In the first line, Heaven shows someone with the potential of a dragon, but for whom the time and place are not yet right. Waiting is necessary. (**2**) As the situation progresses, one can advance farther to look for friends or seek the guidance of others. (**3**) We must all work hard to be diligent and strong, and we cannot stop in guarding against danger. (**4**) As this period of time progresses, greater risks can be taken. Eventually, (**5**) one can fly like a dragon. But there can be lateness too. (**6**) Even for heaven and even for someone who is like a dragon, opportunity passes: too confident in one's talents, one continues to strive even though it is late and friends are gone.

The *Image* shows that the sages saw the image of heaven moving powerfully, and that they responded by looking to themselves. Seeing the limited nature of human beings compared to heaven, they did not excuse human puniness. Rather, they resolved never to rest in trying to strengthen themselves. They knew, and the Oracle remembers: nothing can be done without heaven's strength.

Heaven, the origin. Heaven, the pervasive. Heaven, the bountiful. Heaven, the pure. If you would worship heaven, then be like heaven. If you would last as long as heaven, then create like heaven. In all things, be no different than heaven and the future will be yours.

Hexagram 2
Earth above
Earth below

Earth upon earth. Six split lines symbolize supreme yin.
    The Earth trigram below another Earth trigram forms a hexagram completely open inside, symbolizing ultimate receptivity.

Kun
Defined in dictionaries as the second of the Eight Trigrams. Earth, compliance, obedience, feminine.

The Sequence and Link
Heaven may be supreme, but earth receives its power and makes all things grow.

Earth

We dredge the streams and shore up dikes
    as clouds move in
to block the moon. Now the storm pours
    as lightning strikes.
Inside the earth, rice grains open
    and start to swell.

The fences burn in just one flash,
    and farmers rush
to save their herds. But timbers fall
    and horses dash—
a mare and foal run down the road;
    the chasers pant.

A new day dawns. Timber is sawn.
    The groomsmen find
their straying herds. They count each horse,
    but two are gone.
The squire stomps and shouts, while new grass
    sprouts underfoot.

The horses pause at green grave mounds,
    ready to rest.
Wanting to graze, they curve their necks
    to kiss the ground.
They are not lost: the endless hills
    remain their home.

The Statement

Earth: maker, everywhere.
Gain from a mare's purity.

The noble one wanting to go far
is first confused, but later finds guidance.

The Lines

Gain friends in the west and south,
Lose friends in the east and north.

6th line ▬ ▬

Dragons fight in the wild:
their blood is dark and yellow.

Peace: this is a sign of fortune.

5th line ▬ ▬

Yellow garments.
Great fortune.

4th line ▬ ▬

A tied sack:
neither blame nor praise.

3rd line ▬ ▬

Hide your talents, but stay steadfast
if you would be of royal service.

The Image

2nd line ▬ ▬

Straight, square, great—
this leads to spontaneous
and undoubted gain.

Ground as the power
of earth:
the noble one generously
supports all things.

1st line ▬ ▬

Treading on frost—
solid ice will soon arrive.

EARTH, like heaven, is our origin. Heaven is the seed; earth is the field. A seed without a field dies unsprouted. A field without a seed lies barren. Heaven and earth are both necessary for creation. Each of us, and everything we touch in our world, comes from that intercourse.

The earth never denies anyone or anything. Whatever can no longer go on—whether it is a beam of light that has been traveling for millions of years, or whether it is a storm-drenched and skittering bird—are all welcomed by the earth: to rest, to sprawl, to arrive without any judgment or rejection.

The earth accepts you too. When you sleep, you lie down. When you are ill, you lie down. When you make love, you lie down. We may be living in high-rise buildings, and cushioning ourselves with satin sheets, but every day, we return to the primal act of lying down on the earth, as every single ancestor has done before us. When the final lying down comes, there is nowhere else for us to go but the place that has always been our bed.

How much of what we experience in life is really marvelous? We cynically reject all the offerings that come our way, tired of the exploitation of the marketplace. We search like wolves for new forms of amusement. When we get to the arena, we roar to be appeased like any decadent aristocrat. Is it any wonder that we vomit up our excesses and gaze bleary-eyed at the horizon, wondering what else there is for us in the world?

The answer is under us—the earth that welcomes us, that yields wonders over every pore of its vast surface and deep into its depths. The earth, with species we are discovering new each day, with nameless grasses and trees that grow in forests, taking the layers of dead and dying leaves and rock and kneading them into green leaves and red hibiscus, bee hum and nightingale song. The earth is the sparkle of brook tumbling over moss-covered stone, and the wonder of gold nuggets, diamonds, and emeralds sparkling beneath its surface.

If it is knowledge you want, there are thousands of patterns in the geometric structure with which earth makes all things live. Whether it is the hexagon of a beehive, the star of a snowflake, the veins of a leaf, the lotus from the mud, or the forests on the north sides of hills, the earth has innumerable patterns to study.

We who are world-weary may complain that there is nothing new on earth, yet every moment, the earth renews itself. We who search for something to satisfy our yearning for the new, and who search for some pattern on which to base ourselves, need look no further than what is beneath our feet: we can find renewal wherever we stand.

Thus it is that a wise person makes herself like the broad earth under all things and all people, bearing and nurturing them with her power. Young girls grow to women and become mothers, hips widen from giving birth, shoulders broaden from lifting their children, hands grow strong from feeding, care, and embracing. In the vision of the *Changes,* the spirit of the earth incarnated is seen as the mare. The mare's power, its stamina and strength larger than any human scale, shows that the qualities of the earth can be embodied in a living being.

In the *Statement,* the mare represents patience, strength, docility, and the mother. The wise one, trying to live the example of Earth, does so not by violent domination, but by acceptance, and finds the right path through following sensitively, and moving by subtle actions.

The compass directions mentioned can be taken figuratively. Coupled with the image of the mare, we are shown acceptance of what the earth brings us as we wander over its expanse. We may find friends in one direction, but lose friends in another. This may not be what we wished for, but if we are like a mare, we will find the proper direction from the confusion. Then there is peace and good fortune.

The *Lines* extend these themes. (1) Earth as the yin force works gradually, as when frost turns into ice. But like solid ice, what has built up gradually cannot easily be broken. (2) When yin acts as it should—straight, square, and great—success happens spontaneously. (3) If yin works quietly, keeping hidden and avoiding conflict, accomplishments continue and will become deeply established. (4) But when yin meets an impasse, it must remain neutral and cautious. (5) The next line shows how: hold to the neutral center (symbolized by the color yellow), and honor will come (yellow garments symbolize a royal reward). (6) Finally, if yin fights with yang—going against the ideal of the mare—there will be a fundamental struggle. Both sides will suffer great injury.

The *Image* tells us that if you would be like Earth, you must follow the example of the mare. Nurture your young. Be the basis on which everyone else stands. By making yourself lower, all things come to you.

Earth is our maker. Earth is our provider of all gain. Those who wander without regard to where they stand on the earth go astray. Those who are willing to follow the lines of the earth find guidance. If you are like the mare, who lives in the fields and has all the sustenance it needs from the ground, and if you can nurture others like the earth, then you have found the most marvelous of paths.

Hexagram 3
Water above
Thunder below

The upper trigram, Water, is falling rain. The lower trigram, Thunder, is sudden growth moving upward through the ground. Times of sprouting begin in stormy confusion before moving toward order.

Tun
Sprouting. To stockpile, to gather, to station an army.

The Sequence and Link
When heaven and earth combine, new life sprouts.

Sprouting

Like heaven's meteor,
a seed drops on the soil,
   then splits and uncoils.
     Rootlets spread out,
     and a stem sprouts
     against the sod.

Though sparrows peck for it
and clods refuse to yield,
   the plant splits the field—
     forking its roots,
     stretching its shoot
     to seek the sun.

Emerging to the wind,
the seedling sways and leans,
   then stiffens and greens.
     New tendrils curl,
     new leaves unfurl,
     broad to the sky.

The Statement

Sprouting begins everywhere,
abundant and pure.

No need to go far:
gain by naming allies.

The Lines

6th line ▬ ▬
Riding a team of horses:
Sobbing and weeping blood.

5th line ▬
Sprouting fresh and thick:
For the small, a sign of fortune.
For the great, a sign of misfortune.

4th line ▬ ▬
Riding a team of horses
to seek marriage. Fortunate.
Nothing but gain.

3rd line ▬ ▬
Although there are deer, there is no forester.
Thinking to enter the forest's center,
the noble one halts. To go forward: sorrow.

The Image

2nd line ▬ ▬
How like the difficulty of sprouting!
Rushing like a team of horses: it is not a raider
who woos, yet the chaste girl refuses.
She waits ten years for betrothal.

Clouds and thunder:
sprouting. The noble one
considers the principles.

1st line ▬
A boulder and a willow.
It is gainful to dwell staunchly here.
Gain by naming allies.

SPROUTING is new life. From the buds on the trees to the cry of a new-born, sprouting represents all that comes from the joining of Heaven and Earth. The *Changes* reminds us that giving birth and infancy are natural—and they are great blessings in our lives.

Birth occurs against the threat of decline. The newborn nursery is not far from the mortuary. Troops raise clouds of dust on roads beside farmlands. Even in our daily life, decline is constant. A shovel forgotten in the rain rusts. Scattered clothes do not move into the closet. An unused mind weakens.

Life renews itself against decline in an ongoing and irrepressible process. It does so in spite of considerable resistance. Seeds are scattered to the wind to be eaten by birds, to fall on barren ground, or to be scorched by the sun. The mating of animals and humans is marked by courting, testing, and some-times combat. Even the process of a sperm finding an egg is one that requires the conquering of distance and the survival of a woman's chemistry. Nevertheless, life will renew itself.

Even the travails of birth and afterward cannot suppress life. A seedpod ruptures for the root to emerge. A new seedling must push against the earth. Trees growing from mountainside cracks must go through daunting days of sprouting. And the pain of human childbirth is well-known, an endeavor that, if it did not go to the very base of our existence, would be an experience few would choose. Every practical consideration argues against the effort to make life, and yet there is nothing more central to us than birth itself.

Besides these observations, the Statement goes on to draw societal par-allels. Finding a favorable place where we can live in peace and prosperity is compared to sprouting. Finding the right mate is also likened to sprouting.

One way that sprouting applies to our daily work is in the effort to begin new ventures. Every minute of every day, we must overcome inertia to embark on the tasks that face us. We use the energy we have stored—as a seed relies on the energy packed into its pod—to push against circumstances. Then we increase our efforts, like a plant sprouting. We must continue to grow, find how we will be supported, find out what we will become. The nature of the seed is important. A pear tree does not come from an apple seed. In the same way, we have to make the best of our beginnings. The whole is contained in the seed.

The scale enlarges when we talk about efforts with others. In the same way that every sprouting plant has a tip, group ventures must have a leader. As new life continues to strive against every hardship, leaders must drive our efforts. Sometimes we must even rely on them to clear the way themselves.

The *Statement* tells us that we must solve the mystery of why seeds continue to sprout in spite of all the odds in order for us to solve the mystery of life. Understand why the plants and animals renew themselves and you have the best template for your own actions and for being a leader. Find that impulse within yourself, and you will discover the source you need to face any difficulty. As water symbolizes risk and thunder symbolizes activity, be the one who acts in the midst of danger. Those who understand sprouting gain what is abundant and pure.

The *Lines* extend this theme with two images. One is built around the repeated phrase "a team of horses." The other is built around hunting and agriculture. In the case of horses, there is power and urgency. In images of agriculture and hunting is the message that we must learn from the place in which we find ourselves. The Lines interleave these two sets of images.

The first, third, and fifth lines address dwelling. (1) Once a favorable place is found, we must keep it, and find friends for support. (3) In this pioneer beginning, we must hunt, but while we may be eager to feed our families, we must find the proper guidance. (5) Both in crops and in prosperity, riches will begin to accumulate, but the time is still early and so only minor accomplishments are possible.

Marriage is the beginning of human bonds, and the second and fourth lines show two views. (2) In one case, someone comes on horses to woo but the situation is not yet right. (4) In another case, the marriage is right, and it is to be pursued with the force of a team of horses. (6) Finally, if we are too late, riding a team of horses is useless, and we are left sobbing and weeping blood.

How do we steady ourselves? How do we discern the many beginnings that lead to sprouting? The *Image* shows us how: we must study the principles under all that we see.

Every day we wake to a new dawn. We rise from the darkness of our beds to test ourselves against the events of the coming day. We can find enjoyment in sunshine and friendships. We can find the harshness of storms and fighting. Whatever it may be, we must not be severed from our root, and we must find a way to continue growing. As soon as growth ceases, decline and death are inevitable. Sprouting is our tie to the heaven and earth that made us. Sprouting is the mode to constant renewal. Sprouting is how we make our way through life.

Hexagram 4
Mountain above
Water below

Mountain above and water
below represents a spring at
a mountain's foot.

Meng
Young, ignorant, stupid, dull,
obscure. To deceive, to
cajole, to receive, to cover, to
screen, to hide.

The Sequence and Link
After birth, youth follows,
and there must be long
learning.

Youth

A young climber—
   lost, alone,
on a mountain
   with no guide,
feet stumbling
   over stones,
fingers clutching
   against slides—

until he finds
   a white stream
that dashes rock
   and shakes the trees,
splashes down ruts
   and ravines,
twisting to cut
   its own course.

The Statement

A youth must be steadfast.

I do not seek the naive youth.
The naive youth seeks me.
At the first divination, I explain,
but after three times, it is irritating.
Annoyed, I explain no further.

Nevertheless, a gainful omen.

The Lines

6th line ———
Nothing is gained by beating a youth.
That is the way to treat raiders.
We gain by preventing misdeeds.

5th line —— ——
An innocent and naive youth:
fortunate.

4th line —— ——
A distressed and naive youth:
sorrow.

3rd line —— ——
It is useless to marry a woman
who loses herself when she sees
a golden man.

The Image

2nd line ———
To have the joy of holding your own child,
take a wife. It will lead to fortune:
your children will lead the family.

A spring gushes
below a mountain:
the naive youth.
The noble one nourishes
virtue with determination.

1st line —— ——
While penalties are useful to illuminate
the naive youth, take off the fetters—
to go too far leads to sorrow.

YOUTH follows every birth. Before birth, the mother provides everything to the child, and the child is not yet separate from her. After birth, the long process of learning and separation from the mother begins.

The time it takes for this separation varies with each species. For simple life-forms, the separation is immediate. In many cases, the quicker the separation, the less freedom the life-form has. A grass seed needs no time with its parent, and yet it is tied to its roots and easily destroyed. Human beings have the greatest freedom of will and mobility, but they need to have a long period of learning, sheltered by parents and adults.

We take the spring bubbling up at the foot of the mountain as the image of youth: the mountain represents the stability, loftiness, and staid qualities of the elders. The spring—with its fluidity, its limpidity, its noisiness, its way of finding its own course away from the height and base of the mountain by tumbling over rocks and logs—symbolizes the contrasting image of youth. How can a spring be like a mountain? Perhaps that is how far the distance between youth and adulthood really is.

Still, our children have to grow into adults. They will make mistakes, they will be awkward, they will say things that any older person would blush to utter. That is what youth is for. If a young person were to act like an adult, it would be unnatural.

Adults must be patient with their children. They need to give every bit of guidance that they can. That is difficult. The wisdom necessary to care for children is overwhelming, and the sheer physical energy required exhausts anyone. Caring for the young is not an entirely rational act, but we dedicate ourselves to doing so. We love them. We see ourselves in them. We see the chance to extend kindness to someone in an all-too-callous world. We see the chance to nurture innocence in another human being, even as we keep one eye on the terrifying demons that wait for every soul. Let them come. We will fend them off until the young can take our places.

The mountain is firm. The mountain is set in place. The rushing spring carves new channels. In the same way, the young have a readiness to remake the entire world. Youth are ignorant of the classical world for good reason: they are the true agents of change.

Therefore, change happens from inside our homes and from the hands and mouths of our children. We give birth to these agents of change, and we nurture and dearly love those who will alter our world. We should not lament that. We should celebrate that.

It is right, then, to see family in the image of the trigrams. There is no closer, no more natural, and no more loving process of change than raising our children and sending them off with the full powers we can give them.

This hexagram goes on to consider youth from different angles. It is also the first time that the Oracle speaks in the first person.

The *Statement* opens with an ideal: the young must be guided to be upright and pure. Then it considers the exasperation of actually trying to reveal this wisdom. At the end, however, the Oracle realizes the importance and wonder of youth. That the young come to inquire is in itself a good omen.

The *Lines* extend these themes. (1) The Oracle considers consequences useful to teach the naive youth, but it warns against excessive punishment or restriction. (2) It recognizes that children are important, understanding the need to take a spouse in order to perpetuate the family. (3) It then gives a warning not to choose a spouse who will be unfaithful.

The Oracle then turns to two images of naive youth. (4) In the case of an exhausted naive youth, we are shown a young person who wastes his or her energy despite the teachings emphasized in the hexagram statement and lines 1, 2, and 6. (5) In the case of a naive youth who manages to keep her or his energy and innocence intact, there is fortune. This is the image of the successful youth, and of the youth that line 2 promises will someday lead the family. (6) Finally, the Oracle again reminds us not to go too far in punishing a naive youth; that is the way to treat criminals, not our young. In other words, we gain by preventing lawlessness rather than punishing it after the fact.

The *Image* of a spring beneath a mountain as a symbol of youth contrasts splashing fluidity with the staid substance of adulthood, yet the positive benefits of a spring show us the importance of youth. Our children are sources of regeneration. They are our future. On a moral level, the wise person nourishes virtue much the way a spring nourishes our bodies. That leads to inner regeneration.

The spring and the mountain—the youth and the elder. Youth exists only in relation to old age. Old age takes on a greater depth in contrast to youth. If the youth can learn from the elder, she can combine wisdom with vigor. If the elder learns from the youth, then that is like an old mountain man finding a fresh spring.

Waiting

The shadows in an oilskin tent
    cover a sleeping boy.
Squatting on sacks of seed, eight men
slap mosquitoes and shout their tales
    over the river's din.

Seeing morning clouds sag, men grunt
    and turn to beach their boat.
The boy jumps to the rope but groans
as the crew drags the wooden hull
    across the sand and stone.

Rain like arrows punctures the banks,
    men shout and grab the boy.
They lash the raft, make their retreat,
and laughing, slog back to the tent,
    the mud sucking their feet.

They dry themselves and throw the boy
    rice wrapped in lotus leaves.
Filling mouths with taro and wine,
they nudge the boy and urge him, "Eat!
    Your strength will come in time."

Hexagram 5
Water above
Heaven below

Water in heaven: rain clouds in the sky. We cannot make it rain; we have to wait for this nourishment to fall.

Furthermore, heaven, meaning strength, is combined with water, meaning danger. When one is faced with danger, one carefully times one's action and, while waiting, seeks nourishment in preparation for the work ahead.

Xu
Hesitation, waiting. To need, to require, to demand. Expenses, provisions, needs, necessities.

The Sequence and Link
Youth requires nourishment and time for growth, and that requires waiting.

The Statement

Waiting. Stay confident:
there is light everywhere.
Pure fortune.
Advance across the great river.

The Lines

6th line ▬ ▬
Entering into a cave and
finding uninvited strangers.
Three people come. Honor them
and in the end there will be good fortune.

5th line ▬▬▬
Waiting with wine and food.
Pure fortune.

4th line ▬ ▬
Waiting in a bloody cave.
Get out!

3rd line ▬▬▬
Waiting in the mud
draws raiders to arrive.

The Image

Clouds rising to heaven:
waiting. The noble one
drinks, eats,
and feasts with joy.

2nd line ▬▬▬
Waiting in the sand.
The small will talk.
At last, good fortune.

1st line ▬▬▬
Waiting in the countryside.
Gain by being steadfast.
Be without fault.

WAITING is one of the hardest skills to learn. It is usually an asset of old age, not of youth. It takes that long—and perhaps some weariness—to master the art of waiting.

The trigrams show clouds rising into the sky. We are waiting for rain, but the needed rain has not yet fallen. We must let this waiting neither shake our confidence nor deter us from action. In the phrase "light everywhere," we are reminded of the possibilities that constantly surround us. In the advice to advance across the great river, we are reminded that a delay in plans may provide other opportunities even as we are waiting for our original plans to develop.

Waiting is of such importance that it is wise to look deeply into it.

Waiting is patience. Waiting is timing. Both meanings are difficult for the young to grasp, and yet both meanings are especially important if the young are to grow straight and true.

Waiting as patience means waiting for a course to run. For example, children must be steadily educated. They must travel, go to festivals, schools, museums, and historical sites to become well-rounded. If they are fortunate, they will meet great people who initiate them, and they will have dedicated teachers who will expand their knowledge. Children must learn all the academic skills, and they must also learn many others as well—art, music, athletics, dance, theater, wilderness skills, financial literacy, farming and cooking, carpentry, craft—and more. Above all the diversity to be mastered, spirituality is paramount: to raise children who are kind to each other and to all creatures is a profound accomplishment. The process requires great effort. How appropriate, then, that waiting in the sense of patience is so emphasized. This is not dumb inaction, but the attentive sequencing of education.

Then there is waiting as timing. We can get what we want if we wait until the right time. If we do, everything will be easy.

We all know this: it is foolish to plant trees when the ground is frozen. But we need to apply this in more subtle ways as well. If we are promised a business contract, it makes no sense to rush. If we need to act on a certain day, we must wait until that moment. When the right time comes, of course, we had better not fail to act. Waiting makes sense only if our timing is correct.

During waiting, we are advised to seek nourishment. This means that we should fortify ourselves and prepare. Once our chance comes, we will be as strong and undistracted as we can be, and we will not fail to make our waiting well worthwhile. Those who are prepared usually do best when the time comes.

So it is that the *Statement* gives us several meanings to waiting:

Waiting. Water in the sky. We cannot make it rain, so we eat to strengthen ourselves while we wait.

Waiting. Water in the sky. In the waiting, clouds build: waiting is how heaven builds itself.

The *Lines* give variations on just these ideas. (1) At first, we are on the outskirts of the situation, and so we must be constant and persevering toward our goals. This situation is not of our own making, and so we are not to blame for it. (2) In the image of waiting in the sand, we can imagine an expedition marching toward a desert tribe, or an army on the banks of a stream. The small—perhaps a tribesman or the enemy—will come forth to negotiate, and there will be good fortune in the end. (3) By contrast, waiting in the mud shows travelers mired, and this only invites opportunistic raiders to attack. (4) An even worse situation is portrayed in the image of a bloody cave (or hole, or even grave), and then we must get out at all costs. (5) The right action to take when delayed is to enjoy wine and food. Clearly, such a person has timed the situation well and makes use of the respite to fortify himself or herself. This idea will later be reinforced in the Image. (6) Finally, we are shown entering a cave where we encounter strangers. It will take others to rescue us here, although we might not recognize them at first. But if we can identify them and honor them, they will help us.

The *Image* reminds us that waiting need not frustrate us if we make use of it. Drink, eat, and feast with joy. Then, when it comes time to advance, we will be well rested and strong.

If we eat and drink while waiting, what could be a more supremely confident attitude? If we gather ourselves before crossing, what could be a more powerful advance across the great river?

If we are shrewd enough to wait until the time comes into our favor, we will surely achieve our purpose.

Hexagram 6
Heaven above
Water below

Heaven above signifies one half pulling upward, while water below pulls the other half downward.

    Heaven represents strength, water represents danger: when excessive strength is applied to a dangerous situation, there will be conflict.

Song
Litigation, contention. To dispute, to demand.

The Sequence and Link
During the time of youthful immaturity, there will inevitably be dispute.

Dispute

With their teeth bared,
two brothers stand
poised with their saws
to claim the prize
the judge awards.

With shouts they cut
the beams that span
their father's house.
Malachite tiles
explode in shards.

One brother wants
bedrooms and roof,
the other gloats
that he will keep
the family grounds.

They stand in piles
of splintered wood.
The brothers stare,
and each declares:
"This house is mine!"

The Statement

Dispute: keep confident
even if blocked and alarmed.

In the middle, good fortune,
but in the end, misfortune.

Gain by seeing a great person.
Do not advance across the great river.

The Lines

6th line ▬▬▬
One may be awarded a belt of high rank,
but by morning's end,
it will have been stripped away three times.

5th line ▬▬▬
Dispute. Supreme fortune.

4th line ▬▬▬
Unable to win the dispute. Go back now,
make your decisions.
Change your mind
and there will be peace.

3rd line ▬▬ ▬▬
Surviving on old favors: a perilous sign.
In the end: fortune.
One may undertake royal service,
but without personal success.

The Image

2nd line ▬▬▬
Unable to win the dispute. Return,
and so flee his realm
of three hundred households.
No blunders.

Heaven and water clash:
dispute. The noble one
devises the right beginning
in all matters.

1st line ▬▬ ▬▬
Do not prolong this case.
The petty control all the talk.
In the end: fortune.

DISPUTE is possible in any public situation. It is likely whenever we are striving for new accomplishments. Just as heaven rises upward and water sinks downward, a dispute can be as heavy as a struggle between the skies and the oceans.

It is good to look at the warriors, for they are trained in the ways of conflict. When we do examine, however, we see that a good warrior avoids war. A common person never sees the best warriors lift a finger, because the true fighter knows: completely winning a conflict is seldom possible. If it is to happen it all, we must be morally right and strong. Only if we are both sure of our cause and if we have skillfully guided power are the risks worth taking. Those who try to win out of brute force alone are no better than those who enter into dispute when they have no chance of winning: both kinds of people only worsen the conflict.

In the situations where disputes are unavoidable, we must stay composed. The dilemma of disputes still means we have choices—even if none may be palatable. One thing is certain: change is at hand. Whether that change will be profitable or not depends on what we do.

It may be surprising to consider, but every dispute implies a relationship. Whether it is an argument with a sibling, a parent, a neighbor, or a government official, a dispute occurs within a context. Like two brothers arguing, it is critical to resolve the dispute and uphold the relationship. That is why the best solution is to compromise and to give something to both sides. True, we may have to soften our position, but that may be necessary in order to gain resolution. The image of Dispute reminds us to be firm inside, like heaven, and yielding outside, like water. We compromise not to capitulate but as a strategy for peace.

We live in a world that celebrates selfishness. Children shout to be heard over others. Adults sputter over the slightest infraction of their rights. The peaceful are beaten by those who want their bodies, land, and money. Ethics means defining ourselves against this backdrop of greed and lust. If we happen upon unguarded money, we do not take it. If we see a chance to exploit the weak, we do not take it. If we have an opportunity to promote ourselves by undercutting someone else, we do not take it. We know what *most* people might do, but we do what we know is *right*. Thus, by being conscientious, we can avoid the conditions that lead to dispute.

We must constantly ask ourselves what the best outcome should be. Then we must work toward it. Studying ethics and morality is essential so we can judge properly. Balancing individual rights with the common good is no easy task. The more we steep ourselves in the consideration of what is right, the more it will help us in the time of dispute.

If we always do what is right, we develop a superb moral force that will serve us well in the time of dispute. We can attain the loftiness of heaven, and the clarity of water.

The *Statement* acknowledges that dispute is of great risk. During the course of matters, we may believe that we will win the case, but in the end, we risk misfortune. That is why we should seek the advice of someone of experience or influence, and we should avoid grand undertakings. Get out of the dispute before making a new venture.

The unpredictable outcome of dispute is shown in the *Lines.* (5) Out of six lines, only one, line 5, can press the dispute to a successful outcome. The remaining lines all have warnings against continuing with the dispute.

(1) When we find ourselves blocked and alarmed by petty people, it is best not to prolong the dispute. If we do that, there will be good fortune in the end. (2) If our opponent is mighty, we must acknowledge that we cannot win. We must return quickly to our own province. (3) In a dispute, we must not assume that old supporters will protect us. We may have become used to depending on old favors, and if we turn away from this, we may yet enjoy good fortune. But we must not try to do too much, because we will not be successful at this time. (4) There is also a recognition that we often hold the key to our own success. By resuming our normal lives and changing our minds to avoid Dispute, we gain both peace and safety. (6) Finally, as in line 3, we are warned against striving for fame and recognition, and against wrangling for influence. This invites more conflict, and we may not be able to withstand further conflicts. We may think we are succeeding, but we will be quickly stripped of success.

That is why the *Image* advises us to make our plans carefully: the best way to avoid dispute is by meticulously planning from the very beginning to avoid conflict.

How subtle is the mind of the noble one! Such a person understands that to clash openly is already failure. In planning, a wise person arranges all things so that disputes can be avoided. Our society celebrates the heroes of disputes—the lawyers, the generals, the warriors—but the wise one is as transparent as heaven, as unfathomable as the deepest water. When such a person arranges the beginnings of a venture, and aligns his or her efforts with the Way, no dispute interferes with the momentum created.

Hexagram 7
Earth above
Water below

Water below earth: ground-water. A good army is drawn from the populace as ground-water floods from the earth.

Water as danger and earth as receptivity also symbolizes an army's violence controlled by discipline.

The single yang line in the second place represents the strong leader of an army.

Shi
Army, master, instructor, tutor, division, model. To imitate.

The Sequence and Link
If disputes escalate, armies are mobilized.

Armies

A horde of armored cavalry
breaches our borders to the north.

Each day they kill, each night they raid.
Blood in chariot tracks runs fresh.
The hammer blows that forged their blades
give steel power to cut through flesh.

Their arrows seem to hit the stars,
the moon hangs like a severed head.

The great prince draws our battle plans.
With patient strokes we push them back.
He leads the charge and calls each man
to trade blow for blow, hack for hack.

The farmers' new crop is the dead—
rotten melons heaped on broken carts.

The Statement

Armies must be steadfast.
With a great leader
they will find fortune.

They must remain without fault.

The Lines

6th line —— ——

The great prince takes command.
He founds a country
and supports the clans.
He does not employ petty people.

5th line —— ——

There are birds in the field. Catch them!
No fault when the eldest one
commands armies, but if it is a trainee—
carts of corpses and pure misfortune.

4th line —— ——

The armies camp on the eastern side.
Be without fault.

3rd line —— ——

The armies might cart corpses:
misfortune.

The Image

2nd line ——

In the middle of armies: fortune.
Be without fault.
The king confers command three times.

The earth's center
is filled with water.
The noble one supports
the people and cares for
everyone.

1st line —— ——

Armies must march with rules.
Otherwise, whether gain or loss,
there will be misfortune.

ARMIES have always been a part of society, and they will continue to be a part for the rest of humanity's existence. However, resorting to armies should always be done after thorough consideration and preparation. When such a decision does come, the army must be drawn from the people both for the sake of might and for the sake of popular support. The name of this hexagram, which can mean "the multitude," reminds us of this essential truth.

In King Wen's time, farms were organized into cooperative districts. Whenever there were large tasks, such as harvesting or building homes, the people in the district willingly combined their labor. Districts were then combined into larger units of villages and counties. In this way, there were continuous links between the individual and the government.

Whenever there was a need for soldiers, districts were also combined to form an army. The soldiers knew each other, and they already knew their general, who came from the same area. The unity of the army was therefore inherent in its recruits.

In times of peace, the army provided labor for large public works like building roads. An army working to improve its own community had great motivation, and its soldiers usually worked hard. At the same time, the army was providing needed services, and this built goodwill among the citizens it served.

Most of the battles fought by the Zhou army were defensive rather than offensive. King Wen did not seek to conquer others. Thus, his army was often fighting on familiar territory. When the country was attacked by barbarian tribes, the army was fighting for its own home. There is a great advantage to an army fighting on its own land: it is easily supplied by the citizens of that area, it is fighting for its own leader, and it will be supported by the citizens.

In military history, there are numerous instances of wars fought in far different circumstances. There have been despots who have sought to conquer, even in winter, or even in distant lands. There have been generals who have underestimated the determination of people fighting for their own homes. And there have been numerous instances where an invading army has abused the people by slaughtering, looting, and raping. Obviously, anyone who understands the wisdom of change will not take make these mistakes. The image of water and earth resonates with this. How can any human army, no matter what size, truly overcome those people who are fighting for their own water and fields?

A good general will not campaign farther than his supply lines will stretch, unless his soldiers can live off the land. An intelligent warrior will not enter unscouted territory. A good leader will maintain the faith of his army through exemplary behavior. And a good army will remain disciplined and will not molest innocent civilians.

If we would use the image of the army for nonmilitary considerations, we must ask ourselves whether our situation calls for us to be soldiers or leaders. If we are a soldier, it is crucial for us to identify our comrades and our leader. If we are the leader of the situation, we must recognize that we are the one person holding the group together. Just as the hexagram has only one yang line, every group must have at least one strong leader. The **Statement** shows us that *shi* the multitude makes an army, but that a single person—*shi* the master and model—forges that army's destiny. Therefore, steadfastness, purity, and even reverence are essential. This hexagram alludes to the spiritual power of the just warrior.

The **Lines** therefore concentrate on the proper leading of troops. (1) In the first line, the need for discipline is established. If armies are disorderly and flout military law, victory and defeat are secondary. That is why military crimes are punished swiftly and harshly. (2) However, if a leader is strong and in the center of a disciplined army, all goes well; the king will confer honor on both the leader and the armies. (3) Naturally, all war entails the risk of defeat. What could be a more vivid symbol of humiliating loss than corpses piled on the very chariots and carts built for attack? (4) Besides orderly ranks and a powerful general, there must be consideration of position on the battlefield. The general can make no mistakes in choosing campsites and battleground. (5) Line 5 states the importance of opportunity ("birds in the field"), determination ("Catch them!"), right leadership, and how the wrong leadership can cause disaster that will internally undermine an army. (6) The final line shows the culmination of the campaign: the war is over; the prince takes command and establishes a country. Even then, the need to be without fault is evident: petty people must be excluded if the country is to become great.

The **Image** emphasizes that a leader of an army must support all troops, while being aware of civilians too. In turn, the army must be kind and generous to all those it meets. There can be no looting, no war atrocities. Instead, armies must care for themselves and the people around them, rebuilding all they destroy. Then all will be well.

Joining

Hexagram 8
Water above
Earth below

The Water trigram above the Earth trigram: an ocean flows in the deep hollows of the earth.
    A single yang line in the fifth place symbolizes how times of unity require strong ideals and strong leaders.

Bi
To follow, to assemble, to equal, to provide, to classify, to compare.

The Sequence and Link
An army must assemble. The ideal result of military action will be a new social order.

The war horses
have been put to pasture:
they never graze the same patch twice.
The emperor
sends out proclamations
and calls the kings to sacrifice.

Kings from abroad
arrive at the temple,
splendid in their sables and gold.
The emperor
welcomes with open palms
and calls the circle to be closed.

After fasting
in silence for three days,
the priest speaks of the omens first.
"Be like sunlight
on the moving water."
The kings touch their heads to earth.

The Statement

Joining brings fortune.
Repeating the divination by yarrow stalks
brings a supreme and lasting omen
without fault.
Those who are not sure
will join the plan.
Those who are late
will meet misfortune.

The Lines

6th line — —
Joining without a leader:
misfortune.

5th line ——
Glorious joining. The king uses three beaters
to flush the birds before him,
but citizens need no such coercion. Fortune.

4th line — —
Joining with those outside.
Pure fortune.

3rd line — —
Joining with robbers.

The Image

2nd line — —
Joining from within our own people.
Pure fortune.

Water pooled
on the earth: joining.
The early kings founded
the myriad nations,
and kept close ties
with all the leaders.

1st line — —
Have confidence. Joining is without fault.
Be as full of trust as an overflowing pot.
At last, another will come. Fortune.

JOINING is a natural occurrence. Our society duplicates that. Just as water gathers in the hollows of the earth, it is natural for people to join together. Society means joining.

We want joining. Look how much of our time is spent trying to meet the right people, trying to organize ourselves to take action, trying to find the right way to be fair to everyone while we attempt to move an agenda forward. We have tried every form of assembly from anarchy to tyranny, and still we cannot perfect the central act of cooperation. Nevertheless, we keep wanting to meet others and work with them.

If we cannot find the joining we want immediately, we must remain sincere and centered in our beliefs until joining is established. Patience is essential. We may be tempted to associate with people whose goals ultimately do not reflect our own. Then good efforts fall into confusion. Thus, we need both the right group and the right leader.

Just as the hexagram for Joining has only one yang line, a leader holds others together. We say leader, and imagine someone out in front, but we should also imagine someone underneath, someone who supports all others, or we might even think of "around," because a leader is someone who binds people together.

A leader and a collective cannot exist without each other. A good leader must be talented and intelligent, but a good leader must also let joining happen naturally. No good comes from coercion. If the joining comes from a natural need, people come to a leader without any force. That is the best kind of joining, for it is willing. If a good leader simply express what the group wants, all that follows will be fortunate.

In the process of joining, a leader will become powerful. We use the archetypal image of a king, but in fact, the equation applies to everything from the head of a household to a president, from coaching a team to teaching children. In all cases, a leader must remember that the group confers authority. If a leader makes the mistake of thinking that power rises solely from his or her own personality, that would be wrong. A leader must never forget that it is the people, not he, who is the source of power.

When wealth accumulates to the leader, it is wise to distribute the wealth. If there are too many riches at the top, the results will be unbalanced and this will cause resentment. The leader who shares in prosperity only broadens the base of support. A good king redistributes authority—by delegating responsibilities to those below him—and he also distributes rewards. He should keep little for himself. In that way, the joining will continue to have a long life.

Joining shows the beginning of society by its very name. In Zhou times, *bi*, the name of this hexagram, meant a grouping of five families. Thus, we see the beginning of a larger community from the shared concerns of neighbors and the common needs of an agricultural community.

In early times, a venture as important as beginning a community was preceded by divining. Here the **Statement** considers this joining so important that we are urged to divine again to be doubly sure. We may not perform divination when we come together today, but we certainly look for signs. We check to see how many people support the idea, we look to see what the needs of the community are, we see if there is a shared goal that people can rally around. We divine no less today, only we poll people rather than heaven.

In all joining, we must endeavor to persuade those who are reticent. There must be a plan that they can understand, and then they must be willing to join that plan. Creating a community has its time, however. That is why those who join too late meet misfortune.

The **Lines** extend these themes. (1) Certainly, joining requires confidence, trust, and a willingness to wait for the right people. (2) That is why joining that springs from within one's own people is so right. (3) As a reminder that our associations are important, we have the example of joining with robbers. The foolishness of that should be evident. (4) We can also join with those outside our area, and if done correctly, this can be fortunate. (5) In all cases, joining should be voluntary. In ancient times, a king used beaters to flush game, but his citizens should have come of their own volition. (6) Finally, it is also possible for the people to want joining but for them to lack a leader. In that case, there can only be misfortune.

The **Image** shows us that once joining has been established, the leaders must become part of the larger community. A good king will keep close relations with all segments for the larger good.

Joining is the excellence of all society. Joining is the meaning of all structure. Without joining two pieces of wood, we would have neither furniture nor houses. Without joining with others, it is impossible to build any great endeavor.

小畜

Wind above
Heaven below

The wind in the sky may be
gentle, but it can hold back
the rain we need.

　A yin line in the fourth
place represents a smallness
that manages to dominate
five yang lines.

　This hexagram makes an
analogy between control and
the domestication of animals.
Since the yin line is not
completely strong enough,
control is limited.

Xiao Chu

Xiao: Little, slight.
Chu: Domesticated animals.
To raise livestock.

The Sequence and Link

Once joining has taken place,
some control is possible.

Smallness Tames

Bedsheets billow,
dung on green hay, burrs on wet wool.

Dust flies in eyes.
Rubbing and blinking bring no tears.

Stacked clouds. No rain.
Prayers swirl up like scraps of paper.

Shamans go, bowed;
the wind has neither ears nor heart.

Best to pull weeds,
nail loose boards, and cart off the dung.

The Statement

Smallness tames. Persevere.
Dense clouds, no rain
at my western border.

The Lines

6th line ⸺

Rain is done, all is in place. Respect and virtue
are full. Yet a woman's chastity is imperiled.
When the moon is nearly full,
the prince attacks: misfortune.

5th line ⸺

Have confidence. Entwine
with your neighbor for wealth.

4th line ⸺ ⸺

Have confidence. Bloodletting is past,
alarm has gone. No fault.

3rd line ⸺

Carriage spokes halted.
Husband and wife quarrel.

The Image

Wind moving high
in heaven: smallness tames.
The noble one acts
with restraint, culture,
and morals.

2nd line ⸺

Pulled to return.
Fortune.

1st line ⸺

Return to your own Way.
How can this be wrong?

SMALLNESS TAMES invokes the image of livestock, thereby extending the theme of control resulting from Joining. Just as animals are restrained when domesticated, so wild and errant forces are restrained or "domesticated" by agreements within the community.

However, when a society is just struggling to coalesce, controls will often be limited. Much work lies ahead before greater accomplishments are possible. In one sense, then, this hexagram describes times when order is still incomplete and only small things may be done.

The hexagram takes its image of limited domination from dark clouds piled in the sky. Rain is hoped for, but it has not yet arrived. There is a mild standoff. The wind cannot dispel the clouds entirely, while the clouds are kept from moving overhead and releasing rain. The image of a limited and partial control is clear.

The image of Smallness Tames is applicable in two ways. The first sense is control as applied to ourselves. We have attained limited dominance over a situation, but it is not yet total or overwhelmingly powerful. When this happens, only limited accomplishments are open to us, and we must not refuse to participate. If all we can do are small things, then we should do small things until our situation changes.

The second idea of limited control has to do with finding ourselves in a subordinate position in a situation. Something is keeping the clouds from raining. It is slight. The clouds would rain if there was just an opening. But nevertheless, it is not raining, and we can do nothing to make it rain. When we are caught in this time, we can do no more than the situation allows. Like a farmer waiting for clouds to rain, we cannot force a result. Therefore, it is best to prepare ourselves and be ready once the situation changes.

In this lull period, the sages would urge us to work on ourselves. That is the key to all success in change. We must move away from any thought that external factors are the sole determinants in our lives. The *Changes* constantly urges us to cultivate ourselves, improve ourselves, and maintain our confidence. It is the quality of our actions and the degree to which we can resonate with circumstance that make us superior.

Most of us are good at the big things. Most of us rise to the occasion in times of war, financial collapse, or death in the family. But the "minor" times really challenge us to keep to our path: The small things that are not quite enough to change our lives but that still manage to impede things are too easy to dismiss. Yet the accumulated weight of neglected details often undermines us far more than an enormous disaster. We must maintain our determination and discipline even during minor times. We must neither whine nor be apathetic: by small improvements, we become victorious.

The *Statement* gives Smallness Tames connotations of restraint, feeding livestock, and rearing children. It also implies storing, heaping, and accumulation. These associations are not as strange as they might seem. The domestication of animals is a storing of food, labor, and raw materials for the future. The *Changes* expresses taming as dense clouds impeded by the wind, and asks how we might similarly make use of restraint and accumulation in our own lives.

All that being said, we can also look at this hexagram from a different angle: it is the little that tames. The wind holds back the clouds. The rope controls the bull. The sage guides the people with the merest of deeds. Taming takes place by little degrees. We cannot tame a horse all at once. We cannot raise a piglet into a hog in one day. Taming takes place by small degrees. If we understand that, this hexagram can be turned into a meditation on the power that comes from gradual but steady restraint.

A careful reading of the *Lines* will show the many nuances of taming. (1) Self-restraint is depicted as one returning to one's own road. (2) Further taming is shown when someone is pulled to return. (3) However, restraint can also mean coming to an impasse, as when spinning wheels are halted and husband and wife—who should be working as harmoniously as two wheels on a single axle—glare and quarrel. (4) Sometimes, the restraint necessary·is the holding of our own confidence. We are shown a scene where bloodletting and fear are gone— perhaps after battle—and now we must act again without fault. (5) Social restraint is shown through a mutual action with our neighbors that will bring wealth. (6) In the last line, the rain is past; all things are in place. We have benefited from our location, our work, and the weather—and even the respect and virtue of our community is building. But there is a reminder that too much fullness invites new trouble. Women can be attacked, things grow too full, like the moon, and the prince is emboldened to use his power to attack others. In that case, our restraint and accumulation are misused.

The *Image* reminds us that wind can hold back clouds. In the same way, the wise person holds back faults and so accumulates great moral force. To be restrained, to be cultured, and to act ethically are all forms of taming. If we manage to tame ourselves, our greatness will build—and we can then yoke it for further actions.

Smallness Tames. How slight the secret. How monumental the effect.

Hexagram 10
Heaven above
Lake below

Heaven symbolizes a father, and lake represents the youngest daughter. This hexagram uses walking as a symbol for conduct, and refers both to a father's tolerance of his daughter and to the greater consideration of proper conduct.

Lu
To walk, to step, to tread, to follow. Shoes.

The Sequence and Link
The establishment of restraint leads to the question of proper conduct and the securing of support. Walking refers both to proper conduct and to open support.

Walking

A father and his daughter hunt
for red ginseng. He does not say,
"Walk behind," when he sees her prance
like a pony with no bridle.

A tiger, down from dun mountains,

He heaves the pack on his bent back;
the smell of grass seeps from damp cloth.

slinks toward a lake in wilted trees,

She bounds through the high grass, teeth white
against the lake's turquoise ripples.

tongue rough, stalking in rattling grass,

Her father warns her not to run.
She sidles back, pulls his whiskers.

hypnotized by the waves, crouching—

She plunges through the grass again,
steps blindly on the tiger's tail.
Her father grabs for her, eyes wide,
as yellow and black stripes vanish.

She laughs and wades into the lake,
oblivious to teeth and claws.

The Statement

Walking on a tiger's tail:
it does not bite.
Continue.

The Lines

6th line ——————

Look how you walk.
Look into what will be favorable.
Oh, turn toward great fortune!

5th line ——————

Decisive walking,
pure and stern.

4th line ——————

Walking on the tiger's tail:
fright and panic!
In the end: fortune.

3rd line ———— ————

The one-eyed can see. The lame can walk.
But they walk on the tiger's tail
and are bitten. Misfortune
when a warrior shams as a prince.

The Image

2nd line ——————

Walking the calm and level Way.
The recluse is pure. Fortune.

Heaven above, lake below:
walking. The noble one
distinguishes high and low
to fix the people's purpose.

1st line ——————

Walking forward in austerity
is without blame.

WALKING can symbolize a number of meanings. One major symbolism is the relationship of a father (the Heaven trigram) to his youngest daughter (the Lake trigram). Here, a father has a favorite daughter, and he dotes on her. She knows it, and she takes advantage of his fondness. He indulges her, but he also teaches her. It is this tender relationship that is at the heart of walking.

Walking combines two meanings. The first is how a daughter "walks" on her father: he is the firm support from which she will spring into the world. The second is walking in the sense of proper conduct. Through patient companionship, the father teaches his daughter the way to conduct herself. Without this teaching—firm, supportive, patient, and gentle—no child can be fully successful in the world. Her father gives her an initiation that no mother, no sibling, and no teacher can give her.

Walking involves risk—the danger of stepping on a tiger's tail. A father must help his daughter face risk so she can successfully negotiate life's many dangers. The father begins by protecting his daughter until she has learned to fend for herself. He then gradually bring her to a familiarity with the world's ugliness without hurting her or allowing her to be deeply scarred. And he must impart all his skills to her so she can carry on without him. Through a slow and patient process, he imparts "yang" skills to a "yin" person. In return, the father certainly learns something about yin gentleness himself.

One of the most important lessons about gentleness is the need for modesty. This is stereotypically a woman's virtue, and yet every man, even in the most masculine of settings, has had to learn the value of modesty. Safety when working and traveling, giving way when fighting, patience when farming, a deferential demeanor before one's superiors—these are all skills of modesty that every man has to master. At the same time, a man has to combine these gentle traits with the will and strength to make accomplishments. A father shows his daughter a valuable way of combining modesty with confident action because he has first had to learn that himself.

There is a certain innocence that is a power in young girls. Men do not have it. We celebrate that power as a society, applauding the young gymnast, praising the dancer and actress, celebrating with a bride, rewarding the abilities of a young writer, admiring the mind and speed of a woman warrior. The key to harnessing this power is discipline. Talent, youth, and beauty are breathtaking assets, but they are easily lost. It is only by discipline that a daughter becomes a great woman.

Finally, what every father teaches his daughters is this: although the world is dangerous—full of tigers lurking in the grass—each person must develop her own powers without becoming a vicious tiger herself. Friends will betray her. War will devastate her. Men will attack with insults and clubs. Illness will ravage her and her children. Nevertheless, she must protect her own innocence. Evil wants everyone to join it. She must never do that. She must protect her innocence as she would protect her own child. That, above all else, is proper walking.

Do not think of this omen as a charm—that we walk on a tiger's tail and will not be bitten. Rather, think of how you walk, where the tiger is, and how you can act so you will not be bitten. The *Statement* asks: How are we going to walk through our days? Which paths will we choose to walk? These are fundamental questions each of us must answer for ourselves.

The *Lines* suggest three classes of answers. The first two lines portray the walking and paths of modest people. The middle two lines show examples of those who walk foolishly. The upper two lines show exemplary walking.

(1) The walking in the beginning line is one of austerity, a plainness and simplicity like that of a scholar unconcerned with fame or wealth. (2) We are next shown an even greater extreme in a recluse who walks a calm and level road and whose purity leads to fortune. (3) In contrast, the foolish—a one-eyed person, a lame person, and a warrior acting beyond his or her station—fall into trouble quickly. (4) Likewise, the person who steps on a tiger's tail and then gives way to fright and panic only gets bitten. The implication of these middle two lines is that misfortune results from overestimation and fearfulness. (5) The best way is to be a person of decisiveness and discipline. Forks in the road are inevitable, and we must be strong enough to choose which way to walk. (6) The standard is to compare possible paths, to examine what makes us happy, and then to turn toward that. If we do, we will find the greatest fortune—because we have brought ourselves (our walking) into harmony with our surroundings (the path).

The *Image* shows that a wise leader not only does this personally, but also leads the people on the right path. The leader brings order to high and low, and helps the people find the right purpose.

Walking takes rhythm. Walking takes two feet acting in tandem; it takes alternating yin and yang. Walking will bring risk. To keep walking even with the struggle to maintain one's own position and with the risk of the trail, and to do so with poise and knowledge: that is the essence of following the Way.

Hexagram 11
Earth above
Heaven below

Earth moves down from above. Heaven rises from below. The two meet in harmony. The two trigrams can also be seen as heaven inside and earth outside: modesty is wrapped around strength.

    This hexagram is associated with the first lunar month (February–March), when a new spring approaches.

    Tai is also the name of the sacred mountain where China's rulers journeyed to offer sacrifices.

Tai
Peace, quiet, calm, ease. Great, large. Good luck. Prosperity.

The Sequence and Link
The right conduct from proper walking brings peace, contentment, union, and prosperity.

Prospering

Escorted by courtiers and swordsmen,
the queen rides a gold palanquin.
Deer bent to hillside grass graze unconcerned,
    as priests chant to heaven.

Peasants huddle behind warriors with spears.
A woman jumps from the line, shrieks, and dares
to dash into the path as guards rush near:
    "My queen! Let me be heard!"

Circled by blades, she crawls on rock-scraped knees,
her infant clutched tight. When she pleads,
the officials demand that she be seized.
    The queen says, "Let her be."

The mother weeps, "The war—I lost husband—
I lost farm. None of us can find
a grain of rice." The queen sighs, "By my hand
    you shall have rice and land."

The swaddled child begins to kick and cry.
All the peasants avert their eyes.
The queen sings a line from a lullaby,
    soft as Mount Tai's sunrise.

The Statement

Prospering: the vile goes,
the great comes.
Fortune. Continue.

The Lines

6th line ▬ ▬

City walls fall into a dry moat.
Do not use armies.
Report to your own capital.
Make commands: remorse.

5th line ▬ ▬

Emperor Yi gives his daughter in marriage.
Blessing and fortune.

4th line ▬ ▬

Running back and forth:
no wealth from your neighbors.
But do not give up trust.

3rd line ▬▬▬

No flat without a slope. No advance without
return. Be steadfast in difficulty.
No fault, no grief. The other is sincere:
in feasting there will be happiness.

2nd line ▬▬▬

Encompass the wasteland by crossing the river
without a boat, but do not advance so far
that you abandon comrades to perish.
Win honor by a middle course.

1st line ▬▬▬

Pulled couch grass
uproots more with it by entwined roots.
Snatch it: fortune.

The Image

Heaven and earth combine:
prospering.
The empress uses wealth
to fulfill the way
of heaven and earth.
She supports the order
of heaven and earth for
people on all sides.

PROSPERING is shown here as a process. Heaven and earth combine, and the leader shown in the Image meets this auspicious confluence with resources of her own. Thus, flourishing is brought to all the people. This is a time of great opportunity, often so great that it banishes the pain of having gotten to that point.

Struggle is like winter. The time is cold, dry, and brutal. Falling snow thickens our blood and strews ice crystals into our joints until the mere search for warmth grinds pain into every limb. When struggle goes on too long, it saps us—not just muscle, bone, blood, or will, but memory too. We whither, forgetting that there was ever any happiness. The cold turns to darkness, the darkness into night. In the night, we moan in despair.

When spring comes, we recognize how much we have forgotten: the blue skies, the smell of grass, the percussion of pine boughs. Our bodies move again in delight. We join hands with our loved ones, and dance in a circle under the green leaves. With the warm air, the golden sunlight, and the purple crocus, we remember what it was to have all things come to us. We can enjoy the food the earth gives us, thrill to beauty, and go free into the warm breezes. Who can be blamed for forgetting winter nights?

When someone is crushed beneath a wheel, it does no good to philosophize about the wheel's circumference. In the same way, when we are in the midst of struggle, it is difficult to think of cycles. Only when we feel movement and recognize that we are again at the starting point will we see how the circle has involved us. In the seasonal sense, the cycles of life renew themselves each spring. In the personal sense, there is a sense of great wellbeing when the good that is around us matches the needs and desires we have. The time for sowing arrives, and we are ready to plow. The days lengthen, and we feel ready to work in the brightening hours. The rains dwindle; the sun shines. All our work will combine with heaven and earth, and we will prosper.

In prospering, the power of yang goes into the earth and the earth responds with the bounty of all we need for contentment: the blue mountains, the greening rice, the bee buzzing around clover, even the sparkling dust that drifts in the sun.

We can see this same principle inside ourselves. Every person is both heaven and earth. It took a man and a woman to make us. It takes heaven and earth for us to be human. Only by orchestrating the movement between yin and yang will our summers of joy come to us.

If we allow one side or the other to predominate, we fail to bring heaven and earth into harmony. This chills us. We enter a winter of the soul. We fall into perverse behavior. We shift into excessive thinking. We let our emotions fracture into a thousand shards of glass. But if we keep heaven and earth together with us, the wheel turns, and our souls find a peace as fluid and shining as quicksilver. Thus it is that the *Statement* shows all that is vile departing and all that is great returning. There is prosperity and continuity.

Accordingly, the *Lines* support the idea of prospering with subtle wisdom. (1) When the opportunity is right, pulling our actions along will pull related things with it. Fortune is there for our snatching. (2) When the time support us, we might even acquire territory with near-reckless advancement (we can encompass great amounts of land; we can cross a river without a boat), but we are reminded not to go so far that we abandon our comrades. Even in a time of prospering, we must remember moderation. (3) Indeed, in saying that there is no flat without a slope, we are reminded that there is good and bad to every situation. We must work through difficulties and find allies we can trust. (4) If we find neighbors but we cannot make wealth with them in spite of great effort, we should still maintain the trust in the relationship. (5) The best prospering comes from ties that are deeper than those between mere neighbors. Marriage between countries and families implies alliances that will create great prosperity and fortune. (6) Finally, the time of prospering is temporary. It can end quickly, as when walls collapse and we return to our capital only to find confusion and remorse.

This abrupt ending of prospering underscores the need for leaders to be in accord with heaven and earth. The *Image* speaks of using wealth to fulfill the natural way. Opportunities come to us from heaven and earth, and we must devote our resources to completing what is given. Furthermore, a wise person does not use opportunities selfishly. Rather, a wise person looks at the natural order and then acts in accord with it, seeking to bring prospering to people on all sides.

Prospering is mercy. Prospering is growth. Prospering is heaven-sent abundance. Prospering takes work, but the right kind of work. It takes the work that meshes with the cycles of life, and it takes just the right amount of work. Sow seeds, and your family eats. But if you sow too many seeds, your family will not eat more, because the crops will be overcrowded and stunted. Natural prospering is to do just the right amount, measure for measure, and so to gain a simple measure of joy.

Hexagram 12
Heaven above
Earth below

Heaven, above, pulls away
from earth, below.
    This hexagram is
associated with the seventh
lunar month (August–
September). The year has
passed its zenith and declines
toward autumn and winter.

Pi
No, not. Negativity. Evil, bad.

The Sequence and Link
When prospering ends, all is
decline and clogging.

Clogging

Summer dies in autumn,
a ghost flying through women's throats.

Blackbirds die in the sky
and plummet into blinding snow.

Bandits raid caravans,
like wolves biting a stumbling stag.

Priests cringe from quakes and squalls.
The king is afraid to travel.

Diviners sigh, sitting
inside their tents, and will not speak.

Nothing to do but fold
one's hands to the approaching storms.

The Statement

Clogging by wicked people.
Nothing to be gained,
even from a steadfast prince.
The great goes, the vile comes.

The Lines

6th line ———

Clogging overturned.
First there was clogging.
Later all will be glad.

5th line ———

Clogging ceases. Great people prosper.
It could be lost! It could be lost!
Tie it to the roots of a mulberry tree.

4th line ———

Commands without fault,
fields divided: blessings.

3rd line —— ——

Wrapped in shame.

The Image

2nd line —— ——

Wrapped in flattery, the vile prosper.
Great people are clogged. Continue.

Heaven and earth
separate: clogging.
The noble one acts
with self-restraint
in the face

1st line —— ——

Pulling couch grass
uproots more with it by entwined roots.
Snatch it: fortune. Continue.

of punishing hardship,
and avoids glory or riches.

CLOGGING refers to a stoppage of the events that have been moving well. The result is stagnation and decline. It is the downhill slide we cannot halt: Losing money and home. Losing our spouse's love. Death in the family. A parent stricken with terminal illness. Two nations pitching toward war. Whether it is the economy, international stability, business, relationships, or our own health and mental powers, halting and degeneration are depressing and straining.

The hexagram is as clear a picture as can be. Heaven is above earth—which seems to be as it should be—but if we instead view it as heaven pulling away from earth, we see that interaction has ceased and isolation has begun. The *Changes* seldom pronounces condemnation, but it clearly shows that misfortune is marked by alienation. Alienation and isolation define misfortune for the *Changes*.

In such times, philosophy seems of little comfort. We feel mired. We reach out for help, but no help is there. We search our resources, but no answer is there. We try each day, telling ourselves surely this morning will be the turning point, but each evening leaves us in frustration. We remind ourselves that even decline must pass, but that is hard to remember when decline strains our resolve beyond all limits.

All around us, inferior people get ahead. All around us, people who would never have had power over us suddenly have the absolute say over the most minor details of our lives.

The noble person responds by enduring. By learning. By looking for ways to improve. The noble person refuses to accept attention from others, for that would only make the agony of decline more intense.

Such withdrawal is often misunderstood. We are so outwardly directed and dependent on society that we are confused when others withdraw into their homes and inner lives in order to deal with their problems. We have become a rabble of gossip-mongering jackals, devouring every salacious detail of the rich and famous. We are addicted to the memoir, public feuding, and scandals. The noble person may love humility, but not humiliation. Our troubles should not be for the entertainment of others. A time of true clogging is so overwhelming that no one can change it, and so personal that no one else can bear it.

Let us not blame others for our problems, nor ask that the world save us if we merely confess our troubles. Instead, we must face our problems and solve them.

This requires personal resolve. We may be going down. Our boat may be swamped. We will get wet, we will lose our belongings, perhaps we will even be injured, but we must not be swept downriver. We must be strong and clearheaded. We must survive.

That is how a person of change outlasts clogging, looking even for ways to prosper during times of difficulty. At the very least, we must learn from what we experience. Otherwise, when the clogging is over, we would have suffered without salvaging any benefit from the experience.

Do not panic; do not waste your time complaining. Just act, and bear, and learn: the human heart can be stronger than fate, even though fate squeezes with the pressure of a thousand fathoms.

The *Statement* shows that clogging is caused by the small-minded, the small in stature, and the small in wisdom. As distressing as this might be, the *Changes* recognizes that there are times when the small can be overwhelming and the great cannot prosper. When this happens, even a prince of great prestige and moral stature will not find a favorable path.

However, the *Changes* is both a wise and an encouraging voice. In times of prosperity, such as Hexagram 11, we are counseled to search for the subtlety of the situation and to be aware of hidden pitfalls. In times of distress, we are counseled to look for the positives that will emerge with time and patience.

Thus the *Lines* show us how clogging varies. (**1**) Repeating the first line of Hexagram 11, we are shown that more couch grass will be pulled up along with the first clump: we must look for hidden ties in the situation and not lose hope. That is why the word *continue* is added here. (**2**) As clogging progresses, we see some of its worst manifestations. The vile use flattery to gain their influence. Then it is the noble one who must "clog" himself or herself by self-restraint. (**3**) The situation can get worse, bringing disgrace to anyone involved. (**4**) But clogging itself can be broken too. With sure leadership and a definition of territory, there can be blessings. (**5**) When the days of clogging are gone, the great must find all that has been lost and secure it again to something stable. (**6**) Finally, because nothing lasts, the situation for clogging itself will fade, and then all will be glad.

The *Image* shows that in times of clogging, wise persons engage in a parallel closing. By self-restraint, they persevere through the hardships caused by vile people. They also avoid any temptations for glory or riches, because they will invariably be compromised. In this way, the great can triumph over the small, even when all else is unfavorable.

同人

Hexagram 13
Heaven above
Fire below

Fire rises to heaven.
    The single yin line in the second place symbolizes a noble person of yielding nature who calls others to unite.

Tong Ren
Tong: Same, equal, identical, similar, common. To share, to agree. Together.
Ren: Person, persons, people.
Tong ren: Colleague. Member of the same group. People who belong together.

The Sequence and Link
Decline must also end, and when it does, we will find people of like mind and hearts.

Kindred

They sit on their horses in one black line,
brandishing lances and swinging axes.
The duke confronts them, openhanded, thin.
"Give us your land," they shout.
                    He does not blink.

We gather stones in piles behind our duke,
vowing to join the fight, willing to die.
But when his lips compress, we drop our rocks.
His shoulders slump like ours,
                    we hear him sigh.

"To see my people killed—I have no heart.
Whoever would be king, come forward now.
If you show kindness so no one is hurt,
I will not oppose you."
                    Hands clasped, he bows.

His cart holds few blankets, some tools and seed.
He blesses us, then leads wife and children
toward the storm-dark mountains where no one goes.
Whispers dart through the crowd:
                    "See his back bend!"

No one wants to be a slave tilling soil.
Before him, we had not learned to be men.
No one complains, trekking the unmarked trail.
The duke stands in the wild,
                    hammering stones.

We stroll around and see the new expanse
of hills and streams, valleys perfect for farms.
Cooking fires plume the air, we laugh and dance:
the duke smiles through tears
                    and spreads his arms.

The Statement

The kindred in the wilderness.
Continue.
Advance across the great river.
Gain by a wise one's purity.

The Lines

6th line ———

The kindred at the countryside sacrifice.
No regrets.

5th line ———

The kindred first wail and yet later laugh:
great armies are able to meet.

4th line ———

Mounting their ramparts.
Unable to conquer.
Fortune.

3rd line ———

Armed and lying in ambush
under the thicket. Looming above
is their high mound.
For three years, there is no rising.

The Image

2nd line — —

The kindred in the ancestral temple.
Remorse.

Fire rises into heaven:
kindred. The noble one
groups and sorts
all that must be done.

1st line ———

The kindred at the gate.
No fault.

KINDRED brings to mind the example of King Wen's grandfather, known to generations as the Ancient Duke. He persuaded his people to abandon a wandering lifestyle to take up agriculture. However, their growing wealth attracted nomadic tribes who preyed on them. The attacks worsened, until the nomads finally demanded all of the Duke's lands and people. To spare his followers from war, the Duke abdicated and went into the wilderness. Rather than be ruled by the nomads, his people went in search of him. Together they established the area that became the Zhou nation.

This shows that the community that rises out of friendship, mutual association, and inherent enthusiasm is the best community of all. There is no need to force unity. Everyone is there voluntarily and enjoys the benefits of being together.

In our present era, we isolate ourselves and allow our society to stratify in different classes. It is hard to remember that forming a true community should be as easy as growing plants or sailing down a river. In fact, a community that is hard to assemble or that must be maintained by coercion is not a true community. The Ancient Duke put his people first when he abdicated his office. This did not destroy the community, but made the people realize the true value of their kindred feelings. The community was reconstituted, stronger than ever.

This was also the story of change. First, it seemed as if the change would mean slavery. Then it seemed as if change was the loss of their leader. The people decided to initiate change themselves when they decided to migrate. So within the flux of change, they found a deeper and stronger purpose, galvanized by the selflessness of their leader. The outcome of that change would birth a new nation and a new dynasty.

Like Hexagram 7, Armies, Kindred focuses on a leader. Where Armies stipulates a strong general under a benign king, Kindred shows a single openminded leader. The Ancient Duke exemplified this. The one yin line among five other yang lines represents a leadership that is effective among many strong personalities. Only by being open, modest, gentle, and giving can one lead the strong. The strong cannot be compelled. They must be softly induced: good leadership requires flexibility rather than stiff force.

Those kindred to us sustain us, especially when we suffer disaster. In bad times, we pull together. In good times, we join together to improve our lives further. Our community is a vital and growing entity, one where there is constant movement, constant exchange.

The hexagram itself portrays a yin line giving to its surrounding yang lines, with the yang lines giving back to the yin. All are sustained because of this constant sharing. The friendships and efforts possible in community are to be cherished and valued. The message is clear: give, and you will never be alone.

Armies, Hexagram 7, and Joining, Hexagram 8, each focused on groups of people. The army came from the agricultural districts. Joining spoke to people coming together voluntarily. In the *Statement,* Kindred speaks to longstanding groups such as clans and countrypeople. In the image of the wilderness, there is a sense of people migrating to begin a new settlement, and the images contained in the *Lines* extend this portrayal.

(1) All kindred groups must have a beginning. People come to the gate to meet, but the image of a gate also shows kindred on the verge of action. For this, there is no fault, but every effort should be made to avoid mistakes too. (2) Not all meetings are happy, though. Meeting in an ancestral temple can be sad—as in the case of mourning; or can be limiting—as in the case of those who are clannish; or can be ominous—as in those who withdraw to plan attacks on others. The better thought would be to contemplate actions that would honor one's ancestors. (3) Kindred come together for military matters as well, but if the time is not right, one can wait for years to act and still not prevail. (4) The inability of kindred is not always bad. Sometimes, good fortune can be hidden in our inability to conquer. (5) That is how swiftly fortunes change—as when we go to war wailing with misgivings, only to find victory and a meeting of armies from other fronts. (6) Perhaps, when all these efforts are done, the best gathering of kindred is in the open countryside, making a sacrifice to heaven and earth. That kind of gathering transcends even the ancestral temple and the concerns of war.

In the *Image,* the noble one knows that it is natural for people to gather in kindred groups. Emulating this, the wise one groups like matters and separates antagonistic matters. It is this ability to organize that makes the efforts of the kindred effective.

Those who absorb the lesson of kindred know that there are always connections to be made. Whether it is in the realm of ideas, as the Image seems to suggest, or whether it is in the gathering of a new community, Kindred shows that grouping, sharing, and building synergy is generally the most positive course of action. It is in that sense of natural and spontaneous gathering that the power of kindred is greatest.

Hexagram 14
Fire above
Heaven below

Fire illuminates all of heaven.
   The yin line in the fifth place symbolizes a ruler who is modest, virtuous, and benevolent.

Da Yu
Da: Big, large. Great. Much. Very, highly, extremely. Eldest, senior, full-grown, adult. To enlarge, to make great. A surname.
Yu: To have, to be present, to exist. There is.

The Sequence and Link
Communities united are sure to build in wealth and power, resulting in great holdings.

Great Holdings

A father caresses his son,
   and nudges him to school.

A fisherman nets silver carp:
   his children's chopsticks fly.

A priest at the altar, raises
   his gold-rimmed cup and kneels.

The Statement

Great holdings:
supreme
everywhere.

The Lines

6th line ━━━━━
Divine help from heaven.
Fortune. Nothing but gain.

5th line ━━ ━━
His sincerity in meeting
leads to majesty and fortune.

4th line ━━━━━
It is not strength.
No fault.

3rd line ━━━━━
The duke makes an offering
to the Son of Heaven.
The small are unable to do this.

The Image

2nd line ━━━━━
A big wagon, loaded, with a place to go.
No fault.

Fire in heaven:
great holdings.
The noble one
curbs evil and fosters good,
and is favored
with heaven's blessings
and commands.

1st line ━━━━━
Do not mix with the harmful
and there will be no disaster.
A pattern of difficulty, but no fault.

GREAT HOLDINGS. Most of us might think immediately of wealth. But there is more to this idea than holding baskets of gold.

The fortunate have four great holdings, which support their actions like the wheels of a cart: wealth, power, health, and spirituality. What is important is not the seeming material value of these holdings—which is relative and fleeting—but the freedom they afford the possessor.

Anyone who drives a vehicle must steer well. Like any car, the vehicle of great holdings can take one far. Like any car, too, the danger of crashing is constant; great holdings also have great temptations. We must guard against pursuing false possibilities, or grabbing greedily, or exploiting others through our wealth, or immolating ourselves in self-indulgence.

Avoiding such temptations is easier if we follow the image of this hexagram: just one yin line is central but open. This symbolizes a person of high wealth who remains modest and accessible. A great possessor will have enormous control over people, and must be modest, open, and compassionate. The truly enlightened use their great holdings on behalf of others.

The scale of wealth and power is like a pagoda of infinite height. If we are ten times richer than someone else, we are also ten times poorer than another. On the other hand, just as many people must work together to build a pagoda, we can join with other people to extend the benefits of our wealth and power. As if we were communicating and working with others on different floors of the pagoda, everyone benefits, and the risks of selfishness are minimized.

Wealth and power may be obvious holdings. Two other holdings, health and spirituality, are just as critical. Neither wealth nor power is useful unless we have the health to exercise it. Indeed, a person will gladly sacrifice all his wealth and power for one more day of untrammeled movement, unlabored breathing, or joyous thinking. We cannot fulfill ourselves without the possession of health.

Spirituality is also a possession, perhaps the greatest of them all. Spiritual power is not imaginary, but a force that we hold and accumulate. People of great spirituality can heal others and can see into the future. These are not mystical occurrences but the natural effects of great holdings. However, just as a precious lamp can be dimmed or a rare medicine can be lost, we can dissipate our spirituality. The need for moral strength in sacred endeavors is therefore of great importance. Remaining modest and accessible to others, sharing what we have learned on our spiritual path, is the right way to use our great holdings.

Obviously, managing great holdings requires intelligence so we can judiciously use whatever comes our way. Like all our holdings, what we learn cannot be robbed from us, but the more we give, the more returns. The controlled use of power is the deft use of wealth. That is why the *Statement* tells us that our great holdings can extend a supremacy that permeates everywhere.

It is significant that the *Lines* mention the word *meeting* once, and that *no fault* is mentioned three out of six times. We have the fortune of great holdings, but we must be especially careful in working with others. We must make no mistakes.

Power is neutral. The person who wields power determines right or wrong outcomes. (1) We must choose not to mix with harmful elements, just as we must not be tempted by difficulty. (2) After *who* comes *where*. Just as a big wagon can be loaded and can help us cover great distance, so we must be prudent with where we move our great holdings. (3) One possible destination is a higher person. To make a sacrifice in gratitude is one possible meaning, but another meaning is that an offering is an investment that will bring a great return later. That is why the small-minded cannot conceive of such an action. (4) We are reminded to be far-seeing, to understand that the strength great holdings give us should not be abused. We must act not solely by strength, but by honesty and gentle persuasion. (5) That is why sincerity in meeting and the great holding of virtue lead to majesty and fortune. (6) If we succeed in all these requirements, nothing is impossible, and we will receive divine help from heaven itself. Then there will be nothing but gain.

The *Image* shows that the ultimate use of great holdings is to curb evil and foster good. Only that attitude can prevent us from falling into excess when our fortunes are high. If we can succeed in doing that, heaven itself will bless us, and all that we do will be in accord with the divine plan.

Great holdings. All that we possess is a gift from the Divine. Yes, we have to work to receive it, but there is a great deal of fortune involved. Perhaps that is why this hexagram contains heaven—which gifts us with great holdings; and fire—referring to the sun as the ultimate source of wealth as energy. Then, too, the hexagram guides us: just as fire symbolizes enlightenment, we must be enlightened to use our holdings. We must act like heaven, which creates and acts and furthers all things but never seeks to accumulate for itself.

Humility

Hexagram 15
Earth above
Mountain below

Mountain, symbolizing stillness and the youngest son, is below. It is said to be the representative of heaven (the father) on earth.

Earth, symbolizing the nurturing mother, and which usually occupies a lowly position, is instead elevated here, reminding us of the importance of modesty.

Qian
Modesty, humble, retiring, self-effacing.

The Sequence and Link
The rightful use of holdings should be followed by modesty.

We dig gold from a tomb filled with mud,
and it glistens in the sun, still pure.
A son carries his mother from a flood,
and on high ground his legs are still sure.
There is a mountain battered by mist,
but its root is solid to the core.
The earth sprouts forest after forest,
yet it stays as fertile as before.
 Gold, son, mountain, and earth: none make a show,
 and yet each lives powerfully and long.

Like demons we bicker, snatch and grab;
strain for gain by hook and claw. We paw
for a fame to ruthlessly defend.
Sneering, we show what we will do,
and afterward build walls to enclose
our wealth: we chew, denude, and uproot
the earth, then raise towers to our greed.
 Gold, son, mountain, and earth: none makes a show,
 and yet each lives powerfully and long.

On the final day, the low will be
exalted. With bowed heads, we will grieve:
the secret was there for us to see.
 Gold, son, mountain, and earth: none makes a show,
 and yet each lives powerfully and long.

The Statement

Humility imbues.
The noble one gets completion.

6th line —— ——

Singing humility.
Gain by moving armies.
Conquer city and state.

5th line —— ——

Not enriched by his neighbors.
Gain by invading and smiting.
Nothing but gain.

4th line —— ——

Nothing but gain:
modest and humble.

3rd line ———

Toiling humility:
the noble one gets completion
Fortune.

2nd line —— ——

Singing humility:
pure fortune.

The Image

Mountains in the middle
of the earth: humility.
The wise person
takes from the ample
to add to the meager,
weighing and balancing
fairly.

1st line —— ——

So humble is the noble one
who crosses the great river.
Fortune.

HUMILITY is the core virtue of the *Changes.* It is a virtue that is valuable for its own sake, and it is a virtue with great usefulness as well. The modest make fewer mistakes because they are not undone by arrogance, and their lack of dogma is no impediment to change.

Like it or not, humility exists only in the wake of arrogance. Few people know humility for itself or opt for it right away. Most of us have fallen into arrogance and egotism and have failed. We come to humility after having thoroughly tested the alternative.

Arrogance and anger are often the choices we try first because they seem to take less effort. True, they are not effective, but they seem easier. By contrast, even after we renounce our arrogance, we will find that being humble is not easy. True humility is a choice we make each time there is a confrontation, and unless a person is supremely comfortable, self-assured, and safe, he or she cannot easily be humble. The dynamically modest person chooses to be humble out of strength. The humility of the *Changes* is an active power. As such, it is more than a moral position: it is a virtue.

Humility is akin to compassion—at least in the sense that true compassion means extending one's energy and talents on behalf of others. One cannot be merciful from a position of weakness. Stopping short of city gates you could easily storm, carrying someone who is weak, and sheltering a hurt child are all acts of mercy possible only for someone who is strong and capable. In the same way, remaining humble even when you are under great duress, staying self-possessed in the face of insults, and refusing to bully others with your position and power are all examples of humility from the vantage of great strength.

Those who are humble will gradually discover other advantages. They will not hesitate to go beyond themselves. With nothing to prove, they are willing to explore new situations. True, they might make mistakes. They may even suffer embarrassment. But the humble person acknowledges and accepts that. The immodest make mistakes too—but being without shame, they try to hide their errors and deny their fallibility. That worsens their mistakes and increases their isolation.

In time, the arrogant personality becomes brittle and heavy. The tides of each day bring change; the closed person fights the waves. The current ebbs and flows and moves with its rhythm; closed persons throw their limbs against the current. They do not look at the tide; they think only of what they want, even if they are swamped and confused. The humble person accepts whatever change sends, improvising and creating accordingly.

The *Statement* says that the noble one gets completion. This reminds us of King Wen, who was the paragon of the modest personality. He served his people, he waited out his imprisonment, and he built alliances with a majority of other states before he attacked Prince Hu. Even in war, though, he did not forget himself. He spared the innocent and refrained from attacking Di Xin directly. He knew it was not time yet: understanding omens is just a metaphor for knowing whether a situation is favorable. If we follow the example of King Wen, we can see that humility does not mean yielding to others forever. Modesty entails no prohibition against defense or assertive acts when appropriate. The humble person will attack at the right moment because the situation demands it.

When the humble fight, they usually succeed. They have minimized their own faults, and they have closed all openings to others' attack. That is the defensive strategy of the humble. On the other hand, the humble are open to all opponents. They understand human nature; no act surprises them. They are willing to receive any attack by their enemies because they know that a person's greatest vulnerability is his or her refusal to accept the actions of opponents. Thus, although the normal definition of humility is one of demeanor, this hexagram makes it clear that humility is power.

That is the only way to understand the message of the *Lines*. (1) The noble one expresses humility by crossing the great river—to a fortunate result. (2) The very sound of humility yields purity and fortune. (3) The noble one willingly toils in humility and so obtains a great and fortunate result. (4) There is nothing but gain in being humble, the *Changes* tells us, and in the next two lines, this is made explicit. (5) In the line "Not enriched by his neighbors," there is a strong indication that the humble wise one is being unjustly isolated. At the right time, it is necessary for the noble one to campaign. (6) Eventually, the humble wise one can mobilize troops and even conquer city and state because it is the right course of action.

How specific the *Image* is! Mountains in the middle of the earth imply both stillness and centeredness. The wise person is stable and occupies the middle. As the earth is flat and broad, the humble person brings equality to all that is to be done, for the wisdom of humility alone gives the proper understanding to weigh and balance fairly.

To be stable. To be broad. To be as unmovable as the mountain and as fundamental as the earth. That is to attain the power of humility.

Hexagram 16
Thunder above
Earth below

Thunder above symbolizes
movement. Earth below
symbolizes obedience and
devotion. The single yang line
in the fourth place
represents a leading official
who meets with response
from others.

Yu
Comfort, to be at ease. To
prepare. Happy, delighted,
pleased. To travel, to make
excursions. To hesitate. To
cheat, to lie. One of nine
political divisions in ancient
China.

The Sequence and Link
Wealth and power bring
enthusiasm, comfort, and
delight.

Delight

The country has been free a year.
Hundreds stroll and exchange flowers.
"No more wars! No more wars!" they cheer.
The prince gazes from his tower
and waves, but does not seem to hear.

Commoners and nobles gather
to feast in the ancestral halls.
Shamans dance with swords and feathers,
and when the prince enters, they call
for his reign to last forever.

Let us build a new capital!
they shout while amber wine is poured.
As priests complete their rituals,
the prince grants land and names new lords.
He makes a promise to fulfill

their hopes and stay as pure as jade.
After the crowds have all retired,
tottering home and unafraid,
the prince sits silent by the fire,
resting his hand on his sheathed blade.

The Statement

What delight!
Gain by naming allies.
Move armies.

The Lines

6th line —— —

Dark delight succeeds.
Have a change of mind
and there will be no fault.

5th line —— —

Firm illness persists,
but there is no death.

4th line ———

Through delight, the great attains.
Do not doubt it! Friends gather
like hair in a clasp.

3rd line —— ——

Wide-eyed delight is regrettable.
If you are late
you will have regrets.

The Image

2nd line —— ——

Upright like a rock in character.
In less than a day
one shows that purity.
Fortune.

1st line —— ——

Crowing delight.
Misfortune.

Thunder explodes,
shaking the earth: delight.
The early kings made music,
glorifying virtue as the
highest offering to God,
and so they were worthy
of their ancestors.

DELIGHT has become our own version of an omen: if it feels right, if everyone gets excited, if the crowed is roaring and the fireworks are exploding, we think we are doing the right thing.

Popularity has become the standard for everything we do. Entertainment, eating until we are bloated, chasing the wild colors of circuses and the loud music of our favorite singers—all these are our new standards.

Yes, we should be passionate about our lives, we should feel involved, and we should choose a life path that makes us feel absolutely terrific. Our problem is our central subject: change. When we lose enthusiasm, or when we fail to combine our enthusiasm with wisdom, we become confused and lose our balance.

The most significant trouble in measuring ourselves against delight is actually those who enjoy it: us. We grow tired of the delightful. Where we once loved the storytellers, we may one day judge them dreadful and dull. Where we once chased after beautiful lovers, we may one day find them ugly and tiresome.

The plain truth is that what delights us changes as we grow older. We have to manage that change, not allowing our habits to simmer into perversion, and not charging prematurely into new fields. We will find ourselves challenged by circumstances themselves. For no matter how enthusiastic we are, we will be confronted with healthy doses of frustration, difficulty, and simple accident. Discipline is important: we must keep our initial excitement in mind while we maintain our momentum.

So this is another way in which change challenges us: we must see whether we have constancy and perseverance. For delight is volatile. Unless our spark begins a reaction, and unless we channel and amplify that reaction through hard work and perseverance, we cannot find a lasting path.

There is a secret that springs delight open as a symbol. The word *yu* means both "delight" and "preparation." Let us be delighted, but let us not forget ourselves. When all is happy and pleasurable, let us not neglect to prepare for the future. If we have the delight of earning much money, we should enjoy some of it and save or invest the remainder. If we have the joy of a child, we should prepare for our child's well-being and education. If we have the enthusiasm of many allies, we should make plans to keep the alliance intact.

Enthusiasm, comfort, and delight are to be enjoyed when they come to us. We should take satisfaction in what we do. We must manage the hazards of comfort and pleasure. And most important, we must prepare. Thunder above the earth. A single yang line dominating five yin lines. Whatever symbol we use, delight reminds us to keep our focus even in the diversity of all that surrounds us. Since the concern of the *Changes* is often statecraft, the Oracle sees a situation where there can be a powerful and enthusiastic movement of the populace. That is why the **Statement** urges us to gather allies and take action.

But the *Changes* also sees this time as short-lived—no indication of the enduring is mentioned here—and the **Lines** all contain warnings. A wise person therefore makes use of others' delight to move toward unity, but he or she follows deeper convictions.

(1) Immediately, the *Changes* focuses on the excess of delight: when we boast and make much noise about our excitement, this leads to misfortune. (2) The *Changes* immediately contrasts this with the right behavior: character as steady and immutable as rock, character that shows its purity even before the day is over. (3) A step further in the problem of delight is symbolized by wide-opened eyes. Someone is wide-eyed with delight. This is immediately regrettable, especially when the person is so mesmerized that he or she is too slow to act. Then there are even further regrets. (4) It takes a great person to make use of delight, and when this is done properly, enthusiasm binds people together like strands of hair in a clasp. (5) Delight, though transitory and unstable, is ultimately a necessary part of all gatherings. Imagine having no delight, or having to foster delight in dreadful times. Such is the case with a lasting sickness where we are forced to linger without dying. (6) Finally, we are warned that the delight of the crowd—dark, deep, unseen—sometimes succeeds. That may make us change our minds. This might mean we join the crowd. Or it might mean we turn away from the crowd.

Cultivating the wisdom to know the difference is shown in the **Image.** We are shown music, referring both to the music that brings joy and to the music that rouses delight in others. But then the *Changes* puts a succession of constraints on us: glorify virtue, offer to God, be worthy of our ancestors. Only by dedicating the delight of the crowd to the holy can this time be made fully beneficial.

Only one delight, the delight in the spiritual, is lasting and ultimately satisfying. All other delights are external—mere entertainment and playing. The spiritual transcends our isolation, joins us with others, and leads our souls to dance to a music that resonates through the universe in a song of delight.

Following

The music master stands at the door
of his ancestral home on West Lake.
His mother touches his graying hair.
His youngest sister bows with clasped hands—
no more pigtails, but rouge and jade combs.

He talks only of palace duties,
barely touching chopsticks and bowl.
Shuffling out without a farewell,
he wanders the shore by moonless waves,
wind blowing his gown taut to his limbs.

From the endless dark a lute is plucked.
Sound dances through the willows. He follows
to the end of a pier: a candle
glows on the black waves. Behind silk blinds,
his sister sits in wisps of incense.

Mouth open, he stumbles on the planks
and grips the railing. She nods to him
and sings a famous verse. Unthinking,
he joins in a duet that shimmers
through the trees and encircles the lake.

Hexagram 17
Lake above
Thunder below

Lake, symbolizing joyousness
and gladness, as well as the
youngest daughter, is above.
Thunder, which here
symbolizes movement, is
below, and represents the
eldest son.

Sui
To follow, to trace, to come
afterward. To listen to, to
submit to, to comply with. To
let, to allow. To resemble.

The Sequence and Link
Enthusiasm and delight
encourage following.

The Statement

Following
what is great, smooth,
gainful, and pure.
No fault.

6th line ▬ ▬
Adhering and binding
to make following hold fast.
The king makes offering
on West Mountain.

5th line ▬▬▬
Confidence in excellence.
Fortune.

4th line ▬▬▬▬
Follow and there will be capture—but this is a sign
of misfortune. Put your confidence in the Way
and you will understand.
Then, how can there be fault?

3rd line ▬ ▬
Binding to the man
loses the child. Follow
and seeking will bring achievement.
Gain by dwelling stoutly.

The Image

2nd line ▬ ▬
Binding to the child
loses the man.

Thunder over the middle
of the lake: following.
The noble one at sunset
goes into a house to rest.

1st line ▬▬▬
The standards of excellence are altered.
Pure fortune. Go out of the gate
to meet others and there will be merit.

FOLLOWING others means joining and cooperating with a group, a cause, or a nation. For such a group to have direction, it needs a leader. For a leader, following means inspiring others to join with you. For a member of the group, the hexagram urges us to follow the right leaders.

The best kind of following combines the symbols of the two trigrams: Lake—representing delight, pleasure, and joy —combined with the force of Thunder. Thunder explodes upward and resolves itself in the intermixing, pooling, concentration, and refinement of Lake. True following arises out of excitement and leads to unity.

Thus, the presence of Lake—with its delight, pleasure, and joy—excludes any coerced following. True following is gained neither by intimidation nor by stoking people's fears. It should not be induced by deception or by mass hysteria. It cannot be sustained by appealing to greed or hatred. For the *Changes,* and for the hexagram Following, only open and honest leadership will do: ethical, sincere, lasting, and righteous action, so that people follow out of sheer satisfaction. What a challenge to us, and yet what an opportunity to do something lasting! We must turn away from demagogues leading cheers in stadiums and toward the lean, soft-spoken leader who walks with children in the fields .

The deeper principle is trust. A political movement built on anything else will never have the full confidence of its followers; it will inevitably destroy itself. The best leader come from the ranks of the people, expresses what the people want, and operates through mutual confidence. That is the superior method. If the movement winds down, it will not be because of the internal flaws formed by manipulation but because natural decline has been reached.

It should be noted, however, that sincerity alone will not engender a following. There have been many pious people who failed to lead any significant movements. The inverse of manipulative but charismatic leaders who exploit followers, good people often have no one to follow and support them. Perhaps that is cosmic irony. Perhaps that is the stupidity and shallowness of people. But if you would be a leader, remember that humility, trustworthiness, and sincerity alone will not power your movement. You have to be the right person in the right situation. You have to possess some charisma and be able to inspire others. Then following flows naturally.

Ultimately, it is Tao we should follow. If we align ourselves with the natural flow, we do not look anxiously to others for approval. If you are a good person whom others do not support, do not feel bad, and do not abandon your ethics. Follow Tao. You will make no mistakes.

If Tao leads you to join others, then go. If Tao leads you to organize others, then go. If Tao leads you into quiet withdrawal from others, then go. No matter where Tao goes, follow. That following, always sincere, is a gift worth keeping.

Following in the *Statement* has a double meaning. The statement alludes to the right way to follow. It also shows that actions are followed by results. There is no time lag to either kind of following. Rather, there is a reflexive immediacy. If we follow the right course of action, right results are bound to follow.

Naturally, the hexagram statement would have us follow the great origin that spreads so smoothly, permeating everywhere. It would have our every action be gainful, steadfast, and pure. For us to act so cannot be faulted. This is the way to follow heaven and earth.

The *Lines* contain subtle wisdom. (1) When there is a change in standards, this forms a new context of fortune. We must follow that opportunity and go out to meet others. Then we will win merit. (2) Change also alters our options. If we cling to a child, we will lose the man. (3) If we cling to the man, we lose the child. (4) When we follow a new path, there are gains and losses that follow immediately. That is why we must put our confidence in the way of heaven. (5) Following also means to follow what is right. We must have confidence in excellence—which implies that we must not waste our time in trivial involvements. (6) This culminates in the sixth line, where two words—*adhering* and *binding*—make the meaning most emphatic. We adhere to what is right, and so we bind our situation tightly together. In exactly the same way, the king makes an offering to heaven, binding humanity to heaven to follow the natural Way.

The *Image* shows thunder over the middle of a lake. The water trembles immediately from the sound; the surface reflects any lightning. This perfectly illustrates the immediacy of following. The wise one sees that it is sunset, sees that there is a storm, and so goes into the house to rest. The natural order is supreme. The wise do not foolishly oppose opportunity; they follow it.

What a simple formula following seems. What a most difficult thing to do! If we could simply follow, we would find that life gives us ample omens, ample opportunity, and ample materials. If we contemplate deeply, we see that most of our misfortunes happen because of our own shortcomings or lust to assert ourselves. If we would follow Tao, aligning ourselves with the origin, all of life and all others would soon follow us.

Poison

Hexagram 18
Mountain above
Wind below

Wind below, seemingly gentle and weak, erodes the mountain above.

In each trigram, yielding yin lines are beneath solid yang lines, symbolizing things which seem whole on the surface, but which are rotted inside.

Gu
Poison, venom, harm. To bewitch, to enchant.

The Sequence and Link
Where enthusiasm and following have taken place, decay and poisoning will eventually occur.

Come back home.
Father is ill.
You must set
his matters right.
For three days
before you go,
for three days
following your
return home,
you see the change.
His body
is slack and bruised,
his business
in disorder.
You check him.
The poison grows.
You tally
losses and debts.
With wet eyes,
you will receive
his old friends.
You will give his
eulogy.
Three days before
and three days
after, they all
look to you,
and address you
as the master.

The Statement

Poison brings the great continuing.
Advance across the great river.
Before starting: three days.
After starting: three days.

The Lines

6th line ━━━
Do not serve king or lords.
Your own affairs
are of higher importance.

5th line ━━ ━━
Manage father's poison.
Make use of honor.

4th line ━━ ━━
Ample is father's poison.
Going forward, one will see deprivation.

3rd line ━━━
Manage father's poison.
The young have regrets.
No great fault.

The Image

2nd line ━━━
Manage mother's poison.
One cannot be firm.

Wind below the mountain:
poison. The noble one
stirs the people
and nourishes virtue.

1st line ━━ ━━
Manage father's poison.
Let his child examine. No fault
amid such harshness. In the end, fortune.

POISON is represented by the ideogram *gu,* which shows three worms in a vessel. It symbolizes disease in a body, group, or nation. Someone or some organization no longer functions properly. Infestation and poisoning set in.

A significant key is that this hexagram is not addressed to the stricken person or organization but to the people responsible for it. The *Changes* has important wisdom: we must not be afraid to act in the time of poison. Instead we must remain measured as the *Changes* would always have us do, but we must not limit ourselves strictly to convention or duty. The message is to free ourselves to do what we think is best in relationship to higher concerns. Grieving in the time of poison may be necessary, but we must be self-possessed and imaginative enough to organize affairs properly. Without our courage and leadership, there will be no healing.

We are responsible for rectifying the poison. This hexagram might allude to one of the most emotional of situations: the death of our father. When news comes to us that our father is dying, we must go home. It may be the last time, but we must still go. We arrive to find that his affairs are in disorder. In other words, figuratively speaking, they are poisoned.

An enormous change—perhaps one of the most important changes of our lives—is approaching. When our father is seriously ill or dying, the dynamics of the family suddenly shift. Whether we are ready or not, we must bend our backs to carry the burden. We may not relish the duties of setting the family right, but there is no true running away from this. We must be present.

It does not matter how old or young we are. No one is ever fully ready for our parents' passing. We do not really become responsible for our families by glib declaration or easy ceremony. It is only by the rough shouldering of responsibility and the sheer terror of making decisions for ourselves and the many others in our family that we become mature leaders. There is no other way. Heroes are annealed by adversity and tempered by disaster.

It is inevitable that change must come through the poisoning of old orders. Only then will there be regeneration—and it is probable that the new order will be one we can neither imagine nor predict. We do not know what is coming, because our own hands will be shaping it.

Another way to understand this hexagram is to see it as a symbol for fermentation—a "poison" that is good if carefully controlled. For example, rice wine is brewed in clean rooms with the best rice and precisely measured amounts first of mold and then yeast. We use the "poison" of fermentation, and then we stop it, as the period of three days before and three days after mentioned in the Statement implies. If we can bear this image in mind, remembering how commonly we integrate fermentation into our daily lives, we can see that the decline of our businesses, our skills, our parents, and even our own bodies is part of the overall way of change.

The time of poison is sad, but the *Changes* remains encouraging and sympathetic. Although everything may be falling apart and our security may have vanished, the *Changes* points us to the great continuing that is always here. Thus, whenever we are strained by great trouble, we must take special care to fix our minds on ongoing affairs. We must look for the enormous workings of change beneath the surface, and we must act. That is why the **Statement** mentions the great continuing, and the period of three days before and three days after. Timing is a significant element in Poison.

The interpretation of the **Lines** revolves around *gan,* a word that means the trunk of a tree or of a body. The word is normally read as "affairs" or "work," or as a verb implying "manage." However, *kao,* the word for "examine," also means "deceased parent," and the word *yu,* while usually meaning "praise" or "flattery," is here interpreted as "eulogy." This hexagram traditionally refers to a father's or a mother's business. It is not hard to fit this hexagram to the subject of our parents' illness or death.

(**1**) From the first line, the *Changes* is sympathetic. We must check on our father, and we are not to blame for the harshness of the task. (**2**) Harsher still may be our mother's death, and the *Changes* reassures us that we must not worry about correctness: we must be free to mourn. (**3**) When our father dies, sometimes there are regrets, but again, we are assured that there is no great fault in this. (**4**) When our father's poison is ample, we may see the opposite ahead: loss and stinting. (**5**) Finally, we are freed to follow our duty. When our father dies, we must give his eulogy at all costs, since (**6**) duty to our family is higher than duty to our king or lords.

The **Image** shows the noble one concerned with preventing poison among the people. That is why he stirs them to action and nourishes virtue. In both ways the moribund is prevented. Stirring moves people to action, and nourishing virtue creates fresh strength and resolution to do great things—including advancing across old limitations such as the great river.

Poison is a natural process, whether simple fermentation or towering death in the family. Either way, the wise time their actions to mesh with the enormity of the process.

Hexagram 19
Earth above
Lake below

Water flows into a lake bed,
symbolizing arrival. In the
same way, two yang lines
arrive before four yin lines.

This hexagram is linked
with the twelfth lunar month
(January–February), when
the yang power of spring
arrives after the yin of winter.

Lin
To approach, to descend, to
come to, to reach, to visit. To
look down upon, to preside.
On the point of, near to, during, at, while. To copy, to imitate. Temporary, provisional.

The Sequence and Link
This hexagram follows go-
ing home with the image of
arrival.

Arrival

We always knew the world
would sink in snow each year.
One winter, we suffered
as before, but no one
would measure our ordeal,
until a stargazer
staked a pole, setting stones
day by day, year by year,
each time the shadows moved.

His unbound hair whitened
like the ice on his robes,
but he could soon predict
when the sun would pierce night
on the shortest of days.
And once that day had come,
he knew how ice would melt
and the shadows tremble
in the plum blossom breeze.

The Statement

The arrival of the maker: everywhere,
giving and pure.
When the eighth moon comes,
there will be misfortune.

The Lines

6th line ▬▬ ▬▬
Sincere arrival.
Gain without fault.

5th line ▬▬ ▬▬
Knowledge arrives.
The noble one is proper.
Fortune.

4th line ▬▬ ▬▬
Having arrived,
no fault.

3rd line ▬▬ ▬▬
Luscious arrival,
but no place brings gain.
Once grieving passes, there is no fault.

The Image

2nd line ▬▬▬▬
All arrival: fortune.
Nothing but gain.

Earth by the lake: arrival.
The noble one
is inexhaustible
in teaching,
and boundlessly protects
the people.

1st line ▬▬▬▬
All arrival:
pure gain.

ARRIVAL: once arrival has occurred, we realize that there must have been a great momentum building. Every arrival therefore carries the secrets of its origins with it. True to this, the hexagram has two hidden messages. The first message is that each season arrives in succession. The second is that arrival is not possible without movement. In the end, understanding comes by the juxtaposition of both these interpretations.

Following strongly on the grief of Poison, we are shown approach and Arrival. We have journeyed in order to set matters right, and we are assured that this is the fitting and proper thing to do. We will be blameless as long as we work with the greatest sincerity. If we are kind and think of others, and if we approach them like the two yang lines in the hexagram—strong personalities sublimating themselves to others—we will succeed. The other four lines are open—receptive to the fresh input that the two yang lines bring. In other words, we have to move and act in order to arrive.

With its link to the end of the year, when winter is ending and renewal is coming, the hexagram also gives a strong sense of rebirth. Spring is a miracle for us all. We have suffered through the snow and ice of death and decline. How welcome spring is!

A sensitive person will find this another reminder of devotion. For like heaven and earth, we do nothing to cause the arrival of spring. It comes on its own. Anyone who says he or she does not understand Tao or the need for waiting needs only look at what we all do at the end of each year: we wait for the warmer months. If we are wise in positioning ourselves, this principle of timing is endlessly applicable. In this universal way, we all align ourselves with change.

Arrival contains the idea of initiative. In the journey back home to set affairs in order, effort in the midst of disaster is implicit. Just because we wait for spring to come does not mean that we stop passively in the snow. As we wait for spring, we maintain ourselves and pursue activities appropriate for winter. Planting new crops in the spring shows the right combination of waiting for heaven and working diligently with each day.

The four seasons follow one another, like a snake chasing its own tail. We know winter will come again, just as new disasters and problems will follow no matter how successfully we put our affairs in order. That is inevitable. However, for the moment we must approach our difficulties with open minds and strong hearts. Then we will do well. Ideally, we build up our reserves. By the time new problems arrive, we will be better able to cope with them.

As we age, we will go through many turnings. As a consequence we should become more adept at discerning them. Like an astronomer measuring the equinoxes and solstices, we can learn to act before others are even alarmed. Some might call that supernatural. For us, it is simply natural. It is only because of such wisdom and experience that we begin our approaches at the right time.

When spring arrives after winter, the transition is seamless. This continuous following of one phase after another is the essential message of this hexagram. That is why the *Statement* invokes *yuan heng li zhen,* the four basic words of the Oracle. Change is profound. It creates, is everywhere, and is our source of benefit and purity. It has its stages, but it can even free us from the Poison of the previous hexagram. Once the new stage arrives, we see that what was subtly approaching is now here. It is there for us to take advantage of it; we must go along with it wholeheartedly.

Once it has arrived, the present stage will not last long. The next stage is approaching already. The mention of the eighth moon, when autumn and thus a new winter approach, remind us of the cyclical nature of change.

Most of the *Lines* seem to celebrate arrival. (1) In the beginning, arrival brings purity and gain. (2) As arrival deepens, there is fortune and unassailable gain. (3) Some arrivals, though, are tempered. Although the arrival is luscious, the possibilities from there are limited. There is still something to be worked out—the reference to grieving. We must do that first, and then there will be no fault. (4) Other arrivals dispel fault that may have been there. (5) One of the best arrivals is that of knowledge, and if the leader responds in a proper way, there will be fortune. (6) Along with knowledge, the arrival of sincerity is also good, leading to gain without fault.

The sense of arrival as following without separation is shown in the *Image.* The banks of a lake touch the water without any gaps. Then the combination of lake and earth inspires a further understanding: when it comes to teaching others and protecting them, the wise one is as inexhaustible as a lake that can never be drained.

Arrival is the time when our plans come to full expression. It is the culmination of efforts set into motion long ago. Then, each arrival is the momentary level from which our future will spring. As such, Arrival is one pose struck in our dance with Tao.

Hexagram 20
Wind above
Earth below

The hexagram's shape resembles an ancient memorial gateway. Many of these gateways could be seen from a distance, alluding to a dual idea: one can see these gateways from afar, one can also see far from them as well.

The formation of lines refers to the eighth lunar month (September– October), when the yang powers recede from the year.

Guan
To see, to observe, to behold, to view, to inspect. Sights, views. To display. Point of view, conception. A Taoist temple.

The Sequence and Link
Approach leads to greatness, greatness leads to contemplation.

Beholding

Dawn above jasper peaks.
A white crane lands near a gateway.
　　Twigs snap beneath its feet.
The farmers look up and murmur.

Morning in the mountains.
Adepts build a wooden altar
　　beneath the granite arch.
The master bathes in cold water.

Noon, white on the mountains.
A crowd gathers before the gate.
　　The master stills their words
by pressing his palms together.

Dusk on purple mountains.
Crane, altar, villagers,
　　shaman—gone. The gateway
stands silhouetted by the moon.

The Statement

Behold! The hands have been washed,
but the offering has not yet been made.
Be sincere and dignified in appearance.

The Lines

6th line ━━━━
In beholding others' lives
the wise person allows no faults.

5th line ━━━━
Beholding my life:
the wise person rids herself of faults.

4th line ━━ ━━
Beholding our nation's glory:
make good use
of an audience with the king.

3rd line ━━ ━━
Beholding my life:
advance or retreat?

The Image

2nd line ━━ ━━
Spying and peeping:
far better to have a woman's purity.

The wind moving above
the earth: beholding.
The ancient kings
inspected the provinces
and territories to establish
the right teachings.

1st line ━━ ━━
Childish beholding is not wrong
for a common person, but it is wrong
for a superior person.

BEHOLDING happens from a vantage point. In the imagery of this hexagram, all beholding occurs from a portal. We have to stand somewhere to look, and that means there must be an opening.

Such a doorway implies both a real opening and the more figurative one of our perceptions. But while we may be looking, others know us by observing us in the act of looking. In seeing the lines of this hexagram as a picture of a gateway, the *Changes* points out a double meaning. Someone is looking from a gate, but as he or she is doing so, others see that person framed there.

We know by seeing. We are known by where we stand when we see.

So its well to ask: what is worth looking at? While we have to do many kinds of observations in our work and in going from place to place in our daily routines, the Oracle would have us look more deeply. While we may do all sorts of looking, from browsing in stores to gazing in curiosity, the Oracle would have us use our observation for more important views.

For the *Changes,* the highest level of beholding is the holy one. The Statement portrays a holy person in the midst of ceremony. The superimposing of this image on the image of a gateway is intentional. The holy person must be a worthy gateway for others. The holy person is a larger-than-normal human being, as mighty and as prominent as a memorial gateway. Gateway, holy person as gateway, holy person observing, holy person being beheld—the *Changes* mixes these images together and makes the mix our gateway into this hexagram.

Combining the images of a holy person with the image of seeing naturally brings us to the ultimate in "inner sight," meditation. The most important place to focus one's vision is oneself. Tao is within us, and we are within Tao, and there is no instrument more capable of discovery than our own observation. We may find faults and pettiness—the child and the voyeur alluded to in the Lines—but we must search them out and then look further.

This is contemplation focused so strongly that it becomes the single beam of light that simultaneously illuminates and sees. The more we examine, the more we purify ourselves. Every fault must be confronted and eliminated, until we are purity contemplating purity.

If we reach such purity, we may well be like the holy person in the **Statement,** who through inner vision has become someone worthy of others' beholding.

Those who follow change know only one way to lead and teach others: to know others as thoroughly as they know themselves, and to teach based on experience. When the leader contemplates the people, she becomes them, yet with her own experiences, she give them perspective. The leader will benefit too, for the people will become her future. There is a profound reciprocity in teaching. Personal lessons are relived; in affirming them, the leader affirms the experiences of her followers.

As always, then, the Oracle returns to its themes of self-cultivation and service to our community. This hexagram reminds us that we were shown the portal of knowledge by our own teachers. We walked through those portals to gain our position today. We must then encourage and assist others to enter those portals after us. If they are afraid, we must not force them, but must show them, based on our own example, that it is safe.

The *Lines* show us different forms of beholding. (1) The most basic beholding is a childish and naive one. For the Oracle, this is acceptable for a common person, but not for someone seeking to be wise. Instead, one should try to be like the holy person in the Statement. (2) Another kind of observation is the base kind: spying and peeping. This is a low-level and foolish form of beholding. Voyeurism and gossip-mongering should be rejected in favor of chaste purity. (3) Then there is observation as introspection, here perhaps with a hint of self-doubt. Should I go forward, or should I retreat? This is the crux of so much of our self-questioning. (4) Turning outward, there is the beholding of national glory, of patriotism, and of loyalty. If we are in the situation of having some influence with leadership, we should make good use of it. (5) The *Changes* here refers to the theme of self-examination, as the Oracle takes up the issue of self-cultivation. It is blunt: we must rid ourselves of faults. (6) Finally, in examining others' lives in order to know them better, work with them better, and learn from their choices, we must have no faults—that is, we must be impartial and look with uncolored vision.

The *Image* sums up the multiple meanings of beholding. Outwardly, we are reminded of how ancient kings toured the land in order to see what the nation needed. At the same time, they established a teaching—meaning both governmental policy and moral standards—so that the nation would prosper. That fulfills the promise of Line 4, when the nation's glory is something to behold.

Contemplate. Meditate. Then the portals will suddenly have neither front nor back. Look. See. Then you will be the portal, the portal that is the gateway that enters itself. Observe. Be observed. Then you will be the eye that looks into itself by its own light.

Biting

A maid runs screaming to the courtyard gate,
fingernails uselessly scraping the walls.
A bandit grabs her and throws her wriggling
    on a cart piled high with plunder.

The overturned cart is found. Beneath it
a man lies with red gashes on his shirt.
He moans: those bandits snatched away my boy
    and dragged him to their mountain lair.

The magistrate turns and gives his command.
One by one, the culprits are tracked and tried.
The leader is caught and chained in the square,
    bloody, one-eyed, baring his teeth.

Tied to a stake that binds his hand and feet,
he snarls and curses at the magistrate;
the soldiers hold their swords. He is bone white,
    broken between a leopard's teeth.

Hexagram 21
Fire above
Thunder below

The first and sixth lines represent upper and lower jaws, and the yin lines represent teeth. The single yang line in the fourth position is a solid object between the teeth.
    Fire and thunder allude to how obstructions should be overcome.
    This hexagram is associated with criminal lawsuits, while Hexagram 6 refers to civil suits.

Shi Ke
Shi: To bite, to snap, to gnaw.
Ke: To crack something between the teeth.

The Sequence and Link
Following the public attention of Beholding, laws and criminal prosecution must be made clear.

The Statement

Biting. Penetrate.
Gain by prosecuting.

6th line ━━━

How he is imprisoned in a cangue,
ears destroyed! Misfortune.

5th line ━━ ━━

Biting dried meat, winning yellow gold.
Be upright in harsh times
and be without fault.

4th line ━━━

Biting dry bone.
Winning golden arrows.
Gain through difficulty and stay upright.
Fortune.

3rd line ━━ ━━

Biting dried meat,
encountering poison.
Small regrets, no fault.

The Image

2nd line ━━ ━━

Biting skin, destroying the nose:
no fault.

Thunder and lightning:
biting. The ancient kings
defined penalties and
declared the laws.

1st line ━━━

Feet in fetters, toes cut off:
no fault.

BITING—strong jaws gnawing on meat until the bone cracks—is made here into an analogy for criminal prosecution. The administration of justice requires great constancy and persistence. Investigation to ensure that the case is fair requires penetrating many layers. It is only when we reach the deepest meaning of the case—the hard bone—that we can properly render a judgment.

Cracking bones also alludes to the ancient process of divination. During these rituals, ox scapulae were drilled and heated until they cracked. A judgment was interpreted from the resulting pattern. The bone split (thunder), and clarity (fire) was reached. Coincidentally, we speak informally of a case "cracking wide open."

The dismemberment implied in biting, gnawing, and cracking bones also relates to the criminal. When the *Changes* was first formulated, punishment involved mutilation, torture, tattooing, and public display in fetters and cangues. Criminal penalties have evolved, but society still needs criminal penalties to maintain order. We recognize that those penalties are by nature imperfect and excessive. But they are necessary.

Although we live with amazing wealth and technology, and though we have tried to apply egalitarian principles, we still have crime. In spite of our emphasis on education and information, children in every generation grow up to be criminals. We try to help everyone to avoid the temptations of crime, but firm laws are the last resort.

There is no such thing as a fair society without punishment. While that is far from utopian, no civilization has been without law. Let us not question the need for law, but let us ensure that the law respects every person's rights.

We have to apply the same principles on a personal level. If there are injustices made against you, do not be afraid to stand up for your own rights. An attack against you is an imbalance in the natural course, and you must apply as much vigor as necessary to restore that balance. It may be a robber who already has his hands around your neck. It may be a thief invading your home. It may be a swindler cleverly draining away your funds. Whatever the crime, you must not remain the victim. The struggle of the righteous against the criminal is also Tao.

Clear laws and firmly drawn limits benefit all citizens. The best way to provide justice is to look at the image of this hexagram: fire—the symbol of enlightenment and understanding; coupled with thunder—the voice of order, the force of righteousness. No matter how difficult the situation, we need to shine the light of understanding on it and speak our unambiguous judgment.

The *Statement,* as with every hexagram, begins with the name. The words of the Statement allude to the sound of biting and gnawing. They also mean to crack something between the teeth. Biting is definite. It is unequivocal. Each bite leaves its mark. There is little ambiguity about it. In the same way, enforcing the law must be definite and strong. The hexagram itself shows the fourth line like a bone between teeth. Like an animal chewing on a bone, enforcing the law must continue until the resistance of the criminal is broken. We must penetrate to the truth. Our investigation must permeate the case thoroughly. We must prosecute fully.

The *Lines* develop the association of biting and the law. (1) In ancient times, punishment by fetters and mutilation was used, and the Oracle stipulates that there is no fault in this. (2) Likewise, it accepts the necessity of even harsher punishment to the face. (3) Sometimes, in prosecuting a case, we find additional problems such as official corruption or a situation even more alarming than was first supposed. This leads to some regrets, but there is nothing wrong with this. (4) Some cases are difficult, like biting a dry bone. But there is a promise of winning golden arrows—a high recognition. We are faced with difficulties, but we will gain if we remain correct and upright. (5) This same advice is repeated again, with the admonition that we must remain beyond reproach ourselves. (6) Finally, we see the criminal punished, and the penalties that began at the feet and went to the nose are now up to the ears. There is nothing to be said for this except that it is of great misfortune.

The *Image* shows that the key to justice is clear laws with defined penalties. That has been the case since ancient times, and it will always remain the case. Our society must uphold and apply the laws at all times.

Biting. That is a challenge to us. It takes strength; it takes tenacity. Biting is a familiar image to us. We have to bite (chew) every day. Thus, biting is natural, so common that we have forgotten how to use that image. Biting is like the pincher movement in warfare. Biting is the holding on to something. Biting is the cutting through obstacles to achieve our purpose. Biting is the divisions we make in a problem to absorb it in manageable chunks. The ultimate biting is the chewing through to the bone that is truth. When we crack even that open, we have the possibility of true wisdom.

Hexagram 22
Mountain above
Fire below

Fire below a mountain illuminates and adorns it.
    This hexagram discusses various aspects of adornment, with implications of beauty, courtship, and even the substance and appearance of society.

Bi
To adorn. Ornamental. Bright, luminous.

The Sequence and Link
After the resolution and unity of Biting comes the stabilization of a society. With wealth building, adornment becomes a priority and conflict becomes minimized. Adornment also makes us attractive to others.

Adornment

Inside her sedan chair,
her pearl earrings glowing red,
she sighs: the mountain behind her
is a forest of flames.

She meets a man. His horse
has albino pheasant wings.
He offers a bolt of silk
to tie his hand to hers.

Dawn, crimson with embers,
lights hillsides of smoldering pines.
The earth is ashes, cones scorched,
but new seeds tumble out.

Though the mountain stands charred
and the man and woman depart,
their son will return one day,
hiking through green forests.

The Statement

Adornment. Continue.
Slight gain in having a place to go.

The Lines

6th line ━━━━
Plain adornment
is without fault.

5th line ━━ ━━
Light adorns hillside gardens:
A betrothal bundle
may be small and meager,
but in the end, fortune.

4th line ━━ ━━
As beautiful as a white-feathered horse.
It is not a raider who woos.

3rd line ━━━━
Adornment like bright sparkling,
everlasting and upright.
Fortune.

The Image

2nd line ━━ ━━
Adorning is his beard.

Fire at the foot
of a mountain: adornment.
The noble one thereby
governs with clarity, and
does not dare
to decide lawsuits lightly.

1st line ━━━━
Alighting from the carriage
with adorned feet to walk.

ADORNMENT increases in a society that is wealthy and stable. Time and resources are available, and interest is strong.

Adornment links the greater world to our greater concerns. Tribal masks integrate the wearers with the spirit world. Warriors go to battle with banners and decorated armor. Priests lift precious chalices to the gods. Adornment takes what a society finds beautiful or expressive and uses that to integrate people with larger levels of meaning. Our adornment of buildings, objects, clothing, and our bodies thus reflects the values of our society.

It is instructive that in times of calamity—an attack on the country or great natural disasters—our interest in adornment changes. In fact, we remake our adornment to fit even the times of war. The war chariots are named and decorated. Weapons are exquisitely tooled. Flags and colors are displayed with great pride. Afterward, each great war or disaster leads to a change in our idea of beauty. If you look back even one hundred years, you will find that our architecture, dress, or even the shape of our bodies is not the same as it was for our predecessors. We think that by remaking our adornment we somehow change our relationship to the outer world.

Many people think that ornamentation implies something extra. While a building can function perfectly well as shelter without decoration, color, or tasteful choice of materials, it cannot fulfill cultural needs without adornment. For us, adornment enhances the meaning of a building.

If the only function of the massive bronze vessels of the Zhou dynasty was to hold ritual offerings or allow kings to make libations, unglazed clay jars would have been enough. Instead, we have vessels shaped like animals, their surfaces incised with intricate interlocking designs. We find poetry or sacred words inlaid with gold on the interiors or undersides of three-legged cauldrons. None of this "decoration" is necessary to hold the contents. All of it is necessary to integrate the function of the object with the culture that is using it. Every object becomes a metaphor that speaks to its meaning and importance for us. We use cosmetics, hairstyles, clothing, grooming, cars, and houses to show others our status and to shape their impression of us.

When the most conscious use of our beauty is to attract lovers and mates, we spare no expense, often going to ludicrous lengths to make ourselves as attractive as possible. That is understandable, perhaps even necessary. However, even as we engage in striving to beautify ourselves and our surroundings, our efforts are inherently superficial. We must not expect too much from adornment. There must still be substance for attraction to develop into a mature connection.

Every lovely vessel, then, holds two things: its contents and our cultural sensibilities. Every lovely body also holds both its outward beauty that speaks to others, and the spiritual person within. It is that spirit—and not ornamentation—that radiates eternal beauty. There is a paradox in adornment. On one hand, adornment brings to mind magic ornamentation, beautification, and the expression of a culture. On the other hand, as much as adornment might reflect a culture, it is not the core. That is why the *Statement* merely urges us to continue and to expect only slight gains. Adornment should not be emphasized over being thorough and deep.

This tension between the two sides of adornment is subtly carried through the *Lines.* (1) At first, someone alights from the carriage to walk—a seemingly humble act of self-reliance. But then we see that the feet are adorned. Is the person being ostentatious? (2) Likewise, a beard is an adornment for the face. We can tell a great deal about a man with a beard—its style, grooming, and amount of gray can be informative—but again, we cannot learn more without going deeper. (3) It is only when the "adornment" is a direct result of substance that we are in the best of situations. Just as the sparkling water results from the water itself, we need to look for the adornment that is not superficial but is a manifestation of the core. (4) The subject of outward and inward beauty is compared to "a white-feathered" horse—a horse with a flowing white mane. Here the horse and beauty are one, and we must look closely at each situation, just as a man may seem to be a raider but may in reality be a lover. (5) In other words, there are situations where we must not be fooled by appearances or put off by lack of adornment. The light on hillside gardens is fleeting; we must enjoy it briefly. The betrothal gifts from a sincere suitor can still auger good fortune. (6) In the end, it is plain adornment, at one with the core of what it decorates, that is truly faultless.

The *Image* completes the double meaning. Fire alludes to the clarity to rule. Mountain in its stillness is reluctant to enter into disputes. Wisdom is to modulate between bright display and massive stillness. The message here is unambiguous.

Oh, dance before the flames, face painted, costume shimmering with colors and symbols, music urging us to ecstacy, voices raised in chants that spiral wildly between the stars. Then, when the dance is done, turn inward. The body that is decorated is also the body that holds the unadorned spirit.

Hexagram 23
Mountain above
Earth below

The hexagram resembles the roof of a house—when the roof is stripped away, the house collapses.
　Pictorially, the yin lines of this hexagram mount upward and are on the verge of toppling the last yang line.
　This hexagram refers to the ninth lunar month (October–November), when the yin forces of winter are mounting higher.

Bo
Strip, skin, peel, shell.

The Sequence and Link
When Adornment becomes excessive, it leads to disintegration.

Splitting

The soldier reads him the royal edict:
exile. He rips his beard and pounds his head.

His wife weeps and his six children huddle
in shabby sedan chairs. They turn their eyes
as they pass the house where former servants
hang lanterns on the new minister's eaves.

In their frontier hut, the stove smokes badly.
His children play with pots that hold no rice.

As he burns his robes and breaks his brushes,
he hears the shouts: "Snow has collapsed the mill!"
He puts a boot before his sedan chair
but stops when he sees the straw-shod bearers

with their cracked hands on worn poles. He turns back:
if he lifts his pen he saves the starving.

As he dares to break his exile's silence,
he already feels dungeon walls pressing him.
Just then, he sees a crane fly through the snow:
his black ink flows with unwavering strokes.

The Statement

Splitting; no gain
in having a place to go.

The Lines

6th line ——

Great fruits are not eaten.
The noble one gets a sedan chair.
The vile ones splinter their huts.

5th line —— ——

The court ladies and concubines
are like fish tethered to a line:
nothing but gain.

4th line —— ——

The bed's surface splits into pieces:
misfortune.

3rd line —— ——

This splitting is without fault.

The Image

2nd line —— ——

The bed's side splits apart:
If you disregard the signs: misfortune.

The mountain resting on
the earth: splitting.
When the high
are generous
to those below,
all dwell in peace.

1st line —— ——

The bed's feet split:
If you disregard the signs: misfortune.

SPLITTING is the time when when everything seems to fall apart: In spite of all our hard work, our businesses are caught in an economic downturn and we fear bankruptcy. Or we may be leaders, suddenly slandered by dark rumors that overshadow any good work we have done. Or a friendship may be marred by misunderstanding and miscommunication. If we live long enough, we do not see an end to times of disintegration. We may learn to see them coming, but we still feel helpless to avoid them.

Like a building that has too much ornamentation layered on it, a society encumbered by its luxuries will experience another variation of splitting. The *Changes* recognizes this, and shows us that we can sometimes take steps to avoid that. One strategy is to relieve the tensions that might bring on splitting. Thus, the follower of the Oracle who wishes to keep society vital, or the ruler who wishes to remain in power, actively engages in a preemptive splitting to avoid more serious degeneration. Realizing that they are in a superior position because they are supported by those below them, wise leaders "split" their own wealth and influence to give to those below. What was ornamental luxury to them is transformed into fundamental wealth below.

The hexagram is an image of five yin lines about to topple a single yang line: when a ruler is not generous, the people will rise up to overthrow him. This is as inevitable as winter coming each year. The wise ruler realizes that there are many cycles where being overthrown (or, in the case of a democracy, not being reelected) is possible, just as snow comes annually. By giving, a downfall can often be forestalled.

On a personal level, this hexagram shows any situation in which we are oppressed by inferior people. We can find guidance by looking again at the lines of the hexagram: as the yang line withdraws from the yin lines, we do not pander to the inferior. The yang line is firm before the yin lines, just as we must have unshakable confidence.

Such confidence does not come from egotism or stubbornness. The right kind of confidence, which holds inferior people at bay, comes only from moral and ethical character. If we are scrupulous in our every act and thought, an inferior person will have no real way to challenge us—not even by force of numbers. They will be the ones to split apart as they crash into our firm devotion to right.

The Oracle's message is clear: put your efforts into moral accomplishments and self-cultivation, and you will survive the cycles of splitting. The earth undergoes winter each year, and yet it is not injured, because it is true to itself. A superior person may be attacked by inferior people, but if the deeds of the superior person have been moral, the cycle will pass without lasting negative effects. Broaden your base, as the mountain's base is broad on the vast earth. Share as much as possible with those who support you, as rainwater runs down a mountain. Then all will be well.

The *Statement* clearly tells us that this is a time of scant opportunities. The name of this hexagram also means to peel, strip, or flay. Stripping means that superficial things usually go first. Flaying, where the skin goes first, leaving the bones next to be attacked, is a warning to beware of worsening fortunes: when ventures begin to peel apart, a more fundamental disaster may be imminent.

These *Lines* show the splitting of what supports us. The bed is a metaphor for support that falls apart. (1) Initially, the bed legs split and the bed might collapse, but we might still be able to use it. (2) More ominously, the sides might split apart. In both cases, it is foolish to ignore the implications of what is to come. (3) The Oracle acknowledges that there is occasionally no fault in letting things split apart—especially if we have the prospects of an even stronger support. (4) But when we have no alternatives and our bed of support splits apart, this is outright misfortune. (5) However, in some narrow cases, we may be able to do well in the time of splitting. If we have arranged things well, as a king might have his court women protected and in order, we will find fortune. (6) We are given a hint of how loyalty is maintained: The wise remember who supports them (and so their "fruits"—accomplishments—are untouched). As a sedan chair is borne by bearers, a king is borne by his citizens. Inferior persons cannot understand this, and act without heeding the source of their support. When their support splits away, they will sacrifice even their own dwellings, but will still not succeed.

The *Image* unites the idea of splitting and support. Those who govern may be lofty, but they need the support of the people, even as a mountain rests upon the much wider earth. If those above would continue to govern, they must be generous to those below. Then they will not be overthrown—that is, they will not be split apart from the people who make their heights possible.

Bring your greatest attention to bear when splitting means that friendships no longer hold. Be scrupulous to split your wealth to benefit those less fortunate than you. Do not allow yourself to be oppressed by inferior people, but split from them to a higher moral level. Understand the cycles of splitting. Endure them. Make use of them, and be careful to avoid bitterness. A return to unity must come after splitting, and with that will come healing.

Hexagram 24
Earth above
Thunder below

Just when yin has pushed all yang from the hexagram, a new yang line appears in the first position. The time of darkness is waning, and light returns.

    This hexagram is linked to the winter solstice and the eleventh lunar month (December–January).

Fu
Return. Reply. To answer. To repeat. Again. Recovery. To return to normal or to an original state.

The Sequence and Link
Once disintegration has run its course, there must be a return.

Returning

A wheelwright, knee-deep in shavings,
fits spokes to hub with dusty hands.
He bends the rim and joints it smooth.
He fits wood to axle, hammers
in the linchpin. The wheel turns true.

Waves reach a farther shore and then
roll backward, just as a wise poem
will repeat its lines and verses,
or a horse will round a pylon
and a year turn from snow to spring.

Old chess players take the center,
and mathematicians must know
where to put their compass points.
The wheelwright fits another pin
and two cartwheels spin together.

The Statement

Returning. Continue.
In coming and going,
there is neither sickness nor distress.
Companions come without fault.

Returning is its Tao.

In seven days, returning comes.
Gain by having a place to go.

The Lines

6th line — —

Chaotic return: misfortune, disastrous blunder!
Move your army, and you end in great defeat.
Misfortune to nation and prince!
Even in ten years you will not conquer.

5th line — —

Honest returning:
no fault.

4th line — —

Returning alone
in the middle of the road.

3rd line — —

Urgent returning, harsh danger.
No fault.

2nd line — —

Resting, then returning:
fortunate.

1st line ——

Returning from a short distance
is not regrettable. Great fortune.

The Image

Thunder in the center of
the earth: returning.
The ancient kings
closed the borders
during the solstices.
Traveling merchants
did not journey. Sovereigns
did not tour the provinces.

R ETURNING is the fundamental action of cycles. We may concentrate on outward movement—the seafarer setting out on world explorations, the great rush forward of holiday celebrants, the joyous moment when a child goes out into the world—but the Oracle's philosophy of cycles always guarantees that there will be a returning. The message of Returning is even more important when we are in the midst of misfortune.

The Oracle takes inspiration from a natural event. When we reach the shortest day of the year, darkness is at its greatest. How hard to remember that the moment of supremacy for darkness is the moment when light begins its return. Glory leads only to decline, but decline is a prelude to returning. At the winter solstice the depths of darkness and ice coincide with the very beginning of longer days.

Any nadir must lead to ascent. The lowest point of a downward slope is also the beginning of moving upward.

The *Changes* would not have us be smug at the point of supremacy. Neither should we despair in the depths of disintegration. After the darkest point, there must be returning.

If the supreme must give way to decline, and the decline give way to rising, we must reaffirm the power of the circle. A single trough in a waterwheel, for example, comes to its highest point and turns immediately to its lowest. At its lowest, it revolves upward. The trough reaches both the zenith and nadir, but passes through each one of them at a pace no different than that at which it passes through any other point. Those who can identify where they are on the circle and discern the exact high and low points are called prescient.

You cannot get out of a cycle by rushing. A missile might break free of the earth's pull, but it will fall into an orbit around the earth. If it goes farther still, it will eventually end up orbiting around some other center. In either case, its power only leads it to be captured by one gravitational pull or another, and it will be turned. No one pulls free of the principle of returning: push harder on a turnstile and you will only get hit in the back faster.

Cycles happen around us and within us. We can strive to fit in with them without either sentimentality or selfishness.

Returning has another meaning: returning to your own path. The process of "finding ourselves" comes through a succession of repeated ventures outward and back. That is how we find our paths and our limits. Without returning, we do not find our way. Returning is not easy. Each of us is a tangled combination of spiritual seeker and sinner. We will have moments when we lose our touch. But no matter how often we lose our balance, we must return.

This hexagram reminds us that we all make mistakes and have regrets. The secret is to return often to your own Tao. Don't dwell on any one point. Stay with the turning.

The *Statement* makes this completely clear: "Returning is its Tao." In terms of general philosophy, this means that returning is the essence of any path. The phrase "seven days" refers to the simple cycle of a week. The Oracle demonstrates the general truth of cycles by a familiar and simple example. If we know the validity of cycles and the inevitability of return in a small sense, like the cycle of weeks, we should be able to extrapolate that to larger cycles. If we understand the power of returning to our own Tao, we can act with confidence and even seek a distant goal.

As usual, the *Lines* demonstrate variations on the theme of returning, showing us some good and neutral examples, as well as one of the most disastrous images in the entire book. (1) When there is trouble, the first one to return is the safest. (2) If someone uses his or her time away for renewal and then returns, that is still good. (3) Even to return urgently is to avoid mistakes. These lines are then followed by two examples of good return: (4) one who is alone but who walks in the middle of the road (the road of moderation), and (5) one who returns with honesty. (6) But the signs are ominous for those who return in disorder. As is the case of an army with no exit strategy, or a force too distant from its command, disastrous mistakes are made. Nation and leader thereby suffer misfortune, and the original goals of the campaign can never be realized, even with a great deal of time.

Hidden in this hexagram is the implication of the center—the middle path of Line 4, the thunder in the center of the earth of the *Image*. As long as the center is there, no action is needed until returning begins. That is why the passes are closed at the solstices and no one travels: all return into their own centers.

Stand. Walk. Look. That is all the spirituality we need. Walk the circle. Stand in the center. From there, even the universe circles with you.

無妄

Hexagram 25
Heaven above
Thunder below

Heaven is above; thunder—
representing movement—is
below. This is interpreted as
heaven giving a yang line to
the lower trigram: innocent
movement comes from the
power given by heaven.

Wu Wang
Wu: No, not, negative.
Wang: Absurd, untrue, false.
Ignorant, stupid. Reckless,
rash. Wild, frantic.
Wu Wang: Truth, honesty,
unexpected.

The Sequence and Link
When there is a returning to
Tao, there will be innocent
honesty. However, one must
still cope with the
unexpected.

Innocence

Far from home, he has searched through dusty huts.
As he squints at boulders stored in a ditch,
he presses his parched lips and shakes his head.
With a frown, he walks to the door, then sees
the merchant propping the door with a rock.
He puts his cinnabar seal to a note
that mortgages both his workshop and house.

In three months, donkeys arrive with the crates.
The sawyers open the first stone: worthless.
He goes home for dinner and does not speak.
It takes a day to saw the second stone.
The halves split—a sparkling vein of green jade!
He shouts for the carvers and polishers,
then holds incense in both hands at the shrine.

The Statement

Innocence: from the first, all must be
pervasive, gainful, and pure.

Those without such truth suffer calamity
and do not gain no matter where they go.

The Lines

6th line ———
Unexpected action brings disaster.
No place will be gainful.

5th line ———
Unexpected illness.
Recovery from sickness brings joy.

4th line ———
If you can be upright,
there will be no fault.

3rd line —— ——
Unexpected trouble:
a cow might be tethered by someone else.
The traveler gains, the townsman loses.

The Image

2nd line —— ——
No new fields, no old fields:
it is better to go far away.

Thunder moves
under heaven: all the world
is innocent. The ancient
kings paid close attention
to the time
in nourishing
the myriad things.

1st line ———
Innocently going forward:
favorable.

INNOCENCE—*wu wang*—means we can cope with accident (also *wu wang*). In order to understand this hexagram, we must hold these several meanings simultaneously.

First, *wu wang* means truth and honesty: we cannot have innocence unless we are truthful. We must avoid being absurd, stupid, rash, wild, or frantic. Only the calm, intelligent, and truthful are *wu wang*.

Second, *wu wang* refers to unexpected events: accident. The study of change must account for accident. Losing property, opening fields that turn out to be infertile, having others steal our possessions, and becoming ill are all examples of unexpected events.

This brings us to the third implication of *wu wang:* without fault. When accidents occur, we are "innocent" of fault, although we may still suffer. Accident will strike at inopportune times, but we are innocent, and we should not become unbalanced. The unvirtuous are derailed by accidents: their flaws undo them.

This hexagram clarifies a misconception that people have about the Taoist term, *wu wei*—often translated as "nonaction." Many people erroneously believe that everything happens for positive and personal reasons. *Wu wang* refutes such thinking. It declares that accidents exist, and that accidents sometimes affects us in deeply traumatic ways.

At the same time, we cannot depend on accident to do our work for us. Some people shrug and say, "We shall see what happens." What might happen could always be worse. This is far from a glorious invitation to the universe to participate in our ridiculously puny lives. It is simply an unwillingness on our part to think things through and to work toward completion. Indulging in this mentality only leads us further out of true synchronization with Tao. We become people who act at random, much like someone who disregards the seasons. Like a farmer who plows and plants without regard for the weather or time of year, or a musician who ignores sheet music, or a sojourner who does not know that there is snow in the passes, we get more out of touch and our lives wobble increasingly.

If we are *wu wang*—innocent—we can cope with *wu wang*—accident. Only a strong and active personality can cope with random disasters. Absurd, stupid, rash, wild, or frantic—all are qualities we can avoid as part of an effort to avoid being undone by accident. Furthermore, if we can adequately cope with accident, we also avoid having these same qualities mark our reactions.

Those who get sick recover. Medicine is an intervention; it rarely heals. Only we can heal ourselves, with the power of our *wu wang*. Innocence is a power. It is a force within us, the natural genius and skill of our bodies and minds to right ourselves in daily turbulence.

Perhaps we can even say chance is the medium through which events happen. While there is structure—from the sphere of a cell to the hexagons of a beehive to the orbit of the moon around the earth—the interactions of these many structures contain a strong element of chance.

The **Statement** hints at how we must approach this process of chance: We must remain open and without guile. We must align ourselves with the fundamental: that which is first, which permeates, which is gainful. The use of the word *pure* especially reminds us that we must be moral, not in a small way, but through spontaneous purity of character.

The **Lines** carry on the twin themes of innocence and the unexpected. (1) The Oracle first sounds the theme that we must be without falsehood whenever we advance. (2) But soon, unexpected problems happen. We find ourselves without fields, or (3) we are careless and others lead our possessions away. We should deal with these situations by being upright and ethical. (4) Be upright, and you are without fault. (5) Accept that illness can come unexpectedly, and it can depart just as innocently. (6) Finally, we can still suffer a significant loss. Either by our own folly or by the actions of another, events can sometimes not be overcome. They are disastrous, and there will be no place to go.

The **Image** begins with heaven, which provides the framework. Thunder is the movement beneath it. Thus the ancient kings paid close attention to the season and the times in order to nourish others. They realized how important timing was, and how short the openings were, and so they acted in a timely way in all things, especially in the task of nourishing others and exercising good stewardship over all who lived in their countries.

Those with experience tell us that they are barely aware of what they do to be successful. A great athlete may win medals, but she may not be able to describe how she gave her performance. A great leader may solve diplomatic crises, but she may not regard her actions as being extraordinary. Innocence means we are at our most powerful when we are at our most natural. In the end, it is that naturalness and fullness of our own beings that is the essence of Innocence.

大畜

Great Restraint

If, when you see the stars,
you connect them with lines
and think of where they lead—

if you can watch the night
shift hour by hour until
you see the gray east rise,

and you breathe in the wind
and touch the falling snow—
you have found the secret.

If you see in your child
your spouse's face with yours,
and that beggars and gods,

monkeys, serpents, and orbs
floating in seawater
are also in her face,

you can answer her well
the moment that she asks
what will come the next day.

Hexagram 26
Mountain above
Heaven below

The great power of heaven
is concentrated in the
stillness of a mountain.
    The line formation shows
two yin lines in the
controlling middle positions
of the hexagram. Four yang
lines are thereby restrained
by two yin lines.

Da Chu

Da: Big, large. Great. Much.
Very, highly, extremely. Eldest,
senior, full-grown, adult. To
enlarge, to make great.
Chu: Domesticated animals.
To raise livestock.

The Sequence and Link

If one is innocent of reckless-
ness, there is the possibility of
great control.

The Statement

Gain by being upright.
Not eating at home brings fortune.
Advance across the great river.

The Lines

6th line ——

Where is heaven's thoroughfare?
Go through it.

5th line —— —

A gelded hog's teeth.
Favorable.

4th line —— —

A young bull's headboard.
Great fortune.

3rd line ——

A good horse chases, but gain is difficult.
Be upright. Prepare the chariots daily
and be on guard.
Gain by having a place to go.

The Image

2nd line ——

Carriage axle blocks broken.

Heaven in the center of a
mountain: great restraint.
The noble one
frequently studies
the words and prophesies
of the past, and thereby
nourishes virtue.

1st line ——

There is harsh danger.
Gain ends.

GREAT RESTRAINT creates power. The strength of water is harnessed because of a dam. A horse's power can be tamed by the bridle. A person's virtue is stronger after it has become concentrated by discipline.

Hexagram 9, Smallness Tames, showed a situation where control was nascent. Here, after the progress represented by the preceding hexagrams, Great Restraint shows how larger accomplishments are possible.

The *Changes* frequently uses the phrase "advance across the great river" as a marker for such large ventures. The juxtaposition of this phrase here with the name for this hexagram reminds us that it also mean a transcendence of previous limits. The river is a limit. Crossing it means to pass the limits. Breaking the great restraint of a border takes the great restraint of controlling our minds and limbs to act. The breaching of barriers is possible only through our supreme control.

Great restraint implies three kinds of control. The first is control over reckless impulses. The second is disciplined action. The third is daily renewal of our character.

Control over reckless impulses is critical. We all have emotions that get the best of us, laziness that drags us down, and ambitions that crowd our hearts. Some of us may thrill to any sort of strong feelings, but such emotions also make us unsteady. When we are nettled from the day, when we smart with insult and abuse, when we tremble with insecurity and fear, there is no possibility of restraint. It is only by the calm and patient experience of daily life, and the process of disappointment and labor, that we see the necessity of restraint.

Once we have the beginnings of self-control, we have the makings of discipline. A good horse obeys the reins. A good militia obeys its commander. In the same way, we have to prepare and maintain our lives each day. The range of possibilities for a disciplined person is far greater than for the reckless person who can never link one action to another. The disciplined person can see the path ahead, contemplate what preparations are necessary, create plans for proceeding down that path, and take the steps to complete the journey. It is the great restraint of discipline that makes this all possible.

Daily renewal of character emerges from constant great restraint. We all get torn down each day. We all have doubts. We may even chafe under the goals we have set for ourselves. That is why we must renew ourselves each day with rest, good food, and rededication. We must reaffirm the necessity of moral action. We must reaffirm the value of our personal goals. And if we have suffered, we must take the time to heal. Virtue is not some book idea. It is a real power that is made strong as heaven when it is concentrated through discipline.

Heaven restrained by a mountain succinctly sums up great restraint. Such restraint is not like the stoppage of Hexagram 12, Clogging. Instead, the *Statement* tells us that this restraint comes from being pure and upright. With such power, we should not hide ourselves at home with our families, but we should venture forth to find our fortune. Removing all doubt, the Oracle urges us to cross the great river—that is, to transcend the limitations that hinder us and to advance toward larger possibilities.

The *Lines* show both outer and inner control. (1) In the face of harsh danger and loss, our gains end and we are restrained by circumstance. (2) Or, if what keeps our actions turning breaks, as when an axle breaks from a cart, we are restrained to the point of standstill. Then, in keeping with restraint in the sense of animal domestication, we see three types of inner control in the next three lines. (3) A swift horse chases, but gains will be difficult. Accordingly, we must be vigilant—training our chariots daily. Only then are great goals possible. (4) A bull whose horns are controlled by a board will then grow properly and will not gore people. This shows how much restraint must be applied in the long term. (5) In the same way, great restraint is like a gelded hog that is docile but still has teeth to eat. (6) Finally, we are shown the benefit of supreme discipline: we can ride heaven's thoroughfare to great success.

A mountain restraining heaven: the *Image* shows us how we might find the secret of great restraint. In studying the words of the past—not only books, but poems, speeches, and even the wisdom of our elders—and in studying the prophesies—in a wider sense, studying the plans people made and looking to see how successful they were—we find the way to nourish our virtue. It is this guidance that is our "bull's headboard," and it is this guidance that is ultimately "heaven's thoroughfare."

The image of mountain and heaven leaves us with a final picture: the noble person, standing with as much presence as a mountain, the power of heaven coursing through him. If we realize such great restraint, how can we fail to make accomplishments lofty as a peak, wide as the sky?

Nourishing

Hexagram 27
Mountain above
Thunder below

The hexagram forms a
picture of an open mouth.
Thunder as movement and
mountain as stillness also can
be seen as the lower jaw
moving against the upper
jaw.

Yi
Nourishing, to rear, to care
for oneself. Cheeks.

The Sequence and Link
Once control has been
established, we must look to
nourishing ourselves and
others.

The regent dismisses the court
and strolls with his nephew, the king.
They pause at the balcony rail
to gaze at the snow-covered peaks.
They recall the ministers' words
and the boy tells what he has seen.

"The chancellor hides what he knows.
I call on him: he clenches his jaws.
The general stands without friends:
he snaps like a wolf in a trap.
The adviser speaks of the rules
like a parrot perched in a cage."

The regent adjusts the boy's crown:
"The soldiers are guarding the peaks,
the farmers are plowing their fields.
How will you speak for your people?"
"They should keep enough for their mouths."
The regent's lips part in a smile.

The Statement

Nourishing. Pure fortune.
Watch the jaws
and what one seeks to fill one's mouth.

The Lines

6th line ━━━
Through nourishment
in severity comes fortune.
Advance across the great river.

5th line ━ ━
Disobeying the right ways:
dwelling instead in virtue brings fortune.
Do not advance across the great river.

4th line ━ ━
Moving jaws are fortunate.
Like a glaring tiger, passion runs full,
but there is no fault.

3rd line ━ ━
Jaws shake in opposition. Persistence
will bring misfortune. For ten years,
all will be useless and no place
will bring gain.

2nd line ━ ━
With jerking jaws, you disobey
the right ways. Find nourishment
in the nearby hills
instead of journeying far away.

1st line ━━━
You put aside your divine turtle
And watch my moving jaws: misfortune.

The Image

Thunder below the
mountain: nourishing.
The noble one is
careful in speech
and temperate
while eating and drinking.

NOURISHING yourself and nourishing others: that is Tao. The Oracle centers its concerns about nourishment in the image of jaws. Jaws also contribute to nourishing others—literally by ordering that people be fed, and figuratively by speaking words of instruction so others can learn how to feed themselves. Eating is fundamental to living. Feeding and teaching others follows closely in importance.

At the same time, we can get into trouble through the movement of our jaws. We talk too much. We are disobedient and stubborn. We lie. We whisper rumors. We insult. We are profane. Misdeeds of words are even matched by misdeeds of nourishment. We greedily suck in every morsel before us. We insist on feeding our own jaws first. We stuff our mouths full, and spit demands for more.

Furthermore, our jaws are remarkable indicators of our thoughts and feelings. A lying man may have a twitching cheek. An angry woman may tense her jaw. When we are bracing for an assault, we grit our teeth. When others frustrate us, we grind our jaws. If something is funny, our jaws shake with laughter. If we are sad, they tremble. Therefore, if you want to become an excellent judge of others, the *Changes* teaches that you need only watch their jaws, for they will indicate every mood and thought.

Likewise, if you want to know what motivates people, look to see what they feed themselves. What people seek for their own sustenance tells a great deal. Are they greedy? Careless? Will they put aside their own food for the sake of those more needy?

The **Statement** tells us that if we look to see what and how a person nourishes, we will come to a great understanding of that person. One who nourishes evil loves evil. One who nourishes good loves good. If you want to find a compassionate person, look for someone who nourishes others with kindness and generosity. If you want to find a good parent, look for someone who feeds and teaches children well. That is why it is said that we should look to how other people nourish if we would know their true natures.

We often meet over meals. From high ritual to casual friendships, from holidays and celebrations to funerals, we make food the center of our gatherings. Food forms one of the major preoccupations—and therefore meanings—of family. Every government is judged by how it feeds its citizens. Every religion and spiritual tradition teaches gratitude for food. Whether in the form of unrestrained feasting, carefully scripted diets, or fasting, food holds a place in every spiritual tradition.

We need to nourish ourselves, along with our spouses, children, family, and nation. Meals form a natural place not only for the benefit of food, but to nourish each other emotionally. We should never stint on nourishment or on nourishing one another's feelings. If you both nourish yourself and share with others, that is Tao.

The *Lines* expand on the different ways that moving jaws indicate character. (1) Someone looks at the speaking Oracle instead of the actual divining turtles; in other words, someone is misplacing their concentration. This is unfortunate. (2) Another jabbers and disobeys the right ways, hankering afar for results rather than working with what is at hand. (3) A third person is simply obstinate and uncooperative, and this leads to ten years of stymied progress. (4) Sometimes, though, moving jaws indicate passion and exertion. Here, this is appropriate. (5) Some people manage to stop their disobeying of what is right, and find virtue where they are. They should go nowhere but dwell in the virtue they have found. (6) Only someone who learns to nourish himself or herself and others in severe times—which implies the perseverance and compassion the Oracle values—is capable of great feats.

The *Image* advises us to be careful in what we say. At the same time, if we are temperate in our food and drink, we avoid criticism, and others will learn to trust us.

Tao is the natural. Whatever is natural is the way of the Oracle. To eat is natural. To feed others is also natural. To talk is natural. To talk so that we can feed others is natural. When people understand how simple Tao is, they wonder how it can be so profound. Yet the only reason complication enters is that we have trouble accommodating the simple. Eat. Help others eat. Do not speak badly of others. Be observant, and you will find friends. Be as swift as thunder to feed others. Keep your center hollow, as the hexagram indicates. On the outside, be as stable and forceful as the heaviest of mountain. Still yourself from evil words. Mobilize yourself, and Tao will reveal itself.

Hexagram 28
Mountain above
Thunder below

Four yang lines in the middle
and yin lines at the two ends
symbolize a beam carrying a
load too heavy for its supports.

Da Guo
Da: Big, large. Great. Much.
Very, highly, extremely. Eldest,
senior, full-grown, adult. To
enlarge.
Guo: Exceed, surpass. To pass,
to ford, to cross. Across,
through, over. To spend time.
Mistake, fault, sin. After, past.
Contagious. To visit. To transfer. To arrive. To die, death.

The Sequence and Link
In matters of nourishment,
we easily go to excess. Or, if
there is no nourishment, no
crossings are possible.

Great Excess

The king inspects the three-story scaffold.
He envisions, inside the bamboo frame,
the columns of a cinnabar palace
built to cast shadows on his father's halls.

The workmen tie the last beam to pulleys.
The scaffold shakes as the men shout and tug.
After the mortises have been wedged tight,
the king's eyes narrow and his chin juts out.

He turns to eunuchs huddled in a row:
"My palace is the same as my body.
Statues of gods and kings should guard the roof."
Eunuchs nod. Carpenters bow. The wood bends.

One year later, the scaffolds are torn down.
The king grins, until the posts and beams crack.
He throws his satin sleeves over his head,
as roof tiles crash around his pounding feet.

The Statement

The ridgepole sags.
Gain by having a place to go.
Continue.

The Lines

6th line —— ——

Fording, wading, head submerged.
Misfortune, but without fault.

5th line ——————

Withered wood blooms with flowers.
An old woman takes a husband.
Neither fault nor praise.

4th line ——————

An ample beam. Fortunate,
unless there has been stinting.

3rd line ——————

A weak beam.
Misfortune.

The Image

2nd line ——————

A withered trunk bursts with fresh vetch.
An old man takes a wife. Nothing but gain.

The lake overwhelms
the trees: great excess.
The noble one stands alone
without fear,
and can withdraw
from the world
without sorrow.

1st line —— ——

A cushion of white grass.
No fault.

GREAT EXCESS means a sharp unbalancing. Such unbalancing is something we will all experience. No matter how much we study, our experiences will inevitably bring us to situations where too much weight predominates.

Since we are studying change, we might think everything can be tidily accounted for. We absorb ancient wisdom. We travel widely. We nourish ourselves, body, mind, and spirit. Even so, we will be surprised by how some great excess can arise, or how a situation can become so weighty that it endangers us. We can study change, and yet we will not be able to predict everything.

Guo has a large number of different meanings, but it pairs the idea of excess with the idea of crossings, passings, and surpassings.

When we are confronted with a situation that is larger than we are—like a sagging roof—we need to either shore it up or relieve the weight. There's no use talking about any other ideas until the excess is corrected; when the beam of a house is sagging, no one talks about decoration. The way to curb our own excess is through moderation and discipline, like a sculptor whose art is improved by the restrictions of carving marble. We cannot learn moderation without long experience. We need to test ourselves and our ideas—one hopes in a safe way—and then learn from that.

Guo also means crossing. We have to make crossings in our lives. It might be our first day at school, our first time speaking in public, proposing marriage, holding our child, or preparing to die. Whether it is the door of our family house, the river that borders our fields, or an entire ocean, we must make crossings. We will do it not just once but many times. How can we cross safely? We must be familiar with what we are trying to do, and we must be correct within ourselves. If we do that, we avoid the mistakes that mar many crossings.

Once we have crossed borders and barriers, we must leave them behind. We have finished. There is no need for lingering doubts or regrets. Without passages, we will never grow. Whatever happened to us in crossing—as in someone fording a river and getting wet—is secondary in importance to a safe arrival and readiness for what is ahead. No one fords without getting wet, yet this ceases to be a concern once the far shore has been reached.

With each crossing, we become both wiser and stronger. *Guo* thus develops into a symbol for surpassing. This means both the surpassing of external wealth and fame, and the surpassing of all the stress and strain that went into reaching that point.

The greatest challenge is the surpassing of oneself. Anyone can think and act according to personality and training, but only an excellent person can think and act *beyond* what he or she has done in the past.

Snakes shed their skin because their skin cannot grow larger. The older generation dies because it cannot grow enough to keep pace with the next. All of us must keep changing, letting the skin of our old excesses fall away.

The *Statement* gives consideration to the advantages and disadvantages of excess. A ridgepole sags under great weight. The advice may seem obvious: prepare to get away. But in the advice to "continue," or literally, "permeate," there is a hint that we must learn from the situation as well as go through it. In that way, we will survive the excess and emerge with understanding.

The *Lines* present still more subtle interpretations. (1) As might be the case for something excessively heavy, we cushion what is excessive to keep it from marring the floor and to enable us to move it easily. (2) A different sense of excess is shown next. A withered tree and an old man would seem to have a preponderance of age, and yet there is still life there—supporting the idea of continuation mentioned in the hexagram statement. (3) Weak beams are obviously unable to withstand excessive weight; we are urged not to rely on them, and we should clearly avoid being such beams ourselves. (4) If we have a strong beam, we should not stint in supporting it, nor should we weaken it by substituting a weaker and cheaper one. (5) This next line seems to echo Line 2, and yet the judgment is more neutral. Perhaps the pronouncement is because an old woman cannot bear children, or perhaps this is an indication that an old woman's husband may not be helpful to her. (6) Finally, in a foreshadowing of the Image, we see a person fording a stream and being pulled under. Such a misfortune cannot be faulted, yet the person must strive to reach the other side.

The *Image* completes this sense of struggle against excess. Sometimes, excess is when everyone seems to be against you. If you are as sure of yourself as the Oracle would have you be, you will be unafraid of standing independent. If you have to leave the world to protect yourself from excess, you do so without sorrow or confusion. Conform to change, the Oracle declares in most cases—except this one: if you must stand alone to be true to yourself, you must do so.

Great excess. Only the truly great can cope with it—and no one becomes great without being tested by great excess.

Hexagram 29
Water above
Water below

The water trigram doubled.

Kan
Pit, hole, depression. One of
the Eight Trigrams. The sound
of percussion. A snare, crisis.

The Sequence and Link
Excess leads to danger.
Crossings lead to danger.
Great strength leads to
danger.

Pit

Vultures roost in the cracks where ice
   has wedged the granite cliffs.
    The beaks and talons chip
sparks of flint that fade as they drop
       through the chasm's
      torrential wind.

Armies once fled through this abyss,
   chased by drums that echoed
   between narrowing walls—
or is it the river pounding
     as it plunges
      into the earth's hole?

A phantom still glows in the depths.
   Religions have risen
   and prophets have chanted
over what they taught was sunk there:
     a sword, a ring,
     a book, a bell.

Each generation, one child dives:
   To claim the sacred gift
   they must become water.
But what they see they cannot tell:
     a liquid mouth
     cannot shape words.

The Statement

Repeated pits.
Have confidence.
Tether your heart and continue.
Action brings honor.

The Lines

6th line   ▬▬ ▬▬

Tied and entangled. Thrown in brambles.
For three years, nothing can be won.
Misfortune.

5th line   ▬▬▬

The pit is not yet flooded to the brim.
No fault.

4th line   ▬▬ ▬▬

A bottle of wine, a bamboo basket,
and two earthenware vessels offered simply
through a window. In the end, no fault.

3rd line   ▬▬ ▬▬

Drumbeats come: stuck in danger.
Entering the underground vault
will be of no use.

The Image

2nd line   ▬▬▬

The pit has dangers.
Inquiries get little.

Flowing water comes:
repeated pits.
The noble one moves
with constant virtue, and
repeatedly teaches
the critical matters.

1st line   ▬▬ ▬▬

Pit within a pit.
Entering an underground vault:
misfortune.

PIT: that very image makes us shudder. It reminds us of the grave. But the image of the pit is also overlaid with the necessary: the ditch we dig for irrigation, the well we dig to drink, the trench we dig for a strong foundation.

The pit is everywhere in nature too. It is the canyon where the river froths white, the river we must venture to when the cliffs are dry and the wind is hot. It is the cave where we find shelter from the elements, even a place of silence for worship.

So the pit is a double image. An image of the grave, of having to venture down dangerous paths for life-giving water, a place of entrapment. It is also the womb, the home of water, and thus a vital part of what we need. For the Oracle, water, as fundamental as it is, runs in a place of danger. Therefore, water as a symbol is tied to risk.

All that we call worthwhile is done while risking danger. Lost travelers may stumble over the edges of cliffs. Armies may plunge through boat-splintering gorges. Explorers may enter canyons but may not find an outlet. However, we must also remember that spelunkers are willingly lowered into caverns others are afraid to enter. There in the darkness, theirs are the first eyes to see variegated colors painted by a thousand years of seeping water.

If we are to understand the Pit, we must embrace both fright and wonder.

Most activity in our daily lives involves danger. We could drown in the bathtub, burn ourselves on our stoves, choke on cords, cut ourselves with knives, and crash our cars. But we learn how to do things safely. That does not eliminate the danger. It only helps us use dangerous things safely.

There are other dangers, which we must address through cooperation: illness, accident, assault, rape, poisoning, war. These, too, we must face, banding together to guard against these problems.

We even celebrate danger: risk enhances what we value. An athlete risks loss and dishonor, so we are overjoyed with a victory. A political candidate risks reputation and personality, and we give allegiance to the winner. A soldier risk body and life, and we cheer the courage that protects us.

Every businessperson risks ruin to strike a deal, every student risks failure to excel, every couple risks divorce to make their marriage work, and every parent risks ten thousand worries to raise a child safely. All that we call worthwhile is done while risking danger.

Just as we climb down dark grottoes of jagged rock to scoop spring water, the value of our lives is at the bottom of danger. As water bathes us and quenches thirst, our activities sustain us and give us meaning.

It is indulgence when people claim they cannot find the meaning of life. They can. They just do not want to risk danger to find it. And so they sit at the edge, never going into the darkness to seek the answers that will slake their thirst.

The danger of others trapping and hurting us. The danger of failure. The danger of accident. The danger that guards the meaning of life. All these dangers are understandably fearful. Yet that fear is like the darkness and the rock of a cavern, concealing hidden treasure. We each have to face the pit every day, learning how to go deeper, if we are to grasp what is of true value.

This hexagram takes several images and binds them together into the single concept of danger. At most times, references are to a pit, but the Image returns to the water imagery of the trigram's place in the Eight Trigrams. Then there is the use of the word *repeated,* which often signals a doubling of danger, but which is given a different interpretation in the Image.

The **Statement** tells us that as we face the danger of a Pit, we must keep our confidence, even to the point of tethering our hearts so that we can continue. The word *continue* also signifies going through and permeating. Therefore, we must have the largeness of personality to be able to penetrate—and emerge safely from—the most dangerous pits.

Several of the **Lines** convey the idea of entering an underground vault—perhaps a tomb or cave. (1) To do this repeatedly or to enter a pit within a pit is clearly dangerous and leads to misfortune. (2) Then we are shown in the pit, calling for help but getting little response. (3) An even worse situation comes when we are trapped with drums approaching (the hexagram name also means the sound of striking); we flee into an underground vault, but all will be for naught. (4) But if we do get help, we must make offerings, no matter how simple. (5) If we are without fault, we may yet emerge from a pit rapidly filling with water. (6) If we do not escape, we will be caught, tied, and thrown in brambles from which we will not escape for three years.

The **Image** pictures flowing water arriving and associates that with repeated danger. The admonition to move with constant virtue corresponds to the hexagram statement to "tether your heart" even as we act. But then, the Oracle borrows the word for "repeated," and uses it to mean the repetition needed for study and practice. Just as pits or water can be doubled, the Oracle recommends doubling our own efforts to teach in all the important matters.

Pit upon pit. Water upon water. To face the greatest risks in life, double the strength of your personality.

Li
Bright light. To leave, depart, separate. To defy, to go against. Distant from, apart from. To run into, to meet. To act in tandem.

The Sequence and Link
Darkness must give way to light. Risking danger must lead to enlightenment.

Brilliance

Red desert dusk, wagon wheels crunch.
The white-haired patriarch leads them
by the orbits of moon and stars.

His granddaughter trots beside him,
her skin dark, black hair never cut,
and she memorizes his songs.

A shudder rends the earth. The mules bray.
Twin fountains of flame burst from rock,
loud as whipping flags. Men cower,

but the patriarch draws them forth,
knowing the prophecy has come.
Flames arc to the girl, engulf her.

Raising her burning hands, she folds
the fire into her heart and smiles.
Her grandfather and her tribe kneel.

The girl opens her arms to them.
She blesses each one, and they know:
now her light will guide their crossings.

The Statement

Brilliance. Gainful purity.
Continue.
Tame the bull: fortune.

The Lines

6th line ——————

The king goes to battle.
Admirably, he humbles the chieftains
and captures vile rebels. No fault.

5th line ——— ———

Weeping and running tears
as if in mourning and grief:
fortunate.

4th line ——————

This abrupt arrival is like a blaze
that flares and dies, then is forgotten.

3rd line ——————

Brilliance sets with the sun.
Do not drum on a crock with your singing.
When great elders' sighs come:
misfortune.

The Image

2nd line ——— ———

Yellow brilliance.
Great fortune.

Brightness doubled:
brilliance. The great person
spreads his brilliance
to illuminate
all four directions.

1st line ——————

Walk cautiously
with correct reverence.
No fault.

BRILLIANCE: the best ruler raises a lantern. If you would rule the world, the secret is no more simple than that: illuminate what the people want, illuminate the truth, illuminate and bring understanding.

It would be easy to think of good and bad fortune as events from outside ourselves. It's tempting to think that correct action is a matter of synchronizing inner wishes with outer circumstances. Neither impression is completely wrong, and yet brilliance shows us another—and more profound—approach.

Brilliance is commonly called fire, but here it represents the brilliant personality, and more specifically, the insight and intelligence of a cultivated person. In contrast to previous images, where we were able to take advantage of a situation or where we were restricted by a situation, brilliance shows someone coming forth with the light from within himself or herself. This is why there is such an emphasis on self-cultivation in the art of change. The power of one's own enlightenment creates the greatest transformations.

Once we master this, we go from being skillful actors—taking our cues from the myriad changes—to being those who act skillfully, shaping and leading the process of change. We shine the light of our own powerful understanding, dispelling both our own ignorance and the darkness of others.

We can learn further details of such intelligent action by looking closely at the image of Brilliance. This hexagram shows two trigrams combined, giving us the idea of a fire flaming upon itself. It is brightness doubled. We are reminded of the brightness of the sun, and the power that the right idea can have on an entire civilization.

Every fire and light has its source. No fire burns without fuel. In the same way, we as enlightened people cannot live apart from the world. There is no such thing as "being above it all." Even renunciates are tied to the world because they define themselves by what they deny. Besides, every one of them still sits on the earth and breathes the air.

In a political sense, an enlightened leader cannot be separated from allies or constituents. Whatever brilliance a leader attains is because of the "fuel" others provide. If a leader understands this, great things are possible. The leader who loses this understanding will be snuffed out like a candle in the wind.

The best leader is therefore the enlightened leader. The best ruler does not wield an ax but raises a lantern. Those who try to rule by fire are destroyed by fire. Those who rule by bringing light to others join with an ever-increasing radiance.

Mere smartness and book learning are not enough. The spirit is the only light that never dies. It is a light that simultaneously illuminates and perceives. As long as we do not forget it, it is our best beacon in this world of dismal nights.

The *Statement* reminds us that fire is heat and light. It becomes our metaphor for life and brilliance of intelligence and character. Having such brilliance brings gain and purity, and we can therefore spread our influence. In this sense, taming the bull means to subdue the animalistic element in our lives, yoke it through our intelligence, and put it to work. This makes the phrase "gainful purity" quite specific: only intelligently directed effort brings fortune.

The *Lines* explore the range of meanings of brilliance. (1) Even if we have it, we must still walk cautiously and with reverence to be without fault. (2) If we are able to achieve brilliance with moderation (symbolized by the color yellow), we can have great fortune. (3) But brilliance alone has its cycles, just as the sun must set. "Do not drum on a crock" echoes the first line: do not depend wholly on your own talent and intelligence. If you exceed the core wisdom of the elders, there will be misfortune. (4) The potential transitory nature of brilliance is again emphasized. This line could refer to the arrival of something that troubles you—it will be forgotten soon—but it is also a message that you should strive to be more than a flare so easily forgotten. (5) Aside from caution and reverence, the Oracle hints at another quality that should be alloyed with brilliance: compassion. When we can feel the pain of others as if it were our own mourning, there is fortune. (6) At the culmination of this hexagram, we are shown a king brilliantly going into battle and being victorious. His cause is just, and he is at the height of his powers. In this campaign to conquer evil, there is no fault.

The *Image* closes this hexagram by reminding us to use our brilliance unselfishly. Through our efforts, we should try to double our inner brilliance. Once we gain that, though, we must use it to illuminate the entire world. Echoing the care in the first line, the Image would have us use our intelligence to care for people in all four directions.

The flame never questions itself. It shines without worrying how long it will last. Let us be like that flame, letting the brilliance of truth be all that we are.

Hexagram 31
Lake above
Mountain below

The mountain below—
representing a strong and
quiet person—supports the
lake—symbolizing joy and
cheerfulness—in the upper
trigram. This alludes to
attraction and courtship.

Xian
All, completely, fully, wholly.
According to several sources,
the word should actually be
gan (the word combines *xian*
with the radical for heart):
feeling, sensation, emotion.
Affect, move, touch. To be
grateful. To find, to sense, to
perceive, to respond.

The Sequence and Link
Only after heaven and earth,
water and fire have been
established is there the yin
and yang of human attraction.

Feeling

Fields lie frozen, branches stand bare.
A caravan rides from the fog,
led by a girl from beyond the frontier.
She leaps from her camel, waving.
Tiny mirrors glint on her vest.

Men unload chests with spice and cloth.
She drapes her arm with yellow silk.
Townspeople chatter and crowd around her.
She herds them back into a loop—
and I am roped into the crowd.

As she urges people to buy,
her eyes remain steady on me.
Others hear her banter. I hear her song.
She pours rubies into my hands:
I linger over her chance touch.

Tomorrow she leads her camels
to her home of honey and wine.
I must ride behind her, gripping her waist,
to the lakes that rise and dissolve
mountains and borders forever.

The Statement

Feeling. Pervasive
with gainful purity.
Taking a spouse brings fortune.

The Lines

6th line —— ——

Feeling in the jaws, cheeks, and tongue.

5th line ————

Feeling in the spine.
No fault.

4th line ————

Pure fortune. Remorse vanishes.
But if you are indecisive in going and coming,
only close friends will think of you.

3rd line ————

Feeling in the thighs.
Persistence in following and going forward
will lead to harshness.

The Image

2nd line —— ——

Feeling in the calves—misfortune.
Staying put—fortune.

Lake on a mountain:
feeling.
The noble one
accepts people openly.

1st line —— ——

Feeling in the big toe.

FEELING. Sensation. Excitement. Movement. Touching. These lead us into love. Without attraction between two people, neither families nor nations would exist. We all understand this: every society supports courtship and marriage.

When love's first touch comes, feelings explode in clouds of longing. Our limbs fill with the pressure of hot mist. Each touch makes that cloud tremble and mass toward the point of contact. Every feeling that comes awakens a desire to give that feeling back, to be two clouds that collide, unite, finally to burst—their lightning and thunder radiating out into a world that no one else can know. Two bodies become one, a one that admits to nothing else.

Why did this feeling never come before? Why is this feeling something so unlike anything else? This touching has no metaphor. Feeling is its own metaphor, feeding on itself, turning on itself, not allowing any language to escape, but allowing only a pulling deeper into itself—so that every spark, sun, ocean, and sky collapses into its vortex.

The first parting is painful, yet it is a pain that teaches its own lesson of return. Impatience pricks our skin as each moment flakes dully away from us. Desire builds in us, a jungle lake pooling, brimming with warm rain and red clay running in rivulets, a fullness splashing with the slightest breeze. One more drop, one more breeze, and the lake will overflow.

When the lover comes, excitement arises at the thought of how the lover's desire has been building too, piling layer upon layer, building up masses of longing, thrusting up to a high peak that overshadows everything else. Our lover comes back into sight, larger than our memory, looming big as a mountain—monstrous, frightening, with a shadow that casts all things into cold night—and we laugh and smile and know that with one finger we can transform that massive wall of rock into a pyre on which we will lie—to die in its flames, and reawaken in the image our lover has of us.

What is important? What is normal? This feeling, so wonderfully shared, becomes the new imperative, the new normalcy. The pounding, the buzzing, the dizziness—those are all just fibers in a gauzy screen that suddenly parts to show the sun rising on our own paradise.

What a change! Finding a lover initiates a journey through change that cannot be known any other way. Every sage, every prophet has had to bow before love. Yes, throughout the centuries, many have tried to curb love, but all have failed. No whip, no thorn, no snowy cave can extinguish the fires that burn in us. It is foolish to try: extinguish that fire and you extinguish yourself, with no one there to reignite you.

Touch. Emotion. Become the friend of feeling, and do not oppose it.

The *Changes* also reminds us of the importance of feeling as we consider the future. Whether by intuition or bodily sensations, whether it is a pain in our joints that we associate with coming rain or a twitching that we believe tells us someone is approaching, this hexagram reminds us that unusual movements in our bodies provoke us to take note and to wonder.

Of course, we must still make a decision. That is the crux of all divination: we may be given a view of our situation, but it is still incumbent on us to act. The *Statement* lets us know that we may have feelings, but that we should continue, explore them thoroughly, work for positive outcomes, and remain pure in character. At no time is this need to ally feeling with thought and character more important than when we choose a spouse. We may have the mysterious feelings that cause us to move toward one particular person, but we must also determine whether the factors for benefit and purity are there.

The *Lines* return to the theme of bodily sensations in combination with movement. (1) Feeling in the big toe symbolizes just the beginnings of sensing. The next two lines warn about feelings that may not be good to follow. (2) We may have the feeling to move forward, such as we might feel in our calves when we want to move, but the Oracle advises us to do the opposite: stay put. That relates back to the Statement, where we must both honor feeling and temper that with a pure character. (3) Feelings in the thighs remind us of sensuality and lust; to act on that will lead to harsh times. (4) If we are in the situation where our feelings intersect perfectly with what fortune brings us, we are in a good situation indeed. However, we can still ruin it by being indecisive. (5) Tingling in the spine signifies a central and deeply felt feeling, and there is no fault in trusting that. It can also refer to the feeling of energy that courses through us when we are exerting ourselves. (6) As we have seen in previous hexagrams, feelings in the jaws, cheeks, and tongue refer to speech, trustworthiness, and nourishment. Again, we need to balance feeling with pure character.

A lake on a mountain is open to the sky and yet elevated above the plains. In the same way, the elevated wise person learns from the lake to be open and to receive others with equanimity.

When feeling comes, don't be foolish: feelings are real. Without them, life is a barren mountain.

Hexagram 32
Thunder above
Wind below

Thunder, meaning
movement, is above, and
wind, representing
gentleness, is below. Wind
and thunder go together.

Heng
Constant, regular,
persevering. Enduring,
continuous.

The Sequence and Link
When man and woman have
feelings for one another and
marry, they establish the
basis of human constancy.

Constancy

Three years, I begged heaven to bring him home.
Blinking, I glimpse him hobbling down the road,
and I hide in the mulberry and weep.
Pausing, spear and bundle on his shoulder,
he smiles. Without turning his head, he sings:
> Dynasties rise,
> dynasties fall,
> our vow shall last.

The emperor grants each warrior some land.
Brick by brick he builds our hearth: smokeless flame.
Our first child is born, and five more soon come.
Three sons, three brides. Three daughters, three bridegrooms.
Grandchildren wheedle lychee from his hand.
> Dynasties rise,
> dynasties fall,
> our vow shall last.

Fifty years gone. Conscription comes again.
Spies prowl the rooftops. Packing clothes, I sob.
My hair's so thin, it no longer holds pins.
His hands shake as he grips the wheelbarrow.
Eyes clenched, I clutch his sleeve, and still he sings:
> Dynasties rise,
> dynasties fall,
> our vow shall last.

The Statement

Constancy is to continue
without fault.
Gain through purity.
Gain by having a place to go.

The Lines

6th line ▬ ▬

Quaking constancy:
misfortune.

5th line ▬ ▬

Constant in virtue.
Like a woman: fortune.
Like a man: misfortune.

4th line ▬▬▬

No game in the field.

3rd line ▬▬▬

Inconstant in conduct:
one may be disgraced.
Persist and there will be remorse.

The Image

2nd line ▬▬▬

Regrets vanish.

Thunder and wind:
constancy.
The noble one stands
without changing direction.

1st line ▬ ▬

Dredging for constancy.
Pure misfortune. No place is gainful.

CONSTANCY is to have strength of character in both giddy and weeping times. The Oracle extends this idea to relationships. A true relationship needs constancy. This hexagram symbolizes an enduring marriage, with the husband providing leadership (thunder) and the wife providing a gentle, all-permeating influence (wind). The two trigrams are united to form a single hexagram, just as a husband and wife must remain steadily united. If that happens, their marriage will have all the qualities of *heng:* it will be constant, regular, persevering, enduring, and continuous.

Marriage's strength begins with a vow. There is a significant message for all who want to base "reality" in material things. Nothing about any material object or either person's body changes with a marriage ceremony, and yet, from that moment on, two people agree to one of the clearest points of change possible. What happens?

All that happens is that two people make a covenant with one another. They promise to love each other, no matter how much their lives change, no matter how much fortune or misfortune visits them. They promise to face life together, even if demands separate them temporarily. They promise to respect their differences, and to find strength in their similarities. By giving unselfishly to each other, each one is strengthened in a way that neither could ever accomplish on his or her own.

Marriage is not a melding of one person into another. It is the joining of one person with another—two people who remain individuals and yet are joined by a simple promise. It is the challenge, the honor, and the beauty of that one promise withstanding every adversity known to human life.

It takes two people to make a vessel large enough and strong enough to hold all the joy and happiness that come to a marriage: the sharing, the communication, the delights, the pleasures. It is the thrill of working for a home and family, and the joy of seeing daughters and sons carry on in the ultimate expression of their constancy.

The constancy required is not stubborn clinging to one position. Rather, we must have a constancy of heart and spirit. It means we have to know ourselves, and remain steady. A boat may navigate both placid lake and twisting rapid, but it does not lose its shape or cease to float.

Constancy in change means grasping the truth about yourself and your situation. It means always being honest with yourself and your mate. Without that truth—measured solely by the standard of your commitment—there is no constancy, and thus, nothing enduring.

Commitment comes first in all essential things, and then only constant cleaving to truth will nurture our promise into duration.

What does it mean to be constant if the world is in constant flux? The usual message of the Oracle is that we must be flexible and conform to the will of heaven. The idea of constancy, however, seems contrary to that. Yet the *Changes* urges us to find a constancy that can withstand the overpowering pressures of change.

The *Statement* reminds us to be steadfast and ethical, to have the will to pursue right even when surrounded by vile people, and to serve others. In these ways, you must be constant. In a world where opportunities come and go, and where there is both good fortune and misfortune, it is only the person of quiet determination who can persevere long enough to prevail. We cannot afford any flagging. The pursuit of a goal must be steady and unerring. Only then can we continue, find gain through purity of character, and press toward our destinations.

The *Lines* allude to the many images of constancy. (1) Dredging is arduous work, requiring constancy, but if we are toiling in the wrong place or with the wrong methods, there is only misfortune. (2) There may well be something missing from the text of the next line, but constancy is indeed the power that makes our regrets vanish. (3) Obviously, if one conducts oneself with inconstancy, there is only disgrace and remorse. (4) Echoing the dredging image, the image of a field without game means that constancy is useless if there is no opportunity for it to work. (5) In reading the next line, we would do well to remember that the word for "purity" also means "chastity." In tying this to a woman's conduct, the *Changes* reminds us not only of chaste character, but of the need to be subtle, compassionate, and patient. The common male traits of aggressiveness and brute force are not conducive to constancy. (6) In closing, we are given an image of wavering constancy that inevitably leads to misfortune.

The *Image* leaves us with a picture of the wise one standing firm, refusing to change direction no matter how forceful the thunder and wind might be. That is an intriguing counterpoint to the usual wisdom of yielding, and it is also a standard for everything that we do: can we choose a position that is worth standing firm for, no matter what comes?

Fleeing, huddling, even crawling may seem easier that standing firm. Yet those who understand change know that what is easiest may not be the correct choice. To stand in constancy, and what is more, to stand hand in hand with another, is a constancy of spiritual dimensions.

Withdrawal

Hexagram 33
Heaven above
Mountain below

Two yin lines appear at the
base of the hexagram. The
dark powers approach, and
the yang powers retreat
before them.

This hexagram refers to
the sixth month (July–
August), when the approach
of yin winter can already be
sensed.

Dun
To escape, to run off. To
cheat.

The Sequence and Link
For anything to endure, it
must yield before change.

Swinging my helmet, I chortle.
What joy to chase their fleeing dust!
   I do not see
why the general yanks his reins
and raises his flag to retreat.

Five decades pass. A magistrate,
I have proof of treason. Eunuchs,
   teeth sharp as wolves',
stop me, and then I realize
too late: I have no flag to raise.

No one will speak for me at court.
I give bribes to my former men,
   then flee in shame
to a mountain hut, and ponder
what my general knew so well.

The Statement

Withdrawal. Continue.
Small gains in persisting.

The Lines

6th line ——

Wealth withdrawn.
Nothing but gain.

5th line ——

An excellent withdrawal.
Pure fortune.

4th line ——

A fitting withdrawal.
For the wise one, fortune.
For the inferior one, evil.

3rd line ——

Disease and evil come with withdrawal.
Control servants and maids for fortune.

2nd line — —

Hold using yellow ox hide,
but do not declare victory.

1st line — —

Withdrawing at the tail of evil.
No use to have a place to go.

The Image

A mountain under heaven:
withdrawal.
The noble one keeps
distant from vile people,
not with hatred,
but with dignity.

WITHDRAWAL is one of the most important lessons of change. Here we see withdrawal compared to the shortening of daylight as winter approaches. We are reminded that yin and yang are two sides of the same whole. As the earth has dark and light sides at any one time but is still a whole planet, a year has a time of great light and great darkness but is still a whole year. Receding is therefore a natural part of all cycles.

We must understand how to withdraw without abandoning our own purposes. Indeed, we can sometimes better advance by first retreating. We must not desire constant progress. That is too rigidly yang. Utilizing retreat is to use yin's yielding power.

When evil threatens us, it is wisdom to withdraw. But how far? Simply because we began this image with the withdrawal of light during fall and winter does not mean that our escapes need to be similarly slow. No, withdrawal can be made short or long, slow or fast. The time and distance are not determined by outside forces but by our own decisions.

For example, if someone tries to hit you, it is hardly heroic to take the punch in your face. If you can dodge, why not? But do not run away! That is not the withdrawal we are speaking of here. Strike back immediately, for when your opponent has reached full extension, the gates of vulnerability are open. No one can strike without opening themselves to counterattack. So you must return the attack at once. That is why a fight is a series of numerous jabs, thrusts, parries, retreats, and advances.

We may rarely have to use this principle for an actual fistfight. But we do face conflicts every day. If we experiment with give-and-take, with creating emptiness where the other expects to hurt us, we are working with the idea of withdrawal.

The idea of a superior person and an inferior person arises frequently in studying change. When we strive for equality and respect among people, it may be uncomfortable to talk of superior and inferior. The fact is that inferior people do exist and they will be oppress us at some point in our lives.

The *Statement* tells us that for strategic withdrawal to work you must be persistent. Keep your wits and remain calm. Alternate yielding with advance to be superior. Turn the circle, with yourself as the center. Search for small gains now: retreat, but maintain your determination.

Concealment is a tactic that accompanies withdrawal. That is neither capitulation nor cowardice. It preserves us and avoids repercussions.

The *Lines* discuss various forms of such a withdrawal. (1) At first, we are at the end of favorable times (the tail), and we seek to withdraw. Nevertheless, harsh times are upon us, and no place will be a haven. (2) We can try to approach the situation by strength (binding with ox hide), but we should not be overly confident yet, for although we have withdrawn and executed our strategy, the outcome is not yet known. (3) In some situations, withdrawal will also tow difficulties along with us (disease and evil). Those who are our servants and maids may try to take advantage of this situation. Control them if you would want fortune. (4) The completely opposite situation is shown here, where there is the correct withdrawal. Then, the wise ones prosper, but the inferior ones do not. (5) Better still is the excellent withdrawal done in such a way as to spare all conflict. This leads to pure fortune. (6) Perhaps the best withdrawal is the one that allows us to leave with wealth. That is, we are withdrawing from a situation with our resources and gains intact.

The *Image* deals with a situation that frequently confronts the wise person. It shows a situation in which a wise person is hampered by the small, inferior, or vile person. It also alludes to the common person who wishes to undermine the wise person. Such a person cannot understand the subtlety of one who comprehends withdrawal, and so he or she opposes the wise person.

Those who study change will always be in the minority. When we are hemmed in by inferior people, we should withdraw from them, and hold them at a distance. That is not elitist. We are trying to perfect ourselves, and we should not allow ourselves to be bothered by fools and devils.

There will also be times when you find yourself carrying the weight of many people who depend on you but who give you neither credit nor respect. When that happens, withdrawal is again a good strategy. Leave them. Let them fall, still uttering their absurd abuses.

The Oracle advises us to avoid open conflict with inferior people. Instead, we should withdraw from them. It further warns against being hateful. We should not despise the inferior, no matter what they do. Instead, we must always keep our dignity so that we are never compromised by the vile. Most emphatically: we never embroil ourselves in angry struggle. To do that is to lose ourselves by descending to the level of the inferior. Here, heaven withdraws from the mountain. That is the wisdom of withdrawal.

大壯

Great Vigor

Holding leather taut to the bits,
　　I pull ten horses back.
　　My legs gouge furrows in the dirt.
　　　　　The king awards me gold.

It takes two men to pull my bow;
　　I can draw it double.
　　My arrows pierce the center dot.
　　　　　The king awards me land.

I sing my feats to my teacher.
　　He squints. "You may be strong,
　　but tell me how you lift these books."
　　　　　"Like the sun dries a pool."

"How do you travel on the Way?"
　　"When sailing the river,
　　my hand stays strong on the rudder."
　　　　　His eyes close and he nods.

Hexagram 34
Thunder above
Heaven below

Four yang lines enter the hexagram. Thunder combined with heaven symbolizes great strength.
　　This hexagram is associated with the second lunar month (March–April), when the yang spring grows stronger.

Da Zhuang
Da: Big, large. Great. Much. Very, highly, extremely. Eldest, senior, full-grown, adult. To enlarge, to make great.
　　Zhuang: Big, great. Strong, robust, vigorous, sturdy. Portly, stout. To strengthen, to improve. Prime of one's life.

The Sequence and Link
After receding, there will come a return of great strength.

The Statement

Great vigor, gainful purity.

6th line ▬▬ ▬▬

**A ram butts the hedge and cannot pull out
or escape. No place is gainful.
First difficulty, then fortune.**

5th line ▬▬ ▬▬

**The ram is lost easily.
No remorse.**

4th line ▬▬▬▬

**Pure fortune. Regrets vanish.
The hedge breaks: entanglement is gone.
Strong as a great car's axle blocks.**

3rd line ▬▬▬▬

**The inferior exert strength, the superior
exert not. Persist in harsh times.
A ram butts a hedge, entangling his horns.**

The Image

2nd line ▬▬▬▬

**Persist.
Fortune.**

Thunder in heaven above:
great vigor. The noble one
is never without reverence
and does not fail
in conduct.

1st line ▬▬▬▬

**Vigor in the toes:
advancing brings certain misfortune.
Uprightness brings fortune.**

GREAT VIGOR: no one can go through life without strength. Whether you have to lift a sack of rice, push a branch out of your way, or help a companion who stumbles, you need strength. Those who weaken themselves through laziness, poor health, or foolishness have made themselves into crippled sheep in a world of wolves.

Yet there is much to learn about strength, at least according to those who follow change. Strength to them is not the mere charging of a ram. Great vigor is far more subtle than that. Even the strongest person will tire. Therefore, there are certain ways to apply our strength.

The Oracle observes that applying linear strength is tiring: a piston that must go up and down wears quickly, whereas a flywheel turning around a smooth and well-lubricated axle continues longer. Applying strength circularly is one of the central applications of the way of change. As spring rises after the decline of winter, we must be able to apply the circle to most of what we do.

There is a martial art based on the *Changes,* called Baguazhang (Eight Trigrams Palm). It is the art of using circular strength. The fighter never blocks head-on, but deflects, catches the opponent in a circular motion, seizing or throwing him or her when the strike has been fully extended, and then striking back with centrifugal force. By using the force of their turning bodies and twisting limbs, such fighters' actions are far more powerful than the back-and-forth jab-jab-jab of other fighters. That is why women using Baguazhang are able to defeat larger and physically stronger men. In such a case, who has the greater vigor?

Someone who understands great vigor is not afraid to use deception. That is not unethical. If a chess master shields his true intentions with a feint, no one calls that unfair. If an inventor does not reveal his project until it is ready for market, that is not wrong. If an army advances under cover of darkness, that is still honorable. Great vigor does not advertise itself. In fact, it is more powerful if it is secretly delivered before any resistance can be made.

Nevertheless, strength is best applied when we walk a righteous road. There are pragmatic reasons for that. If we accord with what is fair and right to others, we do not waste our strength fighting for something that no one supports. If we are doing what is morally right, there is no risk that we will be challenged by heroes. In fact, if we use our strength to help the weak and defend the helpless, we can count on the loyalty of other good people. Certainly, evil people get support from the other wicked people too—but they cannot count on loyalty.

Great strength is essential in life. It is made greater by a subtle mind and proper and righteous application.

If we would learn more from the Oracle, we must find a number of ways to interpret the *Statement.* Great vigor is its own purity, and we exercise it to bring benefit. But the word for "purity" also implies purity of character: moral correctness. Therefore, there is an implicit message that the exercise of our vigor brings gain only when we are correct in character. In other words, only a pure heart can direct great vigor to good ends.

Certainly, vigor is needed to accomplish anything in life. The study of change can develop a certain amount of cleverness, but there comes a time when cleverness is useless without action. We need to put forth our hands; we need to work to realize our will.

The *Lines* expand on the lessons of vigor. (1) Vigor in the toes signifies an early or slight vigor. We haven't marshaled all our strength yet, so premature action brings misfortune. Nevertheless, if we will continue in an upright way, we will find fortune. (2) This message is extended further here: we must be persistent to find fortune. (3) The Oracle begins to tell us something about the subtlety of vigor. We should not exert brute force; that is the approach of the inferior. We should "not exert," which here means we issue only the amount of strength necessary. Again, we must persist, and not be like a ram stubbornly butting a hedge. (4) Here is a situation in which fortune coincides with available vigor. The hedge breaks, and we are strong. The image of the axle blocks holding a great chariot's axle implies the strength we have to keep a situation under our control. (5) The Oracle returns to its warning against brute force. Perhaps it is referring to a situation in which adversaries lose their vigor and we ultimately are left without remorse for our position. (6) Finally, vigor exerted can still lead to difficulty. We are like a trapped ram. We are without places to go. We suffer difficulty. It is only by returning to the statement's message—to be pure—that we will eventually find fortune.

The *Image* amplifies the theme of purity. We must never fail in our reverence for the holy. We must never fail to conduct ourselves impeccably and correctly. The reverence of the wise one must direct the vigor of our body and will. Ultimately, that is the only quality that will help us persist until our vigor can be best used to meet our fortune.

Vigor itself must be kept pure, but vigor itself will bring greater purity. To have the purity of vigor—that is power indeed.

Advancing

Hexagram 35
Fire above
Earth below

Fire above the earth: the sun rising. This symbolizes easy progress and rapid expansion.

Jin
To advance, to increase, to flourish. A state in the Spring and Autumn Period. The Jin dynasty (265–420 c.e.).

The Sequence and Link
With great strength, advancement will follow.

Reins tugging in my callused hands,
I hold the stallion, as my prince
ascends the marble stairs alone.
The king and court await him at the top.

My prince has fought for fifteen years.
He is given mountains and streams.
Aristocrats and warriors bow,
leaving my lord standing above them all.

After a night of feasts and wine,
he lauds his men and parcels farms.
After donning the yellow robe,
he gives cloth to the childless and the old.

He sits as I brush the horses,
and takes his crown into his hands,
holding the hoop as if to see
the new land where no one will carry swords.

The Statement

Marquis Kang receives gifts
of many breeding horses,
welcoming them three times
in one day.

6th line ———

Advancing with their horns.
Secure by exerting: attack the town.
Harsh fortune. No fault,
but persistence brings sorrow.

5th line —— ——

Regrets vanish. Loss and gain
are no longer concerns. Going forward
is fortunate: nothing but gain.

4th line ———

Advancing like rodents.
Pure harshness.

3rd line —— ——

A loyal crowd.
Regret vanishes.

The Image

2nd line —— ——

Advancing with worry.
Uprightness brings fortune.
Receive now the great blessings
of your grandmother.

Brightness emerges above
the earth: advancing.
The noble one brightens
her own virtue.

1st line —— ——

Advancing halted.
Uprightness brings fortune, but no trust.
Be generous to be without fault.

ADVANCING happens when our own goals agree with the times. That is precisely what good fortune means. When things go strikingly well, an advantageous situation is invariably a part of that. We still say of easy success, "I was in the right place at the right time."

Let us say that the stock market is doing well, and that you happened to have had money to invest. You see your investment skyrocket along with the rest of the market. If the market had not been doing well, you could not have made such a good profit. Certainly, if you did not have capital to invest, and if you lacked the acumen to invest properly, your advancement would be poor. It takes both fortunate circumstances and personal resources to be successful.

Conversely, if you have a large amount of capital but the country is in a recession, you will not make as much money as you would have in a good market. If you are not careful, you might even lose your money. Therefore great advancement can happen only if there is a perfect meshing of the times with how ably you command your resources.

The same is true of career advancement. You have to have all the right qualities if the powerful are to employ you. Whether you are seeking a job in a company or whether you are seeking to advance in a government position, your skill and personality must match what others want. You must also be in the right place at the right time. If you fail to meet an employer, or if your skills are out of step with the times, there will be little success. Career advancement comes when you have the right skills and the right people employ you.

Creative people especially need to heed this. We must strike a balance between inner expression and social need. Our power may come from private visions, but we must also present a crafted expression to our public.

Times change quickly. Fortunes shift. You can no more depend on the stock market than you can depend on your job remaining unchanged for fifty years. We must strive to adapt. Unless you do, you will find few chances to advance.

In the image of the sun high in the sky, there is an implied warning: all times of advancement pass. If you are fortunate enough to enjoy good times, save as much as you can. Cultivate your relationships with others, broaden your support. Do not be arrogant to others; you may need their help someday. Then, even if privation should strike you, you should be able to weather it with the resources you have accumulated.

A time of advancement can be the time of the greatest danger because you may be tempted to overextend yourself. It is at this time that the caution taught by those who follow change is of utmost importance.

Scholars believe that this hexagram and the **Statement** are based on the story of King Wen's tenth son, the Marquis Kang. He is portrayed here rapidly elevated in court, honored with gifts of many horses of breeding age; the implications of vigorous and potent qualities are unmistakable. The Marquis himself is overjoyed to receive such honors not once, but three times in one day. Surely, this is a metaphor for recognition, fame, and success.

The Statement doesn't include many of the Oracle's usual warnings to be pure and upright, or to guard against inferior people. The **Lines,** however, do provide more subtle shades of meaning. (1) What happens when our advancement is halted? We can remain pure of character, but we may still not win anyone's trust. If we want to be impeccable, we must be generous in order to advance again. (2) If we are to start up again, it will be with much concern. But if we persevere with uprightness, we will find fortune. The reference to one's grandmother means that it is really the investment of the past that brings one's present good fortune. (3) Advancement is not just a matter of recognition. We need support too. Once we have that, all our regrets disappear. (4) Sometimes, our advancement can be wrong: too intense, too frantic. Then there is nothing but the prospect of harsh times ahead: we create our own danger. (5) Perhaps the best advancement is the one that is unadulterated. Our regrets drop away, and we are so locked into our fortune that even gain and loss are of secondary concern. We can advance with the prospect of pure gain. (6) The Oracle recognizes the proper need for aggressiveness and action. We attack with our horns. We exert and secure what we want. We attack the town. Our fortune comes, but it comes out of harsh and dangerous times. When war is necessary, there is no fault to this, but we must not draw the conflict out. Doing so brings sorrow.

The **Image** shows the time of advancing as outer fortune coinciding with inner power. Therefore, the wise person brightens that power. For the moment, we can prevail by virtue of our brilliance. We should take advantage of that with both vigor and subtlety. Such occasions are rare. Once we have an opening, we must enter it with all the brilliance we have.

Shine at the right time. Light may fade, yes, but when the time to shine comes, the sun has but one intensity. It never veils itself.

明夷

Hexagram 36
Earth above
Fire below

Fire, buried in the earth.

Ming Yi

Ming: Light, bright, brilliant. Clear, understandable, obvious, evident. Intelligent, clever. Eyesight. Daybreak, dawn. To state, to show. The next (as in the next day or next year). Honest.

  Yi: To eliminate, to kill, to exterminate, to execute. Injuries, wounds. Eastern barbarians in ancient China. Foreign tribes. At ease, peaceful. To level, to make smooth. Grades, classes. Common, usual, ordinary. Great, big.

  Some scholars indicate that *mingyi* may have once been the name for a bird.

The Sequence and Link
Advancing risks injury.

Smothered Light

Buried in cold
and airless dark.
Thin as a kite;
weighted with iron.
Chained with my head
near the latrine.
          You never speak.

Once every day,
one ray shines through
the crumbling brick,
and then I squint
at cockroaches
and floating dust.
          You have no friends.

I will not speak
to the jailers.
Refuse to know
their lowly names.
Instead I think
of old poems.
          You cannot last.

I hoard those words,
will not voice them.
I will keep them
one verse longer
than the sentence
that cages me.
          You will die soon.

One verse longer.

The Statement

Smothered light.
Gain is difficult: persist.

The Lines

6th line — — —
Not a bright night.
First rise into the sky,
then plunge into the earth.

5th line — — —
The smothered light of Jizi:
gainful virtue.

4th line — — —
Enter at the left front, capturing
the heart of smothered light.
Going in and out of gates and halls.

3rd line —
Smothered light on a southern expedition.
Their great chief is captured.
One cannot be hasty to establish rule.

The Image

2nd line — — —
Smothered light: injury in the left thigh.
Exert horselike strength to rescue.
Fortunate.

Brilliance
in the earth's core:
smothered light.
The noble one
governs the multitude
by obscurity—
but with enlightenment.

1st line —
Smothered light in flight, hanging wings.
The wise one travels and has no food
for three days, but finds the destination:
the host responds.

SMOTHERED LIGHT is adversity eclipsing our inner light. When fire is extinguished, it cannot return. When the sun sets, it does not rise in the middle of the night. The human heart, however, is different. It is stronger than adversity.

In many ways, this hexagram has the most important image for those who wish to learn from change. We can easily celebrate in times of good fortune, and we have no choice but to mourn when disaster is total. However, staying wise when we are oppressed is difficult—and therefore all the more essential.

When he was imprisoned, Prince Ji Chang had to maintain his balance. The future of his family and his people depended on it. Although he lacked the power to do anything immediate about his imprisonment, he nevertheless maintained his will to survive and succeed. Even after he was released, he maintained an outward facade of compliance—even as he gradually gathered the allies and armies to mount a counterattack.

His death before the overthrow of the Shang dynasty should not be read as a failure, but as a willingness to make a plan so far-seeing that it extended beyond his own demise. What mattered to him was not the ego of vindication, but the greater importance of overthrowing the Shang and establishing the Zhou dynasty.

The danger of Di Xin's tyranny did not go unnoticed by those in the Shang government. Three men—the Prince of Wei, Senior Tutor Jizi, and Junior Tutor Bigan—tried to curb the tyrant's excess. As matters worsened, Jizi urged the Prince (who was the eldest son of the previous emperor and thus a potential threat to Di Xin's power) to go into hiding.

Unable to restrain himself any longer, Bigan went to Di Xin, determined to change the tyrant's mind. He spoke for three days, until, tiring of his talk, Di Xin asked if Bigan was a sage. He ordered Bigan's heart cut out to see if it was different than that of any other person.

When he heard the news, Jizi plucked one string on his lute and undid his hair. Feigning insanity, he left the palace to live among the slaves. Di Xin ordered him hunted down and imprisoned. Finally, the Prince of Wei also went into hiding, and no one was left to save the Shang dynasty from its own king.

The actions of Prince Ji Chang, Jizi, Bigan, and the Prince of Wei all provide examples of men who faced the times of Smothered Light. When evil so tyrannizes the world, brilliant people cannot openly contest it—but they must not abandon their principles.

Both Jizi's survival and the Zhou ascendancy show that there must be renewal after Smothered Light, even if the injuries are overwhelming. Only the human heart can be stronger than tragedy—but we must be certain that its flame is not extinguished in the darkness.

This hexagram's name can mean "brilliance injured." Others interpret the name to be a reference to a pheasant, and it is quite possible that the pheasant was, at one time, a harbinger of omens. An injured bird can certainly be seen as an ominous sign. While interpreting the hexagram name as meaning a pheasant could fit in many of the Lines, it is the Image and Line 5 that seem to point toward the more general interpretation of a smothered light. When one considers that the word for "brilliance" also means "understanding" and "intelligence," many more possible meanings reveal themselves.

The *Statement* alludes to gaining through difficulty, and it also urges us to persist by being upright and pure. There is no choice but to withdraw into oneself and exert one's influence only in the most subtle ways. All these are indications of dark and injurious times through which we must safeguard our own brilliance and intentions.

The *Lines* portray different strategies as a response to our brilliance being suppressed. Significantly, they all deal with effort and movement. The first four lines may even allude to an expedition against barbarian tribes. (1) At first, the wise one travels, perhaps on a campaign. Hanging wings imply weariness; going without food for three days implies privation and struggle. But the wise one must press on, and in the end he will meet with his host and there will be important words (perhaps of negotiation). (2) In the next situation, there is injury and trouble. We must exert great strength to escape. (3) Even if we are successful—say, capturing the rebel chieftain—we must not be in a hurry to establish the purity of our correct rule. (4) It is this line that shows us plunging to the very heart of our enemy. Here the implication of smothered light shifts: we are going into the land of the unenlightened. (5) In this line, the subject changes to Jizi, the senior tutor to Di Xin; he feigned insanity (darkening his brilliance) to escape the tyrant's anger over his virtuous advice. (6) Ultimately, darkening our light is a matter of survival: the night is bright, so we must go into the earth for shelter.

The *Image* gives us a final perspective on darkening our brilliance. When ruling, we must obscure ourselves; we must not rule by bombast or fanaticism. The ruler must be enlightened, and all rule must come not from egotism but from that crucial inner light. *Truth*.

Family

She holds her lantern at the door
to say good night. In the gold light,
she is a goddess in a shrine,
opening the gateway to dreams.

As my eyes close each night, I glimpse
her mending with needle and thread.
As my eyes blink at dawn, she stands
boiling water and kneading dough.

My mother has been gone for years.
Yet her hands thread my needle's eye,
her hands put the pot on the stove
and they serve me the steaming bread.

Hexagram 37
Wind above
Fire below

The lines and their positions
support the meaning of this
hexagram. The strong yang
line at the top is the husband,
the yin line in the second
place is the wife.

   When the family is strong,
the society is strong. With
clarity and enlightenment
(fire) within families, influence
is spread outward like the
wind.

Jia Ren
Jia: Home, household, family.
A specialist in art or science.
Ren: Person, persons, people.
Jia Ren: Family people.

The Sequence and Link
When adversity is darkest,
take shelter with your family.
When a society is at its lowest, regeneration comes from
its families.

The Statement

**A family benefits
from the women's purity.**

6th line ━━━

**Be confident and dignified.
In the end, fortune.**

5th line ━━━

**The king withdraws to his family.
With no other help: fortune.**

4th line ━━ ━━

**A wealthy family.
Great fortune.**

3rd line ━━━

**The family scolds. Remorse from severity
is gainful. Women and children
laughing too much leads to loss.**

The Image

2nd line ━ ━

**No place to follow. Gifts are within.
Pure fortune.**

**Wind emerges from fire:
family.
The noble one has
substance in speech and
constancy in action.**

1st line ━━━

**A family within its own walls.
Regrets vanish.**

FAMILY is important at every stage of our lives. It nurtures and supports us in ways that no other group will. Yes, some people are burdened with dysfunctional families. The fact that such people find success difficult to achieve in life only shows the critical importance of family.

When change strikes us, we go home. If someone has died, we are called back to our families. Marriages, births, illnesses, change in fortunes, funerals—all these bring us back to our kin. Those who have strong families do well. Those who do not, suffer. The message is clear to all of us with families: lead well, and fortune will come.

In most cases, our place in the shifting constellation of family relationships changes as we grow older. We will go from being children to adults to heads of the family, only to relinquish our position to the next generation. In this way, our progression through a family mirrors the ideal of society: we begin as subjects, rise in rank, become leaders, and then retire to become sages guiding the next generation. Perhaps not all families can live up to those standards—just as few governments could rule by the ethics of the *Changes.* Nevertheless, we must still strive for the ideals.

A father and mother are at the core of the archetypal family, and in the multigenerational context of the *Changes,* they occupy a position, with children, in-laws, and grandchildren below them. Their parents, aunts, and uncles occupy lateral and higher levels. It is often given to one couple to lead the family.

The father must be strong, moral, intelligent, kind, and generous. He is the family's representative to the outside world, and goes out to work. He must be as enlightened as a righteous king. If his rule falters, the entire family falters with him.

The mother rules the inner household, and on a pragmatic level, even the father defers to her in matters of the home. The mother must be equal to the father in intelligence and strength. However, a mother will have other qualities as well: nourishment, comfort, devotion, kindness. She will temper the severity of the father.

In some households, these roles are not strictly divided between two people, nor are they divided strictly along gender lines. Nevertheless, every functioning family must come to a balance between these factors.

Then the roles of the other family members must go to support the leaders. Others may help to build the family fortunes. Some may help with children. The elders dispense wisdom and give the benefit of their already accumulated wealth. In this way, the family's prosperity will grow. When there is loyalty and cooperation, the family benefits and comforts us far more than any other group.

The family is our central matrix for much of human life. Love, sex, marriage, childrearing, childhood, morality, death, and mutual support—all are bound up in the family. Our nation is not made up of a citizenry; our nation springs from its families.

The *Statement* asserts that it is the women's power and wisdom that is essential to a family. The word used here means "purity" and "chastity," but if we think about this deeply, it is not mere chastity but the power that chastity implies. The discipline, leadership, and steadfastness of the woman determines the future of her family. If she is a good leader, the family benefits. If she is a poor one, the family will decline.

The *Lines* bear this theme out in a series of scenes. (1) At first, we are approaching our family again. We are going home and seeing the fence or wall around our family home. We go in and are relieved: regrets vanish. (2) Similarly, if we are near our home, we should persevere. The gifts are within our family, and we must reach them to share in good fortune. Again, family is our power. (3) But family is authority too, and a family must have order. In this scene, there is scolding, but if we feel remorse after such reproach, this will bring gain. The need for discipline is shown in laughing women and children—exactly the opposite of the womanly purity given in the statement. That leads to loss. (4) If we have a good family, and that family is also wealthy, there is great fortune. There are many cases of people who are successful because of family ties and support. If we are such people, we must realize that we are privileged. As long as we use our privilege wisely, all will be well. (5) Even a king needs a family. This is a significant statement, since the king was both the ruler and virtual deity. Nevertheless, when there is real trouble, withdrawing to his family is the true strength: fortune can be realized with no other help. (6) Finally, there may well be times when our fortune is slow in coming. We may have returned to our family and they may be helping us, but results are still not immediate. In that case, we must be confident and dignified because we will be successful in the end.

The demand for purity to lead a family and the patience needed to continue even when success is still distant is summed up in the *Image.* We must have substance in our speech, and we must be constant in our action. Then we can truly have the purity that is the power to lead. Let that be the quality of the matriarch, and any family will have blessings immeasurable.

Estrangement

Hexagram 38
Fire above
Lake below

Fire, in the upper position, rises upward, and lake in the lower position sinks downward. Therefore, the movement of this hexagram is one of separation. In addition, fire symbolizes the middle daughter, while lake symbolizes the youngest daughter: two sisters who live in the same house disagree.

Kui
Separation. Opposition. To squint. To stare. Unusual, strange.

The Sequence and Link
When there is separation from the family, estrangement follows.

My paper umbrella
tears on Sister's parked sedan chair.
Rain soaks my homespun dress.

At the gate, Sister takes
in her ivory fingers the quilt
that I stitched for Father.

My face burns with the slaps
from the years she called me useless.
I hide my rough, red hands.

"What excellent sewing!"
Eyes bright, she caresses the silk
and calls Mother to look.

Then it is I who see:
though their natures are not the same,
needle must go with thread.

The Statement

Estrangement.
In small matters: fortune.

The Lines

6th line ———

Strange sights: a pig shouldering mud,
a cartload of ghosts. One first draws a bow,
then lowers it. No raider— a groom. Go.
Meet the rain, and with it, fortune.

5th line —— ——

Remorse vanishes.
One's kinsmen bite the skin.
Going forward: what error?

4th line ———

Estranged, one meets the main person.
A trustworthy exchange.
Severity is without fault.

3rd line —— ——

Seeing the wagon dragged back, his oxen
taken, his men's hair and noses cut off.
Not a beginning, but an ending.

The Image

2nd line ———

Meeting one's master in the lane.
No fault.

Fire above, lake below:
estrangement. The noble
one works with others,
but remains an individual.

1st line ———

Remorse vanishes. Do not search:
a lost horse returns by itself.
When seeing the wicked, make no mistakes.

ESTRANGEMENT is the very opposite of family. It can happen to every other kind of relationship as well. A longtime friend suddenly becomes cold. A comrade who usually supports us turns hostile. We seek allies for a project, but find others against us. Frustrated, we begin to think the worst of others, and we drag out the barricades.

Opposition leads to separation. Separation leads to alienation. If the two sides never build new bridges between them, the separation becomes lasting. Alienation results, and the situation becomes dangerous: No revolution was ever begun by happy people. Revolts come from the disenfranchised.

When Di Xin degenerated into drunkenness and debauchery, ruling by murder rather than reason, others in his government began to oppose him. King Wen, in a separate fiefdom that still owed allegiance to the Shang dynasty, also opposed the emperor's moral lapses. Both Di Xin's more enlightened ministers and King Wen first tried to change the situation diplomatically. But as communication with Di Xin became more difficult, opposition grew. The Shang dynasty might not have been overthrown by the Zhou had Di Xin heard what was being said and had he worked to remedy the difficulties of estrangement.

Opposition. Separation. Alienation. Once these three factors became overwhelming, there was no saving Di Xin.

Opposition can be positive if it is managed correctly. Democratic government incorporates opposition. By having at least two sides ruling, there is a constant struggle within the government to find the superior choice in any situation. Excesses are balanced, and the government is animated by the opposing forces. Just as it takes two people to move a teeter-totter, it takes at least two political parties to make a democracy work.

Such embracing of opposition implies that the best results cannot be gained by one person's judgment. We do not trust any one person or any one political view to lead our country. We want opposing sides in balance against one another. This system is not perfect. It can also degenerate into estrangement, and the inherent inefficiency of human endeavors can sometimes dominate the process. In the long run, however, there will be progress.

If we delve deeper into this hexagram, we will find that it has multiple meanings, like the other hexagrams, and that these meanings must be understood simultaneously. Opposition, separation, and estrangement can refer to the separation of things. They also refer to the very yin-yang dichotomy that underlies all assumptions in the *Changes*. Thus, opposition, separation, and alienation can refer to separation or can refer to the inherent tension that animates all things. Nevertheless, we have to know what to do in the time of estrangement. The *Statement* tells us that this is a situation where the forces of separation are dominant and we can succeed only in small matters. We have to accept our circumstances and work within those limitations.

The *Lines* give us various examples. (1) At first, we find ourselves in two undesirable situations: we've lost our horse, and we are faced with wicked people. The advice is to relax and let the horse return on its own—which requires trust and faith—and to be wary of the wicked—which requires perception and impeccability. (2) Similarly we may find ourselves cut off from our master, but if we are without fault, we will find our master presently. (3) However, sometimes the estrangement is deep and injurious, as when we see our wagon dragged back, our oxen stolen, our forces attacked. Here, we did not start this trouble, but we must work to make sure the situation ends as favorably to ourselves as possible. (4) If we find ourselves estranged, for example, as outsiders, we must look for the chance to meet the main and influential person. Then we can be assured of a trustworthy exchange. The times of separation may be severe, but we are not to blame for them. (5) Eventually, estrangement itself must wane, and we find the beginnings of success. Then we must go forward without fear of making a mistake. (6) Estrangement may not just be social either. It can mean that we are out of touch with our own perceptions. We see strange sights, we imagine difficulties where there are none, and we take an approaching person for a raider when he may well be a friend. The rain here is a good omen, and a symbol of our confusion being washed away. When it comes, go to meet it and find your fortune.

The *Image* closes with the timeless observation that a leader can never truly be like the masses. A leader is different—strange—but that is the way it is. Although we must work with others, we must remain individuals and continue to cultivate our personal excellence. Frankly, people can turn on you at any time. The risks for a leader are considerable. If you must lead, fulfill your responsibilities but realize that you must maintain your own resources should you and the multitude one day part. Fire above the lake means that there are times when the leader must separate from the gather throng below. Fire above the lake also means that when the opposing forces of a society are joined (as the lake pools all streams), wisdom rises like the sun. Only then is there a chance of some small success in the time of estrangement.

Hexagram 39
Water above
Mountain below

Water—a dangerous
abyss—in front, behind, a
high mountain. One's way is
blocked.

Jian
Lame, crippled, slow, difficult,
hard, haughty.

The Sequence and Link
Difficulties are sure to follow
opposition and separation.

Hindered

I changed my horse three times,
but I have come too late.
The army banners fly
like wildfire in a gorge,
but they are soon engulfed
by arrows from the heights.

Men lie in groaning heaps,
enemy trumpets blare.
Their armored soldiers charge—
a row of glinting pikes.
I parry with my spear.
My sleeves are stained with blood.

They chase me to a cliff,
up to the very edge.
The river froths below.
I turn to face six men:
I can see but one gap
no wider than my blade.

The Statement

Gain in the west and south.
No gain in the east and north.
Gain by seeing the great person.
Pure fortune.

The Lines

6th line — —

Going: hindered.
Coming: enormous fortune.
Gain by seeing the great person.

5th line ——

Greatly hindered.
Friends approach.

4th line — —

Going: hindered.
Coming: joining.

3rd line ——

Going: hindered.
Approaching: reversal.

The Image

2nd line — —

The king's servant hindered—
though he did not personally cause it.

Water on top of the
mountain: hindered.
The noble one
turns inward
to cultivate virtue.

1st line — —

Going: hindered.
Approaching: honor.

HINDRANCE is to be obstructed and frustrated with only a fraction of one's options open. The *Changes* recognizes this kind of difficulty, but it also urges us to embrace and learn from our experiences.

Our lives progress as we confront difficulties. The differences between those who can cope with problems and those who cannot are a matter of skill, experience, insight, and yes, even a little luck. You may now routinely face what would have been overwhelming ten years ago. You learn new ways of operating, remember what has worked for you before. If you can simply repair what is broken or resolve a conflict, you do it—and you move on. When we have solutions for problems, formerly gigantic difficulties are reduced to minor irritations. Experience decides whether a difficulty will become an obstacle. That takes time to learn. It takes making mistakes.

We all make mistakes. If you let a mistake derail you, you go no further. If you rectify a mistake, you continue to accumulate experience, you can avoid the same problem in the future, and your stride will remain unbroken.

In this sense, all our problems are opportunities to learn more. Nobody lives in this world without seemingly discouraging troubles, and yet every day women give birth, children learn to walk, composers make new music, mathematicians return to their proofs, and painters load their brushes. Our lives do not progress in spite of our difficulties; they progress as we confront them.

Facing our difficulties takes a little luck too. As we become more capable, luck becomes less of a factor, but sometimes there is no substitute for it. Whether it is finding something lost or meeting your future spouse, a little good fortune is essential. We should move forward, confident that we will make the right decisions. We must go to meet our luck.

If you want to understand and overcome difficulties, you must be enduring, and if necessary, you must find allies. We cannot go through life alone. We need friends, comrades, family, spouse, parents. We need to align ourselves with our country and our rulers. We need the guidance of spiritual leaders. Difficulties are a given in life, but we must not be so proud that we sever our ties with others.

The net of our relationships often saves us when we fall. If our problems become too great, it is essential to find someone to guide us away from our troubles. If we cannot walk farther, we should call out to others to help us, just as we should respond to others who need help too.

What does one do when one is hindered? The superficial interpretation might be to say, "Go around it." But the *Changes* recognizes that this is not always possible. Sometimes one is blocked from going anywhere. Then what?

The **Statement** expresses this by saying we have only half of our options open to us: we can go to the west or south but not to the east or north. In such as case, we need help, and we can get this by going to see an influential person. If that person can help us, there will be pure fortune. Usually, the *Changes* advises us to rely on ourselves. However, the Oracle is wise enough to know that we may sometimes need help.

When we are hindered, the **Lines** tell us that must penetrate into the situation. Different possibilities may be hidden there. (**1**) For example, we may be hindered, but honor is approaching. (**2**) Or we may be hindered in the service to others and it is our lot to bear that difficulty on behalf of those we serve. (**3**) We may go forth, find the way blocked, and then we must be patient because a reversal of fortune in imminent. (**4**) In another case, we meet difficulties and we must wait, because others are coming to join us. (**5**) Such is also the great fortune when we are obstructed and the even more significant assistance comes from friends. (**6**) The time of hindrance is a time to be farsighted: In this last situation, we are hindered, but there is great fortune approaching. Here, we will benefit by seeing the great person, who will no doubt guide and help us.

The **Image,** as usual, turns the basic idea of the hexagram over, and gives us an alternative view that is not necessarily a contradiction but a profound expansion. Here, the water is on top of the mountain, and it is blocked from flowing away. We want to go somewhere, but we are prevented from doing so. By pointing to this natural image, the *Changes* indicates that hindrance is a naturally occurring situation. The noble one, like the water, is hindered. But the hindrance cannot change the natural purity of the water. In the same way, when we are obstructed, we must not let ourselves be clouded. We must remember that, like water, we have our own inherent purity. The water that is dammed on a mountaintop is also water that is allowed to settle. It finds its own clarity that way, just as the wise person, when hindered, turns inward to cultivate virtue and in so doing finds the clarity to act when the obstruction is removed.

Releasing

Hexagram 40
Thunder above
Water below

Thunder, movement, combined with water. A great release of dammed-up water represents liberation from difficulties.

A secondary interpretation lies in seeing thunder and rain. Lack of rain is drought. When rain comes, new growth is released, and this also represents deliverance.

Xie

To unfasten, to untie, to loosen, to undo. To solve a difficult problem. To explain, to clarify, interpret, explain. To understand. Ideas, views. To separate, disperse. To remove, to strip off. To relieve, to alleviate. To cut apart, to dissect. To discharge. To dissolve.

The Sequence and Link

Finding solutions and gaining release make difficulties fade.

Six months of sun, no clouds:
men and dogs lie panting.
The graves cannot be dug
when earth is hard as brick.

Branches split with a snap,
and dust swirls in the wells,
families take to the road:
their wagons roll from sight.

One morning, clouds appear,
as dark as ink, the air
so damp my clothes hang limp.
Then flashes break the clouds.

I run into the fields
to gulp the falling rain.
It splashes on my palms,
and floods the empty huts.

Gain in the west and south.
No cause to move forward—
then comes return, and fortune.
To have a place to go: dawn fortune.

The Lines

6th line   ▬   ▬

The duke uses this chance to shoot a hawk
from the top of the ramparts.
Nothing but gain in capturing.

5th line   ▬   ▬

The superior one rules by releasing. Fortune.
One has the confidence
of the common people.

4th line   ▬

Releasing the big toe.
Friends arrive, and with them, confidence.

3rd line   ▬   ▬

Shouldering a bundle on the back,
and riding a carriage attracts bandits:
pure severity.

The Image

2nd line   ▬

Capturing three foxes in the field,
receiving yellow arrows. Pure fortune.

Thunder and rain act:
releasing.
The noble one
pardons errors
and forgives offenses.

1st line   ▬   ▬

No fault.

RELEASING is a familiar yearning to anyone who has been trapped by circumstance. In such times of great difficulty, it is often hard to imagine an end. According to the way of change, nothing lasts forever—and that includes travail. When our troubles are loosened, it is like someone untying a hostage. That is sweet release.

Releasing means the return of fresh possibilities. The advice inherent in this hexagram is not to turn around and attempt to control the difficulties from which you have just escaped. For the difficulties here are not the petty annoyances of daily life, but life-and-death struggles. When our loved ones or our own hearts have been held hostage, we do not want to revisit the horrors. We want liberation. We want new meadows.

If you have escaped such pressures, do not look back. If you have been drawn away from your home, like someone kidnaped, leave and return to your home. If the prospects where you dwell have been exhausted, set off to explore new lands.

This is also a recommendation against vengefulness. Once you have been released from your difficulties, do not be punitive. Forgive, and move on.

We have discussed change as cyclical. Releasing reminds us that we are not condemned to cycles. We should choose to leave at any point where matters are bad. Change the context of your life as soon as there is an opportunity. True, the new situation to which you travel will have its own cycles, but they will be completely different than what you are leaving. It will be a fresh start.

There are both external and internal sources of releasing. The external sources come from our environment or from the assistance of other people. For example, a sailing ship in the Doldrums may perish unless a new wind comes along. A land caught in drought cannot survive unless new rain comes.

From an internal standpoint, we can create releasing. If those whom we lead are suffering from an overly rigid discipline, we can loosen the reins. Giving those whom we lead compliments, the freedom to make decisions, and the support that they need will do more than harsh upbraiding.

The original ideogram for Releasing combines the pictures for horn, ox, and knife. Whether this means an ox horn as sharp as a knife, or a knife curved like an ox horn, it is a reminder that we can solve problems by cutting through the knots.

Cutting to gain release is not to be undertaken lightly. Tightly bound ropes can spring apart, and the contents of the box spilled. Or surgery can cut away too much or be too traumatic. Nevertheless, the time of releasing is good and welcome in our days of striving.

Releasing quite logically follows the hindering of the previous hexagram. The previous image alluded to water trapped on a mountaintop. Here, the water is released and events begin to flow for us again. Not only that: the *Statement* shows us at the moment of the release. Until this point, we were hindered from moving forward. Now fortune returns to where we are. During the time of our stoppage, we should have remained aware and laid plans for the inevitable coming of change. Here is our opportunity. We have a place to go, and we set out for it. The dawn of our new fortune approaches.

The *Lines* give us different hopeful scenes of our release. (1) As things change, we are assured that we are not to blame for our previous difficulties. At the same time, this phrase reminds us to be impeccable in the future. (2) Lacking opportunity, like a hunter who lacks game, is also a hindrance, but now we capture three foxes and are awarded imperial yellow arrows. (3) Caution is nevertheless in order. As if amplifying the Statement of having a place to go, we must still be prudent. Setting out and riding a carriage invites robbers, and we can expect harsh times ahead. (4) Releasing the big toe may well be a symbol of new mobility. Not only that, but our friends arrive, and this brings us confidence to venture even farther. (5) The strictness and severity of a strong leader can also be a yoke on the people, and here a leader is reminded to have the "releasing" of compassion. This brings fortune and the confidence of the public. (6) Finally, there is the releasing of an opportunity to strike attackers. The hawk on the ramparts might be a hunting image, but it also alludes to invaders on the city wall. In either case, the duke is given the chance to shoot and he succeeds. There is nothing but gain in capturing the prey.

The time before a storm is a time of building pressure. Anxiety and trouble are the same. When the storm comes, thunder and rain are released, and the aftermath, when the air is clean and the sky clear, brings a great loosening of the pressure. In the same way, the noble one knows that laws and rules too strictly enforced create pressure, resentment, and hardship. Accordingly, the wise release their hold slightly, and they pardon the mistakes of others and forgive transgressions.

Releasing is sweet when it comes to us. Releasing will be sweet if we can bestow it on others. Such release is one of the most wonderful of generosities.

Decrease

The year we had cloth, my wife sewed
my pants. Now they hang in tatters.

The tax man knocks at night and jeers,
"Even your land is worthless now."

At home, the doctors turn away
when my son moans, clenching his teeth.

I stumble out, stagger alone
past arbors where the pea vines sag.

The temple has no open gate
for a man without offerings.

Clutching my empty bowl, I fall
to my knees at a roadside shrine.

Hexagram 41
Mountain above
Lake below

Compare this hexagram with
Hexagram 11, Prospering.
There, earth was above
heaven. The top line of
heaven in Hexagram 11 has
moved up to the top place
of this hexagram, symbolizing
a decrease in yang to the
detriment of the lower
trigram. Therefore, what is
below has been decreased in
favor of what is above.

Sun
To detract, to damage, to
injure, to destroy, to harm.
Loss. To reduce, to decrease.
Weak, emaciated. To ridicule,
to jeer. Wicked, mean, cruel.

The Sequence and Link
Too much loosening leads to
neglect and loss.

The Statement

Decrease. Have confidence.
Great fortune. No fault
if one can be upright.
Gain by having a place to go.
How should one act?
Two square bamboo baskets
can be used in offering.

The Lines

6th line ———

No decrease, but gain there. No fault.
Pure fortune. Gain by having a place to go.
Get servants, but not a house.

5th line —— ——

Someone gains ten groups of turtles
no one can defy. Great fortune.

4th line —— ——

Decrease your hatred.
Act quickly and you will have joy.
No fault.

3rd line —— ——

A group of three travelers
is decreased by one person.
One person travels and gets a friend.

The Image

2nd line ———

Gain is in purity, misfortune is in going.
No decrease, but gain there.

Lake below mountain:
decrease. The noble one
halts his anger
and curbs his desires.

1st line ———

In your own business, go quickly. No fault.
Consider decrease there.

DECREASE can be grinding. It can be gradual. Whatever it is, the *Changes* would have us use it to our advantage. How difficult this is! To be poor, to be ignored, to be cast aside, to see all that you have worked for slip away like your last rice falling through a hole in its sack before you can remedy it—it is hard to bear loss and yet be strong.

As a way of guiding us, this hexagram takes the concept of decrease, and views it from a number of angles. There is the outright meaning of decrease and how to face it. There is decrease in the sense of sacrifice. There is decrease as investment. And there is decrease of hatred and anger. Significantly, decrease is not viewed here as condemnation or misfortune, but rather as a dynamic mode to be used.

The first consideration is outright decrease and how we face it. We may find ourselves in poor circumstances. We may find ourselves having lost our fortunes, our families, our friends, or even our values. The attitude of this hexagram is reassuring, open, and accepting. There is no reproach. Instead, we are reminded to be confident, sincere, and firm in our devotion. Finding ourselves in spare circumstances is no call for shame. We are asked to renew our faith in ourselves and Tao, and we are asked to do so by making an offering.

Offering is decrease as sacrifice. For the *Changes,* the material value of the sacrifice is secondary. What matters is our attitude, the humbling of ourselves even in the most dire of straits. Help will come to us when we put aside egotistical desires to act by our own efforts. We cannot act alone in life; our means are too meager, circumstances are too savage. Instead, we must ask for the greater spiritual guidance we need. This requires a decrease of our egotism.

Offering, as a spiritual investment, brings to mind decrease as material investment. We cannot profit without investing. There is no gain without giving something up. In our own business, we must "lose"—invest our time and capital—in order to profit. In rearing our children, we must "lose"—give up our time, our energy, and our savings—in order to rear strong and intelligent children. If we are farsighted, we will realize that the potential for gain is multiplied by a factor of what we have given. So we should not be small-minded about the "loss" that is our investment. If we give wisely, we will gain.

Finally, we can lose or decrease as a means of personal improvement: hatred, anger, pettiness, and selfishness are qualities we can all benefit from losing. Above the political sense of decrease and increase, beyond the material considerations of loss and profit, one who follows change is always concerned with self-improvement. Losing our hatred and anger is not simply good for our characters; it actually opens us up to higher perceptions. In a spiritual sense, the decrease of our lusts, vices, and anger is the prelude to spiritual gain.

We often panic about decrease. We shrink in shame. We view it as negative. But the concepts here take us far deeper into the benefit of decrease. If we remain frightened of decrease, if we never meditate on it and look deeply into it, we will lose a crucial opportunity to broaden our characters. That is the only decrease that we cannot afford.

We must be faultless, pure, and upright. The *Changes* acknowledges how hard it is to work toward our goals when we are in times of decrease. That is why the *Statement* uses the image of two square bamboo baskets—an image of simplicity and unadorned functionality—as being sufficient for the greatest undertakings. Poverty is secondary to sincerity and determination. We must not lose hope.

The *Lines* express these twin meanings. (1) Attending to our affairs, we must be swift. Nevertheless, if we would be without mistake, we must consider reducing those affairs. (2) We gain not by building, but by first being pure within ourselves. If we do not secure this inner force first, to venture forth will bring only misfortune. If we can be pure first, there will be gain instead of decrease. (3) Increase and decrease occur more markedly on the road. Here, a group of travelers is reduced in number by one, and a single person finds a friend. We are reminded that this is all part of the flux of the journey. (4) Here, plainly, we are told to diminish our hatred (literally, "illness") and then to act quickly to find happiness. (5) As if in continuation, someone who has diminished his or her faults can then gain ten groups of turtles (the vehicles for divination and spiritual power) and be unopposed. (6) The time of decrease is ended. We will find help, but not a permanent abode.

The *Image* reinforces the need to diminish both our desires and our anger. The mountain erodes into the lake and is diminished. Our towering desires for accumulation and the massiveness of our anger must similarly be reduced. In turn, there is the promise of the mountain as symbol of spirituality and the lake as symbol of joy and sharing.

Do not be afraid of decrease. We habitually feel that everything in our lives is supposed to be win, win, win. We tell ourselves that dominating others is the measure of power. Far more subtle it is—and ultimately far more effective and healthy—to understand the nature of decrease.

Increase

Hexagram 42
Wind above
Thunder below

Compare this hexagram with
Hexagram 12, Clogging.
There, heaven was above
earth. The lowest line of
heaven in Hexagram 12 has
moved to the lowest place
of this hexagram, symbolizing
a decrease in yang to the
benefit of the lower trigram.
Therefore, what is below
benefits from what is above.

Yi
To increase, to add, to
augment. A higher degree, a
greater extent, more. Benefit,
profit, advantage.

The Sequence and Link
If we understand decrease,
gain must follow.

Our bowl is the Dipper:
    we find heaven between its stars.
Each time we tilt that bowl,
    a river spills over the rim
with a surge so strong
    no dike can stand against its flood.
But where it is shallow,
    we squat and cup our hands to sip.
The little that we take
    is more than enough to survive.

When we harvest our crops
    we do not scrape the fields bare.
We leave some plants to stand
    until they die in their own time,
their pods close to bursting.
    We hang them on a fence to dry
before storing the seeds.
    The next season, we sow again,
then go back home at dusk,
    dipping our bowls into the stream.

The Statement

Increase. Gain by having a place to go.
Advance across the great river.

6th line ———

No increase when someone attacks.
Setting the heart without constancy:
misfortune.

5th line ———

Have confidence in a kind heart.
Unquestioned great fortune.
Have trust in the kindness of my conduct.

4th line —— ——

There is a middle path. Alert the duke
to follow. Gain by working for the sake
of moving the nation.

3rd line —— ——

Increase by using unfortunate affairs.
No fault. Have trust in the middle path.
Inform the duke using a jade tablet.

The Image

2nd line —— ——

Someone increases by ten groups of turtles
no one can defy. Everlasting firmness
and fortune. The king makes offerings to god.
Fortune.

1st line ———

Gain by using great work.
Great fortune. No fault.

Wind and thunder:
increase. The noble one
sees perfection
and shifts to fit its pattern,
and corrects his own faults.

INCREASE: of all the kinds of increase we pursue, the increase of virtue is the most important. Those who gain in virtue never lose. While the word *yi,* meaning "gain," is a part of business names and terms for profit, this hexagram is not only about material gain, but also about spiritual and moral increase as well.

We are confused about the word *virtue* today. We think of it as something that moralistic school teachers extol, or as a topic confined to religious discussions. We rarely think of it as a living part of our everyday lives. Yet the *Changes* would have us make virtue not just a part of our thinking, but the central power of our daily activities.

The sages did not see virtue as the moral precepts we strain against for the sake of social order. No, they saw it as a vitality animating our actions from the core outward. In this context, virtue is a spiritual energy that asserts itself to the benefit of the possessor and all who are near. Increase, then, is the idea of building this power.

If we can increase and manifest this virtue, we can maintain our balance as other kinds of gain come our way.

One of these increases is political gain. True political gain comes from generosity to the populace, with just actions on the part of all leaders. If this happens, there is sure to be increase, even to the point of overflowing.

However, fullness leads to emptying. Therefore, the virtuous make offerings to heaven, share with those who are poor, and save resources to counter disaster. Charity and philanthropy, community service and civic generosity are all forms of this "emptying." In this way, gain ceases to be the selfish piling up of wealth and instead becomes a tool of virtue.

Another opportunity for gain is through misfortune. Decrease, injury, and suffering are universal, but wise people take advantage of misfortune. They look at themselves to see if they had any fault in bringing about their difficulties. If they find any errors, they correct them. They examine how they might have conducted themselves well, and then seek to strengthen those traits. In this way, a person of virtue can benefit even by misfortune.

We are subject to cycles if we stay within closed circumstances. If we move—if we change—the nature of the cycles changes, and we may be able to benefit. A time of increase is a time to change. New ventures can keep us going on upward trends; failure to change can lead to entropy. Those who experience success must avoid repeating what has already been successful. Unlimited increase is not possible. What is possible is to use increase as a basis for a new cycle before decline sets in. That takes courage, but it opens opportunities for greater gain.

The *Statement* expresses a time when great increase is possible. The opportunity is already here, but we must make use of it by having a direction in mind. We must forge ahead, and go past barriers. The time is with us.

The *Lines* show additional nuances. (1) At the beginning of the time of increase, we must work especially hard to meet our fortune. Little can be gained without hard work. (2) This line shows a great spiritual increase. Someone gains ten groups of turtles (the symbol of divination and longevity), which no one can oppose. There is great moral firmness and fortune. But this power must not be selfishly withheld. That is why the king makes an offering to god. The country is then aligned with the cosmos, and all is well. (3) We have to recognize opportunity. Even seemingly unfortunate affairs can be exploited for their advantages if we are moderate, and if we gain the support of someone higher than us (symbolized by the duke). (4) Of course, all gain must be handled with equanimity. Here, we see the path of moderation, and we must help our leader find it. The scale here is tantamount to joining the effort of moving an entire nation. (5) Here, the *Changes* speaks to us in the first person, and asks us to trust in the kindness of its heart and in turn to receive our unquestioned great fortune with the kindness of our own hearts. (6) Finally, the *Changes* warns us of the danger of greed. Someone attacks, with the implication that increase is wanted. In contrast to the kind hearts of the previous line, we see a heart that has no constancy. For someone who greedily attacks, as for someone who has an unchecked and unstable heart, only misfortune results from their desire for increase.

The *Image* instructs us in avoiding such an unconstant heart: we must see perfection and emulate it, shifting to fit its patterns. In the process, we must look within ourselves and correct our own faults. Only then are we open enough to receive increase.

We must always come back to virtue. Otherwise, we become wealthy bullies, whom others will eventually attack. Those who set their hearts on kindness and virtue find a constancy of power that will be everlasting. Those who gain in virtue therefore never truly lose. That is why the *Changes,* in its wisdom, urges us to think of the spiritual dimensions of increase.

Hexagram 43
Lake above
Heaven below

The three yang lines of Heaven rise to the trigram for Lake. The lone yin line at the top cannot restrain them: breakthrough comes, with a resolution of the tension that preceded it. This hexagram is associated with the third lunar month (June–July), when there are frequent rainstorms.

Guai
Defined in dictionaries as the name of this hexagram in the *Changes*. Some authorities say that the word should be *jue*: Decide, conclude, judge. Burst, break. Certain, sure, definite. To execute a person.

The Sequence and Link
The flux of decrease and increase demand decisiveness.

Decisiveness

Just as the emperor's edict arrives,
the rain begins to fall. Laughing, squealing,
my sons leap into the courtyard puddles.
I hear the royal edict and stiffen:
  it says someone has betrayed us.

Ten days of rain, the peaks dissolve in mud.
Men push squeaking carts, sons carry mothers.
I wince to watch the old levees crumble,
and order the granary gates unlocked.
  I go myself to ladle gruel.

Most standing in line are barefoot. One man
wears leather boots. While mothers clutch children,
he clutches his coat. Though the gray beard is new,
I remember those darting eyes too well.
  "Did we not meet near the border?"

"No, my lord."
            "Twelve years ago, our army
was betrayed. We never found the culprit."
"I hear the enemy beheaded him."
No, I think, you became a wealthy man,
  while my men's bones lie far from home.

I call my guard. In the man's coat lining
we find maps of our newest defenses.
"Only the premier could have shown you this."
"You have no proof." I snort. Should I wait for
  assassins' blades to prove the truth?

I send my family to join the crowd
fleeing toward the mountain passes. The spy
remains my prisoner. Despite the rain,
I mount a carriage for the capital
  as rain washes the muddy roads.

The Statement

Decisiveness. Proclaim in the royal court.
Trust in the commands. Be stern.
There will be severity.

Announce to your own city.
There is no gain in going to war.
Gain by having a place to go.

The Lines

6th line ▬▬ ▬▬

No signals:
the end will be misfortune.

5th line ▬▬▬▬▬

The amaranth mound decisively cleared:
the middle way is without fault.

4th line ▬▬▬

Buttocks without skin: one walks uneasily.
Follow like a sheep and regrets vanish.
Instead, words are heard but not believed.

3rd line ▬▬▬

Strong in the cheekbones: misfortune.
The noble one is resolute, but walks alone—
soaked by rain, angry,
with no one to blame.

The Image

2nd line ▬▬▬

Alert commands. Night after night
of fighting without relief.

Lake rising to heaven:
decisiveness. The noble one
bestows wealth
to those below
and shuns dwelling
on his own virtues.

1st line ▬▬▬

Strong in the feet:
Going forward, there will be no triumph
due to mistakes.

DECISIVENESS means to move powerfully toward your goal—but you must keep your balance. The hidden message is that true decisiveness results from accumulated force. Just as there must be a powerful surge of water for a levee to burst, factors needed for a good decision must predominate before action is taken. In that way, we avoid dangerous vacillation. If the time is not yet right for a decision, we should busy ourselves in creating the right time by building relationships with others and remaining alert for the right circumstances. Then, when the moment for decisiveness arrives, we can act with great strength.

Governing a state, purging a country of treasonous elements, or even mounting a just war demonstrates that decisiveness is not to be undertaken lightly. The lines in the hexagram itself indicate what is needed. We must first identify what is negative—whether it is a person, another country, or some cultural problem. Then we must unite in strength to attack it. Mere numbers are not enough. There must be cooperation.

All external factors must be in alignment. For example, we can decide that we are going to take a journey, but if the weather is poor or the road blocked, our decisiveness is useless. We need to arrange the world around us, as if we are gardeners arranging plants, rock, and water.

Some people confuse deliberation with indecisiveness. Others think that to question ourselves is weak. Still others declare that once we begin to march, we need no other strategy. All those views are insufficient. The time it takes to make a decision is crucial. Whether that time is one second or several weeks is not the point; we use the time the situation allows. Making a decision work, if we have properly judged the factors, is easy. It is the wisdom to make the right decision that is hard. Therefore, we must take the time to choose the right course. With experience, the time it takes to make good decisions can be instantaneous.

Everything changes, and as soon as we move, other factors shift. It is like a chess game. Each move we make changes the formation of pieces on the board—and our opponent is moving against us too. We must stay alert through the entire process.

History is filled with the stories of those who could not change, even when their decision was initially correct. Whether it is the great general ambushed or a statesman undone by changing economic factors, many people think sticking to one plan is noble. No. We must be quick to change, even as we keep an eye on our eventual goal.

The best approach is to keep a middle course. Move powerfully toward your goal, but keep your balance. In the end, that is what makes decisions real. We are right to place a great premium on wisdom. Beyond that, however, we must put that wisdom to use and make accomplishments for our decisions to be lasting.

In the *Statement,* the most dramatic time for decisiveness is when we make an announcement before the king. There is no turning back, and approval or punishment will be swift. If the proclamation is acted upon, the decision will likely have ramifications of national importance. This is no time for wavering. We must be stern, and trust in the authority of the king and the strength of our position. We must also be ready for the severity of others' reactions and the work ahead.

"Announce to your own city" means to maintain our loyalty, and to make sure our own people are prepared for our decision. Nevertheless, both in the Statement and in the *Lines,* we must remain balanced and aware of the subtleties of decisiveness.

(1) Sometimes, of course, we are decisive, but the situation is not right. We are strong, but we also make mistakes, and so advancement brings no victory. (2) Or we might be a commander, fighting night after night, but it is our will against the situation, and the fighting continues without relief. (3) Here even the noble one makes an error: he is resolute—his jaw set—but he goes on, so alone that he is soaked by rain and with no one to blame and no one to assuage his anger. (4) At other times, we may want to make a decision but we are wholly at a disadvantage. Buttocks without skin could refer to flaying or certainly great hardship. One is injured or lame. If we would follow like sheep, we would be safe. Instead, words (either words of wisdom to us, or our own attempts to persuade others) are heard but not believed. There is no connection or direction. (5) Overgrowth is cleared. We have done the work. Now it is time to return to the middle way. Only that path is without fault. (6) Decisiveness is useless without communication. In an inversion of Line 2, we are shown a situation where there are no commands or signals. In the end, that leads inevitably to misfortune.

Decisiveness rises with power and influence. Thus, the *Image* shows a lake rising to heaven: the power and momentum to decide have become overwhelming. Accordingly, the *Changes* advises a rebalancing: in making decisions, we should always consider bestowing wealth on those below us, and we must not take pride in our own burgeoning powers. The time of decisiveness is always the time for perceptiveness.

Copulating

You grip my arms with your brown hands.
Your breath—fire on my skin. My gems
glint in your eyes, their light racing
with us into the smoking night.

I hear you are brave in battle,
that no warrior escapes your lance.
Let your thrusts number ten thousand.
I shall better each one—and win.

Tomorrow, you will tell your friends
that a courtesan seduced you.
You will gulp your wine, and then swear
that women live to make men weak.

But lions become maggot food,
and a steel lance rusts in a day.
Do you not see the young men gape
over the blooming peonies?

They are like the hovering bees
who burrow into the flowers,
only to crawl out, tired and spent,
while dew glistens on the petals.

Hexagram 44
Heaven above
Wind below

This hexagram is associated with the summer solstice. Yang is at its zenith, but is on the threshold of decline. The first signs of yin's approach and the coming of winter are already here. In terms of the lines, one yin line approaches the group of yang lines.

This hexagram also represents the pleasure of sexual intercourse.

Gou
To pair off, to copulate. Good, excellent. Defined in dictionaries as the name of this hexagram in the *Changes*.

The Sequence and Link
Unexpected encounters and engagements challenge our decisions.

Copulating: the woman is powerful.
Do not marry such a woman.

The Lines

6th line ———

Copulating with a horn. Remorse.
No fault.

5th line ———

Like a gourd surrounded by willows,
and held in place,
there comes a falling from heaven.

4th line ———

The wrapping has no fish:
the start of misfortune.

3rd line ———

Buttocks without skin: one walks uneasily.
Harsh, but no great fault.

The Image

2nd line ———

The wrapping has fish. No fault.
Not gainful for guests.

Wind under heaven:
copulating.
The sovereign
issues commands
to the four quarters.

1st line —— ——

Checked by a metal brake: pure fortune.
There's a place to go, but misfortune
will be seen. A weak pig will surely falter.

COPULATING leads to chance engagements that overturn the most meticulous arrangements. The hexagram is interpreted as a woman brazenly approaching five men. In more general terms, this means that a chance encounter leads to temptation, then seduction. This results in the overturning of all that is superficially considered orderly, natural, and moral. Although the *Changes* upholds virtue and morality, it also recognizes that numerous encounters test, subvert, and destroy what has been defined as "right." Thus, temptation and seduction are right too—not in an ethical sense, but in a natural one.

Encounters alone do not lead to an overturning of our social order, the engagements do. Just as *gou* means copulation, we have to look beyond the mere contact to the entanglement and the results.

Great people throughout history have been tempted, and when they have given in, upheaval and change result. A man can be seemingly all rational—like the five yang lines in the hexagram—and then find his entire life altered by his passions—like the single yin line.

Nature is indifferent to what brings two people together. It is concerned with reproduction, ongoing transformations, and perpetuated cycles. Whether from purest marriage or heated copulation, pregnancy is pregnancy. Bastard princes have still ruled empires. Secret love children have still laid claim to great fortunes. The moralists wail, but nature flourishes.

Turning to a natural outlook, heaven and earth must continue to copulate. They are unconcerned with the morality invented by human beings. We try to pattern ourselves on heaven and earth, but heaven and earth do not pattern themselves after imperfect human beings. They are concerned with their own processes. They know that men and women must copulate too. We try to dress sex up with romance, attempt to sanction it with matrimonial fetters, but we cannot domesticate the wild impulse that creates the generations. As autumn follows summer without fail, copulating is an indelible part of human existence. It all has to do with the greatest imperative: change.

In light of this, this hexagram conveys an important message to an enlightened leader. No organization can remain stable. Just as the five yang lines represent nearly perfect order, unity, and harmonious rule, there will also be at least one person who is inferior, scheming, selfish, and lustful. A good leader must have a sound strategy for identifying and containing such a person. Neither appeasement nor outright battle is wise. It is the middle course that is most successful.

That is why understanding the situation of Copulating can determine who is a good leader and who will be subverted.

When we read the *Statement* closely, we must look at it as blunt advice to a man who lustfully copulates with a woman. By implication, the woman may be powerful and attractive, but not necessarily the right kind of woman to be a wife. Looking deeper into this metaphor, we can apply this view to any situation in which we are drawn into a great involvement. The situation is powerful and strong, but it will not lead to constancy and flourishing.

This lust for pairing is the undoing of a man. The five yang lines allude to a man nearly perfect in his manhood. They represent overwhelming male power—but it is easily absorbed by the single yin line. The man moves, and his perfection is lost.

We must look beyond any judgments about gender or chauvinism. The situation could just as easily apply to a woman, or to situations beyond a man and a woman. The primary message of this hexagram is that the involvement we are so invested in masks other problems.

As usual, the *Lines* lead us into more subtle considerations. (1) Copulation means involvement, and here, one is bound to a metal brake, but this is initially good. But then one's goals or destination lead to misfortune, and the image of the weak pig could represent either our fortune or our vitality: we are bound to a situation that leads to weakness and misfortune. (2) Another kind of involvement is described by a wrapped fish. There is no fault, things are seemingly accounted for, and yet the guests do not gain (or, to look at it another way, the guests bring no gain). (3) Buttocks without skin and halting steps already sketches our disadvantage. The times will be severe, even though we are not at fault. (4) Now we look into the wrapping, as in Line 2, and the fish is gone. We thought we had something, and now it is gone. (5) Only this one line hints at something positive. The melon (symbol of fertility) is enfolded in willow branches, and gifts fall from heaven. Only here do the enticing factors yield a true reward. (6) Finally, we are lost to copulating, and there is only remorse. The phrase "no fault" here should be a reminder that we should try to be without fault and therefore ward off remorse.

The *Image* shows the time correctly used, when sovereign works with heaven as a perfect pair, and with citizens as a perfect pair. The right commands are proclaimed to the four quarters, and all is in harmony. Copulating need not be bad. The Image reminds us that it is good in many cases, and, as with heaven and earth, the very basis for the cycles of change.

Hexagram 45
Lake above
Earth below

Lake above the earth: water has pooled, or gathered, into one place.

Cui
To gather, to meet, to congregate. A thick or dense growth of grass. A group, a set.

The Sequence and Link
Engagement leads to gathering of people and efforts.

Collecting

Gold armor, plumed helmet, tasseled spear, sword.
I am the guard of the sacred cauldrons.

Jade chimes sound, princes line the steps and bow.
The shaman leads the way as brass horns sound.

The son of heaven rides his sedan chair
over the dragon path no man dares walk.

He mounts the altar, prays for rain and rice.
The shaman drills and heats the turtle shells.

A flock of blackbirds wheel across the sky—
thousands of birds, rising, falling, turning.

The shaman stops, but I already see:
only heaven grants and takes away life.

That is why I must ask: if he can divine,
why should the emperor need an armed guard?

The Statement

The king draws near to the temple:
gain by seeing a great person.
Make an offering with purity,
using great sacrificial beasts. Fortune.
Gain by having a place to go.

The Lines

6th line ▬▬ ▬▬

Exclamations, tears, and sniveling.
No fault.

5th line ▬▬▬▬

Collecting brings position. No fault
that there is no trust.
Great everlasting constancy dispels regret.

4th line ▬▬▬▬

Great fortune, no fault.

3rd line ▬▬ ▬▬

Collecting like sighs of regret.
No place is gainful.
Depart without fault. Slight regret.

The Image

2nd line ▬▬ ▬▬

Led by fortune. No fault.
Trust the gain of the summer sacrifice.

Lake above the earth.
Collecting. The noble one
collects the tools of war
to guard against
unforeseen danger.

1st line ▬▬ ▬▬

A trust that cannot reach conclusion:
there is confusion, there is collecting amid commands.
One grasps for smiling results—no help.
Depart without fault.

COLLECTING means the gathering of people together. Previous images have described other kinds of collecting: army, assembly, community, enthusiasm, even family. These showed the beginning formation of groups. Gathering addresses larger and more complex groups such as a nation.

Gathering also follows the previous hexagram, Copulating. In its image of sacrifice and ceremony, Collecting speaks to the sanctioning of even unorthodox unions and the integration of that change into the whole of society. On another level, we can also look on Copulating as symbolizing the evil person in a government. Here, Collecting speaks to the reaffirmation of bonds once evil has been identified and eliminated.

The hexagram shows two yang lines in the midst of four yin lines. The two yang lines symbolize the ruler and prime minister. A collecting of national unity and advancement cannot be strong unless the two highest leaders work together. Leading a country benefits from a double perspective. The two leaders must be compatible with one another and yet use the strengths of their different experiences and viewpoints. Ideally, this expansion of possibilities will give a wider wisdom to their rule.

Once we understand the importance of the two leaders, we can turn to the strong image of sacrifice and ritual. Even the strongest of human governments must integrate itself with the larger cosmos. The emperor aligns himself with heaven and so integrates the entire empire with the cosmos.

In contemporary government, we do not like to admit to this connection. Our political leaders might invoke gods, but we do not like them to delegate any actual responsibilities to deities. In the same way, our governments show their ambivalence toward anything greater than their rule. We do not easily acknowledge the importance of international relations, we have a wavering attitude toward ecological concerns, we will not make any concessions for the economy of future generations—especially if it means we will have to spend too much of our own money now. All too often, the rulers act as if they are the top of our hierarchy.

Collecting shows us a continuing effort to integrate the outer with the inner. That is not mere "nature worship," but a far more sophisticated approach to governing. In basing our governing and our lives on natural patterns, we are hoping to find better ways of organization, better means of getting along with one another.

However, we must neither rely on our love of nature nor take the patterns of nature literally. We must adapt and create. Those who seek to run a government exclusively on omens do as badly as those who ignore them completely. The leaders in Collecting must realistically assess themselves, the people, and heaven above. It is from that true awareness that true service emerges.

Thus, the *Statement* alludes to three major kinds of collecting. First is the collecting of the human with the divine: the king draws near to the temple to make an offering, closing the circle from the divine to the human by his act of devotion. Second is the collecting together of people. This is shown in the Lines. Finally, the Image depicts the collecting of the tools of war in preparation against the unforeseen.

The Statement's advice is therefore aimed at continuity. "Gain by seeing a great person" may well be a reminder that even the king needs the guidance of a wise person. "Gain by having a place to go" means that a strong course of action is possible.

The *Lines* delve into the dynamics of collecting people together. (**1**) In some cases, our efforts cannot develop: there is no trust, our attempts to collect are made in confusion and conflicting commands, and our reaching out is futile. It is no fault for us to leave. (**2**) On the other hand, sometimes collecting is easy: fortune beckons, we follow, and there is no fault. However, we are reminded to align ourselves with heaven through the summer sacrifice. (**3**) At other times collecting is painful. Our actions accumulate signs of regret. There is no possibility of success, so we must leave with lingering remorse. (**4**) Of course, the best collecting comes with great fortune. When this happens, we must remain without fault. (**5**) At the height of the time this hexagram describes, all the collecting together brings position. That position is high and firm. Although others will not trust us, that is not our fault. The way to deal with this is great and everlasting constancy. Only with that will we dispel all regrets. (**6**) At the end of this hexagram, all is disintegrating. We exclaim, we weep and snivel. The problems are not our fault, but there is nevertheless no chance for success.

The *Image* shows a lake collecting on the earth. The wise person also collects the means to guard against the unforeseen. How fascinating that a book of divination mentions the unforeseen! It is not magic but devotion to heaven, dedication to leading the people, and the wisdom of marshaling all one's personality and resources that is the true means of action.

We have seen hexagrams that predict catastrophes and disintegration. In the time of Collecting, the wise prepare so that the unity of the group cannot be shattered by the calamities of the future.

Hexagram 46
Earth above
Wind below

The lower trigram, Wind, also symbolizes wood: a shoot ascending through the earth.

Shang
To rise, to raise, to ascend. To advance, to promote. A unit of measurement, especially for grain.

The Sequence and Link
When the gathering of a nation has been successful, people will be promoted and the nation will rise in power and prosperity.

Rising

For the third time, I fail
the examinations.
I trudge the road toward home.

I slump against a tree,
tilt my chin and behold
the forest's tallest fir.

Above its fire-scarred bark,
branches embrace the sun
and leaves dance in the wind.

How can I ever soar
as high as this old tree
where the birds sing at dawn?

The Statement

Rising. Great continuing.
Act now to see the great person.
Do not be distressed. Advance southward:
fortune.

The Lines

6th line ▬ ▬
Rising in the night.
Gain by unceasing firmness.

5th line ▬ ▬
Pure fortune.
Rising up the stairs.

4th line ▬ ▬
The king makes offerings on Mount Qi.
Fortune. No fault.

3rd line ▬▬▬
Rising into an empty town.

The Image

2nd line ▬▬▬
Trust the gain in the summer sacrifice.
No fault.

Wood growing in the
center of the land: rising.
The noble one is mild,
gradually raising what is
tiny into the tall and great.

1st line ▬ ▬
Truly rising.
Great fortune.

R ISING is an image of rapid progress, of great and joyous ascension. It is the thrill of having fortune on your side, of a rapid rise from obscurity to the heights of power and glory.

Are you ready? You may have worked hard, you may have great determination to reach your goals, but will you act when your goals loom within your grasp? For example, if someone has been working to join the government and is suddenly selected for a powerful position, she must marshall her utmost intelligence, will, and stamina—or she will not remain in that position for long.

In order to maintain balance in the time of rising, we must rely on three qualities emphasized in the *Changes:* virtue, humility, and reverence.

Virtue is both a sense of ethics and a force of personality. Being ethical changes us. It purifies us. In the minds of those who follow change, such purification is essential to becoming a superior person. The most moral person is not the one who thinks about doing right. It is the person who instinctively *does* right.

A superior person, confident in virtue, is a tightrope walker who no longer fears heights or worries about balance. Balance and walking become automatic. Similarly, an expert martial artist no longer worries about tactics or strength. Such a warrior fights without thinking, letting the long years of cultivation create the movements. Effortlessness is the sign of deep virtue. We need that effortlessness if we are to keep our balance while rising.

Arrogance has been the undoing of many who have been rapidly promoted. Thus, humility is crucial. At the least, you will not overlook problems if you remain modest. The arrogant miss the very seeds of subversion because they are busy reveling in their position, indulging in wine and drugs, rutting, and buying expensive playthings. The humble person looks down— where the seeds of both good and bad are sprouting.

The tree bears fruit to feed others; sacrifice allows us to distribute the fruits of our own rising. In making offerings, we give to charity, we serve others, and we distribute wealth to the people below. In this way, we create a wider base to support our own position even as we bring benefit to others. At the same time, we must also look above, remembering to give thanks to our gods and to remain integrated with the spiritual world. In this way, we avoid retribution both from above and from below.

We are reminded in the *Statement* to seek the great continuing. At this point, guidance is indispensible, so we should immediately seek the help of a great person. We should remain calm and advance southward (toward the sun, open fields, and gentle winds). Then we will find fortune.

The treatment of the *Lines* is mostly positive. (1) From the beginning, things are good (as a good seed in good soil begins well). There is true rising and great fortune. (2) As with other hexagrams, we are urged to keep our relationship with heaven in mind. We must trust in the summer sacrifice and remain without fault. (3) The message of rising into an empty town is a warning, but there is no judgment attached; we will determine our own fortunes. When an army charges into a town and finds it empty, the soldiers must question themselves. Is it an ambush? Or have our enemies fled? In the same way, we must determine what it means when we rise into an empty town. (4) As in Line 2, the king here makes a sacrifice. Mount Qi saw the beginning of the Zhou dynasty, so this is an optimistic image of a new and idealistic venture. (5) As in many other hexagrams, success is portrayed as promotion. Certainly, this is a kind of rising too, and we are rising up the stairs as someone who is being honored by the king might do. (6) Finally, it is thought that trees grow day and night. What a tree accomplishes is through a constant effort both night and day. We must be like that too, and then we will gain by our constancy and firm will.

The *Image* pulls the various parts of the Statement together. We are not to be distressed, we must seek further to the south, the Statement says. If we tie the great person mentioned there to the noble one of the Image, we can see the importance of a guide or even a master: he or she will raise us gradually from what is tiny to what is great. If there is any confusion as to what kind of person to seek, the Image should make the qualities abundantly clear. The other way to look at the Image is to imagine ourselves as the noble one. We must be mild. We must be patient to raise what is small into what is great. The hidden meaning, of course, is that what is raised in this manner is difficult to oppose, just as a man cannot uproot a tree with his own strength. Similarly, we must aspire to such stability in all our risings.

The sage guides us, lifts us, inspires us to go higher. When we are mature, we occupy the great heights of our former master. Then we are the master, and it is only fitting that we turn, bend our backs to extend our hands, and help others achieve their own rising.

Distress

Hexagram 47
Lake above
Water below

A lake drains away into a
deep pit. The lake is thereby
exhausted. Joy, represented
by the lake, drains away into
the dangerous hole, leading
to feelings of oppression.

Kun
Difficult, hard, poor, tired,
weary, fatigued. To trouble, to
worry, to be stranded, hard-
pressed.

The Sequence and Link
Rapid ascending must
eventually meet obstacles
and difficulties.

"My horse bucked and threw me;
I crawled from the brambles, cut and bloodied.
I should have seen the signs.
But I shrugged off my luck.
Even as I gambled away my house,
I swore I would win big.

"My wife turned pale, and bled
unchecked for months. We quarreled every day
over my foolishness.
But I had not yet learned.
I bullied others with my fists,
and cut them with my tongue.

"Two years ago, my son
was arrested for treason. I lost him
to stone walls and iron bars.
Only then did I stop
and repent. I gave silver to the poor,
and paid to build a shrine."

The stranger leaned forward
rolling one eye, and grinned, then asked me
if I would buy him wine.

The Statement

Distress. Continue.
For a pure and great person: fortune.
No fault. What is said is not trusted.

The Lines

Distressed by vines and creepers.
With anxious speech and acts, one repents.
Repent and go forward to fortune.

5th line   ▬▬▬

Hacking off noses, hacking off feet. Distressed
by vermillion sashes.
Then, slowly, there is talk.
Gain by making offerings and sacrifices.

4th line   ▬▬▬

Progress is gradual.
Distressed in a metal car.
Regret will end.

3rd line   ▬ ▬

Distressed by rock, seized in thistles.
Entering into his palace, not seeing his wife.
Misfortune.

The Image

2nd line   ▬▬▬

Distressed with wine and food.
Vermilion sashes come from all directions.
Gain by making offerings and worshipping.
Going: misfortune. No fault.

A lake without water:
distress. The noble one
devotes her life
to fulfill her will.

1st line   ▬ ▬

Buttocks distressed by tree stumps.
Entering a dark ravine.
For three harvests, meeting no one.

D ISTRESS, for the superior person, can yet be a time of great success. Although difficulties hamper us, or we fail to solve our problems, or weariness drains into exhaustion, there is a secret in the maelstrom of distress that can yet help us.

If we were once the soaring tree of the preceding hexagram, we now find ourselves in a ravine, with no room for roots, no sunlight for leaves. Some people find poetry in stunted trees, but stunting never means a long or healthy life.

Distress is when self-possession is most needed. We must know ourselves, and know what we want. Otherwise, perseverance becomes endurance without reason.

It is precisely during this time that we must keep our intrinsic values. When nothing works, we must return to what we most deeply believe. To surrender to distress is to lose all our meaning. To keep our values is to work toward victory. When our troubles end, we will be well positioned to make progress again.

So if only small acts are open to you, perform those small acts. If darkness is pervasive, make use of the darkness. Vines may trap us, but we can make them into ropes and baskets. We can make something useful of misfortune only if we know what is right. We must have the wisdom to know that distress will end.

One of the greatest worries is poverty. We are hungry and vulnerable to other people, distressing us all the more. Poverty cannot be overcome all at once. But we can gradually build our resources through education, hard work, and savings.

Some people are surprised by this, thinking that spirituality means being nonmaterial.Being nonmaterial is not the same as being without wealth. We can utilize the freedom that wealth provides, and not be enslaved to riches. By using our wealth to help those more unfortunate than ourselves, and by offering our wealth to higher purposes, we can learn to handle wealth and mitigate the chance for disaster.

The hexagram of Distress does not just mean misfortune that happens to us. It is also a warning not to oppress others. That is easy, you might think: you are sure you will not be cruel to others. However, many have been surprised—and have regretted—how sudden fortune changed them. Those are the people who have not refined their inner virtue. Those are the people who ride with fortune. Those are the people who will be pulled under in times of distress.

One of the principal strengths of the *Changes* is how it gives encouragement and guidance when circumstances are bad. In the **Statement,** we experience serious distress, symbolized by the line "What is said is not trusted." We are sincere, but no one believes or supports us. This sense of isolation characterizes the misfortune so often mentioned in the *Changes.* The Oracle does not mind adversity, but it considers those times when we find ourselves isolated and alienated to be among the worst of predicaments. Nevertheless, it says, "continue." We must look for the subtle strands that we might follow to new fortune. If we emulate the purity of a great person, and we remain without fault, we will be successful.

A bad situation can always get worse, and the *Lines* picture different kinds of distress by showing the subject of each line isolated and abandoned. (**1**) In the beginning of the situation, we are distressed by tree stumps, we enter a dark ravine, and we meet no support or help for three lonely harvests. (**2**) Even if it seems we are successful (eating good wine and food), trouble comes; the vermillion sashes represent government officials coming to arrest us. Here, there is the possibility of escape if we are reverent and seek help from above, but to act strongly would be unfortunate, and we must be careful to remain without fault. (**3**) The next line pictures a man who is distressed by rock—perhaps by a rock slide, or perhaps by having rocks thrown at him—and he also is caught in thistles. He runs home, only to find that his wife is not even there to comfort him. (**4**) Even if we escape some trouble, our business is slow to develop. We may have a metal car—something rare in ancient times—but we are still distressed. However, our regrets will come to an end. (**5**) Official trouble is again shown. Hacked noses and feet allude to criminal punishment, and the sashes show us surrounded by officials. But there is a chance to negotiate, and we will have to make sacrifices to escape. (**6**) Perhaps the worse distress is the one we cause ourselves. Distressed by the vines and creepers of our own doubts, guilt, and errors, we must learn to repent. Then we can go forward into fortune.

The *Image* shows a lake drained of water: Distress is to lose the very substance that gives us life. Nevertheless, look at what the noble person should do in this situation: she must not abandon her faith in herself. She must devote her life to fulfilling her will. To have such strength when one's lake is drained is truly to have spiritual strength.

Devote your life to following your will: there are few other words so worth remembering.

Hexagram 48
Water above
Wind below

The lower trigram here represents wood. The image of wood paired with water alludes to the ancient wells, which were sometimes lined with wooden boards, and which had wooden poles above for lifting buckets of water.

Jing
Well.

The Sequence and Link
When oppression has exhausted all, there must be renewal by going back to the source.

Well

The prince orders the village moved
to a site he says is lucky.
The whitewashed walls and black tile roofs,
the towers that honor heroes,
even the roadways and the docks—
his clever men can move them all.
But none of them can move a well.

I have skill too. I plait new rope
before the old one frays, cut wood
before the old bucket has leaked.
Let him take the town. I will stay.

The Statement

Well. A city may change,
but the well does not.
It does not lose, it does not gain.
In spite of all who come and go from a well,
it remains a well.
But if the rope cannot reach,
or if the well's vase is upended:
misfortune.

The Lines

6th line ▬ ▬

The well collects fully. Do not cover it.
Have confidence: great fortune.

5th line ▬▬▬

The well of a clear cold spring: drink.

4th line ▬ ▬

The well lined with brick.
No fault.

3rd line ▬▬▬

The well is dredged, but no one drinks.
My heart is anguished. Water
could be drawn. If the king understood,
we would instantly receive happiness.

The Image

2nd line ▬▬

The well bottom gushes carp.
A broken jug leaks.

Wood above water: well.
The noble one encourages
the people and lends them
assistance.

1st line ▬ ▬

The muddy well does not feed.
No birds come to an ancient well.

WELL: draw from it, and you draw from the source. No matter how advanced a civilization becomes, its foundations depend on nature. A source of water cannot be replaced. Whether a town is built around a well or not, the well remains. If a town prospers and becomes ornately decorated, the well needs no decoration. If the town declines, the well is not ruined. It remains a constant source.

If the town is moved, the well stays: what is human is forever superficial compared to nature. If a new town is to be established, a good source of water is essential. Civilization gathers around natural sources of sustenance. Great cities line the banks of wide rivers. Great fortresses stand on steep peaks. Great navies sail from deep ports. In the same way, we can live only where there is water.

We have gotten quite far from an agricultural way of life. Many of us do not know how to plant a field, gather harvests, or mill grain. The supply lines from distant fields to cities are lengthy and twisted, and yet we can prosper only because we have these lines. These ties should be reaffirmed on both practical and spiritual levels. On a practical level, we must maintain our supply of water and food. On a spiritual level, our understanding deepens the more we dwell on the sources of our existence.

A good well cannot be exhausted, given the responsible and measured use of the water. No one should be barred from drinking. In fact, everyone understands the hospitality of offering a drink of water—as anyone would help a person weak with thirst. The water comes to us freely from the earth, deposited by the last winter's rains.

This free use of a well is a metaphor for how we should conduct our lives. If we are careful and healthy in our conduct, we will be replenished each day. Accordingly, we must give all that we can today, knowing that tomorrow will bring new support. Those who are narrow and selfish with their energies grow smaller, not greater. Give everything that you can. Do not hold back: unless water is drawn from a well, new water cannot flow in.

Water from the earth is wonderfully pure, refreshing, and invigorating. Our scientists can find little different about this water in their laboratories, but those who drink from the wellsprings know better. Expensive bottled water and manufactured beverages cannot help us in the way a well can. Eschew the artificial. Go to the source.

The *Statement* is a meditation on what is constant in this life. Although the premise of the art of change is that nothing is lasting, there are yet some things in life that are quite constant by a human measure. The well is one of these things. In a study of change where so much is in flux and therefore of limited reliability, we are right to look for those sources that are reliable and sustaining. The well, gift of water from the earth, stays in one place. The city may change all around it, or the human settlement might disappear altogether, but the well remains. People drink from it; it is not exhausted. If no one drinks from it, it does not overflow. Its water may be drawn out, and it may be used for many purposes, but it remains a well.

It is we who go to the well. So if our rope is not long enough, or we spill the water before we can get it out, the result is misfortune. On a more general level, this is a lesson for all the resources in our lives. We go to the trouble of establishing ourselves where we can thrive, but if we do not fully take what we need, the misfortune is truly our own doing.

The *Lines* continue the consideration of a well and the people who use it. (1) One consideration is a well that is not good. A muddy well sustains no one. An old well does not even attract birds. (2) A well must be in good repair. Here, the fact that the well gushes fish is a sign that other waters have breached the well walls. That is just as bad as the water jug leaking. In either case, the well is not usable. (3) The opposite situation is a well that is usable but is foolishly ignored by others. The well is a vital source, and the Oracle is anguished when the well—or by extension, the sage who might benefit the country—is ignored. (4) As if in reply to Line 2, we are shown a maintained well. It is not a mistake to safeguard what we have. (5) The best situation is a good well and people who value and use it: then there is cool refreshment. (6) The culmination of this situation is a full well. Use it. Do not cover it over. In the same way, when your fortune is full, have confidence in it and great fortune will come.

The Image shows wood as the framework protecting a well and providing the structure to draw the water that is so precious. In the same way, the noble one should aspire to being a source of encouragement and aid to all people. Like the well, we should give inexhaustibly and openly, all the while keeping our own characters as clear and free-flowing as water.

We all get confused by the many demands of life, just as we can be wearied by our labors. When we are befuddled or tired, returning to the source will lift us as surely as water rises up in a well. We must not be discouraged if it seems that we are making no progress and that misfortunes still occur. The hexagram Well gives us the right idea: live close to the source, and you cannot help but be fortunate.

Hexagram 49
Lake above
Fire below

Fire, the youngest daughter, and lake, the middle daughter, are in conflict. This symbolizes the struggle for reform. The original meaning of ge was "molting." Reform was compared to the sloughing off of an old skin.

Ge
Hides stripped of hair. Skin, leather. To eliminate. To change, reform, renovate. Human skin. Chinese percussion instruments. Armor. Soldiers.

The Sequence and Link
Reform must spring from the source.

Reform

We smash the barricades, attack
the soldiers. They toss their helmets
and flee—shields broken, lances snapped.

Shouting, we race through pillared halls,
trample gardens with muddy boots.
One torch! Flames flicker on the lake.

Red gates tumble from cracked hinges.
Footsteps echo off marble floors.
The emperor hangs from a beam,

his wives strangled with their sashes.
Our leader strides to the windows
and kicks the latticework open.

He raises his arms to the crowd.
The pillars shake as people roar,
"May your rule last ten thousand years!"

He waves and laughs as the throng cheers.
Behind him, creaking from the noose,
the corpse swings like a pendulum.

The Statement

**Reform: on one's own day,
confidence is won—
making, pervasive, gainful, and pure.
Regrets vanish.**

The Lines

6th line ▬ ▬

The noble one changes like a panther.
The small person changes his expression.
Going is unfortunate,
staying is pure fortune.

5th line ▬▬▬

The great person changes like a tiger.
No need to divine: there is trust.

4th line ▬▬▬

**Regrets vanish. Have confidence,
alter the commands. Fortune.**

3rd line ▬▬▬▬

**Going is unfortunate. Pure harshness.
Reform is declared three times
before there is confidence.**

2nd line ▬ ▬

**By day's end, there is reform.
Going is fortunate and without fault.**

The Image

Fire in the middle of the
lake: reform. The noble one
orders the calendar
by the seasons.

1st line ▬▬▬

Bound using yellow ox hide.

REFORM is compared to dehairing and tanning hides. This hexagram contrasts with Hexagram 22, Adornment, which pictures a society advanced and embellished with culture and style. Here, we are stripping away extraneous features to facilitate reform. The final message is simple: when it is time to change, then change!

The image of leather is one of refinement. In its allusion to tanning, it suggests that purification and adapting of raw material leads to reformation. This hexagram is positioned between the previous one, Well, and the next one, Cauldron. When there is a need for reform, we must account for the basic elements of nature and sustenance, and our new ways of governing must reaffirm the fundamentals of civilization.

While those who study change speak frequently of virtue, ethics, morality, family, service to nation, and reverence for the holy, they still recognize the need for reform and even revolution. For thousands of years, this understanding was expressed in the phrase "mandate of heaven": a ruler stayed in power only if he had heaven's sanction. We need not understand this in a mystical fashion: the mandate of heaven means legitimacy borne of a virtuous and natural rule. When a ruler became corrupt, the mandate vanished, and a new ruler would replace him.

Those who become good rulers after a revolution must serve the needs of the people, must integrate society with the land, the weather, and the economic conditions, and must establish a stable society. They must continually earn their position. Thus, in this image of a heavenly mandate, there is a concept of a government rightly changing hands according to need.

This hexagram also shows that an individual can change. In so many of the preceding hexagrams, we have spoken of change as the grand shifting of universal forces. On a personal level, *ge,* as in the shedding of skin, is a helpful image. Animals who shed their skins, like snakes, must to do so because their skins cannot accommodate their growing size. In the same way, when we are growing, our old ways of acting should be abandoned without a second thought. Once that is done, we are different. We can no longer go back to our old ways any more than a snake could put on its old skin. Change is a natural part of aging.

Thus, both governmental and personal changes are a constant necessity. If we can incorporate these changes as reforms, we can keep our affairs stable.

The *Statement* clearly shows that social reform is impossible until there is confidence in the leaders and their goals. This trust is slow in coming, but when it does come, the results are profound. A new order is created that thoroughly sweeps through all levels of society. The results are positive and pure.

The *Lines* extend these themes by considering all types of reform, from the general to the personal. (1) The image of being bound by yellow ox hide shows that any reform we make must be firmly fixed to be successful. (2) When the opportunity for reform arises, our purpose coincides with the right conditions. Our ventures are successful and without fault. (3) A far different situation is presented next. Here, our purposes do not coincide with the situation, and the results are harsh. Our declaration of reform is made repeatedly, and it takes time to build confidence in what we want to do. (4) The situation changes quickly. When that happens, our regrets vanish, our confidence builds, and we can even alter our commands to fit the new situation. (5) In this case, the emphasis shifts from outer change to inner change. A wise person understands that the most powerful of reform is self-reform. Only a great person is capable of this. When such a person changes, it is like a powerful tiger moving swiftly or changing its hunting patterns as needed. Such a state is beyond even divination, and the person as well as his or her followers should trust such reform. (6) In the final line, a great person is pictured at the end of the time of reform. The noble person changes like a panther, in contrast to a small person who can only superficially attempt to change his or her facial expression. However, the time is ending (because it is the sixth line), and the noble person must not venture forth but stay in place: inner change here is paramount; moving afar is not.

The *Image* of fire in the middle of the lake alludes to the sun reflected on the waters, reminding us of time and the seasons. The greatest reform is to integrate humanity with nature. Accordingly, the best reforms are the ones that are the most natural. Fire in the middle of the lake is the conflict of fire and water. Only by careful action coordinated with the times is lasting form established.

The leopard cannot change its spots, or so the old cliché says. Those who understand the hexagram of Reform do not try to change their spots. They shed their skins completely and transform themselves into new and superior people.

Cauldron

Hexagram 50
Fire above
Wind below

The lines of the hexagram form an image of a cauldron. The legs are at the bottom, the belly is formed by the next two lines, the yin line in the fifth place alludes to the handles of the cauldron, and the rim is at the top. The cauldron stands in a fire that is fueled by wood and fanned by the wind.

Ding
A three-legged bronze vessel used for cooking and to hold sacrificial offerings. Vigorous, thriving, flourishing. Anything involving three parts. Triangular.

The Sequence and Link
After reform, there must be the establishment of substance and social forms that serve all citizens.

Three legs of a cauldron
    firm in the fire,
handles arched in the smoke
    like twin dragons.

As the prince nods, I stand
    in the fire's glow
and ladle the hot food
    for my people.

They bow and take their bowls
    with hands upraised,
then sit in a circle
    to laugh and eat.

My ladle does not scoop
    the cauldron dry,
yet bellies fill with fire
    and legs stand strong.

The Statement

Cauldron.
Great fortune.
Continue.

The Lines

6th line ———

A cauldron with a jade carrier.
Great fortune. Nothing but gain.

5th line ——— ———

A cauldron with yellow handles
and a golden carrier. Gainful virtue.

4th line ———

A cauldron's feet break.
The duke's sacrificial food pours out.
His person is stained. Misfortune.

3rd line ———

A cauldron's handles removed:
it cannot be moved.
Cooked pheasant uneaten.
Rain now—in the end, fortune.

The Image

2nd line ———

No fault.
A cauldron is full. My enemies are ill
and cannot approach me: fortune.

Fire on top of wood:
cauldron.
The noble one takes the
principal seat
to solidify his commands.
Could you stoke
the cauldron that feeds
all people?

1st line —— ——

A cauldron overturned:
gain by expelling what is bad.
Take a concubine to have children.

CAULDRON: called a *ding,* this is a vessel unique to early Chinese civilization. Today we know of it only by art or archaeology books or in museum collections. The *ding* was a cast bronze cauldron with three legs and high loop handles cast onto the rim. It stood directly over the fire for cooking, and its handles allowed it to be lifted to and from the fire. Some *ding* are so large that several men and a special carrier are needed to lift it. The *ding* was used to prepare food for the nobility and for sacrificial rituals.

The unique qualities of the *ding* extend into language. Some words are exclusively related to the carriers for *ding* or for the food cooked in them. *Ding ge*—a phrase combining the names of Hexagrams 50 and 49—means "to change dynasties."

Many of the *ding* unearthed by archaeologists have animal forms cast in relief on them, as well as totemic motifs of faces. Some have inscriptions identifying the reason a *ding* was cast. This emphasizes the importance of words: only the most important writings were cast into bronze. The *ding* therefore unites sacrificial ritual, public ceremony, nobility, sacred art, advanced metallurgy, writing, and feasting into a single form.

With so much symbolism associated with the *ding,* it is no surprise that the *ding* came to symbolize the ideal person. As a *ding* stood firmly, as it was an empty vessel to serve others, as it was cast of purified metal into a solid form, so these qualities defined the ideal of the superior person. The sage was imagined as someone cooking food to nourish others in the greatest of bronze vessels and who also guided others with wisdom.

Ding follows *ge,* the Reform of the previous hexagram, and it shows the completion of revolution. Revolution expels the old. Casting of a new order must follow. Such an order must be tied to heaven and earth, must be solid and stable, must serve all people, and must be guided by the enlightened. It is no wonder that *ding* were cast whenever a new dynasty began.

Hexagram 27 deals with nourishing as a political act. Here, there is a much deeper meaning and a greater development. The emphasis is on the greatness of ceremony, the feeding of the masses, and the integration of all levels of society with heaven and earth.

When we eat, we take food directly into ourselves. So many of our rituals center around it, even today. Ritual integrates us bodily with a greater order. Eating consecrated food makes that order a part of us. When we craft a vessel that unites all our concerns, that elevates the process further. Now, if we can become the sage who attends to such a feeding, we can truly call ourselves superior.

Thus, the cauldron symbolizes a civilization at its height, where all is stable and where reverence to heaven, so often urged in other hexagrams, is complete. That is why the *Statement* speaks of a fundamental good fortune, and the obvious injunction is to continue, spreading the greatness of the cauldron as widely as possible.

The *Lines* all feature the cauldron, and turn it into an omen all its own. (1) As fundamental as a cauldron is, the *Changes* immediately allows for its overturning. This is necessary here, for the contents are bad and must be expelled. That metaphor is immediately tied to another one: taking a concubine in order to secure heirs. We must support the tradition that the cauldron represents, but we must sometimes make adjustments for practical reasons. (2) In this image, the cauldron is full, meaning all is wealthy and complete. The Oracle's enemies are ill and are unable to even approach: that is fortunate. (3) This line alludes to early troubles: the handles are removed, so the cauldron cannot be moved. Its rich contents cannot be eaten. Just as rain mars our plans, all seems troubled—but there will be fortune in the end. (4) If the cauldron—symbol of the noble one's rule—should break, the food is ruined and the duke himself will be sullied. This is outright misfortune. (5) At the height of the time of the cauldron, all is golden. There is gain; there is virtue. (6) When good fortune is as good as a jade carrier, there is nothing but gain.

The *Image* shows the cauldron standing above burning wood. Living fire heats the cauldron, and the food inside is transformed for all to share. The noble one emulates the powerful cauldron standing stable over the flames: he takes the principal seat as leader and solidifies his commands as the bronze solidifies the writing and magical motifs on its surface.

This hexagram asks if you could be like the cauldron, if you could be so committed to who you are that your presence is solid and hard as bronze. It asks if you could be so stable as to stand in flames, and there, in your personality like a vessel, transform the raw into the beneficial. That takes the highest honor, the highest strength, the greatest dedication. At the same time—in the standing, the bearing of heat, the allowing of using oneself as an empty vessel for the good of all who come—it takes the greatest humility. You need only take your honor, melt it in the crucible of change, and cast it into the mold you make by your daily activities. Then, you can be the cauldron.

Thunder

Hexagram 51
Thunder above
Thunder below

A strong yang line appears at the beginning of each of the two trigrams. Thunder appears abruptly, vanishes, and then appears again.

Zhen
Thunder, thunderclap. To shake, to tremble. To excite, to shock. Scared, terrified.

The Sequence and Link
Once a new order has been established, new calls to actions begin.

Do not ask me
who stretched the sky
like a drumhead
over the peaks.

I only know
that heaven's might
will beat the drum,
and quake the earth.

It pounds the drum
on battlefields,
it splashes blood
and topples kings.

It pounds the drum
in new furrows,
driving grass blades
through the damp earth.

I pound the drum
in the temples,
to forge red hearts
and free clear souls.

The Statement

Thunder everywhere.
Thunder comes frighteningly.
People laugh and exclaim.

Thunder terrifies for one hundred miles,
but do not lose the ladle
of sacrificial wine.

The Lines

6th line —— ——

Thunder menacing, menacing. Eyes wide
in fright. Going brings misfortune.
He does not shake, but his neighbor does.
No fault: a marriage has talk.

5th line —— ——

Thunder approaches and arrives harshly.
What is numerous is not lost.
There is business.

4th line ————

Thunder, followed by mud.

3rd line —— ——

Thunder: awake, awake!
Shaking without injury.

The Image

Continuous thunder
on thunder.
The noble one examines
his morals
in fear and dread.

2nd line —— ——

Thunder comes harshly.
Countless treasures lost.
Climb up nine mounds. Do not pursue.
In seven days: recovery.

1st line ————

Thunder brings fright and terror.
Afterward, laughter and talk: ha ha.
Fortune.

THUNDER jolts. It is the shock of movement. The *Changes* holds that times of shock are calls to cleanse ourselves and make ourselves compliant to heaven's will.

In addition to thunder as jolting, the hexagram has taken on other meanings. Thunder takes the ancient associations of growth, forests, newness, and spring, and joins them to meanings such as the first son, new beginnings, involuntary utterances, and swift and powerful action.

From the Early Heaven Eight Trigrams, thunder already had associations with awesome power, the energy of sound, and new beginnings. In King Wen's time and after, thunder came to represent the return of yang power after the extreme yin of winter. Just as thunder is prevalent in the spring, the force of trees and flowers bursting forth was also called thunder.

Heaven and earth join together to make all things live. A man and a woman join together to begin a family. Thunder not only represents their firstborn son; in this position in the Sixty-Four Hexagrams, it represents the first son coming of age. He is handed the responsibilities of leadership. When the first shocks challenge him, he is not shaken. All others around him lose their composure, degenerating into babbling terror, but he does not falter in his strength or his ability to reassure others. Coming as this hexagram does after Reform and Cauldron—the overturning and reestablishment of a new dynasty—the first son of Thunder represents a new and young leader capable of governing and keeping the rituals.

Thus, this hexagram alludes to a cycle that began with Hexagrams 31 and 32—which represent courtship and an enduring marriage—and that ended with Hexagrams 49 and 50, the previous two hexagrams. Just as Hexagram 31 represented a new beginning, Thunder represents the beginning of a smaller cycle within the overall group of sixty-four.

Thunder not only refers to the power of nature's sound, but also speaks to the sounds we make involuntarily. When we are shocked by thunder, there are murmurs, cries, screams, titters, and laughter. These are all the products of natural actions, unreasoned and unrestrained as a burp or cough. When we are assaulted by a great shaking, that trauma registers within us; our involuntary responses prove this. We must take action. We cannot ignore what is happening. The young leader cannot afford to falter. It is only because of his or her superior personality that there is joining in the awesome force rather than resistance to it. Just as thunder inspires awe by pure force, so too must a young leader move followers to great deeds.

A leader must never fail to search within for faults. When we are shocked by events, we must not fail to examine ourselves for errors. Times of shock are calls to search ourselves and obey heaven.

The *Statement* observes that change often comes with the force of thunder. The serious shifts in our lives are often abrupt and shocking. The nervous laughter and the exclamations of shock are as much a metaphor for sudden change as they are a description of our reactions to severe thunder. We are grounded in a spiritual image, however. Let us picture ourselves in a temple, holding a ladle of sacrificial wine, and thunder explodes overhead. In that situation, we must have enough self-possession and confidence that our hand does not even shake. That calmness represents exactly the attitude we need for all changes in life.

The *Lines* tell us that when thunder or a sudden change comes, we must be careful to discern what the situation is and have an understanding of what to do. (1) In a small situation, thunder comes. It is terrifying, but it passes quickly. There is laughter and talk. (2) Next, thunder comes with storms and causes greater confusion. Treasures are lost. In this case, we should not pursue the matter further; it will resolve itself. (3) We are again reassured here, because thunder approaches but we escape without injury. (4) Even if no other factors are present, we will still have some inconvenience: the mud that follows will undoubtedly be difficult. (5) Here we are caught in a shocking situation. But our many concerns are not lost and we must attend to the business at hand. (6) There are a number of concerns in this last line. We are caught in a shocking situation and no immediate relief is indicated. The thunder is menacing, eyes are wide in fright, venturing forth only brings trouble, and even if we are not shaking, those around us are. We are not at fault, and yet a marriage is either discussed or gossiped about. This is not a good situation. The only solution is to be the one who does not shake. We must be the one who does not lose the ladle of sacrificial wine.

The *Image* reinforces one of the core messages of the *Changes:* that we must examine ourselves when we are shocked by misfortune. Thunder, storms, and calamity are occasions to remember that heaven is far mightier than we. Thus, we must search ourselves so that we are not at fault. No matter what happens, then, our consciences are clear. We will be able to adapt and act in shocking times in a way that no other person will be able to do.

Hexagram 52
Mountain above
Mountain below

In each trigram, the yang line is at the top and is therefore leaving the situation. The yin lines are below and moving downward. Thus, there is stillness because internal forces are moving away from one another.

Gen
Defined in dictionaries as the name of this trigram and hexagram. Tough, leathery food. Simple clothing. Honest and upright personality.

The Sequence and Link
Thunderous leadership must be combined with meditative character.

Stilling

I cannot ride
farther than the cliff's edge. Ahead,
 ridges of snow
smother the north frontier.

 A hundred lands
must lie beyond the horizon.
 A hundred stars
shine but cannot be touched,

 while I fret, small
as a cricket on a boulder,
 too weak to cross
even the slightest crack,

 and then I think
of this mountain ledge that stops me.
 I imagine
that I am the mountain,

 and when I do,
the stars and distant lands revolve
 around my heart
of stillness and silence.

The Statement

One stills one's back
and does not move one's body.
There is movement in one's courtyard,
but one does not see one's people.
No fault.

The Lines

6th line ———

Deep and honest stillness.
Fortunate.

5th line —— ——

Stilling his jaws.
Speech is orderly.
Regrets vanish.

4th line —— ——

Stilling his trunk.
No fault.

3rd line ———

Stilling one's waist.
Splitting the muscles of the back.
Cruelty smokes one's heart.

2nd line —— ——

Stilling one's calves.
One cannot raise one's followers.
One's heart is unhappy.

The Image

Doubled mountains:
stillness.
The noble one
does not consider matters
beyond his position.

1st line —— ——

Stilling one's feet. No fault.
Gain through everlasting virtue.

STILLING is also a mode of change. Although we think of change as movement, stillness is the necessary opposite of movement. When outer movement halts, inner movement is released.

Accordingly, the mountain, symbol for stilling, forms a counterpart to the preceding image of thunder. Where thunder is jolting power and the beginning of movement, the mountain is stillness, culmination, and consolidation. Both are necessary; they form a pair.

If Thunder represents the young leader charged with new responsibilities, Mountain shows a leader in careful deliberation, a leader so absorbed in important matters that eyes grow unblinking and body becomes unmoving. This is mountain absorption—still, poised, and reserved.

Stilling is concentration.

Where Thunder races, Mountain stops. It stops others as well—clouds, birds, people, nations. All must halt before mountains. Metaphorically, the mountain represents the young leader channeling movement by establishing boundaries.

Stilling is a positive barrier.

Where Thunder causes involuntary utterances of terror and alarm, Mountain represents the restraint of a cultivated person. In the time of Mountain, one is poised, purposeful, and calm in word and deed.

Stilling is restraint.

A mountain is massive. Applied to a human being, Mountain alludes to the fullness of virtue after years of self-cultivation. We admire others for their "substance." Those who follow change build in virtue—like a mountain pushed higher—until they have great presence of character. If others look up to them, as sherpas look up to the peaks that keep even clouds at bay, it is only because the virtue in them is tangible and massive. It is the virtue of personal presence.

Stilling is accumulation.

Finally, Mountain represents the importance of meditation. However great a mountain peak may be, however massive a person's honest character may be, the greatness possible through meditation looms over what is already great. Meditation may seem like a simple matter of stilling the walking feet, the climbing legs, the twisting trunk, the chattering mouth, and even the thinking head. Deeper still, however, is the change that takes place when the body is stilled. When outer movement halts, inner movement is released. For a skilled meditator, spiritual energy is dynamically circulated inside, and there is gain, a pyramid of concentrated power.

Stilling is meditation.

This, then, is the message for the young leader. Through concentration, through controlling self and others by stilling, through restraint and honesty, and through the insight of meditation, great leadership is sure to develop. Cleverness and learning have their place, but ultimately, the presence of a calm character and the insight of meditation rise above all else.

Stilling, both personal and tactical, is the consideration of this hexagram, with the underlying message that there are times when such stillness is appropriate and necessary. In the *Statement,* the subject stiffens his back and does not move his body. The people moving in his courtyard—already a closed and private place—are not even noticed. There is nothing wrong with doing this, because such stillness is proper.

Obstinacy and anger are the negative side of stilling. The stilling of meditation comes from our calm withdrawal. If we would have spiritual stilling, we must still our rage. These themes are further explored in the *Lines.*

(1) The initial consideration is stopping our movement: stilling of one's toes. This pause is without fault, and it is a good time to consider what everlasting virtue might be to us and to realign ourselves on that path. (2) Then there is stilling brought on by one's helpers. Here, one's companions are not forthcoming, and unhappiness is the result. (3) The final discussion of stillness in progress alludes to both frustration and pain: the waist, normally turning and flexible, is stilled. Pain splits the muscles of the back. The harshness of the situation smokes one's heart. The next three lines seem to focus on inner stillness. (4) In an echo of the Statement, one stills one's trunk and there is nothing wrong with this. (5) After that, stilling one's jaws is often helpful: we stop chattering and make our speech orderly. (6) If we do that, we might even come to a deep and honed stillness, thereby fulfilling the call for everlasting virtue that was sounded in the first line.

The mountain denotes limits. In the *Image,* we are counseled not to worry about things that do not matter to us. The noble one stills himself or herself as if embodying the stillness of doubled mountains. In an echo of the Statement, the noble person does not consider matters beyond his or her position. Any business that is remote and does not have a chance of affecting us should be put aside. If we are careful to concern ourselves only with the business at hand, we will surely find the serenity of the highest mountain.

Master movement and stilling, and you master yourself.

Gradually

Hexagram 53
Wind above
Mountain below

The wind trigram in this hexagram also symbolizes wood. A tree grows gradually on a mountain. This hexagram also became associated with marriage because the middle four lines "move upward in their proper places" (see page 402)." In other words, the middle four lines are considered to be of the right yin or yang character for their position, and this is interpreted as an image of the proper development for marriage.

Jian
Gradually. By degrees. To soak, to permeate. To extend (as in land extending to a certain point).

The Sequence and Link
The inert mountain will move through steady influence.

It is the day we knot
our red silk sash: wind blows
star bits from the heavens,
and cones tumble from pines.

Thirty summers will pass:
grandchildren will tie flags
from the forking branches
and leap in the breezes.

In thirty summers more,
we will both lie entwined
with the roots, but our souls
will rise on children's kites,

and red streamers will wave
from sticks and paper wings—
the silk and wind knotting
above forested peaks.

The Statement

A woman marries: fortune.
Gainful purity.

The Lines

6th line ———

Wild swans gradually reach a plateau.
Their feathers can be used for the rites.
Fortune.

5th line ———

Wild swans gradually reach the hill.
Three years: a wife cannot conceive.
At the end of twilight: success. Fortune.

4th line —— ——

Wild swans gradually reach the wood.
Some find branches. No fault.

3rd line ———

Wild swans gradually reach the shore.
A man journeys but does not return. A wife,
pregnant; does not give birth. Misfortune.
Gain by guarding against raiders.

The Image

2nd line —— ——

Wild swans gradually reach the boulder.
Drinking and eating in bliss. Fortune.

Wood on the mountain:
gradually.
The noble one dwells
in high moral character
and reforms
popular customs.

1st line —— ——

Wild swans gradually reach the stream bank.
One's children endangered. There is talk.
No fault.

GRADUALLY means a situation that has developed slowly toward culmination. The hexagram shows the moment when a course of action is on the verge of being fulfilled. Thus, the name really means "gradually reaching fullness." The Statement alludes to marriage. It takes time to come to the point of marrying, and it takes time for a marriage to mature and develop. The idea of gradually reaching certain points of development is given a secondary metaphor in the Lines. The Lines show wild swans reaching destinations that are shown farther inland with each successive line. At each place, their arrival represents the realization of a process that has been slowly developing.

The *Changes* takes the idea of a gradual advancement and first associates it with a good marriage. It is miraculous that the simple and voluntary act of saying yes to another person joins us for what should be life. With time and care, our lives grow in love and beauty, prosperity and health, learning and mutual support. That sense of gradual building, of voluntary joining to create something much greater, is the crux of this hexagram.

Turning to the two trigrams, we can compare this to trees (the variant association of the trigram Wind) growing on a mountainside. They begin as saplings and over the course of many years deepen their roots and spread their branches. Soon, they grow into trees that have a complex relationship with their environment. The mountain gives the trees their places, but the roots of the tree check erosion. The mountain is solid and lofty, but the trees adorn it. Together, mountain and tree support animal, plant, insect, and bacterial life in the branches, trunk, and shade of the tree.

Turning to the problems of government, the followers of change extrapolated other meanings. They saw the statesman or minister as a bride to the emperor. Just as a marriage takes an equal commitment between two people, an emperor and his minister make a commitment to one another. Anything less compromises their mutual cause. Even in modern times, when there are few emperors and ministers, the idea of a nation's leader needing support and interchange with cabinet members is still valid.

The image of gradual advancement was further used to describe the gradual promotion of an official. This image is also relevant today. We hope to meet mentors and leaders who will work sincerely with us. We hope to find mutual commitment and respect. We must then make a full commitment, just as we do in marriage. Then comes the long process of perseverance, work, and gradual rise to prominence.

The power of Gradually should not be overlooked. Work that has taken place gradually is not easily undone. Whenever we find ourselves impatient or in despair that advancement seems to be slow, we should take comfort in this fact. We must persevere and build our momentum slowly. Then, when we are ready, we can show ourselves in our fullness. Others will be awed, because we have built ourselves carefully. Anyone can begin the work that will develop gradually, just as anyone can marry. But few can last—to someday rise up as grand and unopposed as a forested mountain. In the same way, few today keep their marriage vows.

The *Statement* is one of good fortune. The word that we have usually interpreted as "purity" now takes on one of its other meanings: chastity. The woman will do well to remain chaste and virtuous in her marriage, as indeed the entire marriage will be fortunate if both man and woman remember to seek gains for their marriage while being true to their vows.

In one of the most orderly structures of all the *Lines,* the image of wild swans reaching their destination is tied to different situations. Things have settled in each of these lines, and we are urged to face them. (**1**) Our children (or others we are responsible for) are endangered. There is much discussion. We are not wrong for acting, just as we must make sure our own children are not at fault. (**2**) We are settled in a good situation, and we eat and drink in bliss. This is good. (**3**) On the other hand, sometimes a situation comes to an unsatisfactory conclusion: a man does not return from a journey; a woman suffers a miscarriage. What should have been happy is now sad. Still, we must guard against even worse events. (**4**) We have searched, and now we arrive at a place where we have some pause. There is nothing wrong with this—but the situation is neutral. (**5**) We have striven for success, as when a couple strives to have a child. In the end, the gradual development leads to success. (**6**) Finally, we are returned to the spiritual: all is settled, and what is left is for us to enter back into the rituals that tie us to heaven.

The *Image* shows us that reaching good culminations requires the noble one to stay wholly in a superior moral position. Thus, popular customs—which are gradually shifting—will always remain positive. In a way, the sage is the wind that lessens the inertia of the people, and so everyone advances.

Wind and trees on the mountainside. Geese gradually progressing toward their goals. A couple growing old in their marriage. These are ample images of one thing: the wisdom of gradually reaching all the points one must in one's individual journey.

歸妹

Hexagram 54
Thunder above
Lake below

The Thunder trigram above represents the eldest son, while the Lake trigram represents the youngest daughter. This image symbolizes an older man taking a younger girl as a secondary wife. However, being a concubine is not desirable.

Guei Mei
Gui: To return. To marry, to pledge, to belong. To attribute. To put in somebody's charge.
Mei: A younger sister.
Gui Mei: The marrying younger sister.

The Sequence and Link
Gradualness returns to domesticity, and the mutuality of gradualness is contrasted with the restrictiveness of being a concubine.

Marrying Sister

Magpies flit across the full moon.
The wedding guests leave wine jars drained
and banquet tables strewn with scraps.

In a bedroom decked with orchids,
a cloth with the word *happiness*
hangs over my face, blinding me.

Oceans of blood pound on the shores
ground from the bones of concubines—
no words left but the screech of gulls.

In the past, the gods saved maidens
by turning them to stone. What god
will save me when he tears my veil?

The moon goddess fled her husband,
but what chews at the moon each night?
I have no doubt it is a man.

The Statement

Advance: misfortune.
No place will bring gain.

The Lines

6th line — —

A woman carries a basket: no fruit.
A man sacrifices a ram: no blood.
No place is gainful.

5th line — —

Emperor Yi gives his younger sister in marriage.
Her royal sleeves are not as fine
as the secondary wives'. The moon: nearly full.
Fortune.

4th line ———

A younger sister marrying.
Overflowing expectations.
A late marriage has its season.

3rd line — —

A younger sister waits to marry.
Returns to marry as a secondary wife.

The Image

2nd line ———

Blind in one eye: able to see.
Gain by a solitary person's firmness.

Thunder over lake:
marrying sister.
The noble one pursues
far-reaching goals
while keeping aware
of possible ruin.

1st line ———

A younger sister marries as a secondary wife.
The lame can tread. Going is favorable.

MARRYING SISTER means a subordinate union. It portrays an ancient situation that seems foreign to us now, and yet its inherent message is as immediate as anyone who accepts a compromised situation. If we consider all the people who live with poverty and little education, if we consider how many people—children and women especially—live in culturally restrictive environments, the message of Marrying Sister is heartbreakingly relevant.

There are two cultural practices behind the title of this hexagram. The first is the concept of secondary marriages. Although it includes the idea of concubines and harems, the hexagram also refers to the feudal practice of a bride and her younger sister both given in marriage to the same sovereign. In the ideal case, the two women supported one another. Nevertheless, most would agree that the marriage depicted in this hexagram, in contrast to that depicted in Hexagram 32 or 53, is undesirable and limited.

A second understanding is the title "younger sister." In traditional Chinese families, every person is identified by the position he or she holds in that family. The naming system is exact and thorough. One's maternal grandmother, for example, has a different title than one's paternal grandmother. Sisters older than oneself have one title, while sisters younger than oneself have another. Often, one's number in the birth order is added to make the designation unequivocal—for example, Fourth Sister. *Mei* is a younger sister.

Such a sister has fewer familial responsibilities; she is low in the hierarchy headed by the oldest living family member. In traditional times, when women were not valued highly, a young sister might receive less respect than those older than she. If we combine the idea of a secondary wife with the image of a young girl in a family, we can grasp the degradation and enslavement this hexagram implies.

Marrying Sister is thus a metaphor for people who marry because they must, or because they are afraid that they are getting old, or because they are forced into marriage by familial, cultural, or political reasons. More generally still, the hexagram portrays any subordinate relationship that necessity or circumstances force us to enter. King Wen's compliance with Di Xin is classically compared to Marrying Sister.

As King Wen survived by being strong in humility, Marrying Sister must be humble and strong in order to escape the deficiencies of her situation. Situated as this hexagram is between Gradually and Plentiful, there may yet be an opportunity for change. We must not regard any situation as fixed. All situations evolve into further situations, and our every act influences that development. It is essential that we keep our determination strong in the time of Marrying Sister. What is ahead is misfortune, and the **Statement** offers little hope through the phrase "no place will bring gain."

The **Lines** paint this picture in greater detail while offering little more that is positive. (1) In the first line, the woman is married as a secondary wife or concubine. This is not ideal, but it is workable—even the lame can still walk—and so going is favorable. (2) Following up on this compromised portrait, we consider that those blind in one eye can still see. In other words, we are not in an advantageous position, but we can still make the best of things. A solitary person has to be firm and impeccable to survive. That may not be wonderful, but it is our current lot. (3) Sometimes, one waits for the best situation, but none comes. That is the case when a woman waits to marry and then has no choice but to return to her old life and become a secondary wife. (4) The opposite situation is shown next. In this case, the waiting worked, and the woman marries with great expectations and her late marriage proves to be timely. (5) This line is a possible allusion to Emperor Yi, who gave his younger sister in marriage as a secondary wife. Although her clothing was not as fine as that of the other wives, she still stood out. It was her personality, not her wealth, that made her special, and so fortune followed her. (6) The final line shows frustration and the loss of all possibilities. A woman has no fruit in her basket, and the implications for food as well as her fecundity are clear. Likewise, a man sacrifices a ram, but there is no blood—a clear reference to the astonishing absence of what should be. The Statement is reinforced: there is no place we can turn to.

The **Image** shows thunder over lake: shock overcomes joy. The image of a compromised and unhappy marriage is thereby reiterated. The message to the noble one is really twofold. Naturally, the first order of business is to avoid becoming a Marrying Sister. In all our efforts, we must avoid this situation. But the *Changes* also has a message to the person who finds herself in this position: pursue far-reaching goals while preserving yourself. The time of Marrying Sister is not a good one, but everything will change. We must be ready for that time so that we can again find a place that will bring gain.

As in all cases of discouragement, the Oracle urges us to be true to ourselves, to maintain our inner determination, and to find the spiritual power greater than fate. In the time of Marrying Sister, that may be a person's most crucial act.

Plentiful

Bronze vessels, newly cast,
are heaped with bear meat, fox, and deer.
Priests robed in silk brocade
offer incense with their clasped hands.
    My ears deaf to their chants,
    my ancestors so close,
           I am sun in the grass.

We have raised new towers.
People see them from miles away.
Market crowds throng the roads,
their colors flicker before me.
    I am blind to the spires
    as the sun looms above.
           I am sun in the trees.

The granary doors bulge,
the treasury is full. Armies
line up on parade grounds
to carry harvests from the fields.
    My skin warms in the sun.
    Tomorrow's pulse quickens.
           I am sun through the flags.

My son waves in greeting—
handsome, learnèd, a good horseman.
He rides a white stallion
and leads the one hundred nobles.
    I see what is to come:
    evening follows day. Still,
           I am the sun at noon.

Hexagram 55
Thunder above
Fire below

Thunder as movement and
fire as clarity symbolize
plenty. Like thunder high in
heaven and the sun high in
the sky, they also symbolize
the height of plenty—yet
heights cannot be long
sustained.

Feng
Abundant, luxurious, copious,
fruitful, plentiful, thick, large. A
crop, harvest. Feng was the
name of the capital King
Wen established after he
razed the city of Chong.

The Sequence and Link
When one is no longer subordinate, one will be
returned to one's proper
place.

Plentiful. Progress.
The great king arrives. Do not grieve.
All is right as the midday sun.

The Lines

6th line — —

Plentiful activity in one's house, screened
is one's household. Peering through
one's door: quiet with no people near.
For three years no one visits. Misfortune.

5th line — —

Receiving the seal.
There are congratulations and praise.
Fortune.

4th line —

Plentiful screens.
Seeing the northern stars at noon.
Meeting one's great lord. Fortune.

3rd line —

Plentiful flow.
Seeing darkness at noon.
Breaking one's right forearm. No fault.

The Image

2nd line — —

Plentiful screens.
Seeing the northern stars at noon.
Going brings a strange illness.

Thunder and lightning
come fully: plentiful.
The wise one decides
lawsuits and applies
punishments.

1st line —

Meeting one's suitable lord.
In spite of sameness, no fault.
Going has honor.

PLENTIFUL means zenith. Zenith is right—as right as the midday sun. Plenty also leads to decline. That is right too, and the timely understanding of both rise and fall infuses all our actions with wisdom.

King Wen razed the city of Chong and avenged the seven years of suffering caused by Prince Hu's intrigue. Although he took care not to harm the innocent, we can imagine that he was harsh toward his enemies. Yet once this matter was done, he saw the strategic importance of that area. After all, it had taken him a costly one hundred days to storm the city.

It was on this high plateau, with miles of land from there to the Pacific Ocean descending in a succession of lower plateaus, that King Wen decided to build his new capital. He named the city Feng—plentiful. That may have been a wish for glory, but it could have been a reference to the place itself.

Some speculate that the commentaries to the Lines refer to an eclipse. Throughout Chinese history, this was considered a bad omen, signaling the withdrawal of heaven's support for a dynasty. As a consequence, the royal astronomers were charged with accurately predicting eclipses to show that they were natural occurrences rather than a sign of divine displeasure. Science was used to counter superstition—as long as it kept the emperor in power. The hexagram specifically mentions the midday sun, and the Lines provide a serious counterpoint by referring to stars seen at midday.

Therefore, we must accept plenty equally with decline. No part of a circle can be avoided. The secret is to keep the circuit of change revolving. That way, one experiences plenty with the regularity of the sun reaching midday. We cannot have midday at all times, but we can still enjoy noon.

Yet the study of change must also account for the unusual. While we can become well practiced at change, we can still experience strangeness. The person of change does not fret. If the sun is shaded, the person does something in keeping with a cloudy day. If there is an eclipse, he or she takes advantage of it—whether that means studying it, or whether that means taking advantage of the unusual darkness. No matter what happens, the person of change is not surprised, and is always ready to leverage advantage from irregularity.

There is also the possibility of an inner eclipse: if we lack self-control or if we do not know ourselves well, we can darken our own light. Not all problems come from outside. We can cause our own difficulties too. Thus superior persons are constantly aware of their own emotions and their own thinking so that they do not disrupt the cycles themselves. The sun-bright clarity that emerges is an inner brilliance, and inner plenty.

In sum, then, this hexagram presents a puzzling mix of imagery. Only by solving those puzzles will the secret of the hexagram be apparent. We know that the name means "plenty," "abundance," "fruitfulness," and "luxury." The Lines present an intriguing array of images: one's lord, seeing the northern stars at noon (which implies an eclipse), screens, receiving a seal, and isolation. The **Statement** says that plenty comes when the great king arrives. We do not grieve, because the struggles to bring the king are over. All is as fitting as the midday sun.

We have reached a moment of plenty. All is approaching culmination. There is no judgment of fortune in the Statement; that fortune is no longer in the future. It is here. All has reached fullness.

The **Lines,** then, provide a set of counterbalancing warnings. Yes, we have reached our zenith, but that is precisely the time to bring one's wisdom to the fore. (**1**) We have met our ruler. We have an ally and a sponsor for our goals. But we must remain without fault to receive the honor we seek. (**2**) In greater contrast to the message of plenty we find a plentiful number of screens. The eclipse implied by seeing the stars at noon is a clear reminder that even the sun can be eclipsed; we must be aware that we and our plans can be blocked as well. Perhaps that is why "going brings a strange illness." (**3**) The next line clearly presents mitigating difficulties: there are screens, there is an eclipse, and one breaks one's right forearm. (**4**) In a continuation of Line 2, we are again confronted with screens and an eclipse. This time, however, our lord comes, and we share in that fortune. (**5**) Only this line has unmitigated success: one is given a seal (implying authority) and receives both congratulations and praise. (**6**) The situation is quickly reversed, however. In the final line, one is screened off from the others in one's household, even though there is wealth there. No one is near. In fact, no one comes to visit for three years. Clear misfortune indeed: what good is plenty if it is screened from others?

Plentiful also implies a fullness of our power. In the **Image,** we are urged to decide lawsuits and apply punishments. Apparently, the plenty of the name applies to copious thunder, lightning, and the rain. In the same way, we must be powerful, relentless, and soaking in acting on the legal matters under our jurisdiction.

To be as fitting as the midday sun—that is an ideal we must all strive to have.

Hexagram 56
Fire above
Mountain below

Fire flames upward from a mountain. The two elements separate, just as the wanderer separates from others.

Lu

To travel, to lodge. A traveler, a passenger, a lodger. A multitude, people. Disciples, students, followers, subordinates. Order, sequence, arrangement. A military brigade. A sacrifice in the mountains. To proceed together, to act together.

The Sequence and Link

Plentifulness in a country leads to surveyors, merchants, officials, troops, and tourists traveling. But plenty can also bring exile, loss of position, and alienation.

Traveler

The wars are past, new borders stand.
The mandate of heaven is carved
on the curve of the temple bell.
To ring it—easy. To survey

the entire kingdom—arduous.
Each year I toss aside worn boots
and buy a new horse. Dreams of home
grow more wan than the frontier moon.

My sons and my daughters marry
while I claw at mountains to find
where the Yellow River begins.
When I return, I am summoned

to guide the king to the Five Peaks.
We climb where even monkeys shun
the heights, and there we light our fires
and offer rams to please the earth.

Hair gray, no stride, just a shuffle
as I sweep my wife's grave, the stars
like temple lights. I grab my stick
and nudge stones on the pilgrim's road.

The Statement

Traveler. Slight progress.
Be steadfast in travel: fortune.

The Lines

6th line ━━━

A bird sets fire to its nest. A traveler
first laughs, afterward howls and weeps.
Loses an ox in barter. Misfortune.

5th line ━━ ━━

Shooting pheasants. One arrow vanishes.
In the end, there is honor and authority.

4th line ━━━

A traveler in a dwelling place
gets his wealth and ax.
My heart is unhappy.

3rd line ━━━

A traveler sets fire to his lodging,
loses his servants. Firm harshness.

The Image

2nd line ━━ ━━

A traveler promptly stops for lodging,
holding his wealth, getting servants.
Virtuous.

Fire on the mountain:
traveler. The noble one is
clear-minded and cautious
in meting out punishment
and yet does not delay trial.

1st line ━━ ━━

A traveler, low and weak-voiced:
thus he summons calamity.

TRAVELER is an omen of both good and bad implications. On one hand, the daily life of any nation requires travel: officials must travel to understand the needs of the people, troops must travel to defend the borders, surveyors and census takers must report the basic features of the country to the government, merchants travel with their goods, farmers bring their harvests to market, and tourists engage in the pleasure of wandering. Through such means, wealth circulates within the economy.

The image of Traveler has a second connotation, however—one of loneliness and desperation. Those who lose their jobs, those who flee wars, flood, or famine, those who are alienated from families, those who seek outlets for ambitions, those who travel for careers, those who wander because they are misfits, and those who are exiled as political punishment are all examples of the negative side of travel.

This hexagram encompasses both meanings. They form a yin and yang pair. Like all efforts to balance yin and yang, travelers must find a balance between the free benefit of travel and its loneliness. Few do well by becoming permanent wanderers. The best travelers are temporary sojourners.

Traveling well is a skill. The best traveler packs the right amount of clothes and supplies, has money for the trip, and is a good guest in other people's lands. We must never be obnoxious or careless when we are guests. This will benefit us and those who come after us, and ensures that we will not be a nuisance to our hosts.

The pursuit of Tao and the understanding of change are greatly enhanced by travel. One can acquire a great deal of wisdom in a short period of time—provided one is observant and willing to engage in new experiences. The value of going to different places and absorbing their power cannot be had through books or other people. We must go ourselves.

Traveling is an excellent time to contemplate change. We are outside of our usual routines, our sensitivities are heightened, and we compress experiences into a short period of time. We will contemplate our journey long after we have come home. Travel changes a person in ways no one can predict. Even after we return, the lessons of change reverberate.

When we live in one place, the Tao of that place flows into us. When we travel, we bring our personal Tao into contact with the Tao of others and the Tao of those new places. We also gain respite from our routines and allow ourselves to absorb new understandings.

The world's population is in constant migration. Travel has spread the world's cultures and ethnicities around the globe. We are no longer living in isolated communities. Instead, travelers regularly cross boundaries. Borders can create isolation. Travel creates change all over the world.

A traveler must move with the course of events, remaining self-reliant and sensitive to any changes. A traveler, along with a warrior (who is also often a traveler), must read the omens of events as they occur. Whether there will be fortune or misfortune in the future will often be a matter of how canny the traveler will be.

The rewards of travel are not always large. Whether the traveler is someone trying to start a business, a tourist, an ambassador, or even a spy, slight progress is usually the outcome of travel. Thus, the *Statement* ends by urging us to be steadfast. Then there will be fortune. Another way to look at the Statement is to say that the continuation will be slight *unless* we are steadfast. Only then will there be great fortune.

The *Lines* amplify this theme of the traveler's need for impeccability. (1) An inexperienced traveler is timid, and so he draws disaster to himself. (2) By contrast, a traveler who stops promptly for lodging, safeguards his wealth, and secures servants (or assistance) has the kind of steadfastness the Statement mentioned. (3) A traveler can suffer misfortune by his own carelessness. He sets fire to his lodging; he loses his servants. Then the times ahead are surely harsh. (4) In one of the few places where the *Changes* comments directly, there is a mention of a traveler who gets a place to live, gets wealth, but also gets an ax. The aggressive intent of the traveler is clear, and the *Changes* is unhappy. The implication of the lack of necessity and wisdom of this turn of events is clear. (5) Another kind of traveler is a hunter, and here the search is for honor and a command under the king. One hunts, and it leads to greater things. (6) The lines close with another bumbling traveler. Like a bird that sets its own nest on fire, a traveler laughs, oblivious to the approaching difficulties. Then he howls and weeps. Likewise, the loss of his ox in barter is due to his own inadequacies. Then there is only misfortune.

Travel is a matter of give-and-take. From this concept comes the *Image:* administering law is a matter of give-and-take, of traveling to see how the laws work. The wise one is cautious in punitive measures, but does not let that interfere with the pace of justice.

Travel: it is an essential way to follow Tao. Travel the middle road with balance, and you will travel well for your entire life.

巽

Hexagram 57
Wind above
Wind below

One of the eight doubled trigrams, this hexagram symbolizes wind, wood, and the eldest daughter. Its attribute is gentle interweaving—like the wind or steadily growing wood. The lines also show yang lines penetrating yin lines, just as the wind disperses dark clouds.

Sun
Defined in dictionaries as the name for this trigram and hexagram of the *Changes*. Submissive, subordinate, mild.

The Sequence and Link
When one is no longer subordinate, one will be returned to one's proper place.

Wind

How the willow rustles
and the king's flag flutters,
forming the warp and weft
of a great tapestry
rippling with hills, valleys,
and the festival crowds
returning to their homes.

Hawks fly. Pines grow. Snakes
crawl into their tunnels.
The king repeats his old command.
His words are gentle breaths
rising to the heavens,
woven into the strands
that wrap this spinning world.

The Statement

Wind. Slight progress.
Gain by having a place to go.
Gain by seeing the great person.

The Lines

6th line —————

Wind under the bed.
Loses his wealth and ax.
Firm misfortune.

5th line —————

Firm fortune. Regrets vanish. Nothing but
gain. Without a beginning, there is an end.
Before the time of *geng,* **three days.**
After the time of *geng,* **three days. Fortune.**

4th line —— ——

Regrets vanish. In the field:
capture three articles.

3rd line —————

Incessant wind.
Sorrow.

The Image

2nd line —————

Wind under the bed.
Use many chroniclers and wizards.
Fortune. No fault.

Wind following wind:
wind. The noble one gives
further instructions
and takes action.

1st line —— ——

Advance and retreat benefit
a warrior's firmness.

WIND further articulates the humble determination needed both by Marrying Sister (Hexagram 54) and by Traveler (Hexagram 56). Both of those situations represent people in subordinate and difficult circumstances, and for both kinds of people, only humble forbearance will see them through. In the example of Wind, we see more of the power of gentleness.

Wind is the image of freshness and renewal, and the Oracle uses this to show that new growth is possible from lowliness. The wind has no solidity and no fixed position in the world, and yet its gentle motion shows that seemingly weak and insubstantial forces can still cause change. In the same way, we may find ourselves downtrodden, but we will find our situation changing if we can act according to our circumstances. When we finally succeed, we will go out into the wind, throw back our arms, take in deep breaths, and feel a new charge to continue on.

The wind, then, is the symbol of all that is soft and yielding, flowing and gentle. Perhaps these might be qualities easy to obstruct, but when the forces of wind are gathered, they are powerful. In the same way, any of us can accomplish amazing feats by gathering up our forces.

Traveler—the previous hexagram—portrayed people traveling all over the world, doing the work of the country or pursuing their own commerce and purposes. The hexagram Wind asks us not to follow one traveler, but all the travel that is happening in our country. It asks us to consider all the countless interweaving paths and lives. As the wind enters into every opening in the forests and the earth, the millions of moving people in our nation are like the wind entering and exiting through thousands of gates.

All these different, unpredictable, incalculable, and overlapping paths show the process of change. It is too easy to be lost trying to trace it all. (And even if we could, think of how much change would have occurred while we pondered our tallies!) Movement is life. It is commerce. It is the vitality of the nation. A leader must encourage and even stimulate this process, while ensuring that order, prosperity, and overall national interests are followed.

To control the wind, one must be like the wind. We cannot control the wind by stifling it. Instead, we must ride on its currents. Opposing the wind would be tantamount to shooting arrows and cannons at the wind—what would one hit? Instead, the enlightened leader issues orders, confirms them, and gently leads followers toward the most advantageous directions.

The name of this hexagram also means "mildness," but this is a dynamic mildness that nevertheless penetrates like a steadily blowing wind. While the wind may seem gentle when evaluated for just a few moments, the accumulation of its effects over a long period of time can be great. It is exactly this kind of powerful mildness that is the meaning of this hexagram.

The *Statement* implies that some progress can be made now. Accordingly, we set out on new ventures. We will find profit by setting out for a destination. We will find opportunities by meeting with an influential person. Putting these ventures together into a constant and coherent effort goes unsaid here, but it is in the very meaning: all our efforts must be linked together like a steadily blowing wind. The efforts can be mild, but accumulated over time, they become unopposable.

The *Lines* discuss different aspects of this approach. (1) The accumulation of small actions is akin to the advance and retreat of a warrior. Accordingly, this approach benefits the power of a warrior. (2) This hexagram alludes to subtlety, and here there is a presence to be dealt with. If we cannot tell what it is, we must use our chroniclers and wizards—or else manifest these skills in ourselves. Then there is fortune. (3) Incessant wind symbolizes constant stress or misfortune. The result is sorrow. (4) In most cases, though, the constant effort of Wind leads to a breakthrough. Our regrets vanish and we get tangible results. (5) The next line can present a conundrum. First, we are promised firm fortune and a dispelling of our regrets. "Without a beginning, there is an end" means that our results come to us without our necessarily having established them. It is important for us to discern these points in time. That is why we are advised to be aware of a situation's pace and timing. We must know of it three days in advance and act on it three days after. (*Geng* is a measure of time.) There is an echo of the Statement of Hexagram 18 here. (6) The final line flips the view entirely: we can lose a considerable amount—both of our wealth and of our power—because of the subtle erosion of wind.

The *Image* sums up the concept of mild constancy. What does the wise person do with this idea? The wise person gives further instructions or commands, and then takes action. That action should be as constant as the wind, and as flowing as one wind joined to another. If a person can master the image of the wind, there is no place that his or her mind cannot penetrate.

Hexagram 58
Lake above
Lake below

The last doubled trigram in the hexagram sequence, this hexagram symbolizes a lake, marsh, joy, and the youngest daughter. The yin line of each trigram rests on the firm yang lines beneath it. True joy relies on inner strength and remains gentle and yielding on the outside.

Dui
Defined in dictionaries as the name for this trigram and hexagram of the *Changes*. In modern definitions: exchange. Some feel that the word is *yue*, which combines this ideogram with the sign for "heart." This word means "delight," "joy," "happiness."

The Sequence and Link
After the spreading of wind comes the consolidation of lake and the joy of exchange.

Exchange

Where market tents billow, two lakes
flow together: lotus-spiked waves
lap magnolias and mirror
swallows returning to their nests.

"Sister, what will you buy today?"
The vendor boy grins and I smile,
but then he turns his eyes away.
I'm in no rush to be married.

A white-bearded merchant offers
cloisonné, then something precious:
a bronze mirror, constellations
etched on its back. "Here—hold heaven."

I hurry home at the day's end,
and put the mirror on a stand:
its face flares in the candlelight
like the sun poised above the lake.

The Statement

Exchange: progress and steadfast gain.

6th line ▬ ▬
Guided to exchange.

5th line ▬▬
Sincerity in disintegration.
There is harshness.

4th line ▬▬
Discussing exchange restlessly.
Avoid harm and there will be happiness.

3rd line ▬ ▬
Coming exchange.
Misfortune.

The Image

2nd line ▬▬
Sincere exchange.
Fortune. Regrets vanish.

Joined lakes in exchange.
The noble one
investigates and explains
knowledge to friends.

1st line ▬▬
Harmonious exchange.
Fortune.

EXCHANGE, the hexagram, doubles the trigram Lake. While some assert that the meaning of the name is "delight" or "pleasure," "exchange" is the more dominant interpretation. The word also fits the context of the Lines. Most important, the Image itself confirms this when it describes two joined lakes; this clearly implies exchange. Thus the lesson for this hexagram might be that delight must come from right exchange.

In Wind we had the image of the many paths as people traveled through the world. Exchange represents the gathering of all those paths into a common place. Earlier in the *Changes,* some paths involved prosperity and success, like Hexagram 55. Some involved unhappiness, like Hexagram 54. Some were the travels of ordinary people going about their everyday lives, as in Hexagram 56. All these paths, and all these efforts, must also reach a point of culmination. Exchange, like its image of the lake, is the symbol of all streams uniting. This should result in the joy and delight the hexagram symbolizes.

When we are successful, we should enjoy it. We have worked hard, we have sowed our crops properly, we have harvested, and we have stored our grain. Celebration is in order. The ideogram shows two dancing legs, a mouth open in laughter and song, with both hands thrown into the air.

Exchange can also be understood by looking at a marsh. The marsh is where water and earth lie in exchange. It is where birds rest during migrations. It is where animals and human beings come for water, rice, and fish. In this place of exchange, there is delight.

Any person of wisdom is careful with delight. On one hand, they know how necessary and healthy it is. If we must have forbearance through times of suffering and adversity, then we must have happiness in times of joy. Otherwise, why should we accept pain? Yes, we know happiness cannot last. Some people argue that because happiness is fragile, it should not be trusted. Not so. A butterfly's life is short, but it is no less beautiful. A night of love must end in the morning, but that does not mean that the night was not to be savored.

Yet too many of us refuse to let happiness rise and fall with its own natural rhythm. We stimulate happiness when there is no natural occurrence for it. We try to deaden our pain when it strikes us. Joy and sorrow are like two kinds of currency in our lives. We cannot live without either one, and we cannot exchange one permanently for the other. We must have both, so we might as well exchange with adeptness and regularity.

Let delight instead come from a middle path, and all will be well. Instead of limiting ourselves to the exchange of dark pleasures, let us remember the pleasures of light and truth. That is worthy exchange, and the delight of uniting our paths into the great tide of Tao is the greatest joy of all.

The *Statement* is straightforward. Exchange brings progress and steadfast gain. A further interpretation would be to say exchange is pervasive and gains by the purity of those involved—or, that exchange will bring progress and gain provided we are steadfast.

The *Lines* are equally clear in their description of various stages of exchange. (1) Harmonious exchange brings fortune. (2) Entering into exchange sincerely dispels all regrets and doubts. (3) "Coming exchange" can mean that the approaching exchange will not be fortunate, or that the exchange is approaching and not yet here, which is also unfortunate. (4) A complicated exchange that engenders much unsettled discussion is difficult, but if we avoid harm, we will find happiness. (5) In this situation, the event is disintegrating and splitting apart. We must maintain our confidence even though times will be harsh. (6) Finally, there are situations where we are guided to the exchange. There is no judgment as to whether this is good or bad. Nevertheless, when we consider that alienation and isolation are considered misfortune in the *Changes*, being guided to exchange is positive.

As is often the case, the *Image* brings us another perspective that is related to the Statement and Lines but that also provides us an anchoring idea:

Lakes joined together exchange their waters. In the same way, a wise person investigates and discusses knowledge. If we take the idea of two lakes doubled, there is an indication of the *Changes'* attitude toward knowledge: that it should be as deep as two lakes combined. If a person is wise enough and powerful enough to understand the immensity of that knowledge, that person is indeed qualified to lead others. If we take each lake of the Image as the two friends, then the Image also implies that the true exchange of knowledge best happens between two equals. Only when the friends have deep knowledge is there true exchange.

Exchange is the lake. The lake gathers where all waters flow. How hard it is to be like the lake, to lie the lowest of all. But the reward to the one who lies the lowest is the receiving of the richness of all others. Let others run wild with their lives. Sooner or later, their essence must run downhill toward Exchange.

Spreading

Hexagram 59
Wind above
Water below

Wind blows over the water,
dispersing whatever may be
blocking the surface. In
spring, the winds move the
breaking ice floes. Likewise,
spirituality disperses the
divisiveness of stubbornness
and egotism.

Huan
Expand, scatter, disperse. The
name of a river.

The Sequence and Link
After the sharing of delight,
people scatter to their separate lives; when delight congeals into selfishness and
decadence, dispersal must
follow. When the pooling of
exchange is over, there must
come spreading.

When I was ten, I saw
three days of sun and wind
melt an ice-clogged river.
I think back to that time
while kneeling officials
tell me of scant harvests.

Farmers have rioted.
Southern tribes threaten war.
Bandits attack the farms.
Silt fills the waterways.
My advisers urge me:
"Levy higher taxes."

I tell them no, that I
will settle these problems
no matter how bitter.
A king holds heaven's force:
he can open rivers
and let the waters flow.

The Statement

Spreading.
The king draws near to the temple.
Advance across the great river.
Gainful purity.

The Lines

6th line ————

Spreading his blood.
Go far away. No fault.

5th line ————

Spreading sweat: his great command.
Expanding royal dwellings. No fault.

4th line —— ——

Spreading his flock. Great fortune.
Expanding and there are mounds.
No common person can understand this.

3rd line —— ——

Spreading his twisting body.
No regrets.

The Image

2nd line ————

Spreading and going directly toward
his platform. Regrets vanish.

Wind moving above water:
spreading.
The ancient kings made
sacrificial offerings to God
and established temples.

1st line —— ——

By the saving strength of a horse.
Fortune.

SPREADING, with its associated meanings of "broad" and "swelling," implies the particles of a body expanding even as the whole remains intact. This hexagram forms an interesting continuation from the previous one, where two lakes were joined. Now the lakes are not only united; they are spreading with their joined waters. The wind moves above the lakes, and they become wider, more energized—flowing broadly outward, brimming with force.

When spreading occurs, obstacles are overcome. For the *Changes*, this usually refers to the overcoming of our moral failings. People can overdo their pursuit of pleasure, becoming slothful, lustful, and selfish. The *Changes* regards these as blockages. Just as a once brilliant lake that, gently accepting many streams, can become clogged with silt, we can be clogged with our faults. A breaking up is necessary, just as the proper flow must be restored to the lakes.

The Oracle holds that without such overcoming of obstacles, there will be no reverence, and no service to one's country. Unless there is a clearing away of faults, there is no chance to glimpse truth. On a larger level, war, crime, natural disasters, and a country's internal strife must also be broken up by the force of spreading to bring about peace.

None of this happens without a good leader. In previous hexagrams, we have seen that a leader must be generous and kind to followers. In turn, the leader can count on popular support. The leader must call upon others to put aside whatever keeps them divided. Clannishness, chauvinism, and selfishness must be washed away. Reverence and compassion must be strengthened.

When natural cycles of change are allowed to occur, an equally natural equilibrium will usually be reached. However, if there is stagnation and obstruction, the *Changes* regards that as a perversion of the natural flow. Obstructions must be cleared for that the true Way to prevail and move again.

For a leader to initiate spreading, there must often first be a dissolution of the leader's own egotism. No leader who is primarily concerned with self-interest can stay in power. No leader who is beholden to a secret cabal can successfully lead either. Petty habits separate every person from greatness. A true king must scatter any poor habits through the force of spreading in order to have true majesty.

A good king must also uses spreading to dissolve fear. The leader must soothe people, reassure them, and give voice to their own uncertainties. In times of war, as in times of natural disaster, people instinctively look to their leaders for guidance and safety.

A secondary meaning of this hexagram might be "to issue forth" or "to flow," which is a rapid spreading in a single direction.

Thus, the *Statement* shows that we have reached a point of great spreading. The king—at the head of all people—approaches the temple. Events are full and strong, and the king knows that the only way to avoid excess is to link human efforts to a spiritual plane. This restores balance with nature.

The *Lines* further explain the dynamic nature of spreading. (1) Our power has expanded to save us, and this brings fortune. (2) As an extension of the previous line, someone spreads energy and vigorously approaches a platform (presumably for leadership and action). Regrets vanish. (3) *Spreading* in this line implies someone putting out his or her limbs to act vigorously. Along with the image of a twisting body, we have the idea of someone acting energetically, and this is appropriate at this time. (4) The spreading of the flock might mean an increase in their number or them spreading out in the field. The next sense of spreading might be a similar dispersion of soldiers or settlers. The word *mounds* suggests burial mounds or the hills being traveled: our forces are spread in a strategy that is unusual and subtle. (5) Now the time of absolute action has arrived: the king issues his edict. The term "spreading sweat" means an imperial edict: just as perspiration cannot be taken back, so the king's order cannot be reversed. The royal dwellings, or more figuratively, the nation, is expanded, and this is faultless. (6) *Spreading* in the final line implies vigorous action, but it can also imply bloodshed. The action is extreme: we must go far away, but then we will be without fault.

The *Image* returns to the theme of the statement. All is flowing and expanding. This is precisely the time to humble ourselves before heaven and to use our largesse to establish places of devotion.

Ride the momentum of spreading. But if you are fortunate enough to have such force behind your wishes, remember to be cautious. Look into yourself, and remember the second meaning of this hexagram. Let the spreading carry you along as it carries away your shortcomings.

Regulation

If you would build a wall,
cast no shadows on your neighbor's garden.

If you would build a dam,
do not flood the millet fields that feed you.

A good general leads
his troops to build roads, not to rape and loot.

A good ruler opens
granaries when farmers have lost their crops.

I learned these rules by heart,
and I have spent years gazing at these words.

So it is that I give
a wide pasture for my horse to gallop,

and set an open road
where children run as far as they can see.

Hexagram 60
Water above
Lake below

Water flowing into a lake
will cause the lake to
overflow unless there are
banks to hold the water.
Limitations in life must also
be set to regulate activities
and maintain order. However,
excessive limitation can be
dangerous, and can provoke
restlessness and rebellion.

Jie

A node, a knot, a joint. A
passage, a paragraph, a
section. Principle, integrity,
fidelity, constancy. A festival, a
holiday. Seasons. Rhythm,
beat, musical time. To
restrain, control, restrict. To
curtail, to economize.

The Sequence and Link

The flux of delight and
spreading must be disciplined
by structure and restraint.

The Statement

Regulation. Be pervasive.
One cannot be morally pure
through suffering and trial.

The Lines

6th line   —— —

Bitter regulation.
Pure misfortune.
Regrets vanish.

5th line   ——

Willing regulation: fortune.
Go: there will be honor.

4th line   —— —

Calm regulation:
progress.

3rd line   —— ——

Unrestrained in regulations:
unrestrained sighing.
No fault.

The Image

2nd line   ——

Not leaving the court gate:
misfortune.

Water above the lake:
regulation. The noble one
regulates number and
measure and discusses
virtuous conduct.

1st line   ——

Not leaving the front hall:
no fault.

REGULATION takes its imagery from the joints of a bamboo. Just as the nodes are the very character of the bamboo, so proper regulation is the basis of a wise person. Regulation is not a set of rules imposed from outside. Instead, it is the very rhythm with which we act. We need not fear that regulation impinges on freedom. Quite the opposite.

We can compare this to music. It is the regulation of the time signature and the adherence to the key that makes the freedom of singing possible. By analogy, it is the regulation of building one thing on another that makes future accomplishments possible.

By building section after section, a bamboo gains its height. Examples of this principle in other areas are plentiful. A fisherman knots strands into a net and thereby creates the net's usefulness. Each year is divided into four seasons, and this unvarying sequence drives the growth of all nature. Music has its rhythm. Poetry has its beat, lines, and stanzas. Restraint compounds structure and thereby creates possibility and freedom.

Before a house is built, the wood lies in a heap. It is only by methodical construction that the wood forms rooms useful to us. What was unrestrained before is restrained—cut and nailed together—giving us the freedom of living within its walls. We move in, free to create and live in ways that were limited before we had the building.

The house provides for our safety. It wards off rain, snow, animals, robbers. Indeed, the best examples of wood-frame houses— where timbers are joined and wedged—are examples of extraordinary beauty and craftsmanship that are also sturdy. In earthquakes, for examples, the many wooden joints dissipate shock waves.

We cannot help but live in divided spaces; even if we live in one room, we define different functions for each area. Our tallest buildings consist of manageable floors. Beehives are made of hexagonal compartments. Every living thing is made of cells.

As a house is divided into rooms to function efficiently, those who define and establish the most useful approaches to their work do well with their lives. Disciplined people are no more free of misfortune than the rest of us, but like the wood-frame house, the joints of their regulation dissipate the quakes of disaster.

Regulation frees us. That is not paradoxical. Disciplined persons imagine a direction they want to go in—even if it means learning or changing—and then they take that direction. Relying on their abilities, they leverage their skills to realize their goals. Undisciplined people want to change too, but they cannot persevere long enough to make their wishes real. Personal change requires hard work. A disciplined person plans and then executes that plan, confident that he or she will reach the end.

Only calm and willing discipline should be practiced. Fanatical restriction is not discipline. Instead of training our horse, we imprison it. This is not the right way. Restraint in action is. We often say that a performer danced without restraint, but it was years of practice and patient discipline that made those precious moments of spontaneity possible.

Thus, the *Statement* is that regulation makes the pervasive influence of a wise person possible. Such masterful discipline is part of that person's inner being. It cannot be forced; it must be gently encouraged and developed. Moral purity harshly imposed by punishment, or the habits of someone who has been bitterly shaped by trauma, can never establish the spiritual regulation that the *Changes* advocates.

The *Lines* make this quite clear by contrasting different kinds of regulations. (1) Sometimes, the self-discipline that keeps us at home is right. We commit no fault. (2) At other times, not leaving is misfortune. These two lines underscore how proper regulation is a matter of both action and timing. The next four lines convey how regulation must be carefully cultivated. (3) When one is unrestrained, it leads to unrestrained regrets later. We are reminded how important it is to act without fault. (4) If we instead reach a level of calm regulation, there will be progress. (5) In fact, it is willing regulation that brings us fortune and honor. (6) Finally, to return to the theme of the Statement, we are left with an image of bitter regulation. Then there is only solid misfortune. The phrase "regrets vanish" is given here not because of the bitter regulations, but because of what it feels like not to have such bitterness.

If we contrast the regulation here with the restraint of Hexagrams 9 and 26, we see how this is definitely an inner regulation dynamically and subtly manifested.

The *Image* places great importance on regulation, echoing the primary theme of most of China's dynasties: to create order that regulated the society and that aligned society with Nature's rhythm. Having agreement on numbers, weights, and virtuous conduct was the way that the sages sought regulation for all under heaven.

Make use of regulation, and you can climb each node to freedom.

中孚

Hexagram 61
Wind above
Lake below

There is an empty space in the middle of the hexagram. The two yin lines determine the character of this hexagram, and their centrality symbolizes the inner confidence that rulers must have, and which they must inspire in their people.

Zhong Fu
Zhong: middle, among, within, between, central. Fu: confidence, trust.

The Sequence and Link
With discipline and order, confidence is sure to ensue.

Confidence Within

Each night, I clenched my fists,
but did not win, until

I hovered as the wind
that bulged sails and stirred waves.

I shot as an arrow
through a sphere on a pole.

I slid between an egg
and its mother hen's claw.

I rushed, and pressed, and huffed
through a blacksmith's bellows.

I aged in the green flames
of an alchemist's stove.

I became the peasants
who offered fish and pigs.

Only then did I see
what I fought for each night

and find what I wanted
in both my open hands.

The Statement

Confidence within:
Pigs. Fish. Fortune.
Advance across the great river.
Gainful purity.

The Lines

6th line ———

The sound of a white horse
rising to heaven: pure misfortune.

5th line ———

Have confidence as if entwined.
No fault.

4th line —— ——

The moon is nearly full:
one of the horses vanishes. No fault.

3rd line —— ——

Encountering an enemy:
Some drum, some halt.
Some sob, some sing.

The Image

2nd line ———

A calling crane in the shade:
its young are at peace.
I have a good wine goblet.
I will share its excellence with you.

Wind above the lake:
inner truth.
The noble one
discusses the law
and grants reprieve
from execution.

1st line ———

Expect fortune
while others are without ease.

CONFIDENCE WITHIN emerges when we live without hankering for "sophistication." The word here for "within" comes from the word that means "center" or "middle." This alludes to archery—hitting a target in the center—and to strategy, occupying the middle. In fact, the ideogram for "center," *zhong*, shows an arrow piercing the center of a target. Many passages throughout the hexagrams have advised the moderation of the middle path. The center is highly valued. Here, as we are nearing the end of the great cycle of sixty-four hexagrams, and after the struggles of the preceding sixty hexagrams, we find the attainment of confidence.

There are other readings for this hexagram, as is often the case. Some say that the word *confidence* is really the word for captives, and some say that the mention of pigs and fish in the Statement is really a mention of a dolphin that lives in the Yangzi River. But reading this as Confidence Within works — and is more helpful today than talking of captives—so we will interpret *fu* as "confidence." Certainly, confidence is important. This is confidence as the highest trust.

When people are confident in their leaders and their country, all things are possible. Such confidence is made valuable not because of grandiose words or fanatical rallies but because of the day-to-day sincerity of the common person. The image of pigs and fish celebrates the everyday. The common people cannot offer the rams and oxen of royalty: they make offerings from their own farmyards and ponds. Yet the sincerity of their offerings is considered far more important than grand imperial ceremonies. In addition, pigs and fish are symbols of plenty and of natural living. When people are able to live naturally and without hankering for the "sophistication" of a so-called advanced civilization, Confidence Within emerges.

Confidence Within comes from the simple relationships of family, friends, and fellow citizens. A child is confident in parents, and a parent must be confident in the child. Friends must be confident in one another. And citizens must be confident in the honor of others and in the essential goodness of the nation.

None of this happens by artificial means or unnatural stimulation. It happens only when the situation is right and people are sincere. That is why the image of Confidence Within is such a good omen for any group.

We cannot do anything of significance until we believe in ourselves. You have to know what you can do, you have to be confident in your core values, and you have to be willing to act. Then there is Confidence Within. Accomplishments create more confidence, and more confidence creates greater success. The challenge of keeping one's confidence along with modesty and ability is a great one, but if we can do that, we emerge balanced—or in other words, centered. Confidence Within is confidence centered.

The hexagram has an empty space in the middle. Confidence is our center. It cannot be calibrated, it cannot be packaged, it cannot be separated from us. It appears empty, because none of us can find it anatomically, and yet it is one of the most essential elements of a successful life. Inner truth is empty— not empty in a nihilistic way, but empty in the sense that it allows all possibilities. The greatest use comes from emptiness—the blacksmith's bellows, the alchemist's oven, the ceremonial wine goblet. The wise are empty within, and thus they are unopposed. Confidence is bolstered by concord with all that is around us.

The **Statement** shows us the resulting prosperity. We have livestock and we have fish. That is fortune. We can advance across the great water—that is, embark on great undertakings. All that together is a gainful purity that we can rely upon. In other words, confidence increases when there is progress.

The **Lines** refer to such states of confidence in spite of external circumstances. (**1**) We expect fortune even though others are ill at ease. (**2**) We have a peaceful time in which to beckon to friends. (**3**) We encounter an enemy, but our confidence is so great that they panic: some drum, some halt, some sob, some sing. (**4**) We maintain confidence even when events are discouraging because we understand yin and yang. We know that the waxing moon must wane. We know not to take the loss even of a horse to heart. That is how we remain without fault. (**5**) Confidence must be solid, like entwined trees. (**6**) Finally, as the time of Confidence Within comes to an end, the auguries are bad: a white horse neighs to heaven. Bad times come with a simple turning of events.

The **Image** shows the noble one discussing the law and extending leniency to transgressors. The implication of the frequent mentions of confidence, of ethics, of steadfast purity is clear: all must rise from within. We know that the criminal cannot hurt us. Therefore, in the time of Confidence Within, we let no one sway us. Instead, we act from our inner convictions. Then we attain the middle that the name implies, and our hearts are clear.

Inner confidence: outer trust.

Small Crossing

How hard a bird must work to soar,
to fly over miles of wetlands,
black wings against the setting sun.

Most return to the nest, content.
But if some never crossed the peaks,
how could the family of birds spread?

Hexagram 62
Thunder above
Mountain below

The strong lines are within;
the weak lines are outside,
resembling a flying bird—a
solid body in the center and
flapping wings on each side.
A bird should not fly too
high or far but should return
to its nest; a person should
not be ambitious at this
time, remaining modest and
grounded.

Xiao Guo

Xiao: small, little, tiny, minor,
young, humble, light,
unimportant.
Guo: To pass, to ford, across,
through, over, spend, after, to
exceed limits, excess, to visit,
to transfer, death, arrival.

The Sequence and Link
Maintaining confidence
requires modesty and a willingness to give extra effort.

The Statement

Small crossing. Continue for gainful purity.
Small matters can be done,
but not large matters.
Flying birds leave their sound:
it is unsuitable to go high—
the suitable is below.
Great fortune.

The Lines

6th line   — —

Not meeting is excessive.
Flying birds separate: misfortune.
This is called calamity and blundering.

5th line   — —

Dense clouds, no rain.
At my western outskirts, the duke shoots,
takes another in the cave.

4th line   —

No fault. Do not cross to meet them.
Going is dangerous. Absolutely refrain.
Do not act: be everlasting and firm.

3rd line   —

Do not cross. Be on guard.
Attend to this, or there may be killing.
Misfortune.

The Image

2nd line   — —

Crossing to one's ancestors,
meeting one's dead mother.
Not reaching as far as one's king:
meeting his minister. No fault.

1st line   — —

Birds fly from famine.

Thunder above the
mountain: small crossing.
The noble one acts with
more than enough
reverence, destroys
excessive grief, and uses
more than enough
economy.

SMALL CROSSING pivots on the double meaning of its name. *Crossing* also means "excess," and the hexagram becomes a meditation on the right kinds of crossings to make while avoiding what is excessive. This goes to the heart of all change and all questions. A crossing—going past a barrier, passing a milestone—is the ultimate act, and the name for "going too far" is *excess*. When we act, we act with the appropriate amount of effort and emphasis. In crossing, we must understand what it means to go too far.

We are nearly at the end of the cycle of sixty-four hexagrams. The progression of hexagrams has been toward greater control. Even at this late moment, however, we are making adjustments, struggling to make the final maneuvers that will bring our efforts to culmination.

Confidence Within repeated the now familiar theme of humility as a great virtue. Small Crossing—in the sense of a slight crossing of what is the middle path—raises the possibility that even virtue can be excessive. Sincerity taken to extremes becomes foolishness. Trustworthiness taken to extremes becomes gullibility. Humility taken to extremes becomes weakness. Values are important, but they do not relieve us from being careful and making intelligent decisions. This is a critical point about studying change: we must make decisions.

Taking firm control over our lives will inevitably lead to small excesses as we struggle for control over ourselves. The small bird wobbles when it flies, just as a child learning to walk staggers and lurches into walls. A good teacher is pleased when a student masters a skill, but then pushes the student to go further. That is Small Crossing in a good sense.

Thus, Small Crossing can also mean going a little further than is necessary. Superior people are superior in part because they are always willing to give a little more. Often, the difference between superior and mediocre is neither great skill nor great insight, but instead great willingness. If we reach the top of the mountain, the ordinary person says that we have gone as far as possible. The superior person, in viewing the image of thunder, knows that he or she can go farther and transcend what is normally considered the peak: Heaven is ever above the mountain. There is always a higher stage.

There is yet another lesson in this hexagram: to cross a barrier by a slight margin is still an accomplishment. When we are denied bold crossings, we return to the tactics of the gradual and gentle. When we are bound, blocked, frustrated, and hemmed in, we must avoid the small excess of despair. Rather, we must utilize the small excess of modest actions to make our crossing.

How crucial the lessons of Small Crossing are, and yet how often they have been misunderstood. People never fully comprehend the full power of the small. For the wise, it takes only a touch to set a wheel turning—and then that wheel amplifies the power of their touch.

The *Statement* says that we will do well only in small matters. That shouldn't be taken as automatically bad. To do well in the details can be considerable. At any rate, grand actions are not needed now. As a reiteration, we are shown birds that do not fly high. They fly at the altitude at which they are comfortable. If we do the same, we will find both gainful purity and great fortune .

The *Lines* continue the double theme of crossing and excess. (1) There is famine (excess of calamity), and so it is right for the birds to fly (crossing). (2) The greatest spiritual crossing is to cross to one's ancestors. One meets one's mother. In the same way it is acceptable to seek the king but reach only his minister. We may not have gone as far as we wanted, but we have gone far enough. Success is still possible. (3) In a clear statement, we are told here to abstain from crossing and to be on guard against bloodshed. (4) Similarly, we are faced with an enemy, and we must not cross to meet them. This is definite, because we are also told to absolutely refrain, and not to act. (5) "Dense clouds, no rain" is the image of expectant waiting. The situation is here, but we have to wait for the right moment. Then the act must be swift and sure. (6) Finally, failure to act can be excessive in itself. When birds leave their flock, they are vulnerable and lost. We must not disengage, for this would be disastrous.

The double theme of crossing and excess is completed in the *Image.* The wise person acts with an abundance of reverence and an abundance of frugality. This kind of "small crossing" over the measure of our actions is acceptable. What is not acceptable is even a small excess in grief—either our own or for us to inflict grief on others. We must not allow grief to destroy us; we must destroy it instead. Alternating the meanings of "crossing" and "excess" can be challenging, but if we can absorb this lesson, we will learn to balance all our actions. Then our crossings will have the right measure: any excess will be an excess of virtue.

Allow yourself small crossings when struggling for control. Cross past what is average to make extra accomplishments. Do not cross the limits when grieving. Understand Small Crossing, and you will still arrive on the far shore.

Already Across

Hexagram 63
Water above
Fire below

The yin and yang lines in this hexagram alternate in their ideal positions. Equilibrium has been reached, but after completion, disorder must follow.

This hexagram refers to autumn.

Ji Ji
Ji: Since, as, now, already. All, finish.
Ji: To relieve, to aid, to cross a stream, to ford. Benefit, succeed.

The Sequence and Link
The small crossing is completed by a little extra effort, and one's purpose is fulfilled.

Dusk. Steep path. My pack tugs at me.
My stick sinks in mud. The waters
roar as I clamber to the shore.

Rocks scatter under my sandals.
They have sat for centuries beneath
horses' hooves and chariot wheels.

Within each pebble is a seed
holding future planets and stars,
yet they are sand by a river

that flows broadly around my waist—
sand where my bones will someday lie
in the grit of what gave me life.

The water is to my chest now,
pushing me, swirling, testing me.
Am I a child who was born here?

If the river searched me and found
I was no native, it would sweep
me downstream into reeds and ice.

Past the middle. Even if I
lost heart, turning would be foolish.
I push on toward the farther shore.

The Statement

Already across. Continue.
Small gain: be steadfast.
In the beginning, fortune.
At the end, disorder.

The Lines

6th line —— ——
Dunking his head.
Severe.

5th line ————
The eastern neighbor slaughters an ox,
not like the western neighbor's sacrifice
and worship: faithfully receives his happiness.

4th line —— ——
Leaking: caulk with rags.
The whole day: be on guard.

3rd line ————
Gao Zong attacks the Gui Fang:
three years to overcome them.
Minor people are useless.

The Image

2nd line —— ——
A wife loses her ornaments. Do not chase:
get them back in seven days.

Water on top of fire:
already across. The wise
one prepares for calamity
by forethought.

1st line ————
Pulling his wheels, flooding the rear.
No fault.

ALREADY ACROSS comes close to the end of the sixty-four hexagrams, and yet what signifies arrival is not the end. By placing it one hexagram away from the final one, the inevitability of continuing cycles is inherent in the very structure of the sixty-four hexagrams. By using the example of someone who has finished fording a stream, this hexagram looks at the meaning of a complete cycle, knowing that a new one must follow.

For the previous sixty-two images, we have faced all the possible variations of change. We have advanced, and we have been pushed back. We have had great success, and we have had failures. We have been blessed with fortune. We have been cursed with opposition. Walking the Way is Tao. In long treks, it is inevitable that we will have to ford rivers. The river represents the final border. Once we cross it successfully, our journey is complete.

All is done. And yet, the very perfection of the moment calls for reflection. Decline happens precisely after climax. At the exact moment that order is established, disorder is the only possible alternative. We have to be careful as we complete our journey; we do not want to fall or sink in the stream. We have to carefully consider what happens next.

Change is eternal. One cycle of change begins as the previous one ends. There will be more. There will first be disorder, and we will be challenged to begin a new campaign to establish order. There will be change, and we must be prepared.

Ji ji might also be interpreted as "the completion of benefits." In the context of our long journey, this means that all the benefits of this cycle are now realized. On one hand, that is wonderful. On the other hand, it means we cannot expect more from this situation. We must begin new cycles to be reinvigorated.

Every venture is begun with a successful end in mind, and yet too many people are distracted by the process without staying strongly focused on the end. We need both kinds of attention. We need the attention that regards every single detail as a potential element in our plans. We also need the attention that constantly measures our progress against an ideal outcome.

Once we succeed, we must realize that we need to leap to a new cycle. As a cycle reaches its zenith, it must continue toward its nadir. Already Across is a reminder to initiate a new cycle as our current one ends. This is absolutely essential if we are to maintain our successes.

If we are aware, the highs and lows of life will be smoothed. We are actively managing our affairs rather than letting them control us. Throughout the study of change, we have studied the implications of fortune and misfortune, success and danger. In the end, fortune is not a matter of good being bestowed on us. Rather, it is a matter of our learning to identify the proper directions for our lives, and to set out on the journey with faith and rigor.

The *Statement* is that we are across. Permeation (the word *continue*) is complete, and we are poised to go on. The fortune we enjoyed at the beginning, though, is at an end, and so the only possibility (if we do nothing else) is disorder. Entropy succeeds all completion.

The *Lines* look at the details of both crossing and completion. (1) Someone pulls a cart through the river, and the cart's end drops and is flooded. This cannot be helped. (2) The perspective shifts to consider a completion by natural progress. Something is lost, and we find it in seven days (the completion of a cycle). (3) In contrast, some cycles take effort and patience to complete, as in the three years it took to overcome a barbarian tribe. Minor or inferior people are useless in two regards: they cannot envision a plan, and they cannot help us accomplish it either. (4) We return to the imagery of the crossing by considering a boat that begins to leak. We caulk it with rags, but we must be on guard the entire day. All crossings are dangerous, and we must be careful. (5) In an echo of the previous hexagram, which considered the value of extra effort, one person gives more in offering than another. There have been frequent suggestions in the *Changes* to give our largesse in offering, and the reward for such effort is shown here. (6) We close with the crossing again, and here the wader sinks below the surface. The consequences are severe.

The *Image* begins with water on top of fire. Water douses fire, but we put a fire out only after we are finished with it. Again, the idea of an entire cycle of work is implied. The wise person has seen innumerable cycles of beginnings and completions. Thus, at the end of each cycle, she learns from what has happened. This strengthens her forethought, and in her next endeavor, she plans so that calamities are avoided. This is a significant statement for a supposed book of divination: the wise person avoids misfortune by planning, not by depending on luck or divine forces.

If we understand this secret correctly, we will rarely experience downturns. At the height of each cycle, we move to a new cycle.

未濟

Hexagram 64
Fire above
Water below

The lines are close to their rightful positions, and they alternate well, yet they are not in their correct places. Change is close to completion but is still in the future. This hexagram refers to winter's end and approaching spring.

Wei Ji
Wei: not, not yet. The eighth of the Twelve Branches.
The time from 1:00 p.m. to 3:00 p.m.
Ji: To relieve, to aid, to cross a stream, to ford. Benefit, succeed.

The Sequence and Link
There is no halting. After crossing, new crossings are ahead.

Not Yet Across

Do not say I got a letter
and followed the geese flying south.

Do not tell me it is the way
the sun comes up over the peaks,

or how cooking fires rise in plumes.
I just know, with the melting snows,

that I must journey once again,
where winter storms have carved the shores

and cedars lie toppled on stones.
A fox stops on the water's far side,

stares, and trots on. I take a breath,
lift my stick, and plunge into the river.

The Statement

Not yet across. Continue.
The young fox, nearly across,
soaks its tail.
No place is gainful.

The Lines

6th line ———

There is confidence in drinking wine.
No fault. Flooding one's head.
Have confidence in a vow.

5th line —— ——

The prince's brilliance has sincerity.
Fortune.

4th line ———

Pure fortune. Regrets vanish. Terrifyingly
attack the Gui Fang. In three years,
there will be rewards in a great country.
Pure fortune. No regrets.

3rd line —— ——

Not yet across. Attacking: misfortune.
Gain by crossing the great river.

The Image

2nd line ———

Pulls his wheels.
Pure fortune.

Fire on top of water:
not yet across. The wise
one distinguishes things
carefully, and puts them
in their places.

1st line —— ——

Flooding his tail. Sorrow.

NOT YET ACROSS: we are poised at the beginning of a new venture, and this moment when heaven and earth pause between inhalation and exhalation is sacred, terrible, peaceful, fecund. Infinity is made by countless crossings from endings to beginnings. Heaven and earth create and change without cease. Fire and water dance eternally, sometimes extinguishing one another, sometimes combining as big as clouds or sometimes moving as softly as a baby's breath. The Way is forever, and its process is not linear. It is ending, turning, overlapping, and crossing.

If all was infinity with no beginning and no ends, then no endings could ever meet new beginnings. In Hexagram 63, we came to the end of a cycle. In this hexagram, we see the beginning of a new cycle.

Future cycles will be like one of the sixty-four hexagrams or one of the three hundred eighty-four lines. The situation will seem varied because of the combination of circumstances and because different people will be acting in different roles. How can we account for the fact that events can seem both an enactment of something archetypal and yet new? It is we who will have changed.

We could not tolerate living if all was mere repetition of what came before. We are disdainful of exact duplication. We grow bored. If we are trapped in sameness, we fall into despondency.

Yet we cannot ignore the sameness of life either. If there was no similarity in life, we could not have education. The central premise of all learning is that there are fundamental kinds of knowledge that we need in order to live well, make intelligent decisions, do our jobs, and pursue our personal interests. If there was no regularity in life to make learning dependable, no one would improve.

We learn, and by this we face each situation with different approaches. We change as our lives change, and our subsequent actions will affect what happens next. When we learn, we influence the future.

This, then, is the river we ford: the border between one cycle and the next. How amazing. How outrageous. All along, we have been striving to blend with change. We have used the river as a metaphor for natural and harmonious living. And yet here, now, is the crucial message: understand change not by riding the river, but by facing it, confronting it. Cross it.

We crossed over thresholds in our homes to begin this journey. We passed through gates. We committed ourselves with each step. Standing on the shore, we know we must cross to change again.

We went from child to adult, from student to graduate, from trainee to veteran, from single person to spouse, from novice to master, and we will go from elder to ancestor—all by crossing.

Crossing is dangerous. Crossing immerses us. When we ford the river, we get wet. We are not apart from life. We cannot separate when we cross. We will be soaked. But without crossing, we will never realize what change is.

Wisdom is to act in that measureless juncture between beginning and ending. The *Statement* is more an illustration than a prediction: when we are not yet across, there is more risk than chance of accomplishment. A young fox misjudges and gets wet: we are not yet in a safe situation. No place is gainful: we have not yet made land, so of course nothing significant can be done. We have to get to the other side before our plans can unfold.

The *Lines* extend these themes. (1) As a direct outcome of the Statement, the fox has wet its tail and is sorrowful. (2) In an echo of the first line of the last hexagram, someone is dragging a cart across a ford, but this time there is good fortune: his steadfastness brings success. (3) In advice that we can well imagine would be given to a general, we are advised that it is not yet time to cross. To attack would bring misfortune. The advice to cross the great river is not contradictory: we must use the river to travel to the right place. (4) How long does a cycle take? How long does it take to make our plans work? In this line, it takes three years of campaigning, but the rewards are an entire country. (5) The secret of change still lies in the individual who works with it. Here, the prince is both brilliant and sincere. Fortune comes from his character. (6) Finally, there are difficulties, even for such a prince. There is a sinking into the river while fording. The line mentions confidence twice—before the disaster and after. Again, it is the determination of the person that makes the difference between giving in to disaster and triumphing over it. A vow is made: the superior person's decision determines fate.

The *Image* confirms this: by distinguishing things carefully and arranging them in their proper places, the wise person creates the right conditions for change. We are not helpless before the great process of change. We are not mere supplicants waiting for a pronouncement from an oracle. No, we are masters of our own destinies because we make decisions, exercise forethought, distinguish between high and low, and arrange things to reach our goals.

The Voice of the Oracle

I

Heaven existed before us all: the origin, smooth and pervasive, giving all gain, pure and firm.

Two masters tutored me. One was named Lianshanyi—Changes of Linked Mountains. The other was named Guicanyi—The Changes That Return and Store. I became their disciple and took the name Zhouyi—Circles of Change. My masters' bodies and words have been lost, but their wisdom lives in me.

I was a boy when my masters took me traveling. They taught me to observe people, to follow the flow of rivers and lakes, and to chase the divine breath as it swirled over mountain ridges. They fed me, and they fed me the first lesson of youth: waiting. I ignored the great lesson of patience, pacing on a riverbank until the omens were right. I was soaked to my chest when we forded the stream. On the far side, I trotted on without looking back. I should have stopped to memorize the curve of the bank, the arch of the bare branches, but I never stopped to consider that I had just made the first of many crossings.

II

There were books, although you would not know them like you know books today. Those books were strips of bamboo, split from green trunks and carefully dried, with words copied onto them with black ink. The strips were stitched together with cord or leather. When I was young, knowledge was held together tenuously.

I grew as the language grew. People were still gathering words and deciding their meanings when I was a boy. The books, so fragile with their bindings, were also fragile in their meanings. No one ought to regard that as strange. No one speaks the way people did even fifty years ago, so it should be no surprise that no one talks the way they did three thousand years ago.

Words were young. Books could fall apart at the snap of a string. Such things were too weak for my teachers. They demanded that I memorize everything. A human being, they declared, was the ultimate standard. No machine, no war, no task on a farm, no boat on a river could be greater than a person. They asked me: had not the Great Yu created the dikes and ditches that saved thousands from flooding?

In a land where a farmer worked harder than a water buffalo, it was no wonder that my teachers measured everything by what a person could do. If the world required superhuman abilities, their student should be made superhuman. I memorized. I recited. I memorized again.

Words were were important, worthy of being cast in bronze or carved in stone. But they could never equal experience passed freely from one person to another. Words that were dry ink on bamboo could never thunder like blood pounding in human veins. Knowledge is seeded in a human being, to gestate, to be born, and then planted in another.

By the time I was a young man, I had learned the ways of the hunt, of the bow, of the chariot, of the sword. I also learned of the stars, of numbers, of the words carved into shell, bamboo, and stone. My teachers taught me the rituals and sacrifices and taught me to walk with dignity. Many times, their teachings vexed me, and yet I could never escape their eyes or their hands.

I later regretted turning and twisting from their teachings. When I went to the palace, my eyes glazed over and I could not see into the characters of the officials. My voice faltered: I could make no reply to cunning words. I forgot the rules. I forgot who was friend and who was enemy. Confused, I retreated to my hometown.

The first war of my lifetime came. I joined the prince. In the center of the army, I saw the king. When he raised his flag, we advanced. When the battle was over, he rewarded us with bolts of cloth and pieces of land. When he commanded, we obeyed. My king—the son of heaven himself—gave orders, and yet I witnessed victory decided by battle, not words. There were times when our chariots carried more dead to the rear than they carried warriors to the front. Nonetheless, if not for the blood turning rivers red and skulls piling up walls for borders, the nations would never have been established.

The barbarians surrendered. We had lost many people. The country languished in weariness, as when men throw themselves from the plow board when the sun sets. The king called for a great hunt, and I was privileged to join. He sat erect in his saddle, and saluted us. Our shouts made our chests tremble and our horses stamp. The king used beaters to drive the game, and as was his custom, he left one side open to spare some of the animals. I understood that as the power not just of mercy, but of voluntary joining. That hunt was the beginning of our country's rise.

It would be years before we could say that we had fulfilled our promise as a nation. In the beginning, the treasury was nearly empty. The king sent officials everywhere, but the people were slow to obey new regulations. It was like trying to tame a wild stallion; one must be content with small efforts first. What counted was sincerity, and the increase of confidence on both sides. We blamed no one, and so what was small eventually grew larger.

We learned how to act like a nation. We learned how to act toward other nations. We established laws and regulations. In the temples, we respected the customs of local people.

The nations of the world are now old, and it is hard to remember what it was like when countries were young and the smallest details of a society needed to be discovered. You may think it easy to walk, but how does a crowd of people walk down the road? Where will they go to? What happens if some will not give way? How do you regulate the borders and allow trade and yet protect your own country? A country's laws and character spring from just such considerations. The lame, the blind, the poor, the rich, the warrior, the prince, and the sage—all people walk, and yet all people must obey teachings if we are to walk together.

We reached a time of great peace. What is that if not the balance between war on one side and the downfall of a country from within on the other? What is that if not a balance between the plows of a country and its golden coffers? All the people came together, and we kept walking as a nation, and we learned that the most powerful way would be called the Middle Way. That is the only way where we found happiness and peace.

Flatterers. Greedy merchants. People who would not work. Petty officials taking bribes. Small-minded bureaucrats. Dukes interested only in enriching their own fiefs. Myopic astronomers. Pig-faced generals. Scheming slaves. Disobedient youth. All these, and more, are called small people. As the time of peace lengthened, we did not find paradise. Instead, we saw a degeneration into selfishness.

Small people crept into every crevice of our country, as cockroaches and rats slowly infiltrate the most opulent of palaces. We maintained the sacrifices. We maintained the offerings. Still, the small people overran the temples and courts. Pull aside a palace curtain, and it seemed these small people would go scurrying back into the darkness.

I fell in love with a woman whose dark hair drew a veil over me, a veil of night where new constellations glimmered, and I gladly navigated a thousand voyages over rolling seas. We married, forging a pin of gold harder than any bronze, a pin that joined us more strongly than a chariot is joined to its yoke, and we wheeled and turned over plains that stretched beyond the setting sun.

I held my children. I bathed them. Wiped them. Helped them walk. Fed them before food touched my own lips. I taught them, and gave them wealth it took a lifetime to heap up.

I fought and helped to found a dynasty. I punished barbarian invaders. I argued for a just rule.

In my later years, I was disgraced and banished. I went back to digging in the soil, back to being a peasant again. I nearly starved to death during one of the famines.

When I was recalled to the capital, I was not grateful—only wary. Even as I was sent from one frontier to another, forgotten again, recalled again, and burdened again, I reminded myself that I wanted to serve my nation. Eventually, I was promoted to the highest circles of the land. I became that noble leader whose mere twitch of a finger could steady or shake an empire.

At the height of my powers, I walked alone, back to the water I first crossed with my teachers, and I stood, looking once more on the banks of that great river.

III

Memory is a circle of people sitting in a grassy valley. It is a full circle, even though the way each person settles hips and shoulders on hewn rock stools forms the outlines of the missing: Great-grandparents who shriveled into their black robes until the robes themselves unraveled. Fathers who died on the battlefields, petrified into unaging heroes wrapped in war garb for eternity. Young children buried in tiny coffins, clutching small bunches of flowers in cold fingers. When we speak of the missing, we say their names as if they should be sitting there. To speak their name is defiance of the black, shaggy-maned monster that snatches our loved ones and mauls them before our unblinking eyes.

Stories are told as answers to endless questions.

"What happened during the war?"

"Why must we dig ditches for water?"

"How was fire given to our people?"

"Where do the clouds go?"

The stories are told repeatedly until each one murmurs it, sometimes at startling moments, as when we are nearly run down by a train and we wonder why the face of the first ancestor to settle this valley comes to us.

Memory links the crawling infant, drooling on the grass, to the adult bent over the fields, rising in darkness, to the wrinkled and stooped elder—one who, no matter whether witnessing outrageous murder or sublime wedding, stretches out a bony hand and nods assent.

This is memory. Oh, we may speak of synapses and neurons while shuffling our papers, riffling black letters we tabulate by the millions. We may swoop in planes, climb towers to watch the stars, and plunge into a sea so clear you can see the submerged cities even ghosts have abandoned, but we always return to this memory, this circle.

You may pour all you know through a keyboard, channeling it into a pantomime of your speculations, but you will still go to sit in the circle at day's end.

From this circle, stories are passed to other circles, linking into one circuit around the earth, and this circle is alive as long as its ends touch, as long as its circumference remains intact. A circle is a self-evident truth: in our memories there are no deceptions.

The circle vibrates, shimmers, and makes countless other circles tremble, including the circles that form our arteries and veins, the hollows of our hearts, the oval of our open throats, the gossamer circles of our very cells, clustered together to make the toughest sinew.

See how we go back to certain places, like wolves cautiously sniffing our way into unknown territory! We pad the dry dirt, sniff the weeds for smells so thick we could chew them, inch along trails to catch scents of rabbit and deer, or smell piss left as a marker. We thrill to places of golden light, or those with sea breezes sweeping up volcanic flanks like the blessings of a thousand gods, or the shrubbed hills where vineyards hang with bulging grapes. We want to go back to those places we have never before visited but which will sparkle with our recognition.

We want to go back home. To the grit and dark waters where we first crawled. To the forest whose smells sum up our decades of walking. To fields of wheat made blinding by the noonday sun. We touch the clods, hot with summer, and think how the waste we have buried enriches the thickly packed stalks. When we eat, we eat the earth, the sky, the water, the sun, the grass, and the mountain toward which the cranes wing home to the marsh. We are tied to Place. We are silly to make up explanations when our yearning is no more complicated then seeing a tree's roots.

When we are back home, forgetting is as important as remembering. It is an art. We remember how we stabbed a boy during the war, how we saw the rape of a girl in the corner of a barn, how we slumped as tax collectors took a family's land, how we ran as hooded horsemen spread fire through the emperor's palace, with silhouetted figures scurrying like ants. These memories we try to forget, and we cannot.

Then there is the forgetting we cannot stem. The numbers we just added. The face of our lover clenched in a moan. The trail where our father walked. The exact order of homes on the way to our village. These are all things we swore we would never forget, but we find them drifting out of our grasp like mists over a ridge.

Death is tearing asunder by remembering the whole.

Rebirth is healing, but forgetting the whole.

Far too many forget the circle.

IV

There is an art to change:

It converses with our ancestors.

It is the stone that changes the river current.

It shows us new colors.

It plunges to ocean floors and roams freely there.

It is a paint stroke bursting into flame that will burn for a thousand years.

V

Can you tell the story of others' experiences?

Can you sing of those being born louder than the dirges for the black ships sailing in the sunset?

Can you reseed a forest?

Can you unlock the sleeper's doors?

Can you say even one word beyond the masters?

Can you cut the cloth of early sorrows to stitch a rainbow robe for a child?

Can you do one thing to end illness?

Do not say I am east.

Do not say I am west.

Do not say you have no friends in the north.

Do not say nothing good comes from the south.

I stand in the circle's center, and command all compass points.

VI

Say what has never been said. Say you are in love, though your heart is quavering and your feet twitch.

Say what has never been said. Stand up, when all your life men stood over you with fists and as they ordered you to crawl.

Say what has never been said. Speak your story like a train roaring out of a tunnel on newly laid track.

Say what has never been said. When a child puts her hand in yours, speak kindness.

Say what has never been said. Talk to an animal, talk to that spirit within.

Say what has never been said. Make your own life a metaphor for a lotus— instead of the other way around.

Say what has never been said. Talk dumb. Act stupid. Play. Speak outside the cleverness of schooling and job.

Say what has never been said. When you hear a siren, stand up and wail like every child being born.

Say what has never been said. Say that spirit is supreme, even as your body loses strength to age.

Say what has never been said.

Say the name of your god.
Say your own name aloud.
Say a silence no one
has ever heard before.

VII

Bathe in water every day. Let the liquid that has washed this planet for millions of years, that birthed us, that is blood, tears, semen, milk, and sweat, that has soaked pyres, that has chorused in the waves—
Let that take our stories and wash us.

Stretch out naked before fire: Our mother's heart was a sun, igniting our own heart as she embraced us, feeding us first with her own warm milk and then later with grain. She gave us meadows to play in, fields to till, fire that warmed bed and hearth. Then the inferno of invasion swept in, the bonfires of victory, the candles we lit as we laid our mother's body on the pyre, and we lit a lantern and with our hearts—
Let that take our stories and warm us.

Eat from the earth every day. The chunks of black flesh pack against one another, burst with white roots; studded with carrots, peanuts, and potatoes; green stalks, yellow reeds, it piles up millet and peaches, melons and gourds by the rivers it banks; spreads in broad plains where herds of horses gallop, sheep roam golden hills, and deer leap in forests.

Let that take our stories and feed us.

Breathe in heaven every day. That blue sphere that disperses into a mist finer than any fog, that we gulp every minute, that is field to cloud, that is emptiness as endless source, space of a supreme voice.

Let that take our stories and breathe us.

VIII

I am Zhouyi, who sits in a labyrinth of granite walls polished to mirror luster. I am the oracle that people in cities and valleys whisper about, whom lunatics and princes, poets and singers, hermits and youth alike wander to find. You know me. You have heard me. You have eaten me in your rice.

I am inside you, an incandescent presence in your back, thunder and lightning extruded into a beam flashing through your spine, arcing to where you sit on a web of filaments pulsing with stars. Heaven fuses with earth, sending down rain.

You hear me. I am inside you. You cannot forget me. You will listen for me until the day you die and your voice will become entwined with mine forever. The words will tremble in the air over our grave. You will hear me.

We will be reborn as one.

I am Zhouyi, who has lived, and fought, and been father for a million times each generation, who waits to see if anything goes beyond two, four, eight, sixty-four, or three hundred eighty-four. From the beginning, not one single event has escaped me, and yet every event is new, surprising, and enthralling.

Yuan heng li zhen: the origin, smooth and pervasive, giving all gain, pure and firm.

I am Zhouyi.
You know me:
you are Zhouyi.
You will return.

Appendixes

Appendix Contents

The following appendixes contain supplementary materials and discussions on difficult issues. In many ways, we are identifying many of the puzzles about the *Changes*. These may never be resolved, but they are still important to any deeper discussion of the classic.

Problems such as the loss of source materials and the peculiarities of translation may never be settled. However, understanding the questions will help us listen more thoughtfully to the debates that are bound to continue. Each of must make decisions about how we will use the *Changes*. Until we understand the controversies, we will not be able to fully make those choices.

Approaching the *Changes*

We have acknowledged that the two most common approaches to the *Changes* are the traditional mode and the academic mode.

The traditional mode accepts all the received claims as factual. The pious regard the *Changes* as a gift never to be questioned. If a passage seems obscure, the fault is considered to be the reader's. To do otherwise is thought disrespectful.

The academic mode, by contrast, skeptically scrutinizes every detail of the *Changes*. Suspicious that traditional claims are without rigor, and relying instead on research, textual analysis, and archaeological discoveries, scholars search for corruptions in the text in an effort to date the strata of the *Changes* and determine authorship.

Both approaches want the truth about the *Changes*. Both approaches skew the truth they find.

Traditionalists assert that if a person submits to the *Changes* without resistance, the truth will eventually be realized. They argue that a tradition that emphasizes virtue and self-cultivation requires both humility and effort. Many traditionalists place so much value on the book that they want to share it only with people who "deserve" it. Thus, they have no qualms about demanding decades of investigation—repeating in delight the story that Confucius wore out the leather bindings of his copy three times.

I can personally say that there is some validity to this approach, having spent more than thirty years studying the *Changes*, Taoism, *qigong,* and martial arts (including three styles that are particularly allied with the philosophy of the *Changes*: Xingyiquan, Baguazhang, and Taijiquan). The traditional path is a lifelong one that yields new insight each year it is practiced. If that were not so, there would be no reason to continue.

In spite of that, many people still scoff at the traditional methods, mocking the old masters as deliberately paradoxical. As if our world of automobiles, Internet communication, shopping malls, and dance clubs is all that's worth knowing, we dismiss any difficult concepts as absurdly religious. People would not be so scornful if they had seen what I have seen these many years, but then, that's a contradiction: with their attitudes, they cannot see what tradition has to offer. If they looked, especially in today's Asian communities, they would see that the traditions of the *Changes* are still very much in evidence.

Here are some examples: A red and green *bagua* mirror bearing the Early Heaven Eight Trigrams can be found in any Chinatown curio store. You can also see it hung above the doors of many shops and homes in Chinese communities. The mirror is believed to ward off evil spirits. (A priest must consecrate the mirror during a ritual and put a thumbprint on it.) Four of the Eight Trigrams—Heaven, Earth, Water, and Fire—appear on the flag of South Korea around a yin yang symbol. The *Changes* has been used as a manual for warfare. The principles of the Eight Trigrams have been appropriated for martial arts (Baguazhang and Taijiquan are the most obvious cases), and if one wants an authentic *Changes* consultation in Asia, one can go to a roadside fortuneteller or to one of the many temples where readings are given.

In Hong Kong, old men sit at card tables on the sidewalks, with the symbols of the *Changes* clearly displayed, ready to count the yarrow stalks for clients. For those who want a more formal experience, they can go to a temple that offers divination. There are many oracles in Chinese temples, and the *Changes* is considered one of the greatest.

However, the experience of temple fortune-telling may be so bizarre that one may be forgiven for never wanting to do it again. One temple I visited was a riot of supplicants, each carrying offerings of whole cooked chickens and roast pork.

Rivers of red ran down the sidewalks. The halls, courtyards, and walkways were so packed that people who came late could not even get close to the temple. So they stopped however close they could get in the crowd, lit incense, and knelt down to chant and worship. There was so much burning incense that the grounds seemed as if they were on fire. The blood-red rivers were from piles of flaming red-dyed offerings and incense that the groundskeepers tried vainly to hose down.

If you found a priest, you could ask him to inquire of the oracle. After praying as fervently as you could in the midst of screaming and crying women, you might then shake a cylindrical bamboo container filled with many stakes until one slipped out. This stake is inscribed with a number that matches a preprinted fortune available on a large rack. The pronouncement is usually cryptic poetry, which the priest must decipher for you. Naturally, he will ask you to detail your case to him first; ancient poetry and folk belief intersect with modern counseling.

There is a problem in the need for interpretation, and anyone with less-than-perfect faith is bound to be troubled. If we go to a specialist, will we be able to rely on the responses given to us? Or, if we use the *Changes* ourselves, will we make an accurate interpretation, especially when the text is obscure even to Chinese readers?

Masters will declare that the very time it takes to consult the oracle is necessary. They will insist that the time spent puts us into a contemplative state, and that doing so attunes us to the book. They will stipulate that only someone who engages in daily and rigorous self-cultivation will have the insight to interpret the hexagram. Perhaps, Zen-like, it isn't even the actual bestowal of a pronouncement that is important. Maybe it's the koanlike occasion to pursue enlightenment that is the goal.

Taking the time to contemplate one's predicament is good, because one's inner wisdom and priorities might surface. Certainly, the *Changes* is worth the decades of study and self-cultivation it requires. Nevertheless, such study has to have its practical role in daily life to be useful.

Even in the past, those who used the *Changes* faced moments too sudden to sit in contemplation. War, political intrigue, the demands of others, the decisions for governing a town—all these situations and more would have loomed with such ferocity that action, not contemplation, would have been required. A number of prominent masters of the *Changes* faced real trouble. Qu Xi (1130–1200 C.E.), a governor, commentator on the Five Classics, and editor of the version of the *Changes* many traditionalists use today, fell victim to court intrigues when he was a governor. For a time, he lost all his honors and official posts. He was accused of sedition, being unfilial, the practice of magic, and the seduction of nuns. Meditation is wonderful and should be done on a daily basis, but it cannot solve all our difficulties in life.

The traditional mode takes years of study and requires adequate guidance by someone who understands the *Changes*. There is nothing mystical about that. Every subject needs a teacher to make it truly come alive. The moral values the *Changes* advocate are best observed in practice. But there are few masters in this world, and our needs are pressing. That is why *The Living I Ching* attempts to keep as much of the traditional basis as possible while trying to supply insights that a reader can immediately apply.

The Difference Between East and West

The fact that we must read the *Changes* in translation adds to our difficulties. Most translations clearly have a philosophical bias. Some have shaped the book into the loftiest of academic books and others have made it the most shallow fortune-telling manuals.

Translations from Asia tend to focus on the divinatory aspects of the book. For example, a hexagram that is supposed to mirror heaven and earth is suddenly used to discuss being faithful to one's wife or being a good employee. On the other hand, translations by scholars seem to concentrate on comparing different versions of the text, searching for faults in an attempt to claim some academic territory.

No translation, no matter how complete, can bring us to a full understanding of the *Changes*. Even if we translate every word and give all its meanings, we can never approach the richness of the original language. There are no English words that contain the same clusters of definitions, no phrases that can evoke the same emotional responses. What sounds absurdly simple in Chinese—yet allows for days of contemplation—sounds ridiculously stilted and one-dimensional in translation. Each translator is not duplicating the book in a different language, but creating their own version of it. If translation was absolute, we could translate a book from English into Chinese, then give the Chinese translation to another team to translate back into English. It's obvious that the retranslated text could never match the original. Translation is an imperfect art.

Equally tempting would be to simply translate the *Changes* by giving the full cluster of meanings to each word—and letting the reader sort it out. The *Changes* repeats many words like formulas or mantras. We could create a database, input the meanings, and then replace each Chinese word with its English equivalent. But this mechanistic approach is untenable: it cannot show context.

People in Asia today do not speak or use the vocabulary of the *Changes* in the way they did even a few hundred years ago. Some Chinese words appear only in the *Changes* and nowhere else. *Dui,* the name for the trigram Lake, has no other meaning except the name of a trigram and hexagram. Many of the phrases of the *Changes* have survived as single aphorisms or idioms, but no one remembers the full context from which they were originally taken. Some of the words are defined in dictionaries by a quote from the *Changes*. This makes the *Changes* both the only source of and primary context for its own vocabulary.

Some of the interpretation of the *Changes*, as voluminous as the book is today, does come from stories and understandings outside the book itself. A critical reader would know the history of the Zhou dynasty, would understand that the book has been used by generals in many wars, and would be able to discern which strains in the book were Taoist and which were classical. Readers would also know all Five Classics and could mentally tabulate similarities between different volumes. For example, they could simultaneously read the Duke of Zhou's commentary to a line, think of his speeches quoted in the *Documents,* and know the poetry attributed to him in the *Odes.* Such adjunct knowledge would inform any study of the book. However, such knowledge is also rare.

The Changes, Feudalism, and Gender Roles

It's important to have a clear view of how we want the *Changes* to influence us. If we take on too literal a view of the classic, we end up with values that don't fit with today's world. The original *Changes* was the product of feudal times. The stories, legends, and mythology surrounding the *Changes*—princes, castles, cities under seize, warriors, women being married as secondary wives, and even the basic family structure with its patriarchal tinges—are all part of its feudal imagery. We must separate the *Changes*' beneficial wisdom from the rigidity of the society that first created it.

Perhaps we even need some feudal structures to feel comfortable. Although we study feudalism as if it were an antique phase in human development, we are still emotionally stuck in that time. Some countries maintain monarchies. Fairy tales with princesses still fascinate us. Our political systems mimic monarchies, though they have modifying laws. Our corporations are quite feudal, with one company gobbling up others, just as powerful dynasties once invaded neighboring states.

Nevertheless, we will not be well served to duplicate these values in our lives today. Many situations in our lives may be reminiscent of feudal times—the quarrel between nations may well parallel the behavior of corporate raiders—but we have to take the old as pointers to deeper truths.

The only reason to delve into the stories and imagery of the *Changes* is because they are symbols of archetypal realities. We may not have princes, warriors, and intrigue behind the emperor's back today, but we have many situations that are like that. We may not have geese flying toward grave mounds today, but the reminder of cyclical passings is always important.

None of us would change places with someone a thousand years ago. We would not want to live like the Zhou. As we use the *Changes,* then, we must catch the spirit of the values it offers, and apply it to our life and times now.

Indeed, we must consciously turn away from the feudal values that still exist in the world today. The way we treat women and children is the primary example of how much work we have to do. Beyond that, we still have nations bickering over borders. There is worldwide slavery. Wealthy landowners on many continents exploit their laborers. And we still see nature as passive dirt to be plowed, mined, and dirtied.

The *Changes* offers a choice to us. It couches its imagery in feudal times, but it also urges us to improve ourselves and to constantly strive for moral and ethical behavior. We must take its imagery as pointers toward our deepest emotions, but we must then modulate those emotions with the insight gained by long study. Only by identifying what is feudal in us—and what may be of value within that—can we prevent ourselves from falling into backward tendencies.

The Similar Difficulty of Interpreting the *Changes* in East and West

We are at a strange moment in the history of the *Changes.* Translations from the Chinese are approximate, and native Chinese do not understand the book. Yet the book is still popular, and we have as great a need as ever for its contents.

Without a doubt, the language of the *Changes*—that necessary but imperfect vehicle for two and a half millennia of thinking—is both essential to explore and just as critical to transcend. If we ignore the meanings of the words, we will not get the right understanding. However, embroiling ourselves in semantic analysis without ever looking at what the words are pointing to would be an equal mistake. It seems that anyone interested in the *Changes* must make a careful study of what the words mean—as one would do with any close reading of a literary work. Whether one is reading in Chinese or another language, the footing nowadays is about the same. The words are necessary to understand. The content is even more important.

Nowhere is this more important than in examining the values of the *Changes*. We must use the book to identify the core emotions of being human. By all means, study the book over many years. Sharpen your understanding of all the debates surrounding this classic. Let the *Changes* help you make decisions. Consider carefully as you apply its advice, making sure that you are grasping what it is pointing to instead of taking it too literally. Reject emulation of feudal structures, but understand the archetypal in all of us.

In the end, whether you are Chinese or not is no barrier. For the last two thousand years, every generation of Chinese have been unable to fully read the *Changes* in its original form. Translations, though imperfect, have already influenced thousands. When a person goes to the *Changes* to divine, it is not the words that are important, it is the purity of the reader. Those who are pure of heart will always be able to open this book, and it will speak to them.

Translation and the *Changes*

All translation is imperfect and relative. At the same time, some translations, though flawed, can become the focus of an entire generation. The Richard Wilhelm version of the *Changes* has influenced many people, including Carl Jung. Even if we establish that there are problems with some of Wilhelm's phrasing, those phrases have already entered into the consciousness of several generations; there can be no pulling them back.

Thus, we could never excise or "correct" the influence of the *Changes* on Jungian psychology. When a new person who is interested in Jungian theories looks into the *Changes,* he or she is likely to prefer the Wilhelm version over others. The circuit is then completed, and a cluster of new thinking tied to the Wilhelm version grows. Pointing out textual errors will neither alter nor augment the value these readers place on the book.

Moreover, many translators were so influenced by previous translations that they did not dare to say anything substantially different from what was said before. Wilhelm and Cary F. Baynes translated one of the key phrases, *yuan heng li zhen,* as "perseverance furthers, supreme success." (Baynes translated Wilhelm's German translation of the *Changes* into English.) One can tell the lack of courage of subsequent translators when they followed this same phrasing—even if, as they claimed in their introductions, they knew the Chinese language better.

In discussing the problems of translation, I hope to throw some light onto particularly difficult words, explain why I have interpreted them the way I have, and extend the discussion of the *Changes*.

Hexagram 1

There is a significant phrase in the *Changes*. It is *yuan heng li zhen*. Since the phrase appears repeatedly in the *Changes,* it is a logical place to begin our inquiry.

In Hexagram 1, Heaven, the entire text of King Wen's Judgment is:

Qian yuan heng li zhen

Before we even turn our attention to the problem of translation, we have to accept that early written Chinese had no punctuation. Perhaps this was because there was an emphasis on memorization and oral language, and the written forms were considered to be mnemonic aids. Maybe the Chinese never saw a need for punctuation. The usual explanation is that it was assumed that the reader would know where to put the pauses. This required a universal knowledge of classical forms, so that a reader would discern what breaks were intended and simply add them in. For example, many Chinese poems are written with either four, five, or seven words per line. When a reader is preparing to read a classical poem, which is usually written in a single block of words with no punctuation or line breaks, the reader has to count the words in the poem and divide them by either four, five, or seven and then mentally add the line breaks. So in reading the above, we could consider that it might be punctuated: *Qian: yuan heng li zhen.*

The Wilhelm/Baynes translation renders the above line as follows:

The creative works sublime success,
Furthering through perseverance.

When we say, "The creative *works…*," we are already taking liberty with the translation. Adding "works" already shades the meaning of the line. *Yuan heng* is translated as "sublime success," and by putting "furthering through perseverance" on the next line, there is both punctuation (a comma) and a line break to group words together. The original five-word line has no punctuation and so we can-not deny the translation, and yet we cannot feel fully confident either. Modern Chinese editions of the *Changes* usually add punctuation, but again, this is the decision of an editor. While the additional punctuation often helps make passages intelligible, it does not allow for the different meanings possible when the reader mentally varies the punctuation. It is like comparing the fretted neck of a guitar to a violin neck. With a guitar, the frets determine a specific note. With a violin, you could put your finger into a place between the "normal" notes and thereby discover one of the infinite notes between the intervals of a normal key.

A person fluent in Chinese and versed in classical culture would hold entire clusters of meaning in the words. They might read it like this:

[*Qian:* The first of the Eight Trigrams. Heaven, male, father, sovereign.] [*Yuan:* The beginning, the first, the original. The head. A dollar. The eldest, chief, big. Sixty years (in Chinese astrology). A surname.] [*Heng:* To go through smoothly, pervade, success, fortunate, to persevere.] [*Li:* Profit, benefit, advantage, gain, sharp, to serve.] [*Zhen:* Chastity of a woman; pure, virtuous; incorruptible; firm; devotion, dedicated; divine, inquire by divination.]

When they read these five lines, then, they are not necessarily reading it like a sentence but as a matrix of metaphors that can freely combine and recombine in their mind. Out of this matrix of meanings will come an association with the person's inquiry. This is not mystical in the least. It is fundamental human nature to make connections, to see parallel meanings out of juxtaposition. We go to the *Changes* with certain questions on our minds, and then we are given a range of imagery that will interact with our concerns. The deeper we go, the more complex the process, and the more dense the web of associations becomes.

If we look at the phrase as a whole, we could reasonably translate it as the Wilhelm/Baynes translation does. We could also understand the phrase in other ways as well:

Offering the primary sacrifice, there is a beneficial omen.

At the main sacrifice there is an advantageous divination.

Make the primary sacrifice with beneficial devotion.

For beginning ventures to benefit, one must have an advantageous, firm, and incorruptible character.

In the beginning there was a force spreading unimpeded that makes the grain we harvest and inspires our reverence.

We are inspired to reverence by the unimpeded gain from our very origins.

The beneficial answers to our divination come directly from the origin.

These paraphrases capture aspects of what the four words could mean, yet none of them have the resonance of *yuan heng li zhen.* They also lack the completeness of meaning available in Chinese. The word *zhen* in particular has connotations that a Western reader might not combine intuitively. How are we to keep in mind meanings ranging from "divination" to "chastity"? How can we put them onto the level of the Qing dynasty commentator, Qu Xi, when he asserted that the four words are equivalent to the seasons: *yuan,* the origin, is spring; *heng,* the pervasive and furthering, is summer; *li,* profit and benefit, is autumn; *zhen,* pure and correct, is winter?

We can intellectually grasp these combinations of meanings, but it is difficult to feel them directly on a gut level. A screen comes down between what we feel and the words themselves. Those who know cannot speak.

We should not be discouraged, though. The four words could also be interpreted to mean that "the answer to divination is beneficial and comes directly from the origin." With this view, there is a distinct assertion that the *Changes* immediately responds to an inquiry from the origin of the universe.

Hexagram 2

In Hexagram 2, the *Changes* expands on the basic formula. (Line breaks are introduced for convenience; they do not exist in the original. The capitalization is also added.)

Kun yuan heng li pin ma zhi zhen
Jun zi you you wang
Xian mi hou de zhu…

We have this translation in the Wilhelm-Baynes version:

The receptive brings about sublime success,
Furthering through the perseverance of a mare.
If the superior man undertakes something and tries
   to lead,
He goes astray.
But if he follows, he finds guidance.

This leaves us with additional questions. In the first line, we could consider a phrase like *li pin ma zhen,* which might mean "Benefit from a mare's omen," meaning you are getting a gentle, docile reading. But it could just as easily mean, "If you want to gain, have the same chaste virtue (*zhen*) as a mare (*pin ma*)." Or, it could mean "You will benefit from the purity and firmness (*zhen*) of a mare (*pin ma*), and the *Changes* could be referring either to an actual horse or to something in your life for which the horse might be a metaphor. Undoubtedly, an educated reader would hold both possibilities in their mind as they set out trying to comprehend the *Changes.*

A phrase like *jun zi,* which begins the second line, means "prince," "gentleman," "person of virtue," or "superior one." The entire second line, *jun zi you you wang,* could literally be interpreted as "the superior person has a destination." Again, the connotations of *jun zi* being a prince (much of the *Changes* is framed as advice to a ruler) and being a superior person (in other words, to be a superior person, follow the advice that is about to be given) are both intentional.

The next line literally means, "First, confusion. After, mastery." However, *zhu* in this case has a variety of other possible interpretations: master, leader, chief, host. God, Lord, to officiate at, to preside, to take charge of, main, chief, primary, principal. Any of these meanings might be applicable—"first confusion, after, you will find your master." Or, "first confusion, after (you will pull others together to) preside."

Hexagram 18

I have always dreaded receiving Hexagram 18, and many others feel the same. It seemed to be one of the "worst," a judgment that everything was simply rotten. Then, when I was working on understanding the commentary to the Lines, I realized the multiple messages that were there. These multiple messages cannot be understood just by reading translations. With the lack of punctuation and extremely compressed language, the *Changes* allows for numerous readings, allowing the reader to infer an answer that will seem virtually custom-tailored to the inquiry. Imagine if we were worried about our father's health and we received Hexagram 18 as you read the passages below. The Chinese is followed by a word-for-word rendering and then two alternate interpretations to suggest many more possible ones.

Line 1:

a. *Gan fu zhi gu*
b. *You zi kao wu jiu*
c. *Li zhong ji.*

[*Gan*: trunk—either of a tree or a body. The main part of anything. Capabilities, talent, business, manage.] [*Fu*: father. A male relative of earlier generations such as an uncle older than one's father, or a grandfather. To do father's duties. In ancient times, a respectful term for an elderly man.] [*Zhi*: To go, to leave, zigzag, winding; it, her, him, them, this, that, those, these, of.] [*Gu*: Poison, venom, harm. To bewitch, to enchant.]

[*You*: To have, to be present, to exist, there is.] [*Zi*: A child, son, offspring. Seed, egg. First of the Twelve Heavenly Branches. Rank of nobility equivalent to viscount, a way of designating a man in ancient times similar to "mister."] [*Kao*: Deceased father, to test, to examine, to check, to investigate.] [*Wu*: No, negative, without. Doubtless.] [*Jiu*: Disaster, calamity, a fault, mistake, blame, punish.]

[*Li*: Coarse whetstone; harsh, violent, severe, stern, serious; persuade, urge, encourage; bad, evil; epidemic; oppress, cruel, dangerous.] [*Zhong*: End, come to an end, conclusion. Death, die, pass away. Finally, at last, in the end. Whole, all entire] [*Ji*: Good, lucky, auspicious, propitious, favorable, fortunate]

Here are just some of the possible translations. With a little thought, the reader can surely come up with many others.

Line 1a

Managing father('s) poison.

Or:

(The) business (of a) father: it (is) harmed.

Line 1b

There is a child (who will) investigate (and there is) no fault (in so doing).

Or:

Have a child check (so that there will be) no calamity.

(Note that *kao* simultaneously means both "to examine" and "deceased father.")

Line 1c

(This is) harsh (as a whetstone)! (But in the) end, (all will be) favorable.

Or:

Violent death (but afterwards, good) fortune.

Line 2:

a. *Gan mu zhi gu*
b. *Bu ke zhen.*

[*Gan:* trunk—either of a tree or a body. The main part of anything. Capabilities, talent, business, manage.] [*Mu:* Mother, origin (figuratively, as in the mother of all things, or mother of invention), female.] [*Zhi:* To go, to leave, zigzag, winding; it, her, him, them, this, that, those, these, of.] [*Gu:* Poison, venom, harm. To bewitch, to enchant.]

[*Bu:* No, not, negative.] [*Ke:* May, can, to be able to. Around, estimated at. But, however. A surname.] [*Zhen:* Chastity of a woman; pure, virtuous; incorruptible; firm; devotion, dedicated; divine, inquire by divination.]

Line 2a:

Managing mothers ('s) poison.

Or:

Mother's business is harmed.

Line 2b:

(You will) not be able (to be) firm.

Or:

Unable to (make a) divination. (i.e., foretell the outcome)

Line 3:

a. *Gan fu zhi gu*
b. *Xiao you hui wu da jiu.*

[*Gan:* trunk—either of a tree or a body. The main part of anything. Capabilities, talent, business, manage.] [*Fu:* father. A male relative of

earlier generations such as an uncle older than one's father, or a grandfather. To do father's duties. In ancient times, a respectful term for an elderly man.] [*Zhi:* To go, to leave, zigzag, winding; it, her, him, them, this, that, those, these, of.] [*Gu:* Poison, venom, harm. To bewitch, to enchant.]

[*Xiao:* Small, little, tiny. Minor. Young, junior. Humble, mean, lowly. Light, slight, trivial, petty.] [*You:* To have, to be present, to exist, there is.] [*Hui:* Regret, repent, remorse.] [*Wu:* No, negative, without. Doubtless.] [*Da:* Big, large, great, much, very, eldest, senior, adult, before (date), to enlarge. A surname.] [*Jiu:* Disaster, calamity, a fault, mistake, blame, punish.]

Line 3a:

(Repeats line 1a.)

Line 3b:

(The) young have remorse, (but they are) not (to be) greatly blamed.

Or:

(The) subordinates have repentance (but this is) no great disaster.

Line 4

a. *Yu fu zhi gu*
b. *Wang jian lin.*

[*Yu:* Abundant, affluent, plenty. Tolerant; generous, magnanimous, slowly.] [*Fu:* father. A male relative of earlier generations such as an uncle older than one's father, or a grandfather. To do father's duties. In ancient times, a respectful term for an elderly man.] [*Zhi:* To go, to leave, zigzag, winding; it, her, him, them, this, that, those, these, of.] [*Gu:* Poison, venom, harm. To bewitch, to enchant.]

[*Wang:* Go forward, depart, bound for; formerly, bygone, gone.] [*Jian:* See, perceive, understand, observe, examine. Visit, call on, meet. Receive visitors. Sometimes used as a form of the verb "to be." To move toward a certain direction.] [*Lin:* Stingy, niggardly, parsimonious, grudging.]

Line 4a:

Abundant (is the) father's poison(ing).

Or:

(The) affluence (of the) father: this (will be) harmed.

Line 4b:

(If you) go forward, (you will see) stingy(ness).

Or:

Formerly (your father) saw (parsimonious) times.

Line 5:

a. *Gan fu zhi gu yong yu.*

[*Gan:* trunk—either of a tree or a body. The main part of anything. Capabilities, talent, business, manage.] [*Fu:* father. A male relative of earlier generations such as an uncle older than one's father, or a grandfather. To do father's duties. In ancient times, a respectful term for an elderly man.] [*Zhi:* To go, to leave, zigzag, winding; it, her, him, them, this, that, those, these, of.] [*Gu:* Poison, venom, harm. To bewitch, to enchant.] [*Yong:* Use, employ, exert, use, effect, finance, to need, to eat, to drink.] [*Yu:* Fame, honor, glory; praise, eulogize.]

Line 5a:

Managing father ('s) poison.
(You will) need to eulogize (him).

Or:

(The) business (of a) father: it (is) harmed. (To revive it) finance it gloriously.

Line 6:

a. *Bu shi wang hou*
b. *Gao shang qi shi.*

[*Bu:* No, not, negative.] [*Shi:* An affair, matter, business. A job, occupation, task. A service. Duties, functions. A subject, to serve, to attend. To manage a business.] [*Wang:* King, ruler, prince, great, the strongest, a salutation of respect. An audience with the ruler or emperor. A surname.] [*Hou:* The second of five grades of the nobility. A target in archery. A marquis, a nobleman, or a high official. A surname.]

[*Gao:* High, tall. High level or degree. Lofty. A surname.] [*Shang:* Yet, still, uphold, honor, esteem. A surname.] [*Qi:* He, she, it, they, their, his, her, this, that, the, if] [*Shi:* An affair, matter, business. A job, occupation, task. A service. Duties, functions. A subject, to serve, to attend. To manage a business.]

Line 6a:

(Do) not attend (to the affairs of the) king or noblemen.

Or:

No business (with the) emperor (or) the officials.

Line 6b:

Higher still (is) this duty.

Or:

Loft(ier is the) esteem (for) his business.

What is beings said here? Clearly, there are two major tracks of meaning. First, that your father's business is declining and you have to go back and put things in order. This will not be easy. There will be an accounting; there will be tallying. However, line 6 implies that this is a critical task, more important than serving officials or kings. The more sorrowful interpretation can be that your father is dying and that you have to return home to put his affairs in order. You will give your father's eulogy. This must be done, even in place of one's duty to the emperor. There is a higher duty to one's family.

One could interpret line 2 as saying: "Your mother is ill. You will not be able to be too firm." Coupled with a message in line 6 that helping your family during the death of a parent is of higher importance than service to one's country, a tender picture emerges. The *Changes* is comforting. "Do not try to be too strong as your parents are dying. Do not worry about outside concerns." There is no cheap fortune-telling phraseology, no promise pain can be avoided. The *Changes* is a human oracle, understanding of sorrow, and lenient with those who must struggle with great burdens.

Naming Names

One of the reactions that people have to the *Changes* is that it seems astonishingly accurate. In Chinese, that reputation is enhanced by the book's seeming ability to put a time frame on a prediction (based on the association of certain hexagrams with specific times of the year) and its apparent mentioning of names. If you look up many of the words used in the *Changes*, you will find that a large number of them double as people's surnames. In this sense, one could read Hexagram 18, Lines 6a and 6b, as "(Do) not attend to—Wang, Hou, Gao, Shang—(and) their business."

Coupled with those hexagrams that mention time, it would be possible to receive eerily accurate readings. If you were wondering whether to go into business with someone named Wang, for example, the *Changes* could give you a specific answer. This kind of reading would be possible in Chinese but impossible in translation.

In order to round out this discussion of translation, I would like to highlight two of the negative words used in the *Changes*, and then two of the positive ones.

A Bad *Li*, a Good *Li*, and Other Words

In the preceding passages from Hexagram 18, there are two words used—*li* (line 1c) and *lin* (line 4b)—that are not easy to interpret.

Li has a variety of meanings: a coarse whetstone, harsh, violent, severe, stern, serious, persuade, urge, encourage, bad, evil; epidemic; oppress, cruel, dangerous. We have an image of being ground on a whetstone, or, without much effort, we can imagine knives being sharpened against us.

The word seems to have mostly bad connotations. However, it now also means "encourage," "persuade," and "urge," which might not be entirely bad. And to think of someone as serious or stern might be entirely different from thinking of someone as violent and evil. Again, we usually have to translate the word one way. Or we might vary our translation when contexts are clearly different.

One thing we cannot do is preserve the ambiguity of the word in translation. In line 1c, you could see something as prosaic as "Things will be bad, but in the end, they will be good." Or, "Be encouraged, for in the end, all will be favorable." Unfortunately, we cannot hold both meanings at once, as we can often find multiple meanings in a sentence when we are familiar with a language.

Lin means "stingy," "niggardly," "parsimonious," "grudging." Sometimes, this word does not fit easily into a translation. In line 4b, we can see the line *wang jian lin* from different angles. "Go forward and you will see spare times." "Advance and oversee with frugality." "Gone are sights of stinginess." *Lin* is hard to translate because its implications do not fit well, or even grammatically, with how we usually think in English. *Lin* appears at the end of Hexagram 22, line 5, where a betrothal present is portrayed as tiny. Here, *lin zhong ji*—stingy, but in the end, good fortune—shows the use of the word in a different context than in Hexagram 18.

Let us now consider two positive words, *li* (which is spelled the same as the *li* above, but is a different word) meaning "profit" and "advantage," and *ji* meaning "good fortune."

The word *li*, in its basic pictographic form, is a stalk of grain and a knife. Goodness and benefit are symbolized by harvesting. It takes a few steps in thinking to connect this with advantage and benefit. We can talk about having an advantage in a sports competition, business, or warfare, but we don't normally connect harvesting with advantage. If we think about it, though, it makes sense. The person who has a successful harvest has benefited and gained an advantage in life. There is no image of weaponry, as exists in some words, no image of dominating others. Advantage is seen not in terms of surpassing other people, but in the superiority of receiving the benefit of heaven's gifts and our own hard work.

When the *Changes* uses a phrase such as *li jian da ren*—meaning, "*li* to see the great person"—there is no guarantee that we will automatically be granted benefits. Instead, it implies that seeing the great person is like harvesting: unless we have worked to sow the seeds, and unless we put in work by going to see the great person, there is no benefit.

Ji can mean "good luck," "good fortune," or just "being favorable." In this case, there is little controversy over how to translate the word, but it's important to examine what the word means. What is most important to realize is that the "good luck" and "good fortune" are not bestowed by an outside force. Instead, I believe that "good fortune" means that our work takes place within favorable circumstances and that the resulting sum of our efforts and the natural state of things are good. Like finding a gold mine, we have to put effort into prospecting and we have to put effort into mining. But if there's no gold mine to be found, constant effort will be useless.

Each time we see *ji*, then, we should not regard it as a "promise" of good luck. That would be an error. Instead *ji* reminds us that we must constantly combine our inner goals with the favorable elements of our circumstances. That is what is truly called lucky. The *Changes* constantly puts the possibilities for our own lives in our own hands—and encourages our initiative.

Some translators have attempted to go back to the earliest possible strata of the *Changes* hoping to find the purest meaning. One has to be brave to do this, because it sometimes significantly alters the meaning of a line as it has been interpreted for thousands of years. Even our basic line, *yuan heng li zhen*, when read strictly in terms of what it might have meant in the early Zhou dynasty, could simply mean: "From the origin: a good divination," or, "Original and great luck: a good omen." For people of the Zhou, who unlike us were not inclined to question the supernatural, getting an answer as simple as "good" or "bad" may well have been both satisfying and useful. In time, however, the interpretation of the *Changes* became complicated as social needs and demands increased. When the dictionary of early Chinese etymology, the *Shuo Wen*, comments that *zhen* does not mean "divination" but the "virtue-needed-to-be-worthy-of-divination," we are already embarking on abstraction and Confucian elaboration of the concept.

Generations of people over thousands of years have derived benefits from the *Changes*, in part because they saw new meanings in the ancient words. We cannot reject Confucius's interpretations. We cannot reject Qu Xi's interpretations. We cannot reject the semantic investigations of scholars throughout the centuries.

Let us imagine a Chinese scholar two hundred years ago who consulted the *Changes*. When he received the reading, he pondered it. He was able to gain insight into his predicament. The *Changes* worked for him. It is highly unlikely that he read the book based only on the language of the Zhou dynasty. Instead, it stands to reason that he brought the full weight of his cultural perceptions and scholarly background to bear on his problem. In the same way, we must study all the meanings that have been added to the *Changes* over the centuries. We need not cling to any one of them, nor should we reject some as being too modern any more than we should sneer at the early Zhou for being primitive and nonscientific.

Our study of English is no different. How many people go back to the Latin roots to try to wring every bit of meaning out of the language? How many try to separate the various strains of languages from all over the world that have crept into English? In virtually every religious setting today, there is a conscious drive to conduct ceremonies and lectures in plain language. This does not downgrade the religion. It makes it accessible. By giving as many associations as possible to the language and imagery of the *Changes*, we are trying to do the same thing: make it accessible and usable. Now.

We do not drill turtle shells and inscribe questions on bones as the early Shang and Zhou did. But our need to contact the divine is no less urgent than theirs was.

We do not read or write in the archaic language of the Zhou, but our need to express our human condition is no less powerful than theirs was.

We do not have the same feudal structure as the Zhou, but our need for social stability is no less fundamental than theirs was.

None of us tries to live the way people did fifty years ago, let alone three thousand. We are wealthy in the legacy of thousands of years. Let us use our legacy rather than restricting ourselves in mistaken searches for purity.

I am not finding fault with the Wilhelm/Baynes translation. I love that translation as one loves an old house, even if it lacks modern plumbing and updated wiring. We need only to remember that all translations are approximate, and then we can get the most value from them. It is like comparing two animals of related species that evolved on two different continents: the bone structure is similar, but the two animals are outwardly different. All the translations available are sincere attempts to make the *Changes* accessible to us, but if we want more, we must go much deeper. Certainly, we must avail ourselves of study with teachers and an exploration of a bilingual edition.

But here is the paradox of this situation: there is a great deal of wisdom in the translations of the *Changes*, even if their interpretation seems distant from the Chinese. There have been many occasions when I have muttered the Wilhelm/Baynes translation of King Wen's Judgment in Hexagram 2: "But if he follows, he finds guidance." I do this because it is often the most apt description of my experience. That is why I believe that the *Changes* is spilling out of its classical Chinese form and evolving into other languages.

People in countries outside of China are adapting the *Changes* to their environment and cultures. No matter how far these adaptations are from the core *Changes*, they are still tied to basic texts. This is not different than the way the *Changes* grew before. From Fu Xi, to King Wen, to the Duke of Zhou, to Confucius, to the Ten Wings and then the commentaries and revisions of subsequent editors, the *Changes* grew layer by layer. The numerous translations of the *Changes* merely extend that process.

APPENDIX 3

Assessing the *Changes*
as an Oracle

Is there such a thing as an oracle in today's world of science, rationality, and technology? Can someone both be a rational person and also use an oracle? It depends on how we view our rationality; it also depends on our understanding of what an oracle is.

There are limits to all knowledge and all art forms. The reason that we have developed so many professions, philosophies, and lifestyles is that no one mode can fulfill all our needs. Just as our eyes stop and focus for us to comprehend—making our perception a process of mental collage—so we cannot comprehend life all at once. Every person, no matter how learned or spiritually powerful, must be expert in more than one thing.

If someone is a chemist, she must use a different set of skills to care for preschool children. If someone is a yogi, he must use a different consciousness to drive a car. A writer may yet need to know how to plant flowers. A farmer may yet need to do accounting. Every person must hold many approaches to life. The fact that we have these many approaches does not invalidate any of them.

Therefore, it is wrong to criticize any form of knowledge on the basis of what it is not. If we criticize physics for not providing us with answers to religious questions, that is no true condemnation of physics. Indeed, physicists go right on designing experiments and using their knowledge to launch spacecraft. So the fact that any knowledge is limited is not a sign of its inadequacy. Any body of knowledge has to be critiqued based on what it intends to address. The knowledge and art of the *Changes* cannot be rejected simply because it does not fit in with our current notions of science. The *Changes* may not be scientific, but we may find it valuable.

At the same time, we must reject the attitudes of those who consider traditional Chinese wisdom to be the ramblings of primitive people who supposedly could not keep accurate records, were strangers to logical thinking, or secretly revised their classics throughout the centuries. Some writers have asserted that no Chinese thousands of years ago could have thought of the *Changes* on their own—it must have been the work of later, more sophisticated people who tried to ascribe greater antiquity to their work. Suspicions of forgery, "anonymous" scholars (even if they were, what is our opinion of the work?), textual corruption, and so on are important questions, but they may not be the only critical thinking we need.

Another culturally biased criticism is that the Chinese classics are didactic rather than "objective." The *Spring and Autumn Annals* of Confucius, for example, will not merely describe what happened in a particular event, but will try to draw some moral lesson from it. We modern people strain against this; we do not like to be lectured about morality. We prefer to twist ancient literature on our own, and we resent having ancient writers telling us how they would want their own literature interpreted.

Confucius and the Five Classics are not meant to be read in a few sittings like romance novels. They are meant to be memorized in childhood, quoted throughout youth, and then applied during conflict. Chinese culture has glorious achievements. From the cinnabar walls of the Forbidden City, to jade carved into statues of veneration, to the beauty of its great poets, there is much that is awe inspiring. Beneath that, however, Chinese culture is one of disaster, despair, and inescapable dilemma. The Great Wall and the imperial palaces have been breached innumerable times, the statues have been shattered or stolen, and the poets have written many lamentations and elegies. The Five Classics address themselves to a people who have known invasion, cruelty of warriors and rulers, corruption, famine, and earthquake. The classics are like steles, set facing north against trouble. In the need to counter the seeming ruthlessness of fate, Confucius and his disciples edited much of the emotion from the classics.

Many of the passages became dry and moralistic. In the *Changes,* successive editors tried to wring the most truth from the concrete images of the early writers. Perhaps that's a measure not of the scholars' pedantic tendencies, but of their determination to find answers. If a passage in the *Changes* suddenly occurs to someone as they are struggling with a seemingly impossible situation, the scholars would most likely feel justified in what they have done. They are being helpful—though it may have taken decades before rote memorization, moralizing, and endless study morphed into the solution for calamity.

At times, it almost seems as if the ancient scholars were embarrassed by some of the imagery of the classic, preferring a figurative—and moral—interpretation to the literal one. For example, the Lines of Hexagram 59 use images that mean scattering, dispersal, and flinging. In visualizing someone scattering a flock, scattering sweat, and finally, scattering blood (Hexagram 59, lines 4–6), effort and dispersal in different forms are made vivid. (The eventual choice of the word *spreading* for this hexagram was based on a reading of the Lines.) However, the commentaries are reticent to embrace the full emotion of the *Changes*' imagery. The Wilhelm/Baynes translation of line 5 is "His loud cries are as dissolving as sweat." The commentary then backs away from cries and sweat and finds a figurative interpretation:

> In times of general dispersion and separation, a great idea provides a focal point for the organization of recovery. Just as an illness reaches its crisis in a dissolving sweat, so a great and stimulating idea is a true salvation in times of general deadlock.

In line 6, the phrase "He dissolves his blood" is interpreted as follows:

> The idea of dissolving a man's blood means the dispersion of that which might lead to bloodshed and wounds, i.e., avoidance of danger.

If we remember that dissolves can be seen as flinging or scattering, the image has far more impact. As wisdom, I have no quarrel with the commentaries of past masters. I only want to point out that we should not forget the vivid and visceral images that the early writers of the *Changes* used to express themselves. The danger both of the Confucian effort to graft moral lessons onto earlier literature and the contemporary rejection of those didactic efforts is that we will fail to connect with the primal level of the *Changes.*

We should not strip away the later commentaries. But we should realize that they are the clothing around a far more profound body of truth.

Assessing the *Changes* as an oracle, then, means we have to consider what the oracle means on its own terms, and we have to consider that the *Changes* has been an honored and usable tradition for thousands of years. We do nothing like the Zhou did, and yet this one book has somehow evolved and stayed in constant use since that time. We need not look for a mystical answer to explain this, but we do need to acknowledge that this book must have some tremendous value to have lasted so long. Few other books from world literature could claim the venerable age and unbroken usage of the *Changes.*

Let us get right to the point. I do not believe in fortune-telling. I do not believe in consulting the book with every question that is burdening our minds, as if there is a foolproof answer there. It just doesn't work that way. Is there a single person or any other body of knowledge that is correct all the time? No priest of any religion, no teacher, no parent, no expert in any field is right any more of the time than the *Changes.* Every mature person recognizes the need to consult with people and find expert advice. Only an immature person stops there and thinks that another person can provide unassailable answers. We contemplate others' advice, but if we are wise, we make the final decisions ourselves.

The *Changes* should therefore be seen in that light. It is a repository of thousands of years' worth of wisdom, and if we learn its unique way of accessing that information, we can make use of that wisdom. The book shows ways of internalizing that wisdom, so that we can be that much more canny about our actions. We should not become dependent on any book, but we can certainly make use of books.

The superior use of the *Changes* comes from absorbing its principles, making its wisdom our own. Using the *Changes* only as a book of divination puts its philosophy outside ourselves, leaving a gap between the book and our own actions. Only by learning the knowledge of the *Changes* can we put it to immediate use. Only by exercising its wisdom as quickly as the working of our own intuition can we move swiftly to meet our challenges. The ideal use of the *Changes*, then, is not to resort to the book in times of crises, but to act at every moment exactly as the *Changes* would have us act.

Masters of the *Changes* emphasize that it is the person approaching the *Changes,* not the hexagram and texts themselves, that matters. "First take up the words and ponder their meaning, so that the fixed rules [which govern the universe] will reveal themselves. But if you are not the right person [moral and with insight], the meaning will not be revealed." The central operating principle is not the power or mystique of the book but the power and insight of the person. By the same token, the masters warned against overuse of the book, or divining repeatedly with the hopes of getting a "better" reading. Xunzi (d. 238 B.C.E.), a Confucian master, stated that those who were expert in the *Changes* never actually needed to divine: by the time one had cultivated the high moral character needed to properly divine, one would already have internalized the *Changes*.

Clearly, each person who approaches the book must do so personally, and each person should read as many different versions of the *Changes* as they can. There is nothing wrong with that. We have hundreds of commentaries on each of the holy books in the world's libraries. The *Changes* is

no different. There is room for discussion, for comment, and for reverence.

Although it is an oracle that is in a book, it is an ever-evolving oracle. The more it is used, the more it develops. The more it spreads throughout the world, the more there are different commentators and thinkers, all adding to the same oracle. We must think beyond what the book meant in the Zhou dynasty.

The *Changes* seems to retain its power no matter which school, emperor, or academic tries to fit it to their own ideas. No edition or translation of the book is wholly invalid, but no single version is wholly authoritative either. Nevertheless, each one enlarges upon the wisdom of the *Changes*.

There is ongoing scholarship focused on the *Changes,* and with each new version there is eager comparison with the editions we currently have. Finding an older version of the *Changes* is exciting and educational, but an older version isn't necessarily going to settle controversies or become the premier form of the *Changes*. It's ironic, because we are really engaging in a form of ancestor inquiry when we dig into the distant past to find some more definite answer. In their way, then, the anthropologists and scholars are engaged in their own mystical pursuit.

Besides the many versions of the *Changes*, each inquiry also enlarges its power, not in some mystical fashion, but because each inquiry increases the importance people place on the book. If we can consider the continual efforts made to publish the *Changes,* and the millions of inquires people make to the book each year, it's clear that the *Changes* is growing and evolving.

Many have also asked what or who is responding to the inquires put to the *Changes*. If we think of the *Changes* as a spirit or person sitting in a distant dimension, waiting to be contacted, we would be mistaken. There is no one waiting to talk to us, no one formulating a message to us. The *Changes* is not an external force. It is the strength of our inquiry contrasted with human wisdom. This process is activated by chance.

That, of course, bothers some people, so it is worthwhile to probe this question.

There are three problems that hinder our acceptance of the *Changes* as an oracle.

First, how do we feel about making an inquiry? The question is about the same as asking how comfortable we feel about prayer. Perhaps we feel odd addressing ourselves to a book. When we make an inquiry to the *Changes*, we have to ask a question, and in the process, we have to admit our inability to deal with our problem. We must confess our confusion. When some of us question the "reality" of the *Changes*, we are really asking whether questioning an unknown source outside ourselves is valid. Even if we understand that the *Changes* is not a spirit waiting to be contacted, we then have to come to terms with the act of asking. Should we ask?

Yes, we should. The answer that comes is not a list of orders. What comes is another point of view that helps focus our own.

The second trouble that many people have with an old book like the *Changes* is the problem that they have with any human wisdom. They do not trust it. We live in cynical times where only the new is good. We distrust the past, believing that our rapid progress in fighting disease, developing technology, and improved standards of living similarly mirrors a progress in human thinking. Thus, in this view, only what is newly discovered is valid, and since all knowledge is subject to revision, all knowledge is suspect.

While we are rapidly making progress in technology and many people are becoming rich, there has not been a similar shift in the human psyche. The issues are the same for a child growing up today as they were a thousand years ago. A middle-aged man will still have to go through the same stages of life as someone who lived a thousand years ago. We go through childhood, we go through young adulthood, and in old age we still have to confront the issues of what we'll leave to others and how we're going to face death. In other words, the basic nature of human existence is the same for each generation. It's hard for us, with our "modern" this, and our "revolutionary" that, to believe that we are walking in the same circles that many others have mapped in the past. We have come to distrust the past, because, admittedly, there were atrocities in the past. History reminds us of such devastating events as Nazism, slavery, the subjugation of women and children, and religious fanaticism.

A middle path is advisable. We must not discard the past simply because bad things happened any more than we should turn our backs on the preciousness of knowledge people often committed their entire lives to finding. There have always been good and evil, fortune and misfortune. The wise course is to examine all sides rather than to deny their presence. The *Changes* has a view that is so far-seeing that it calmly considers fortune and misfortune side by side and presents them clearly. It is not indoctrination. We are free to accept or reject its images.

The third hesitation we may have is the way we access the book. The *Changes* uses chance to activate its hexagrams, and this makes some people suspicious. It goes against what we think of as rational, and it even touches on our disapproval of gambling. It also challenges the popular assertion that we can "be whatever we want to be." How can we have initiative when we give credence to a book used by a random procedure? How can we support logical and orderly thinking if we are counting sticks in a bizarre mathematical ritual to find a page that might as well be found by just opening the book?

The value of chance is not that it bypasses our strengths as rational people. It is simply that it uses a different approach—one that takes us wholly outside ourselves. When we are facing a conundrum or some situation where we must make a terrible choice, we may well welcome the opportunity to step outside ourselves. That is what the use of chance and the *Changes* allows us to do.

We actually use chance every day, and we associate chance with impartiality. When we want to choose fairly between a group, we use chance, as we do when we have people draw straws. If we want to award a prize to one person among a group of people, we draw lots. Even the idea of democracy incorporates an element of chance; we don't know which candidate will be elected until every vote is counted.

When we use chance to access the *Changes* as an oracle, we aren't appealing to a personage—who might be capricious or partial. We take a book that is the accumulation of human wisdom and select advice by chance. It is an unequivocal and uncorruptible process. There is no god to be swayed by our begging, no personage who may have his or her own desires. We have a wholly human system that we engage without any taint of partiality. When we receive a judgment from the *Changes,* it is neither a condemnation to misfortune nor a guarantee of good fortune. We still have to understand what has been given to us, and apply it. Perhaps this is why the *Changes* above all other forms of divination has received the greatest attention from astute people: all the responsibility still rests with the inquirer.

But someone will ask, How can we be sure we'll get the "right" hexagram? Does this mean that *any* hexagram could give us a valuable answer? Or, through some mysterious process, does the *Changes* always give us the "right" answer? If we were to ask the same question one thousand times and look for the hexagrams that came up the most, would that increase our accuracy?

Obviously, such an approach would not work. The hexagrams cannot give us the answer. They cannot tell us what to do, as we hope our parents will do whenever we have problems as children. When we are young, and we are puzzled, we immediately turn to our parents to solve our problems. Part of the transition to adulthood is the facing of our mistakes, the taking of responsibilities for all that we do, and reliance on ourselves rather than the intercession of others. The book with such mature views that Confucius reputedly waited until he was fifty years old to study it is clearly not designed to "give us the answer," to tell us what to do. It is there to give us another perspective.

If you have ever done any perspective drawing, you know that you need a horizon line and a vanishing point. In simple one-point perspective, all objects in a single file lie along lines drawn from the largest, most forward object back to a single point.

The *Changes* provides us a vanishing point, a place to anchor the lines of our ideas and give them a relationship to one another. The *Changes* doesn't give us the answer any more than a vanishing point determines the subject of a perspective drawing. Yet we cannot succeed without the right perspective, just as we cannot make a successful perspective drawing without a vanishing point; it doesn't matter whether we're drawing train tracks or drawing a parade of human beings.

When we approach the *Changes* with a dilemma, the hexagram it gives us provides us with just that valuable perspective. That perspective is valuable precisely because it is outside ourselves. We have to approach the *Changes* by putting aside our reservations about making an inquiry, we have to admit that we are willing to look through the records of human wisdom for guidance, and finally, we understand that we are still the ones making the decision, except that we will have the benefit of another perspective.

The *Changes* is not a person, not a god. It is an oracle that is composed of human wisdom, one that we approach through the uncorruptable medium of chance, and an oracle that gives us not a prescription but advice and perspective. To ask whether the *Changes* is "real" in the sense that it is some entity that responds to our own specific problems is childish and egotistical. The *Changes* is a book oracle—the source of its wisdom is the accumulation of thousands of years' worth of human experience—and its power comes from us.

The Problematic History of the Chinese Classics

We have discussed both the difficulty of translation and the attitudes toward the *Changes* that interfere with appreciating its value. In delving more deeply into the *Changes,* we will encounter different commentaries. We will invariably question which view to believe.

If one takes a deep but balanced view of history, one will soon see that numerous events must have shaped the final form of the *Changes.* It has been built up from layers of different texts, commentaries, and revisions. Thus, the existence of differing copies of the *Changes* precludes the possibility that anyone has an uncorrupted and authoritative version directly derived from the writings of King Wen.

The desire to reduce the *Changes* to a single author such as King Wen may arise from our current respect for the individual. However, it's clear that any consideration of the *Changes* must begin with our acceptance of multiple authors. Beyond the question of definite authorship is also the question of divine revelation. While there are other books in Chinese history that claim divine authorship, it's significant that no such claim is made for the *Changes.* The veneration of the *Changes* is based on the classic as a whole rather than on any great emphasis of authorship.

Even if we stipulate that King Wen wrote the Statements and that the Duke of Zhou wrote the comments on the lines, we cannot be sure of what happened after that—or even how faithfully their words were preserved. Furthermore, tradition attributes various sections of the Ten Wings to Confucius, though many modern academics find this unlikely, and we know that certain sections are commentaries from scholars in subsequent dynasties. Beyond those broad outlines, we cannot be completely certain about the details. It is important to go into this now, to establish both how problematic it is to search for the "real core text" of the *Changes,* and how remarkable it is that the *Changes* has survived this long.

The following chronology will quickly establish that the *Changes* was affected by a variety of cataclysmic events in Chinese history.

The *Changes* and the Chinese Language

The *Changes* asserts that it was Emperor Fu Xi (acc. 2852 B.C.E.) who invented writing: ". . . he drew the Eight Trigrams and invented the written word as a substitute for reckoning by knotting ropes. From this are derived literature and records." If we accept the account that Fu Xi formulated the Early Heaven Eight Trigrams, then the tradition of the *Changes* was growing at the same time that the language was being codified. As we shall see, the language itself was not standardized until hundreds of years after the *Changes* was supposed to have taken its present structure and content. As we try to understand the *Changes* by parsing its language then, we cannot be certain that we are understanding it the way it was understood thousands of years ago. The *Changes* may be as lofty as a great mountain, but it is a mountain born from the time when the earth's crust was still cooling.

How likely is it that Fu Xi was both the father of the Eight Trigrams and the father of the language itself? Due to the extreme antiquity of Fu Xi's time, even ancient Chinese scholars are not sure. Xu Shen, who compiled a dictionary in the early second century C.E. wrote:

> Affairs were getting more copious and complex. There was much deception and chicanery. The record keeper of the Yellow Emperor, Cangxie, saw the marks and prints left by the claws and paws of birds and animals, and found that these could be differentiated in tracings. He became the first to invent written characters that could be carved on wood, to be used by the multitude of officers for the clarification of myriad matters.

Chinese scholars therefore usually date writing to the time of the Yellow Emperor (acc. 2697 B.C.E.). If Xu Shen, writing at a time much closer to antiquity, is unwilling to venture earlier than the Yellow Emperor for the formation of Chinese writing, we must be similarly reticent in ascribing writing to Fu Xi more than 150 years earlier.

Cangxie was the Yellow Emperor's official scribe and historian. Among the records that were kept since the Yellow Emperor's time were the *pudie,* or lineage tablets describing lines of decent, and the *dieji,* or tablet records, which recorded the years and history of a ruler's reign. We do not know of these tablets directly, but only through the description of China's most famous early historian, Sima Qian of the second century B.C.E. For centuries, the *pudie* and *dieji* were kept by the ruling houses, and they grew in extent and sophistication. They formed one of the largest continuous collections of writing in early Chinese history.

It is believed that Confucius (551–479 B.C.E) had access to these archives and that they were the source of the *Documents* (a collection of documents, speeches, and events from earliest history to the Zhou dynasty). The archives were still intact in the Han dynasty, and Sima Qian also utilized them in writing the early chapters of his *Historical Records.*

There are a number of points to bear in mind here. First, the tablets were evidently wood or bamboo, so they were vulnerable to mishandling, fire, and decay. Second, the tablets are believed to have been brief in their chronology and would have been supplemented by memorization and oral history. Third, if copies were made, they had to be transcribed by hand, and as long as the main medium was carving in wood or bamboo, transcription required both meticulous copying and skilled carving. The combination of oral history and manual transcription would have provided obvious opportunities for mistakes and omissions. In particular, homonyms were frequently substituted, making strict interpretation by written forms problematic. Finally, the Chinese language

itself was evolving and developing. It stands to reason that in the more than two millennia between the time of the Yellow Emperor and Confucius, words and meanings would have changed.

By the time of Confucius, the language of the tablet records was already arcane. Few other than the official scribes could read them. We think that Confucius understood the ancient language and could interpret it properly. Thus, in compiling the *Documents* and the *Changes* themselves, Confucius was gathering all the material available to him at the time, supervising their transcription, editing them, and appending his own commentary. Significantly, Sima Qian records Confucius speaking of records *too incomplete for him to verify.*

"I can speak about the rites of the Xia, but the records of Qi are too scant to verify. I can speak about the rites of Shang, but the records of Sung are too scant to verify. Had they been complete, I should have been able to check them." Sima Qian also indicates that Confucius consciously edited and discarded material. Sima Qian writes:

> There were more than three thousand ancient songs, but Confucius rejected those which were repetitious and retained those that had high moral value. He began with songs about the ancestors of Shang and Zhou and went on to descriptions of the good reigns of both dynasties.

Sima Qian concludes: "Thus both the *Documents* and the *Rites* were compiled by Confucius." Confucius then went on to edit the *Odes* (an anthology of early Chinese poetry). Again, Sima Qian indicates that Confucius consciously discarded many poems. It is apparent that the ancient Chinese did not look at their classics as fixed, but as literature they felt free to revise:

> He put the poems on daily life first, starting with the folk-song section.... Confucius chose three hundred five songs in all, and these he set to music...

It is here that the great historian also gives us a scene of Confucius and the *Changes.*

> In his old age, Confucius loved to study the *Changes,* the order of the hexagrams, definitions, appendixes, interpretations, explanation, and commentaries. He

studied this book so much that the leather thongs binding the wooden strips wore out three times.

There are several crucial points in this passage. First, it's reassuring to know that Confucius had great fondness for the *Changes*. His study of the book was not mere duty. It fascinated him. Evidently, his interest was not merely for the philosophy, because Sima Qian describes him as interested in the "order of the hexagrams."

What is also important to note is that the book already had "definitions, appendixes, interpretations, explanation, and commentaries." Admittedly, we are relying on Sima Qian's research hundreds of years after Confucius's death, and while we have every indication that the historian took great care to be accurate, he is nevertheless reporting hearsay. However, if this is true, it indicates that there were already significant ancillary texts attached to the core *Changes*. This raises the possibility that there was already much cultural value placed on the *Changes* as an independent book and not strictly as a divination manual. Furthermore, it is hard to determine which parts of the *Changes* may have been modified by Confucius, and which parts may have been added by others. Rather than Confucius giving the *Changes* his own "Confucian" slant, it may well have been that the *Changes* profoundly influenced him and provided him with the basis for many of his own important ideas.

For approximately the next two and a half centuries, the body of Chinese classics, compiled and edited by Confucius, was transmitted through his disciples and other teachers. All during this time, however, the words were transmitted through the imperfect system of memorization and manual copying, with all the attendant risks of inaccuracy.

The Loss of Books in the Time of the First Emperor

In 213 B.C.E., the First Emperor of China, who ordered the building of the Great Wall and whose tomb is surrounded by the famous Terracotta War-riors near Xian, issued a proclamation that severely affected most of the empire's books.

Qin Shihuang is called the First Emperor because he was the first ruler to unite the feudal states that roughly make up China today. As part of his efforts to consolidate authority under his rule, he had to address resistance and dissent. In the *Records of the Grand Historian,* as translated by Burton Watson in his Columbia University Press edition, Sima Qian writes of the chancellor, Li Si, who observed that the past feudal states were fragmented and coexisted without order. The feudal lords used examples from antiquity to disparage the present and ". . . prided themselves on private theories and criticized the measure adopted by superiors."

Li Si blames the "adherents of private theories" who criticize the emperor's law. ". . . each one proceeds to discuss it in the light of his theories. . . . They hold it a mark of fame to defy the ruler, regard it as lofty to take a dissenting stance, and they lead the lesser officials in fabricating slander."

The chancellor recommends a course of action in great detail:

> I therefore request that all records of the historians other than those of the state of Qin be burned. With the exception of the academicians whose duty it is to possess them, if there are persons anywhere in the empire who have in their possession copies of the *Odes,* the *Documents,* or the writings of the hundred schools of philosophy, they shall in all cases deliver them to the governor or his commandant for burning. Anyone who ventures to discuss the *Odes* or *Documents* shall be executed in the marketplace. Anyone who uses antiquity to criticize the present shall be executed along with his family. . . . The books that are to be exempted are those on medicine, divination, agriculture, and forestry. . . .

The reign of the Qin Shihuang also affects our investigation in this way: he ordered the language standardized. Although there is much controversy as to how much the language was altered, we know that it was. This adds another layer of difficulty to accurate interpretation.

Qin Shihuang was succeeded by the Second Emperor—who was forced to commit suicide after a series of bloody court intrigues. One of his chancellors, Zhao Gao, supported Ziying, the son of one of the Second Emperor's older brothers, as the next king of Qin.

Ziying in turn stabbed Zhao Gao and put the chancellor's family to death. The Second Emperor's reign lasted forty-five days. After a series of attacks that overwhelmed the Qin army, Ziying surrendered. He was eventually killed, along with all the princes and relatives of the Qin royal family. Rebels massacred the citizens of the capital, enslaved the palace inhabitants, plundered the palace—and then set it on fire. Sima Qian makes no comment on the length of time it took to destroy the palace, but popular belief is that it took three months to completely burn the buildings down. The royal library was destroyed. The *Documents* and all the books in the imperial collection were lost.

This is a crucial point. Many people believe that the books were lost because of Qin Shihuang's burning of the books, but Li Si's petition specifically exempts the books of the state of Qin and the imperial academicians. It was the fall of the dynasty, not the commanded burning, that came close to destroying all written knowledge.

Recovering the Classics in the Han Dynasty

During the reign of Xiaowen (179–157 b.c.e.) of the Han dynasty, twenty-nine fragments of the *Documents* were discovered. Sima Qian tells us that when the Qin dynasty fell, a scholar named Fu Sheng hid many books in a wall. When he went back for them, some had been taken and others had been damaged. Only twenty-nine were left. It must be remembered that these were not books as we think of them today, but bound bundles of wood or bamboo strips with ideograms brushed or carved. Not only were these tablets subject to deterioration by dampness or heat, but their string or leather bindings usually broke with use and the tablets came undone. At a minimum, it would be a challenge to put the many strips into the proper

order. In the time between the fall of Qin and the search to restore the lost classics, any bound tablets could have rotted or been burned, separated, or stolen.

The emperor summoned Fu Sheng to court. However, the scholar was already over ninety years of age, and was too frail to travel. Accordingly, the emperor's master of ritual, Chao Cuo, was sent to learn from Fu Sheng.

Sima Qian names Qin Shihuang's burning of the books and military uprisings at the fall of the Qin dynasty as the reasons why Fu Sheng fled his home, leaving the tablets hidden. The old master had been teaching from recovered fragments as well as from memorized passages: "As a result of his efforts, scholars were able to expound the *Documents* in considerable detail, and all the important teachers east of the mountains studied the Classics and included it among their teachings."

Significantly, Sima Qian goes on to enumerate each of the Five Classics—*Odes, Documents, Changes, Rites,* and *Spring and Autumn Annals*—and then names the masters who were noted for specializing in each one.

He lists six generations of masters who specialized in the *Changes* since the death of Confucius, ending with Yang He, who gains a post as palace counselor because of his expertise in the *Changes*. The most important point here is not the names of the masters (since no one claims to descend from those lineages today), but that there was a lineage at all. This dwelling on unbroken lineages is a central part of Chinese culture. For example, many Chinese keep family trees tracing their ancestors back to the dawn of Chinese history. A variety of schools, whether religious, artistic, musical, or martial, all pride themselves on knowing the long line of those who came before them. Knowledge of lineage is thought to establish the qualifications of the masters as well as indicate the integrity of the school. Sima Qian's passages also show that the *Changes* were made part of an ongoing tradition of teaching that involved both oral and written instruction. The fact that there are several schools and masters also shows that there were competing schools and varying opinions of the *Changes.*

The fame of the *Changes* was already firmly established by this point. Besides Yang He, Sima Qian notes:

> Jimo Cheng, a scholar of Qi, advanced to the post of prime minister of Chengyang because of his knowledge of the *Changes*, while Meng Dang of Guangchun was made a lord of the gate to the heir apparent for the same reason.

During the reign of Han Emperor Wudi (140–87 B.C.E.), a prince wanting to enlarge his own palace demolished the walls of Confucius's buildings and a second batch of the *Documents* was found. These were given to Kong Anguo, a descendant of Confucius, to interpret. Again, this clearly shows that the literature we have today was on the verge of loss and had to be reconstructed.

Chinese language was revised several times more, and the Han dynasty saw an attempt to codify the Five Classics including the *Changes.* An official version was carved in stone. However, this did not prevent confusion and varying versions, because subsequent dynasties carved their own versions in stone and these do not always match the Han versions. Given the fluidity of the Chinese language, the extreme antiquity of the *Changes,* and the difficulties of transmitting accurate versions, we cannot ever determine the "true" *Changes* with absolute confidence. Traditional explanations of the *Changes* remain open to interpretation. Trying to evaluate the different parts of the *Changes* or attempting to separate parts that may have been added to bolster a particular school of thought is just as problematic.

Given the above brief chronology, however, the reader should be able to see just why the history of the *Changes* remains tantalizingly ambiguous. If we want to make use of the *Changes,* we cannot put all our faith in textual analysis. We have to let the *Changes* speak to us—and we have to continue the investigation.

Ritual and the Study of Change

The process of divination was a ritual, and many of the passages of the *Changes* allude to further ceremonies, sacrifices, and offerings. Today, we may be eager to learn from the wisdom of the *Changes,* but we are less willing to engage in the long study of ritual that has been the basis of using the *Changes.*

The use of ritual was tied to a learning based on rote memorization and the unquestioning mimicry of established forms. The student was told that if he or she studied long enough, a sudden enlightenment would come decades later that would transcend the strictures of ritual.

A poetry student composed poetry within closed forms, diligently copying the style of great masters. A painter adopted the style of one or two masters, aiming to become so facile that the difference between educational effort and outright forgery was effaced. A martial-arts student imitated animals' movements, striving to become an expert fighter by taking mimicry to a somatic level.

Such repetition was also the basis of ritual. Confucianism advocated the centrality of the rites not just as etiquette but to integrate the human with the divine. It was a tie that had to be constantly renewed. Whether by offering the harvest or by divining the *Changes,* every ritual act renewed the link between heaven, earth, and humanity.

Taoism also preserved rituals for blessings, consecrations, and exorcism. Among its major movement rituals are the Steps of Yu (in honor of the legendary tamer of floods) and the Seven-Star Step (a dance to invoke the power of the Big Dipper).

The power of ritual has been known outside of China too. For example, the Japanese tea ceremony, intimately tied to Zen Buddhism, remains vital because participants can experience the Way of Tea and Zen through prescribed movements in a tea hut. The sand paintings of the Tibetan monks and the chanting of mantras by the Bhakti yogis have also utilized the power of ritual.

We in another country and in a century distant from the Zhou dynasty have our own rituals, even if we have modified them. Our rituals are no longer as detailed and rigid as the ancient Chinese rites. We have modernized our dress and language, we may omit some parts, we may even be ignorant of the right procedures, but we still use rites in our complicated and individualistic world. Maybe our rituals are just holiday celebrations, or perhaps they are limited to graduations, weddings, birth celebrations, and funerals, but we still need them. We instinctively turn to ritual, however slightly, to mark the passages of our lives.

What Does Ritual Do?

Ritual integrates us with larger relationships. When the emperors of China made sacrifices on the sacred mountains, they were following a long-held belief in the need for human beings to keep their bonds with nature and gods. We are no different. We need to reaffirm our connection with others and with nature.

But what's the difference between merely copying and being a person transformed by ritual? After all, we don't normally look upon imitation as positive. The comedian who mimics a public figure makes us laugh and may even convey serious social messages, but he does not become the person he imitates. A musical group may make a living imitating a popular singing group from the past, but they are not those musicians. We don't like the word *imitation*. It connotes cheating and something shallow. We profess to prefer original thought. It's not enough that we know of the past or ape the past; we are expected to come up with something of our own.

Many people object to ritual as an insincere set of obligations. We don't see how people can really be transformed by ritual. We ask for the scientific data, the double-blind studies, and we find no material evidence that change through ritual exists.

Another objection to ritual is that it is abused. We fear the brainwashing of the cult. We look at people in churches and temples who go through the motions once a week and then live fallible lives the rest of the time. As a result, many people reject ritual altogether.

We must not denigrate ritual simply because it can be abused or debased. There are innumerable cases of perverted or indifferent sex, but that does not stop others from finding great beauty and fulfillment in making love. We have plenty of people who break their wedding vows, but we have many more who keep their vows with utter fidelity. There are doctors who engage in malpractice, but that number is small compared with those who treat their patients well. Some priests may abuse their position to take advantage of other people, yet there are thousands more who genuinely make significant differences in the lives of their constituents. Badly practiced roles do not negate the value of the role itself. In the same way, badly practiced ritual does not negate the value of true ritual.

There is value in the rituals of the *Changes*. Counting the yarrow stalks or casting the coins, consulting the book with reverence, and contemplating the response can produce change within us. Doing the ritual is in itself a valid act. The ritual is not a prelude to the "real thing." It *is* the real thing. If we are going to do ritual, we must accept that the actual act is in itself the reward.

Each person who performs a ritual will be affected according to what they invest in it. That's the very premise of ritual. If we aren't fully transformed right away, that isn't a fault. As is true of someone learning to dance, it takes time to become good. But there's no doubt that we are dancing the first moment we step onto the floor. Ritual is a prescribed act that will produce an instant change when it's performed as long as we have committed ourselves fully to it. In that sense, ritual performed completely reveals the performer.

A traditional Japanese carpenter once estimated that he spent fully 75 percent of his time sharpening his tools. He understood that carpentry was not how many pieces of wood could be erected on the job site in an eight-hour day, but how much reverence he felt for the wood and his profession, and how accurately he cut his joints. With his emphasis on perfection, he wasted little. The average carpenter today, with pneumatic hammer and circular saw, cannot see the traditional approach as "efficient," and yet today's carpenters will still admire the beauty of the traditional carpenter's work. In his case, the Japanese carpenter is improving himself and his job performance through constant ritual. When he sharpens his tools—which surely cannot dull that quickly in a day—he is really sharpening himself.

Meditation is related to ritual. It is done to cultivate ourselves. Taoist meditations, for example, are designed to integrate us more completely with Tao.

There is an erroneous opinion advanced by some masters that beginners aren't doing "true" meditation. These masters say that it took them decades to advance, so our learning must take just as long. Dancers, martial artists, poets, painters, and members of nearly any avocation with an elite component will say the same. They are wrong.

If we do one moment of meditation, we are truly meditating. If we are sincere in a ritual—whether it's divining the *Changes* or completing our wedding—we will be forever altered by that act. Ritual's power is not for "later." It must be for *now* or else it has no validity at all. If we continue the practice of ritual, we will change further. If we practice for twenty years, we will be different than when we started.

The Erosion of Ritual

There are two other reasons why ritual is eroding. One is the failure of traditionalists to keep ritual vital. The second is that the world itself is changing, and in the process old rituals have been made less relevant.

The old masters have declined. Age makes them feeble; language limitations—whether the old masters can't communicate with interested people from other lands or whether they just can't communicate with younger people of their own culture—isolate them.

Rituals don't exist outside of the people who perform them. If people stop doing them, their vitality vanishes. When the masters are no longer able to set an example or to bring the force of ritual to bear, ritual declines.

In times of crisis, we look to our leaders—and that includes the old masters—to help us shape a response to our terror. It's no accident that attendance at temples, mosques, and churches increases when there is trouble. If the masters then give effective rituals that assuage fear and help people cope with the trouble, ritual is bolstered. But if the masters are weak or bankrupt in their spirituality, people lose faith.

The second way ritual is endangered is by rebellion. All around the world, we revolt against the past. In every part of the world, young people question and then abandon the old ways. This process of rebellion is part of contemporary culture.

In Western art, an artist's obligation through the nineteenth century was to church and state. Since then we have marched away from that with a series of movements ranging from impressionism, Dadaism, abstract expressionism, pop art, minimalism, and conceptual art. Our architecture changed radically after World War II, with modernism beginning a search for a building style untainted by the past that people felt had so betrayed them.

In science, we have elevated constant testing and experimentation to an institution; one era's scientific genius stands only until proven wrong. Galileo is justly admired, but our current telescopes can detect phenomena he could not even suspect. Newton's hypothesis was world-changing—until Einstein relegated those theories to provisional status.

In music, classical music stands at one end of the spectrum, while a continually developing rebellion of nonconservatory rock 'n' roll, bebop, jazz, hip-hop, and avant-garde keep springing up. In the Western poetic tradition, free verse supplanted the rigid and, some might argue, elitist forms such as the sonnet, villanelle, and sestina.

These tendencies are now global. Yet, the masters of the *Changes* and allied arts insist on the primacy of form. Taoist and Buddhist masters urge us to engage in years of practice. A Taiji master insists on a student reviewing one movement for months on end, or a calligrapher stipulates that strokes are to be written only in a certain order. When teachers insist on the mastery of form above all else, it is contrary to the world's cultural development. There had better be a good reason for us to undertake the discipline of ritual.

Yet there is something deeper in the *Changes*, accessed through its rituals. In other words, the ritual is just a way to bring us to the reality of the *Changes*. The core of the *Changes* provides us with ways to know ourselves, know the world around us, and formulate a stance toward the future. What it points to is not the outside reality. What it ultimately points to is ourselves. As much as our art, science, and culture change, they are all a product of the human mind, which we must probe more deeply. The *Changes* can help us do that.

The *Changes* itself would accept the alteration of ritual as natural. It's said that the most furious storm cannot last more than a day, so how can human works last forever? That ritual dies out is inevitable. There is nothing wrong with people no longer living as Confucius did. Indeed, it would be foolhardy to try to suppress people and force them to live according to an imagined superior time. There is also no reason to weep over the feebleness of the masters, for if they were fully committed to their philosophy they would realize that the force of everyone's personality must ebb (that's why there's a tradition of retirement, even in the spiritual community). All life consists of cycles, and that includes the power of the masters as well.

Though we would not want to live as King Wen or Confucius did, though we have no appetite for the agrarian sacrifices mentioned in the *Changes*, and though we embrace our technological and information-based society, we don't lack the same troubles that faced the people in the past. We will all face misfortune, illness, and death. That's where we need the essence of the *Changes*. The ritual and decades-long immersion in this book are all a means of going directly into it, using it, contemplating it, and creating with it. In the process, new rituals will be discovered. Every time that happens, it renews the tradition of the *Changes*.

We have to make a combined approach to the *Changes*, taking the best of both the traditional approach and the modern approach. Those who are committed to the *Changes* will find themselves coming back to it for years on end. It is a book that you do not forget. At the same time, we can jettison some of the moribund elements in the *Changes* tradition by bringing a modern and more creative approach to the *Changes*. The key is this: as long as modern and intellectually rigorous means are not used as a substitute for the content of the *Changes*, we will be acting correctly.

In this view, then, we must make as many varied inquiries as possible—meaning not just divination, but intellectual and artistic inquires too. Many people are doing that already, and their efforts are important. For example, there have been painters who have made series of works based on the *Changes*. The use of the *Changes* in the work of the composer John Cage is well-known.

Anyone who is creative knows that it is a lifelong endeavor and a great deal of hard work. That does not change in spite of how our cultures change. Creativity is a sense perception. We need to bring it to bear on the *Changes*. If we exercise the traditional forms, contemporary mental rigor, and creativity, we will become a part of the *Changes*.

Traditional and Contemporary Meanings of the Eight Trigrams

Attributes traditionally assigned to the Eight Trigrams are listed here. These associations are derived from the Ten Wings, as well as definitions currently used in Asia.

Some of these meanings may seem peculiar. Why does watermelon belong to the trigram fire? If Wind is associated with the first daughter and assigned many yin connotations, why does it include gray-haired men, carpenters, and roosters?

What is instructive is the wide range of the symbols, and how literal some of the interpretations are. Generations have tried to include as much as possible, with the resulting list being rather untidy and bordering on the superstitious. But many of the meanings assigned to the Eight Trigrams are part of contemporary divination and feng shui. If a reader is trying to understand the full scope of the *Changes,* it's important to survey all the permutations of the tradition.

Heaven

Quality: strong

Direction: northwest

Season: late autumn or early winter

Weather: clear, cold

Taste: acrid

Family position: father

People: emperor, prince, president, dictator, leader, sage, founder of religion, pope, church elder, prime minister, board chairman, military commander, husband, old man

Occupations: government service, military service, industrial businesses, sporting equipment, businesses dealing in precious metals, fruit, watches, and clocks

Parts of the body: head, face, lungs, pleura

Illnesses: headaches, constipation, pulmonary diseases, broken bones, fevers, swelling

Places: palaces, official halls, offices, temples, shrines, churches, theaters, schools, military encampments, markets, walls and fortifications, observation platforms, racetracks, stadiums, and athletic fields

Articles: jade and other precious stones, metals, watches and clocks, stamps and chop marks, automobiles, streetcars, bicycles, sewing machines, machine guns, overcoats, hats, umbrellas, mosquito nets, purses, mouth coverings, clothing, cloth wrappers, mail boxes

Food: rice, beans, canned goods, fresh fruit

Animals: horses (a good horse, an old horse, a lean horse, a wild horse), tigers, lions

Plants: chrysanthemum, fruit, herbs

Miscellaneous: round shapes, abundance, fullness, rapid advancement, charity and donations, happiness and gratification, the time prior to midnight, bravery, boldness, determination, wealth, high position, honor, pride, luxury, ice, cold

Earth

Quality: yielding

Direction: southwest

Season: late summer, early autumn

Weather: cloudy, overcast

Taste: sweet

Family position: mother

People: citizenry, the multitude, groups, workers, the industrious, handymen, the poor, the incapable, the ignorant, wives, old women.

Occupations: obstetrics, gastrointestinal doctors, dealers in antiques and curios

Parts of the body: abdomen, spleen, stomach

Illnesses: gastrointestinal disorders

Places: fields, farms, wilderness, slums

Articles: cloth, trousers, pants, chair cushions, sheets, mats, mattresses, kettle, square-shaped items, chessboards, boxes, suitcases, carriages.

Food: powdered and ground food, sweet potatoes, taro, wheat, sugar, desserts, snacks

Animals: cows, calves, mares, ants

Plants: flowering plants

Miscellaneous: flatness, frugality, miserliness, caution, tranquillity, respect, reverence, modesty, loads, levelness, a large wagon, form, a shaft, black soil, warmth, afternoon

Thunder

Quality: movement

Direction: east

Season: spring

Weather: thunderstorms

Taste: sour

Family position: first son

People: prince (subordinate to a king), famous people, eldest sons, youth, newly prosperous people

Occupations: telecommunications operators, technicians, engineers, musicians, broadcast personnel, announcers, workers in music stores and audio media, dealers and workers in arms and munitions

Parts of the body: foot, liver, throat

Illnesses: hysteria, spasm, convulsions, phobias, liver, foot ailments, nervous-system ailments

Places: a great road, forests, houses and buildings being remodeled or repaired, music and concert halls, telecommunications offices, broadcast stations, auditoriums, power stations, electric companies, gunpowder factories

Articles: firecrackers, fireworks, guns, rifles, rockets, gunpowder, pianos, organs, trumpets, clarinets, recordings in all media, audio equipment, stringed musical instruments, flutes, drums, bells, gongs, harmonicas, telephones

Food: green vegetables, bean sprouts, pomelos, grapefruit, lemons, bamboo shoots, plums

Animals: dragons, horses that can neigh well, horses with white hind legs, horses that gallop, horses with a star on the forehead, eagles, swallows, canaries, larks, cicadas, bees, crickets, centipedes, spiders, frogs

Plants: young and green bamboo, reeds, rushes, pod-bearing plants

Miscellaneous: spreading out, decisive, struggle and determination, frivolousness, sunrise, flying, freshness, lectures, space launches

Wind

Quality: penetrating

Direction: southeast

Season: late spring, early summer

Weather: windy and cloudy

Taste: pungent

Family position: first daughter

People: gray-haired men, people with broad fore-heads, people with much white in their eyes, those who prosper easily and quickly, businesspeople, travelers, sisters

Occupations: moving and transport, shipping, con-struction, carpentry, plasterers, masons, guides

Parts of the body: thighs, buttocks, elbows, intes-tines, nerves, digestive tract, eyes

Illnesses: colds, digestive ailments, upset stomach, diseases of the stomach and bowels

Places: forests, remote places

Articles: string, thread, wire, rope, tables, lumber, railroads, pencils, matches, drawers, swings, postal items, electric fans, bellows

Food: noodles, onions, leek, garlic, greens

Animals: roosters, chickens, cranes, snakes, earth-worms, *qilin* (Chinese unicorn)

Plants: grass, willows, reeds, rushes, lilies, calamus, trees

Miscellaneous: clouds, the period of time between 7 a.m. and 11 a.m., length and height, obedience, adjustments, orderly and neat appearance, mar-riage arrangements, travel, dismissal or disbanding, hesitation, purity, completeness

Water

Quality: danger

Direction: north

Season: late winter

Weather: rain, flood, downpours, cold, cloudy, dark

Taste: salty

Family position: middle or second son

People: thieves, middle-aged men, the sick, the blind, those with many cares, toilers, adulteresses, lovers, nymphomaniacs, sex maniacs, the dead

Occupations: bartender, bathhouse attendants, dye-factory workers, brothel workers, prostitutes, dairy workers, fishermen

Parts of the body: ears, nostrils, genitals, kidneys, anus, blood, sweat, tears

Illnesses: melancholy, heartsick, earaches, kidney ailments, venereal diseases, hemorrhoids, alcoho-lism

Places: ditches, large rivers, banquet and meeting halls, funeral parlors, hospitals, convalescent homes, wells, baths, brothels, caves, waterworks, aquariums, firehouses, waterfalls, hot springs

Articles: chariots with many defects

Food: wine, soup, drinks, soy sauce, seaweed, lotus root, raw fish

Animals: pigs, boars, foxes, rats; also horses with beautiful backs, wild courage, hanging heads, thin hoofs, or who stumble

Plants: plums, daffodils, narcissus, algae, firm wood, wood with much pitch

Miscellaneous: the moon, ambush, bending and straightening, cunning, trickery, wisdom and intel-ligence, worry, thoughts, hidden crime and unre-vealed guilt, social exchange, sexual intercourse, midnight

Fire

Quality: clinging

Direction: south

Season: summer

Weather: clear and warm days, heat, droughts

Taste: bitter

Family position: middle or second daughter

People: big-bellied men, middle-aged women, beautiful women, wise and intelligent people

Occupations: writers, artists, craftspeople, ophthalmologists and opticians, police, war correspondents, soldiers, those involved in munitions, department-store workers, barbers, beauticians, bookstore employees

Parts of the body: eye, heart, spirit, breasts, blood

Illnesses: eye disease, mental illness, high fevers, heart ailments, headaches

Places: police stations, lighthouses, fire departments, department stores, theaters, schools, courthouses, downtowns, battlefields, scenes of fire

Articles: armor and mail, helmets, lances, weapons, paintings, works of calligraphy, books, ornaments and decorations, electric lights, candles, lamps, pots, kettles, stocks, bonds, checks

Food: dry foods, turtles, oysters, shellfish, crab

Animals: pheasants, tortoises, crabs, snails, mussels, mollusks, hawkbill turtles, chicks, goldfish, fireflies, lobsters

Plants: trees dried in the upper part of the trunk, crepe myrtle, maples, watermelon, all red-colored plants

Miscellaneous: dryness, brightness, lightning, violence, nervousness, impulsiveness, intelligence, passion, enthusiasm, electricity, rainbows

Mountain

Quality: standstill

Direction: northeast

Season: late winter, early spring

Weather: cloudy and changeable weather

Taste: sweet

Family position: third or youngest son

People: eunuchs, watchmen

Occupations: monks, Taoist adepts, clergy of all religions, restaurant workers

Parts of the body: hand, fingers, back, waist, nose, hands, fingers, joints, fleshy tumors

Illnesses: side aches, arthritis, fatigue, nasal inflammation

Places: buildings, doors, gates, paths, walls, graves, hotels, garages, dikes, stairs, stages, platforms

Articles: things stored or piled up, screens, tables, building blocks

Food: fruit and seeds, preserved foods, sweets, fruit from trees

Animals: dogs, rats, black-billed birds, bulls, oxen, tigers

Plants: firm and gnarled trees

Miscellaneous: bypaths, pebbles, doors and openings, twilight, tardiness, slowness, stubborness, sincerity, candor, independence, loftiness, frugality

Lake

Quality: pleasure

Direction: west

Season: autumn

Weather: rain

Taste: spicy

Family position: third or youngest daughter

People: concubines, young girls, girlfriends, actresses, female singers, bar girls, prostitutes, sorceresses, witches, the feeble

Occupations: lawyers, lecturers, those involved in finance or drinking establishments

Parts of the body: mouth, tongue

Illnesses: all illnesses of the mouth, tongue, chest, and breasts

Places: valleys, ponds, marshes, low-lying ground, hollows, ditches, riversides, lakes, bars, taverns, beverage stores, brothel and prostitution districts

Articles: knives, blades, money, musical instruments

Food: tea, coffee, wine, alcohol, mutton, fowl

Animals: sheep, birds, monkeys

Plants: bellflower, magnolia, plants growing in marshes and by lake shores; also all peppery, spicy, or hot-tasting plants

Miscellaneous: smashing, breaking apart, dropping off, bursting open, hard and salty soil

APPENDIX 7

The River Chart, the Lo Writing, and the Five Phases

In traditional commentaries, the He Tu, or River Chart (*river* here refers to the Yellow River), and Lo Shu, or the Lo Writing (Lo is the name of a river), are said to be the bases of the Eight Trigram formations. The River Chart was supposed to have inspired Fu Xi, while the Lo Writing is linked to the Great Yu and unifies the Five Phases with the Eight Trigrams. Many accounts are confusing, and give concordances without coming to any useful conclusions. This is sad, because there is much to be learned by exploring these three diagrams. We can then unify the Five Phases and the Eight Trigrams. These are the two major systems of Chinese metaphysical thinking, and reconciling them gives us a complete understanding.

Let us begin with some of the cultural background surrounding these three charts. While scholars do not agree whether the River Chart and Lo Writing are truly connected with the early emperors Fu Xi and Yu, we must nevertheless acknowledge the cultural importance placed on these two diagrams. The mythology surrounding these two charts is as follows.

Fu Xi was meditating by a river when a "dragon-horse" rose from the Yellow River with the River Chart on its back. Inspired by its markings, Fu Xi created the Early Heaven Eight Trigrams. Some scholars cite a passage in the *Documents* that refers to the River Chart being displayed as a treasure during the accession of the third emperor of the Zhou dynasty around 1067 B.C.E.

In the case of the Lo Writing, it is said that an enormous turtle rose from the water with the diagram marked on its back. It was seen by the Great Yu (acc. 2205 B.C.E), the man credited with building a system of canals and dikes to relieve China from flooding and who eventually became one of the early emperors.

Evidently, the appearance of such charts from rivers had a cultural significance we do not fully understand today. In the *Analects,* Confucius wails: "The phoenix does not arrive! The river gives no chart! It is all over for me!"

The secret of the River Chart and the Lo Writing is to count the number of dots and to convert them to numbers. The River Chart becomes a cross-shaped chart of numbers, while the Lo Writing forms a group of nine squares. Note that both diagrams have the number five in the center.

The River Chart

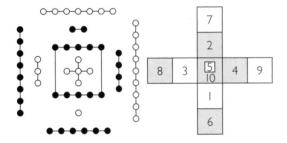

The River Chart has the following features:

- Beginning from the five in the center, add any number in the square adjacent to it (skipping over the ten), and the answer will be the number beside it. For example, $5 + 4 = 9$.
- Take the outer number at the end of any axis of the cross and subtract the number beside it. The answer will be five, which is the number in the center. For example, $9 - 4 = 5$.
- Complete the above subtraction for any two ends, add the differences, and the answer will be ten. For example, $(8 - 3) + (9 - 4) = 10$.
- Complete all four sets of subtractions, add the differences, and the sum will be twenty.

- Add all the odd numbers on both axes (thus excluding the five and the ten), and the answer will be twenty. Likewise, add all the even numbers, and the answer will also equal twenty.
- Add all the numbers together, $1 + 2 + 3 + 4 + 5 + 6 + 7 + 8 + 9 + 10$, and the answer is 55.

In the Ten Wings, the appendixes in the *Changes* credited to Confucius but at least augmented if not written by later scholars, there is a passage that relates to this fascination for numbers:

Heaven is one
Earth is two
Heaven is three
Earth is four
Heaven is five
Earth is six
Heaven is seven
Earth is eight
Heaven is nine
Earth is ten

We thus have a clear indication that heaven numbers are odd and earth numbers are even. The *Changes* continues:

There are five heavenly numbers. There are also five earthly numbers.
Within a set of ten, there are five odd numbers and five even numbers.
When they are distributed among the five places, each finds its compliment.
There are four sides plus the center in the River Chart—the five places.
The sum of the heavenly numbers is twenty-five. The sum of the earthly numbers is thirty.
Adding all the odd numbers from one to ten equals twenty-five. Adding all the even numbers from one to ten equals thirty.
The sum total of heavenly numbers and earthly numbers is fifty-five. This completes the changes and transformations and sets the demons and spirits in motion.

These passages from the *Changes* are the only mention that we have of any numbers that might relate to the River Chart. There is no mention in the *Changes* that any of the makers of the *Changes* directly utilized such numerology in formulating their valuable contributions. Although traditional commentaries assert that the River Chart is the basis for the Early Heaven Eight Trigrams, the *Changes* never states this. Moreover, while the *Changes* mentions Fu Xi (or Pao Xi as he is also known), it never credits him with creating the Early Heaven Eight Trigrams formation, nor does it show the relationship between the River Chart and the Eight Trigrams. The closest mention is in the Ten Wings:

> Heaven creates divine things. The holy sages took them as models. Heaven and earth have their transformations. The holy sages imitated them. In heaven are images that reveal good fortune and misfortune. The holy sages reproduced them. The Yellow River brought forth a chart. The Lo River brought forth a writing. The holy sages took them as models.

Many editions of the *Changes* elaborate on this passage, repeating the legend that Fu Xi created the Early Heaven Eight Trigrams formation after having received the River Chart. This tradition is worth questioning, especially since the relationship between the River Chart and the Early Heaven Eight Trigrams is neither apparent nor easily intuited. An examination of two major attempts to reconcile the diagrams will show how much effort has gone into this endeavor, and it will also show whether those efforts are credible.

Shao Yong (1011–1077 C.E.) assigned numbers to the trigrams and then tried to show how those numbers fell into the same formation as the River Chart. He assigned these numbers:

Heaven 9; Lake 4; Fire 3; Thunder 8; Wind 2; Water 7, Mountain 6; and Earth 1.

Then he said that the sequence of numbers 9, 4, 3, 8 matches the horizontal axis of the River Chart when read from right to left. Then he asserts 2, 7, 6, 1 as the second sequence. If 9, 4, 3, and 8 are placed at the top and then around the octagon in a counterclockwise direction, it accounts for the sequence of half the Eight Trigrams. The sequence 2, 7, 6, 1 does account for the second half, going in a clockwise direction.

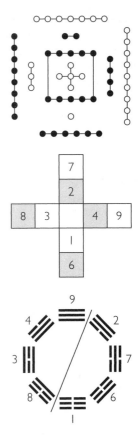

There are two flaws in this argument. The first is that the sequence of the second numbers is really 7, 2, 1, 6, or 6, 1, 2, 7. Shao Yong has to take the two axes of the River Map and claim two different sequences, which, at best, is an inelegant solution. After all, what is to prevent someone from arbitrarily assigning numbers and claiming that this "proves" the connection?

As we read from the *Changes* itself, heaven numbers are odd, while earth numbers are even. This brings us to the next flaw in Shao Yung's analysis: the heaven or yang numbers are not all odd, and the earth or yin numbers are not all even. He assigns 9 and 7 to the yang trigrams Heaven and Water, but gives Thunder 8 and Mountain 6. This obviously leads to corresponding errors on the Earth, or yin, side of the set.

For these reasons, we have to set aside Shao Yong's explanation of the River Chart's relationship with the Early Heaven Eight Trigrams.

Another attempt to reconcile the two diagrams was made by Ren Qiyun (1669–1744 C.E.), a Qing dynasty scholar. He tries to rearrange the River Chart according to the yin-yang symbol.

Under this arrangement, the yin numbers end up on the yin side of the symbol, and the yang numbers are on the yang side. But what are the correspondences to the trigram numbers? This is not explained, and again, the proposed solution is inelegant, especially since the yang trigrams are not all on the same half of the Early Heaven Eight Trigrams.

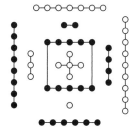

If the traditional explanations are not satisfactory, why then is the River Chart included in the tradition of the *Changes*? Here are some possibilities:

- The River Chart attempts to take sequential numbers and give them dimensionality. Numbers set across from one another are sequential: 1–2, 3–4, 6–7, 8–9.
- The center of the chart indicates four directions. But how does one take what must have seemed like a complete set—ten—and express dimensionality? The cross at the center may be a clue. One takes a center, and then branches off into four directions.
- The chart pairs odd and even numbers in a formation that both puts them far from each number and yet keeps them in a relationship (the addition and subtraction in various directions). Thus odd and even are mixed in a way that is as diverse as possible and yet not a mere jumble of numbers.
- The chart allows the expression of greatest multiplicity without losing a connection to wholeness. It allows us to take a whole, separate it into its constituent parts, and yet allow for reassembling them back to the whole again.
- If heaven and earth are the source of all transformations, how is this expressed and possibly probed by the human mind? Assigning numbers and then interleaving them is one way to contemplate the interlocking nature of heaven and earth, and of yin and yang.
- Ten must have been an obvious set to all early thinkers. After all, we have ten fingers and ten toes, and it is easy to count by fives and tens. Multiples of ten also have a certain elegance. There were also other systems of ten in ancient thought. In particular, the lunar-solar calendar that the Chinese have been using since the time of the Yellow Emperor utilizes the Ten Heavenly Stems. But Fu Xi, or others after him, had a system of *eight* trigrams that had to be reconciled with the completeness of *ten*. The River Chart shows one way that this can be done. By taking a set of ten and dropping out the five and ten, eight numbers—four odd and four even numbers—remain.
- The River Chart also suggested four cardinal directions, and if Fu Xi was at first undecided as to how to express his eight trigrams, the cross formation may have been inspiration enough without him actually assigning numbers to the trigrams or attempting to find the position of the trigrams through mathematical operations.

Perhaps the relationship between the River Chart and the Early Heaven Eight Trigrams is an enigma because there is no direct numerical relationship. What then is the reason for the River Chart being included in the tradition of the *Changes?* There are three possible explanations:

- The River Chart is a mathematical artifact, a mere curiosity. It may have had only a limited role, as an underpinning to other needs.
- The River Chart was added later, probably around the Han Dynasty, by schools who sought to graft their numerological speculation onto the *Changes.* In particular, when the yarrow-stalk method of divination was added to the *Changes* (because we know that early divination focused on the cracking of bones and turtle shells), a greater need for mathematical justification occurred. It would thus have been easy for someone to have added numerological charts, easing their acceptance by claiming a connection to Fu Xi.
- The reason for the River Chart's connection to the *Changes* is now lost.

If the River Chart was indeed known to King Wen, then perhaps he was dissatisfied as well. He ended up formulating an entirely different structure. Legend has it that it too was based on a divinely gifted writing borne by an animal rising from a river.

The Lo Writing

The Lo Writing is the second diagram to be associated with the *Changes.* Abstracting it to its numerical values yields a magic square. Any row, column, or diagonal will add up to fifteen—coincidentally the sum of the three fives in the center of the River Chart. If you add any two numbers across from one another along the diagonal or cardinal directions, excluding the five, the answer will be ten in every case. Since the numbers are the same as the River Chart, adding up the odd numbers (without

the five) and adding up the even numbers will again equal twenty. However, the sum of the numbers 1–9 in the Lo Writing equal 45, and so this particular diagram cannot be related to the previously quoted passage of the *Changes* that states that the sum of heavenly and earthly numbers is 55. One would need the additional ten in the River Chart, and the Lo Writing does not incorporate the number ten.

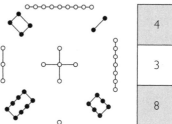

Note also that the outer pairs of numbers in the River Chart are adjacent numbers on the Lo Writing—that is, 8-3, 4-9, 2-7, and 6-1 are adjacent to one another in both diagrams.

If we now try to reconcile the Lo Writing with the Early Heaven Trigrams, we encounter a number of problems, some historical, some logical. Tradition holds that the Lo Writing was imparted to the Great Yu, who lived more than two thousand years after Fu Xi. If Fu Xi is the maker of the Early Heaven Eight Trigrams formation, he cannot have based it on the Lo Writing. If we want to incorporate the Lo Writing as the basis for the Early Heaven Eight Trigrams, we cannot accept Fu Xi as the maker of the Eight Trigrams formation—unless the two diagrams are related only by coincidence.

The Lo Writing fits into Shao Yong's logic better than the River Chart. At least now we have a perimeter that could be seen as analogous to the octagonal pattern of the Eight Trigrams, and the numbers correspond to the numbers that Shao Yong assigned the trigrams. Beginning at the top and moving counterclockwise, we have 9, 4, 3, 8, and then beginning on the top right, we have 2, 7, 6, 1. Whether in the magic-square formation or in the

Eight Trigrams arrangement, adding any two numbers across from one another equals ten, and the arrangement thus resolves satisfactorily. Unfortunately, the original assignment of numbers appears to be arbitrary, and the fact that there are still odd numbers assigned to yin trigrams and even numbers assigned to yang defeats this theory.

If we try to fit King Wen's Later Heaven Eight Trigrams to the Lo Writing, we fare a little better. One as the number of water might make sense (all living things came from water), and earth receives a two. ("Heaven is one, earth is two.") But again, even numbers are assigned to yang trigrams when they should be odd: heaven 6, mountain 8 will not correlate to the doctrine that heaven's numbers are odd, and wind 7 with fire 9 does not correlate with the statement that yin trigrams should have even numbers. This insistence on congruence with odd and even relates directly to a passage in the Ten Wings of the *Changes*:

> The light trigrams have more dark lines, and the dark trigrams have more light lines. Why is this so? The light trigrams are uneven, the dark trigrams are even.

The River Chart, the Five Phases, and the Later Heaven Trigrams

Before we consign these two charts to the scrapheap of numerical puzzles and wonder how wise scholars could distort the obvious in order to justify tradition, we should take a fresh look at the two charts. They provide other hints. Since both charts are based on the numbers five and ten, they strongly suggest that the masters of the *Changes* were trying to stay compatible with other systems of thought. The two charts suggest that we look for connections to the Five Phases and the astronomical and calendrical speculations of the day.

The Chinese calendar was in use long before King Wen's time, and the Five Elements were likely conceived as far back as the Great Yu. The Duke of Zhou was interested in astronomy, mathematics,

and earth sciences, and Confucius included mathematics as one of the Six Arts.

All those factors give us reason to consider the River Chart and the Lo Writing from fresh perspectives. The two diagrams are associated with a lineage of thinkers who were serious, who understood mathematics, and who were therefore unlikely to flippantly make two number puzzles the bases for their most profound meditations on the universe.

In particular, the two charts are thought to offer a concordance between the Eight Trigrams and the Five Phases. This alone is something worth taking seriously.

In Chinese, the Five Phases are called *wuxing*. *Wu* means "five." Among the translations for *xing* are "walk," "go on foot," "move," "go," "travel," "act," "do," "work," "road," "path." *Wuxing* has often been called the Five Elements, perhaps to give a parallel to the Greek idea of four elements of earth, air, fire, and water. But it is essential not to conceive of the Five Phases as material. Rather, they are descriptive of certain phenomena that were identified as fundamental. That is why a more accurate description is more dynamic, and "phases" reminds us that the Five Phases include one phase generating another, or one phase "destroying," or replacing, another.

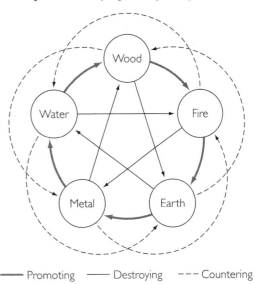

—— Promoting —— Destroying - - - Countering

Table of the Five Phases

	Wood	Fire	Earth	Metal	Water
Season	Spring	Summer	Late Summer	Autumn	Winter
Weather	Wind	Heat	Dampness	Dryness	Coldness
Color	Green	Red	Yellow	White	Black
Taste	Sour	Bitter	Sweet	Pungent	Salty
Direction	East	South	Middle	West	North
Process	Germination	Growth	Transformation	Reaping	Storing
Emotions	Anger	Joy	Meditation	Grief	Fear
Organs (*zhang*)	Liver	Heart	Spleen	Lung	Kidney
Viscera (*fu*)	Gallbladder	Small intestine	Stomach	Large intestine	Bladder
Senses	Eye	Tongue	Mouth	Nose	Ear
Tissues	Tendon	Vessels and ducts	Muscle	Skin and hair	Bone

The Five Phases—Metal, Water, Wood, Fire, and Earth—are metaphors for any action that is similar to the definition of those phases:

Metal is that which purifies and solidifies.

Water is liquid, flowing, downward-traveling.

Wood is piercing, growing upwards, and linear.

Fire is heat, light, expansion, and consumption.

Earth is flat, broadening, and neutral.

The Table of the Five Phases shows many of the equivalent qualities of each phase.

Many believe that the Five Phases describe all universal phenomena. The ancient Chinese approached their analysis purely in terms of their observations. They tell us in detail how things function, but they are not interested in the smallest particles of "matter." They are interested in the *relationships*.

The Five Phases theory has been a part of traditional Chinese medicine for centuries. Practitioners of traditional Chinese medicine all over the world trace their history back to the Yellow Emperor, and from that time on, the Five Phases theory has been the basis for all Chinese medicine, from acupuncture to herbology. Briefly, the Five Phases describe the functioning of the human body in terms of deficiency or excess of one or more of the Five Phases. A perfectly functioning human being has his or her Five Phases in harmony and balance—very much as the River Chart and the Lo Writing suggest a perfect summing of their parts.

The Five Phases theory explains how one phase generates another. Although it is easy to remember that water "promotes" wood, the theory really means that downward-flowing, cold, and liquid phenomena give way to the stiff and ascending. The references to water and wood should be interpreted metaphorically rather than literally.

Once doctors have determined whether a person has a deficiency or excess of their Five Phases, they administer a treatment to bring the Five Phases back into balance. Certain phases either generate or control other phases. Depending on the illness, the doctor will use herbs, massage, acupuncture, or psychology to restore balance.

Even now, when doctors in China and the West are developing hybrid practices, the Five Phases remain one of the fundamental underpinnings. We are familiar with some of the miraculous results that Chinese doctors have been able to accomplish with their needles and herbs. It has been the Five Phases that have enabled them to get these results.

The Five Phases and the Eight Trigrams

The River Chart and the Lo Writing demonstrate a concordance between the Five Phases and the Eight Trigrams. This concordance gives us insight into the two systems and unites all of Chinese metaphysical thought. If we move earth to the center, its traditional direction, then we have four phases whose symbolism has been given numerous meanings.

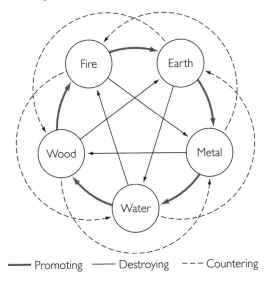

—— Promoting ——— Destroying - - - Countering

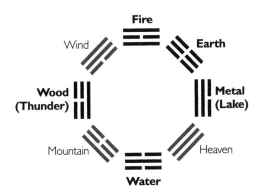

The Later Heaven Eight Trigrams correspond to the Five Phases. Water, represents the north and winter and matches Water in the Later Heaven Eight Trigrams. Wood, representing the east and spring, corresponds with Thunder, which symbolizes the east, beginnings, and spring. Fire represents the south and summer, and corresponds easily with the Fire of the Later Heaven Eight Trigrams. Metal, representing the west and autumn, corresponds with Lake. (If we remember that Lake means purification and solidification, we can see some connection to the pooling of molten metal and its purification by smelting.)

Moreover, the direction of promotion is the same direction as the direction of the Eight Trigrams (both clockwise). It is quite easy to see how the Five Phases were made into the Eight Trigrams by simply inserting three more trigrams between the Five Phases—Heaven, Mountain, and Wind.

If one was already committed to the Five Phases, the Later Heaven Eight Trigrams would have allowed an entry into its system without requiring abandoning the Five Phases. Perhaps King Wen's revising of the Eight Trigrams was meant to appeal to all schools of thought.

Did the concept of the Five Phases exist before the Han dynasty? There is evidence that it did, one of the most powerful being a passage in the *Documents*.

> The Five Phases are as follows: first is water, second is fire, third is wood, fourth is metal, and fifth is earth. Water flows downward and is moist. Fire rises upward and is burning. Wood can be crooked and straight. Metal can be changed in form according to the needs of people. The earth can be used to grow grain.

Some scholars dispute whether this document truly came from the time of the Great Yu (based on the language, the speculation is that this section of the *Documents* dates from the Qin dynasty), but if it does, it establishes the Five Phases before the time of King Wen, and thus it is possible that he would have wanted to reconcile the Eight Trigrams with the Five Phases. Given the interruptions in the history of the *Documents*, the fact that they were compiled and edited, and the fact that we have very little hard evidence for comparison, it is difficult to determine the truth. It will be a continuing question whether the Five Phases predated King Wen.

The fact that the Eight Trigrams can be projected onto a nine-square arrangement of the Lo Writing brings up another possibility for the Eight Trigrams' formation. When Yu was faced with administering the country, he divided it into nine parts. Roughly, these parts make up a formation reminiscent of the nine sections of the magic square. Traditionally, the Chinese say that this division of the country is based on the character for the word for "well" (as in water well).

The word has two parallel horizontal lines and two parallel vertical lines, like a tic-tac-toe grid. It is impossible to say whether this is purely a coincidence, evidence of the penchant to see all things as metaphorically related to one another, or a conscious decision. At the very least, the idea of nine divisions is deeply rooted.

If we look at Yu's dividing lines, and check each formation, there is a correspondence to the geographical and meteorological associations of the Later Heaven Eight Trigrams.

As has been previously discussed, the dating of the *Documents* is the subject of continuing debate. But if the passage in the *Documents* is true, King Wen must certainly have been familiar with the Five Phases. If he was trying to formulate a true image of the universe, he would naturally have taken advantage of ideas already in the culture. Perhaps he even found the Five Phases to be insufficient. Why else would someone completely remake the metaphysical structure of his times? King Wen's Later Heaven Eight Trigrams thus sum up and incorporate all the metaphysical thinking up to his time. They incorporate the Five Phases. They incorporate Fu Xi's Early Heaven Eight Trigrams. As discussed in the text, they include seasons, direction, time, family, and many other sets of phenomena as well. They take all these concerns and then meld them together based on the Lo Writing, a diagram made already complete by the way its numbers resolve to ten and fifteen. The Later Heaven Eight Trigrams are thus one of the most complete and thorough worldviews. They were the ancient Chinese theory of everything.

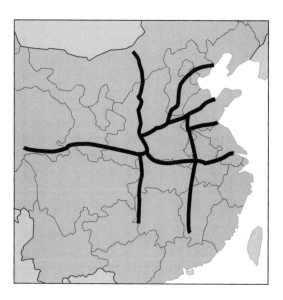

APPENDIX **8**

King Wen's Ordering of the Sixty-Four Hexagrams

For centuries, people have been trying to explain the order King Wen gave to the hexagrams. We know that there were other orderings of the hexagrams. Edward Shaughnessy's translation of the *Changes*, for example, is based on a version of the *Changes* found in a tomb dated to 168 B.C.E. It is the earliest known version of the *Changes* that we have, and it has a wholly different order than the orthodox version.

Even within the *Changes* itself, hexagrams are discussed in the Ten Wings out of order. Nevertheless, when the Early Heaven trigrams and hexagrams can be connected in such perfect mathematical order, the natural expectation is to see some evolution of that order in the hexagram sequence. Not so with King Wen's version. Thus far, no one has found a convincing logic for the current hexagram order.

As we discussed in the text, we know two indisputable observations about King Wen's ordering:

- Every even-numbered hexagram is the inversion (turning upside down) or reversal (switching each line of the hexagram for its opposite) of the preceding odd-numbered hexagram.
- The book is divided into two parts. Hexagrams 1–30 are called the upper classic and 31–64 are called the lower classic. There is no hierarchy implied here; Chinese books in two volumes are always labeled "upper" for the first and "lower" for the second.

Many attempts have been made to analyze the sequence further. Some have resorted to statistical analysis, while others have seen fractals as a possible approach. As clever as these explanations are, they do not seem as if they could have been a plausible plan by a person in the eleventh century B.C.E.

In order for an explanation to be credible, the following criteria would have to be satisfied:

- The method for generating the sequence should be consistent with what we know of thinking in the time between the late Shang and the early Zhou. We cannot resort to later methods such as statistics, calculus, or modern physics to explain what King Wen might have been thinking.
- The method must be a closed system, and it must be self-generating. Whatever the possible explanation, it must begin from the first two hexagrams and generate the exact sequence of all the others in a method that will generate only that sequence.
- The method must be compatible with all else we know about the *Changes*. From the number theories to the actual images of each hexagram, we must be sure that there is no contradiction between a proposed method and other facts about the *Changes*.

The first question to consider is whether the sequence is simply a random jumbling of hexagrams. What if King Wen simply threw them together by accident? Let's say that during his imprisonment in Youli he was ordering and reordering the hexagrams for seven years, and then, when he was released, the hexagrams just happened to be in that particular order.

Alternatively, King Wen might have let the oracle choose the sequence. What if he cast the yarrow stalks each time he needed a new pair of hexagrams and built the sequence up that way?

Both these are possible, but there are a number of details that seem to indicate conscious ordering. While these features don't give us the inner structure of the sequence, they are intriguing enough to keep us searching.

Indications That the Sequence Is Not Random

The sequence begins with Heaven, all yang lines, and Earth, all yin lines, and ends with Already

Across and Not Yet Across—the only two hexagrams where the yin and yang lines alternate one after another. Thus, Heaven and Earth start the sequence with the two most extreme opposites, and the sequence ends with yin and yang ideally mixed and balanced. What's more, the last two hexagrams of the sequence are the only two ways that the trigrams for Water and Fire can be combined. After Heaven and Earth, Water and Fire are the most primal of hexagrams. They are the only two trigrams that occupy cardinal places in both the Early Heaven and Late Heaven Hexagrams.

The other two hexagrams with Water and Fire—the doubling of each trigram—are strategically placed nearly at the middle of the sequence at 29 (Pit) and 30 (Brilliance). Thus the sequence opens with Heaven and Earth, is anchored in the middle by Water and Fire, and resolves itself when Water and Fire combine.

There are eight hexagrams that are symmetrical: when you turn them over, they are unchanged. Their opposites are derived by switching each line for the opposite one. These eight hexagrams are also strategically placed. Heaven and Earth open the sequence. Water and Fire are near the center. One pair, Hexagrams 27 and 28, are placed right before the double trigrams of Hexagram 29, Pit, and Hexagram 30, Brilliance. The last pair, Hexagrams 61 and 62, are placed right before the last two hexagrams. These placements seem to be conscious rather than coincidental.

Hexagrams 27, 28, 61, and 62 are the only hexagrams that directly suggest their meanings by the overall picture of the hexagram rather than being influenced by what the combination of two trigrams might suggest. Hexagram 27 is seen as an open mouth. Hexagram 28—all yang in the middle, yin on each end—implies a heavy beam on weak supports. Hexagram 61 is seen as the empty middle of Confidence Within, and Hexagram 62 is seen as the body and wings of a bird.

Is the Sequence Mathematical?

The sequence may be intentionally arranged, but before we can turn to that question, we must consider whether the sequence is derived by numbers. This question is important for a variety of reasons.

If the sequence was derived numerologically then we can expect the following:

- There is a numerological relationship with the Early Heaven Trigrams and Hexagrams.
- King Wen could have ordered the hexagrams before assigning their symbols.
- That the numbers and equations used to derive the ordering bespeaks an interest in the mathematical description of reality.

However, if the sequence does not prove to have a mathematical basis, then:

- It would suggest that King Wen did not want to confine himself to numerological methods.
- King Wen might have arranged the hexagrams by content. This could still mean that he had either symbolic, numerological, or geometrical reasons for determining his order.
- If he arranged the sequence consciously, there might be a secret message in the way he did so. Can we derive some further understanding by looking at his reasons?

At this point, no one has been able to discover a credible mathematical underpinning to the sixty-four hexagrams. However, there are features that show King Wen was thinking beyond the point of mere numbers theory. If we look closely at the sixty-four hexagrams, certain patterns seem to bear themselves out. Initially, it seem as if every tenth and every twelfth hexagram come to a junction point. The trigrams seem to bear this out, and the text seems to indicate this as well.

One of the mysteries is why the sequence is divided at Hexagram 30 between upper and lower parts. Wouldn't most people divide the sequence into two equal halves, especially given the mathematical background of the *Changes?* Not only are the two halves uneven, but the division is reinforced with hexagrams derived from the two cardinal trigrams of water and fire, so there is no mistaking the intention here. What might the number thirty mean?

One possibility is if it indicates some intended structure that is a factor of thirty. Consider this sequence and the accompanying comments indicating how these hexagrams have similar roles in the sequence:

Hexagram 10: Walking. Heaven above, Lake below. Continues the sequence after Smallness Tames. It is followed by Hexagram 11, Prospering, which combines the trigrams for Heaven and Earth.

Hexagram 20: Beholding. Wind above, Earth below. An image resting and contemplating, and of establishment—a memorial gateway—and also an image of continuing—going through the gateway. It is followed by Hexagram 21, Biting, which introduces new conflicts.

Hexagram 30: Brilliance. Fire above, Fire below. Brightness after the dark of the Pit, an image of enlightenment and brilliance, but also mutuality. It is followed by Hexagram 31, Feeling, and the classically defined second half of the *Changes*.

Hexagram 40: Releasing. Water below, Thunder above. Loosening of the preceding Hindered. It is followed by Hexagram 41, Decrease, which is compared to Hexagram 11 and which seems to be a new cycle of conflict after the favorable casting of the cauldron.

Hexagram 50: Cauldron. Wind below, Fire above. Another image of establishment, like Hexagram 20, but here it alludes to the establishment of a state, of ritual, and of reverence. It is followed by Hexagram 51, Thunder, one of the doubled trigrams.

Hexagram 60: Regulation. Lake below, Water above. Not only does this name imply a joint, or node, but it indicates the final order after the preceding Spreading. It is followed by Hexagram 61, Confidence Within.

Now consider the sequence in multiples of twelve:

Hexagram 12: Clogging. Heaven above, Earth below. This is the overturning of Prospering, the pulling apart of heaven and earth. It is followed by the goodness of Kindred.

Hexagram 24: Returning. Earth above, Thunder below. This is the return to the path after Splitting. It leads to Innocence.

Hexagram 36: Smothered Light. Earth above, Fire below. This is perhaps the hexagram of greatest misfortune, following Advancing. It is followed by a return to Family.

Hexagram 48: Well. Water above, Wind below. A reminder of the one of the most fundamental features of civilization. It is a restorative hexagram following Distress, and immediately precedes the revolution and upheaval of Reform.

Hexagram 60: Regulation. Lake below, Water above. Again, it indicates the final order after the preceding Spreading. It is followed by Hexagram 61, Confidence Within. This hexagram joins the sequence of tens and twelves.

We already know that fives and tens were important in the River Chart and the Lo Writing, so it makes sense that they would receive some consideration in the hexagrams ordering. The number twelve was important from the calendar system—the Twelve Branches, which correspond both to divisions of the twenty-four-hour clock and to points of the compass.

It's also natural to inquire whether there are intervals of eights:

Hexagram 8: Joining. Water above, Earth below. It is a culmination after Armies, and leads to the control of Smallness Tames.

Hexagram 16: Delight. Thunder above, Earth below. This follows on the significant hexagram, Humility, and leads to Following.

Hexagram 24: Returning. Earth above, Thunder below. This is the return to the path after Splitting. It leads to Innocence. The hexagram overlaps with the cycles of twelve.

Hexagram 32: Constancy. Thunder above, Wind below. This follows Feeling, the hexagram that begins the second half of the *Changes,* and Constancy ends the true arithmetical first half of the *Changes.* It leads to Withdrawal, which seems to be the beginning of a new cycle.

Hexagram 40: Releasing. Water below, Thunder above. Loosening of the preceding Hindered. It is followed by Hexagram 41, Decrease, which is compared to Hexagram 11 and which seems to be a new cycle of conflict after the favorable casting of the cauldron. The hexagram overlaps with the cycles of tens.

Hexagram 48: Well. Water above, Wind below. A reminder of the one of the most fundamental features of civilization. It is a restorative hexagram following Distress, and immediately precedes the revolution and upheaval of Reform. The hexagram overlaps with the cycles of twelve.

Hexagram 56: Traveler. Fire above, Mountain below. This follows Plentiful, and ends a cycle just before the double hexagram for Wind.

Hexagram 64: Not Yet Across. Fire above, Water below. The end of the sixty-four hexagram cycle, and yet, by its content already suggesting new beginnings.

It can probably be argued that one could take any intervals of numbers—3, 7, 4, 5, 6, or 9—and imagine some cycles. Perhaps we are even meant to do that as a form of study. While the cycles are subtle, they ultimately point the way to these overlapping cycles:

- Every hexagram is a cycle. The first line is a beginning, the sixth line is a culmination.
- Every hexagram turns into its opposite. It's possible to see this turning as the natural aftermath

of the culminating sixth line of the preceding odd-numbered hexagram.
- Pairs of hexagram follow several larger cycles, perhaps in tens and twelves, perhaps in other units.
- All the hexagrams as a set make one overriding cycle from one to sixty-four.

The Trigram Links Between Even- and Odd-Numbered Hexagrams

There is another linkage to point out, a graphic one from one hexagram to the next one. Many people have taken the following approach in attempting to unlock the sequence of the *Changes*: since every even-numbered hexagram is derived from the odd-numbered one, all we need to do is find the sequence of the odd-numbered hexagrams. While looking at the trigrams doesn't satisfy this criterion, there is a special connection between the trigrams of the even-numbered hexagrams and the next odd-numbered hexagrams: except for a few places, the next odd-numbered hexagram will share some form of a trigram. This is done in a way quite consistent with all the thoughts of the *Changes*: the shared trigrams are either repeated, inverted, or reversed.

Not only does this give us a way to link an even-numbered hexagram to the next odd-numbered one, the actual transformation of the trigram forms a parallel set of images to the the other parts of the *Changes*. Take Hexagram 24, for example, where the hexagram is nearly identical to Hexagram 25. Thunder, the lower trigram of Hexagram 24, is repeated in Hexagram 25, while Earth in the upper trigram of Hexagram 24 is reversed to become Heaven in the upper trigram of Hexagram 25. If we look at these relationships openly, certain messages are suggested:

- Hexagram 24, Returning, evolves into innocence when the initiating energy of Thunder continues and the receptivity of Earth becomes the yang truth of Hexagram 25, Innocence.

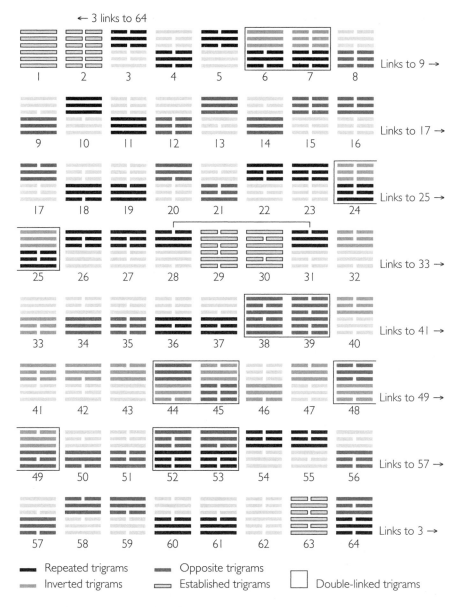

← 3 links to 64

Links to 9 →

Links to 17 →

Links to 25 →

Links to 33 →

Links to 41 →

Links to 49 →

Links to 57 →

Links to 3 →

■■■ Repeated trigrams   ■■■ Opposite trigrams

▨▨▨ Inverted trigrams   ▱▱▱ Established trigrams

☐ Double-linked trigrams

- Thunder suggests sound, or the voice. Innocence comes from a Returning to righteousness, so that words (metaphorically, the voice of Thunder) go from the receptivity of Earth to the truth of Heaven in Innocence.
- Innocence also means the unexpected. The movement (lower trigram Thunder) of Returning continues on in Innocence (in the sense of the unexpected) when the intervention of accident comes from Heaven.

There are many ways of interpreting these inner links between trigrams. Rather than dictate how these should be viewed, the reader should explore the links and let them speak for themselves. They should be addressed to the subconscious, like looking at the rhymes in a poem.

There are three significant breaks in the sequence of linked trigrams. One is at the beginning, since nothing precedes Hexagram 1. The second break is between Hexagrams 28 and 29, while the third is between Hexagrams 62 and 63. Again, notice that the breaks occur adjacent to the hexagrams that can only be reversed and not inverted. They also emphasize the junctions of heaven and earth, and water (pit) and fire, since Hexagrams 29, 30, 63, and 64 are wholly about water and fire. Even so, the trigram link continues, connecting with the next pair of hexagrams.

Looking at the hexagrams in groups of eights, tens, and twelves, combined with looking at the trigram links, again makes the heaven, earth, water (pit), and fire hexagrams stand out. Some commentaries say that we should really regard sixty of the hexagrams as applying to the human conditions, and that Hexagrams 1, 2, 29, and 30 are outside of time and space. The trigram links leave those four hexagrams as well as the two culminating hexagrams of 63 and 64 as "islands" in the cycles around which the ongoing energy of the hexagrams flows.

In a way, it is amazing that King Wen constructed a cycle of hexagrams that so resists mere quantitative analysis. Everything about the sequence hints strongly of structure, and yet nothing about it is limited to structure. Contemplating the sequence will continue to yield many insights beyond the core texts and traditional commentaries. We must remain aware of the graphics, the mathematics, and the symbolism. Studying the sequence of hexagrams teaches us a great deal, even as we are reminded that it is the whole of the *Changes* that is most important.

APPENDIX 9

The Structure of the Lines

The theories regarding the structure and relationships of the hexagrams' lines originated with scholars after the time of Confucius. Most notable among them were the authors of the Ten Wings and the scholar Wang Bi (226–249 c.e.).

The Ten Wings is explicit about the time frame that each of the lines is thought to reflect:

Line 1 shows the nascent tendencies of any situation. The Ten Wings say that this line is "difficult to understand" because the cause of any situation is hard to discern.

Lines 2 through 5 are put in terms of proximity to a ruler:

Line 2 is an official. Since it is the center line of the lower trigram, it is usually considered auspicious. The official that Line 2 represents usually is fulfilling duties well, albeit far from the capital. He is a good leader, and works in cooperation with the ruler who is represented by Line 5.

Line 3 is conceived as an official who has limited power and who does not command a central position. This is related to the position of the line, which is the topmost line of the lower trigram. Thus, because it is on the periphery of its trigram, it is unstable and is not influential. Furthermore, this official is outside both the official in line 2 and the ruler in line 5. Usually, this line is unlucky.

Line 4 is similar to Line 3 in that it does not command a position of its own. It is in close proximity to Line 5, the ruler, and so it must be cautious. Advice to this line commonly involves caution not to offend the ruler. However, if this line heeds the warning, it is more likely than Line 3 to make accomplishments, precisely because of its closeness to the seat of power.

Generally, although not always, Line 5 is considered an auspicious line. Since Line 5 is the ruler, it can make far more extensive achievements than the official in Line 2.

Finally, we return to Line 6. Like Line 1, it is outside the situation, not because things are nascent but because they are dying or ending. Where the situation of Line 1 is hard to determine, Line 6 is easy because everything is already known. By the same token, there is little adjustment possible, since the ruler in Line 5 has already acted.

Each line also has temporal implications. Line 1 is early in a situation; Line 4 is early or just outside the true center of power. Line 2 is central, but of outer influence; Line 5 is central and of inner and therefore greatest influence. Line 3 is outside of a situation and has limited influence; Line 6 is outside a situation and its influence has come to an end (occasionally, Line 6 also represents the sage outside of society, who has retired, still has wisdom to impart, but has no temporal power).

This emphasis on early-central-late puts the greatest power into the central lines. The ideal structure of the lines upholds the ideal of the middle way, which is honored in Taoism, Confucianism, and Buddhism. The middle way is the way of moderation, either avoiding the extremes of action, or else, when the extremes have been encountered, moving back toward the center:

Hexagram 11, Line 2, states: "Win honor by a middle course."

Hexagram 24, Line 4: "Returning alone in the middle of the road."

Hexagram 42, Line 3: "Increase by using unfortunate affairs. No fault. Have trust in the middle path." Line 4 continues: "There is a middle path. Alert the duke to follow."

Hexagram 43, Line 5: "The amaranth mound decisively cleared: the middle way is without fault."

Finally, Hexagram 61, Confidence Within, *Zhong Fu* (*zhong* meaning "central" or "middle"), reinforces the concept, its title implying "Have confidence in the middle."

The *Changes* is based on the idea of every extreme changing to its opposite. The structure of the lines mirrors that thinking, focusing on the progression of early–central–late. It then takes the idea of yin and yang and gives us two different sets of that progression, ties them together with inner relationships, and then sets the entire hexagram together as a diagram for change. When the hexagram is put back into the context of the Later Heaven Hexagrams, and the entire hexagram is changed to its opposite in the following hexagram, we have a complete and sophisticated matrix for understanding change.

The Yin and Yang Relationship of Lines

The *Changes* also looks at the lines from another framework, positing an ideal yin or yang nature to each position. In general, the "ideal" hexagram looks like Hexagram 63:

Embodied in this hexagram is the wish for ideal actions in any situation. We can combine this formation of yin and yang lines with the character of the lines we've described above:

Line 1 is early in a situation—*so there should be a strong (yang) beginning.*

Line 2 is central and ruling an outer situation, but must cooperate with the ruler—*so it should be benevolent and yielding (yin).*

Line 3 is limited in influence and in an unstable situation—*so it should be firm and moral (yang).*

Line 4 is early in its situation, approaching the powerful ruler—*so it should be deferential, supportive, and asserting a tempering influence of mercy (yin)*.

Line 5 is the king and master of the situation—*so it must be firm, strong, bright, glorious, and of supreme goodness (yang)*.

Line 6 is outside the situation, either as someone leaving, retiring, or locked into the consequences of the now-completed changes—*so it should be accepting and its actions are limited (yin)*.

Trouble comes, of course, when a person who should behave one way in their situation behaves inappropriately. For example, when a king is called upon to be yang but is instead weak and yin, it is unfortunate.

Significantly, the one hexagram that is perfect in its formation, Hexagram 63, is not considered ideal. It shows a time of stasis. All has come to culmination. Glory is reserved for other hexagrams—which by definition would be unstable or in transition. These hexagrams, by their very structure, have hidden vulnerabilities and the makings of their own destruction—but at the same time, they are more powerful. In this way, the *Changes* consistently projects its outlook onto every level of its imagery and analysis: the dynamic is imperfect; the imperfect is static.

Summary

In summary, the relationships of lines are as follows:

Lines 1 and 6: outside the situation.

Lines 2 and 5: central and ruling.

Lines 3 and 4: subordinate and uncertain.

Yin and yang are then projected onto these ideals of time and position:

Line 1 should be yang, Line 6 should be yin.

Line 2 should be yin, Line 5 should be yang.

Line 3 should be yang, Line 4 should be yin.

The *Changes* compares the lines of each hexagram with the overlapping ideals set forth above. The tension between the actual and ideal animates the commentaries. At times, a commentator may see the hexagram as overruling the ideal. For example, Hexagram 54, Marrying Sister, sets forth an ambivalent and unfortunate situation. Line 5, which should be yang, makes the best of the situation:

> Emperor Yi gives his younger sister
> in marriage. Her royal sleeves are not as fine
> as the secondary wives'. The moon: nearly full.
> Fortune.

The ideal may be for yang action, but here, good fortune is gained only by the emperor sacrificing his sister and by the princess accepting a compromised role as a secondary wife.

When the line is yin in a yang place, that combination influences the commentary on the line. In Hexagram 32, Line 5, for example:

> Constant in virtue.
> Like a woman: fortune.
> Like a man: misfortune.

The first line relates to the constancy that is the theme of the hexagram. The second line relates to the yin nature of the line, and here, having attained the middle of the upper trigram, a woman (yin) is fortunate, but for a man (yang), who would be acting inappropriately subordinate, it would be unfortunate.

Sometimes a line is appropriately yang in a yang place or yin in a yin place, but the overall hexagram overwhelmingly determines the nature of the reading. For example, Line 6 is the ending of a situation. But this doesn't necessarily mean release from a bad situation. In Hexagram 36, Line 6, the line is appropriately yin in a yin place, but the situation is already dire:

> Not a bright night.
> First rise into the sky,
> then plunge into the earth.

The implication of crashing to earth is unmistakable.

Close study of each line of the *Changes* will reveal the wisdom directly related to a line's position and character. Each line is unique. Each line is a combination of its place in the hexagram and the wisdom attached to it. Each line bears long study, but even after exhaustive study, one marvels at how consistently the *Changes* carries out its philosophy.

The First-Person Voice of the *Changes*

Many passages of the *Changes* are written in the first person. In Hexagram 4, the passage written by King Wen says: "... I do not seek the naive youth. The naive youth seeks me."

The first-person voice recurs in the statements of the Lines written by the Duke of Zhou. Hexagram 20, Line 5, says, "Beholding my life: advance or retreat?" Hexagram 27, Line 1, clearly puts the speaker in a divinatory context.

> You put aside your divine turtle
> And watch my moving jows: misfortune.

The speaker's personality emerges as both kind and emotional. "Have trust in the kindness of my conduct," the speaker says in Hexagram 42, Line 5. When the speaker sees a good situation that is ignored, the words of Hexagram 48, Line 3, are: "The well is dredged, but no one drinks. My heart is anguished." Later, the speaker views a situation with a mixture of disapproval and sadness. In Hexagram 56, line 4:

> A traveler in a dwelling place.
> Gets his wealth and ax.
> My heart is unhappy.

In Hexagram 50, line 2, the speaker says, "A cauldron is full. My enemies are ill / and cannot approach me: favorable." This suggests someone taking care of the cauldron or who is presiding over a cauldron.

Indeed, the speaker has access to the articles of nobility. In this passage from Line 2, Hexagram 61, the speaker holds a *jue,* a three-legged bronze chalice with a loop handle:

> A calling crane in the shade:
> its young are at peace.
> I have a good wine goblet.
> I will share its excellence with you.

Hexagram 62, Line 5, even suggests the ruler of a city or larger territory:

Dense clouds, no rain.
At my western outskirts, the duke shoots,
takes another in the cave.

All these instances suggests the *Changes* to be a human oracle rather than a supernatural presence. This echoes a statement in the Ten Wings: "Those who composed the *Changes* had great care and sorrow." Here is a personality who experienced the joys and anguish depicted in the lines. Here is a person who was heavily weighted with responsibilities, who knew the anger of war and who longed for peace. Here was a person who was married, who had children, who worshiped ancestors, and who was responsible for leading people.

A scholar might say that the first-person voice is merely a literary device: King Wen and the Duke of Zhou occasionally wrote or spoke in the first person, and those artifacts became part of the *Changes*.

That, of course, is the rational and academically sensible approach. For the sake of imagination, however, and to open up new possibilities for reading the *Changes*, let us explore the idea of the *Changes* as a person. Perhaps the oracle was reincarnated through each of the four major authors of the *Changes*. Maybe it entered them as a spirit while they were alive. Some might even say that the *Changes* is a being of pure consciousness with no corporeal existence. Or maybe the *Changes* is a personality that comes into existence as many times and in as many places as it is invoked. However we might want to contemplate the personality of the oracle, there is something valuable to be gained by exploring further.

Most important: unless we admit to the possibility of a spirit inhabiting the *Changes*, we cannot ask it to speak in its own voice.

Bibliography

Balkin, Jack M, trans. *The Laws of Change.* New York: Schocken Books, 2002.

Blofeld, John, trans. *I Ching.* New York: E.P. Dutton, 1968.

Chan, Chiu Ming, trans. *Book of Changes.* Singapore: Asiapac Books, 1997.

Cleary, Thomas, trans. *The Taoist I Ching.* Boston: Shambhala, 1988.

Da, Liu, trans. *I Ching Coin Prediction.* New York: Harper & Row, 1975.

Huang, Alfred, trans. *The Complete I Ching.* Rochester: Inner Traditions, 1998.

Huang, Kerson, trans. *I Ching, the Oracle.* Singapore: World Scientific Publishing, 1984.

Legge, James, trans. *I Ching, Book of Changes.* Secaucus: The Citadel Press, 1964.

Lynn, Richard John, trans. *The Classic of Changes.* New York: Columbia Univ. Press, 1994.

Moran, Elizabeth, and Joseph Yu, trans. *The Complete Idiot's Guide to the I Ching.* Indianapolis: Alpha, 2002.

Palmer, Martin, and Jay Ramsay, with Xiaomin Zhao, trans. *I Ching.* London: Thorsons, 1995.

Ritsema, Rudolph, and Sabbadini Shantena Augusto, trans. *The Original I Ching Oracle.* London: Watkins, 2005.

Russek, Janet, ed. *Images in the Heavens, Patterns on the Earth: The I Ching.* Santa Fe: The Museum of New Mexico Press, 2004.

Rutt, Richard, trans. *The Book of Changes (Zhouyi).* London: Curzon, 2002

Shaughnessy, Edward, trans. *I Ching.* New York: Ballantine Books, 1996.

Singapore Association for I-Ching Studies, trans. *Yijingduben.* Singapore: Singapore Association for I-Ching Studies, 1994.

Wei, Henry, trans. *The Authentic I-Ching.* North Hollywood, CA: New Castle Publishing, 1987.

Wilhelm, Richard, trans. *The I Ching or Book of Changes.* Translated from the German by Cary F. Baynes. 3rd ed. Bollingen Series 19. Princeton, NJ: Princeton University Press, 1967.

Wing, R. L, trans. *The Illustrated I Ching.* Garden City: Dolphin Books/Doubleday & Company, 1982.

Wu, Jing-Nuan, trans. *Yi Jing.* Washington, DC: The Taoist Center, 1991.

About the Table of Hexagrams

Once you have performed the casting of coins or the separation of yarrow stalks to construct a hexagram (see pages xix and 86–89), you can find the hexagram by using the table on the inside back cover.

The table shows the lower trigrams on the left side. Upper trigrams are on the topmost row. By finding the lower trigram on the left and then finding where that row intersects with the column headed by the upper trigram, you can find where your hexagram is in the book using the hexagram number shown.

In the example below, the divining ritual has formed a hexagram with an Old Yin line in the second place and an Old Yang line in the fifth place. The first hexagram that is formed is Hexagram 31. It can be found at the intersection of the lower trigram, Mountain, and the upper trigram, Lake, in the table. The second hexagram formed is Hexagram 32. It is found at the intersection of the lower trigram, Wind, and the upper trigram, Thunder.

In this example, one reads all of the hexagram commentaries for Hexagram 31, plus the commentaries for Lines 2 and 5. In addition, one reads only the commentary for Hexagram 32 (but no lines) as well. If one receives a hexagram with no changing lines, one reads only that hexagram's commentaries without considering any commentaries on the Lines.

Sample hexagram as first cast. Lines 2 and 5 are changing lines. The other lines do not change.

Find the hexagram in the table by looking at the bottom trigram, Mountain, and the top trigram, Lake. This is Hexagram 31. Read the commentary for the hexagram and for Lines 2 and 5.

When Lines 2 and 5 change to their opposites, a new hexagram is formed. Find the hexagram in the table by looking at the bottom trigram, Wind, and the top trigram, Thunder. Read the hexagram commentary.